DATE DUE

			PRINTED IN U.S.A.

Authors
& Artists
for Young
Adults

ISSN 1040-5682

R

Authors & Artists for Young Adults

VOLUME 11

Kevin S. Hile,
Editor

Gale Research Inc. • DETROIT • WASHINGTON, D.C. • LONDON

Kevin S. Hile, *Editor*

Elizabeth A. Des Chenes, Kathleen J. Edgar, David M. Galens, Denise Kasinec, Michelle M. Motowski, Susan M. Reicha, Pamela L. Shelton, Kenneth R. Shepherd, Deborah A. Stanley, and Polly Vedder, *Associate Editors*

Joanna Brod, Jeff Hill, Jane Kelly, Terrie Rooney, and Roger Valade, *Assistant Editors*

Victoria B. Cariappa, *Research Manager*

Mary Rose Bonk, *Research Supervisor*

Reginald A. Carlton, Clare Collins, Andrew Guy Malonis, and Norma Sawaya, *Editorial Associates*

Patricia Bowen, Rachel A. Dixon, Shirley Gates, Sharon McGilvray, and Devra M. Sladics, *Editorial Assistants*

Margaret A. Chamberlain, *Picture Permissions Supervisor*

Pamela A. Hayes and Keith Reed, *Permissions Associates*

Arlene Johnson and Barbara Wallace, *Permissions Assistants*

Mary Beth Trimper, *Production Director*

Catherine Kemp, *External Production Assistant*

Cynthia Baldwin, *Art Director*

Sherrell Hobbs and C. J. Jonik, *Desktop Publishers/Typesetters*

Willie Mathis, *Camera Operator*

The paper used in this publication meets the minimum requirements of American National Standard for Information Sciences—Permanence Paper for Printed Library Materials, ANSI Z39.48-1984.

Library of Congress Catalog Card Number 89-641100
ISBN 0-8103-8025-0
ISSN 1040-5682

10 9 8 7 6 5 4 3 2 1

Printed in the United States of America

Published simultaneously in the United Kingdom
by Gale Research International Limited
(An affiliated company of Gale Research Inc.)

I(T)P™

The trademark **ITP** is used under license.

Contents

Introduction

Authors and Artists for Young Adults is a reference series designed to serve the needs of middle school, junior high, and high school students interested in creative artists. Originally inspired by the need to bridge the gap between Gale's *Something about the Author*, created for children, and *Contemporary Authors*, intended for older students and adults, *Authors and Artists for Young Adults* has been expanded to cover not only an international scope of authors, but also a wide variety of other artists.

Although the emphasis of the series remains on the writer for young adults, we recognize that these readers have diverse interests covering a wide range of reading levels. The series therefore contains not only those creative artists who are of high interest to young adults, including cartoonists, photographers, music composers, bestselling authors of adult novels, media directors, producers, and performers, but also literary and artistic figures studied in academic curricula, such as influential novelists, playwrights, poets, and painters. The goal of *Authors and Artists for Young Adults* is to present this great diversity of creative artists in a format that is entertaining, informative, and understandable to the young adult reader.

Entry Format

Each volume of *Authors and Artists for Young Adults* will furnish in-depth coverage of about twenty authors and artists. The typical entry consists of:

— A detailed biographical section that includes date of birth, marriage, children, education, and addresses.

— A comprehensive bibliography or filmography including publishers, producers, and years.

— Adaptations into other media forms.

— Works in progress.

— A distinctive essay featuring comments on an artist's life, career, artistic intentions, world views, and controversies.

— References for further reading.

— Extensive illustrations, photographs, movie stills, manuscript samples, book covers, and other relevant visual material.

A cumulative index to featured authors and artists appears in each volume.

Compilation Methods

The editors of *Authors and Artists for Young Adults* make every effort to secure information directly from the authors and artists through personal correspondence and interviews. Sketches on living authors and artists are sent to the biographee for review prior to publication. Any sketches not personally reviewed by the biographee are marked with an asterisk (°).

Highlights of Forthcoming Volumes

Among the authors and artists planned for future volumes are:

Bill Amend	The Hildebrandt Bros.	L. M. Montgomery
Isaac Asimov	Langston Hughes	Susan Beth Pfeffer
Margaret Atwood	Zora Neale Hurston	Meredith Ann Pierce
Francesca Lia Block	Hadley Irwin	Christopher Pike
Ray Bradbury	Lynn Johnston	Rob Reiner
Vera Cleaver	Norma Johnston	Ann Rinaldi
J. California Cooper	Diana Wynne Jones	John Steinbeck
Susan Cooper	Rudyard Kipling	R. L. Stine
Arthur Conan Doyle	Ron Koertge	Joyce Carol Thomas
M. C. Escher	Mercedes Lackey	Boris Vallejo
Anne Frank	Julius Lester	Jules Verne
William Gibson	H. P. Lovecraft	Andy Warhol
Joanne Greenberg	Sharon Bell Mathis	H. G. Wells
Stephen Hawking	Lorne Michaels	Robert Westall

The editors of *Authors and Artists for Young Adults* welcome any suggestions for additional biographees to be included in this series. Please write and give us your opinions and suggestions for making our series more helpful to you. Direct your comments to: Editors, *Authors and Artists for Young Adults*, Gale Research Inc., 835 Penobscot Building, Detroit, Michigan 48226-4094.

Authors & Artists for Young Adults

Judie Angell

■ Personal

Full legal name, Judie Angell Gaberman; also writes under pseudonyms Fran Arrick and Maggie Twohill; born July 10, 1937, in New York, NY; daughter of David Gordon (an attorney) and Mildred (a teacher; maiden name, Rogoff) Angell; married Philip Gaberman (a pop and jazz music teacher and arranger), December 20, 1964; children: Mark David, Alexander. *Education:* Syracuse University, B.S., 1959. *Religion:* "Yes." *Hobbies and other interests:* Singing, painting, cats, listening to music.

■ Addresses

Home—South Salem, NY.

■ Career

Elementary school teacher in Brooklyn, NY, 1959-62; *TV Guide,* Radnor, PA, associate editor of New York City metropolitan edition, 1962-63; WNDT-TV (now WNET-TV), New York City, continuity writer, 1963-68; full-time writer, 1968—. Has worked variously as a switchboard operator and a waitress.

■ Awards, Honors

Ethical Culture School Book Award, 1977, for *In Summertime It's Tuffy,* and 1979, for *A Word from Our Sponsor; or, My Friend Alfred;* Best Books for Young Adults citations, American Library Association, 1978, for *Steffie Can't Come Out to Play,* 1980, for *Tunnel Vision,* 1983, for *God's Radar,* and 1985, for *One-Way to Ansonia.*

■ Writings

YOUNG ADULT NOVELS

In Summertime It's Tuffy, Bradbury Press, 1977.
Ronnie and Rosey, Bradbury Press, 1977.
Tina Gogo, Bradbury Press, 1978.
Secret Selves, Bradbury Press, 1979.
A Word from Our Sponsor; or, My Friend Alfred, Bradbury Press, 1979.
Dear Lola; or, How to Build Your Own Family: A Tale, Bradbury Press, 1980.
What's Best for You, Bradbury Press, 1981.
The Buffalo Nickel Blues Band, Bradbury Press, 1982, Alladin Books, 1991.
First, the Good News, Bradbury Press, 1983.
Suds, a New Daytime Drama/Brought to You by Judie Angell, Bradbury Press, 1983.
A Home Is to Share—and Share—and Share—, Bradbury Press, 1984.
One-Way to Ansonia, Bradbury Press, 1985.
The Weird Disappearance of Jordan Hall, Orchard Books, 1987.
What's Best for You, Collier Books, 1990.
Don't Rent My Room!, Bantam Books, 1990.
Leave the Cooking to Me, Bantam Books, 1990.

Yours Truly, Orchard Books/Jackson, 1993.

YOUNG ADULTS NOVELS; UNDER PSEUDONYM FRAN ARRICK

Steffie Can't Come Out to Play, Bradbury Press, 1978.
Tunnel Vision, Bradbury Press, 1980.
Chernowitz!, Bradbury Press, 1981.
God's Radar, Bradbury Press, 1983.
Nice Girl from Good Home, Bradbury Press, 1984.
Where'd You Get the Gun, Billy?, Bantam Books, 1991.
What You Don't Know Can Kill You, Bantam Books, 1992.

CHILDREN'S NOVELS; UNDER PSEUDONYM MAGGIE TWOHILL

Who Has the Lucky Duck in Class 4-B?, Bradbury Press, 1984.
Jeeter, Mason and the Magic Headset, Bradbury Press, 1985.
Bigmouth, Bradbury Press, 1986.
Valentine Frankenstein, Bradbury Press, 1991.
Superbowl Upset, Bradbury Press, 1991.

OTHER

Contributor of short stories to anthologies, including *Sixteen: Short Stories by Outstanding Writers for Young Adults,* edited by Donald R. Gallo.

■ **Adaptations**

Dear Lola; or, How to Build Your Own Family: A Tale was adapted as the videotape *The Beniker Gang* by Scholastic, Lorimar Distribution, 1984; *Ronnie and Rosey* was recorded on audiocassette as part of the Young Adult Cliffhangers Series by Listening Library, 1985.

■ **Sidelights**

"As far back as I can remember, there have been two constants in my life—music and writing," Judie Angell stated in a publicity release for Bradbury Press. "The music was always there as background for the stories in my head, a rhythm to fit the mood." Angell, the author of popular novels for young people of various age groups, recalled the sound of the Victrola playing in the mid-1940s while she, an eight- or nine-year-old, fashioned stories in crayon about a girl who rescues various animals from perilous situations. Angell's concern for animals was eventually displaced by a passion for baseball, but her interest in music continued to develop; the works of Norwegian composer Edvard Grieg and Russian composer Pyotr Tchaikovsky provided the atmosphere as she depicted the painful defeats of the Brooklyn Dodgers. And as an adolescent in the 1950s, the author recorded personal thoughts and feelings in a diary while listening to jazz and pop artist Nat King Cole or the musicals of Rodgers and Hammerstein.

Angell attended Syracuse University, and shortly after graduation in 1959 she accepted a position as a second-grade teacher in Brooklyn, New York. The author's first professional writing experiences involved composing blurbs for *T.V. Guide* and writing for a public television station during the 1960s. In 1964 Angell married Philip Gaberman, a music teacher and arranger specializing in pop and jazz. They moved to an old house on a lake in South Salem, New York, where they raised their two sons, Mark and Alexander. Angell has been crafting works of fiction since 1968, and her musical inspirations have included jazz artists Cleo Laine and Mel Torme, theatrical composers Stephen Sondheim and Marvin Hamlisch, pop singer/songwriter Paul Simon, and classical musician Johann Sebastian Bach.

Novels Reflect Angell's Past

Angell considers each element of her youth and early adulthood helpful in her current work as a novelist for children and young adults. While her teaching and television writing served to strengthen her skills, her childhood stories and musical background inspired many of the characters and events in her books. The author has strong memories of the powerful emotions that pre-teens and teenagers experience and believes this to be her most important asset as a writer. "I take a lot of those feelings, hug them, wrap them carefully in some words, and present them in a book with an invisible card that says, maybe this'll help a little—make you laugh—make you feel you're not alone," Angell related in a Bradbury Press publicity release. The author currently publishes three different categories of novels under separate pen names. She has been writing longest under the name Judie Angell, producing works for and about pre-teens and younger teenagers. Since the late 1970s, she has explored darker subjects for older teenagers under the pseudonym Fran Arrick. Most recently, Angell has adopted the name Maggie Twohill to fashion books suited to a younger audience.

Blending serious emotions with humorous circumstances, Judie Angell's novels explore both common and unique issues that young people face—in their families, with their peers, and with authority figures. Most of Angell's protagonists are experiencing transitions, and they tend to be clever and creative in meeting the challenges involved in moving toward adulthood. Angell's first book, *In Summertime It's Tuffy*, issued in 1977, is based on the author's fifteen summers away at camp as a camper, counselor-in-training, senior counselor, and dramatics counselor. The main character, eleven-year-old Betsy (whose summer nickname is Tuffy), and her friends were devised as "a composite of my friends and young charges during those years," the author explained. Amidst the typical camp activities, including swimming and arts and crafts, Tuffy gets to know her bunk-mates: one of whom is overweight, another obsessively neat, and a third preoccupied with boys and clothes. Tuffy also befriends Iris, a new girl with creative talents and an interest in witchcraft. Iris, Tuffy eventually learns, has wealthy parents who send her to boarding school and summer camp while they travel the world. She is attempting to use black magic to force them to spend time with her. But the girls' more immediate problem is the heartless head counselor, Uncle Otto. Combining Tuffy's wit and Iris's voodoo, the two wage a war against him that lands them in hilarious straits. *In Summertime It's Tuffy* was selected by fourth- to sixth-grade students at the Midtown Ethical Culture School in New York City to receive the school's annual book award. Although some reviewers found the plot and characters trite, Brigitte Weeks maintained in *Washington Post Book World* that the work "abounds with life and is genuinely funny."

Angell's 1979 novel deals with a slightly older age group and a different kind of struggle than *In Summertime It's Tuffy*. *Secret Selves* traces the relationship between an eighth-grade girl and a ninth-grade boy while exploring gender issues on a larger scale. At the start of the school year, athletic Rusty Parmette becomes the object of Julie Novack's first crush. Julie is too shy to speak to Rusty in person, so her more experienced friend Ellen suggests she give him a call. Julie proceeds to do so, but out of nervousness creates fictional identities for both herself and Rusty. She claims to be "Barbara Birdsong" and asks to speak with "Wendell Farnham." Unaware of Barbara's true identity, Rusty plays along with her, and the pretend element makes them both comfortable sharing ideas they generally keep to themselves. After their initial conversation, Barbara and Wendell speak on a regular basis. Julie, whose identity remains a secret, finds Wendell's humor and charm more and more appealing. However, when she

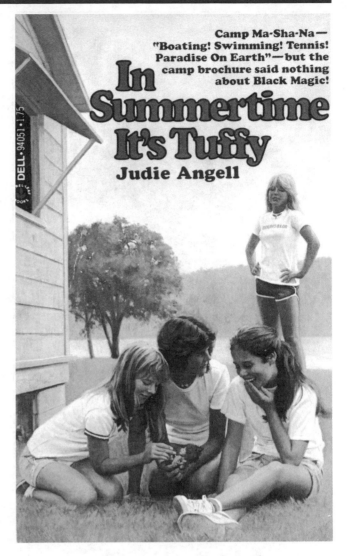

This humorous 1977 novel about a girl's adventures at summer camp was loosely based on Angell's own experiences as a camper and camp counselor.

approaches Rusty in person, he is cold to her and makes rude remarks about girls in general, echoing his father and older brother's sexist beliefs. Julie struggles to reconcile Rusty's two sides, until she finds herself competing against him in a school debate over whether the United States should elect a woman president. At first both Julie and Rusty remain firm on their positions. But then they begin to listen more closely to one another, asking questions and communicating as freely as they do over the telephone. When Rusty concedes that Julie's point of view has merit, the two find a basis for a real-life friendship. A number of critics found the story original and the dialogue natural. For example, lauding Angell's ability to create contemporary young characters, a *Booklist* contributor concluded that the author "reaches a satisfying new level with this engrossing, funny tale."

SECRET SELVES

A Novel by Judie Angell

Angell recounts a young girl's first crush in this 1979 tale of hidden identity and unexpected friendship.

In 1980 Angell published *Dear Lola; or, How to Build Your Own Family: A Tale*. This work involves six residents of an orphanage—ranging in age from five to eighteen—each of whom has been either orphaned or deserted. Although they all depend on each other and are as close as any family, the orphanage continually threatens to separate them by placing the younger ones in foster homes. To avoid this fate, they decide to run away from the orphanage and live in a home of their own. Eighteen-year-old Arthur Beniker—whose nickname, Lola, is the pseudonym under which he writes a nationally-syndicated advice column—orchestrates the plan and provides emotional and financial support for the rest of the Benikers: ten-year-old Anne, who narrates the story, and her twin brother Al-William; eight-year-old Edmund, who is prone to temper tantrums; five-year-old Ben, who is constantly eating small objects; and thirteen-year-old James, whose need for privacy is so great that he rarely leaves his room or makes contact with anyone other than Lola. They travel in a van for three months, stopping at libraries where Lola reads to the group and researches child custody laws. When they are a safe distance from the orphanage, they rent and renovate a house in a small town. In this setting Lola works on his column and tutors James, the other children attend school, and they all help each other work out the difficulties that arise.

But the group attracts the attention of school authorities and suspicious neighbors. They attempt to persuade the community that they are siblings living with their ailing grandfather. But when the truth is discovered, Lola must prove in court that he is fit to be the children's guardian. He explains to the judge that for the first time in the Benikers' lives, they all have a stable, nurturing home environment. The judge is impressed by Lola's intentions, but when he insists that Lola identify his occupation, the resulting publicity costs Lola his job, and this in turn costs him legal custody of the children. The Benikers make another daring escape, however, and wind up picking fruit in California. Reviewers appreciated Angell's exploration of the rights of minors, and praised her ability to promote a willing suspension of disbelief. Marilyn R. Singer commented in *School Library Journal* that the book "will gladden the hearts of many young readers." In her review of the novel for *Publishers Weekly*, Jean F. Mercier described her reaction to *Dear Lola* in the words of poet William Wordsworth: "'surprised by joy—impatient to get on with it.'"

Angell's knowledge of and love for music are evident in *The Buffalo Nickel Blues Band*, her 1982 work concerning a group of sixth- and seventh-grade musicians. Jewish pianist Eddie Levy, black drummer Ivy Sunday, and white Anglo-Saxon Protestant guitarist Georgie Higgins are close friends as well as members of a band. On the advice of Eddie's piano teacher, they concentrate on the blues and enlist two new instrumentalists: horn player Shelby Powell and a bassist who only admits to the name Reese. The two newcomers are somewhat odd and mysterious, but the band improves significantly and becomes better known. Eventually Reese and Shelby reveal their secrets, involving the band members and their parents in humorous antics. Holly Sanhuber asserted in *School Library Journal* that in spite of minor unrealistic elements, "the story is engaging, and readers are made to care for the players."

Grandmother Inspires *One–Way to Ansonia*

In 1985, Angell published *One-Way to Ansonia*, a novel about a Jewish immigrant arriving in the United States in the late 1800s. The work was inspired in part by the experiences of the author's maternal grandmother. Ten-year-old Rose Olshansky and her four brothers and sisters travel by boat from their Russian village to New York City's Lower East Side in order to attend their father's wedding. When they arrive they learn that their stepmother has only been informed about the youngest child, Celia. The apartment is too small to accommodate the others, so Rose and her three older siblings find separate homes with neighbors, working to pay for their room and board. Although Celia attends school, Rose must work at a factory, where she sews twelve hours a day for pennies. At the age of fourteen, she becomes determined to learn to read and write English and begins attending night school against her father's wishes. Walking to class one evening, she meets Hyman Rogoff, a young trade unionist who is attending a meeting in the same building. Later that night, the two walk home together, debating the value of union work versus the importance of education. Unlike most men in their community, who view women only as child-bearers and housekeepers, Hyman appreciates Rose's intellect, and the two become friends. When her father selects a husband for Rose whom she does not like, she quickly proposes to Hyman and convinces her father to permit them to marry. But soon after their first baby is born, Hyman contracts pneumonia and Rose's best friend is killed at a union rally. Sixteen-year-old Rose decides she has had enough of the ghetto. Promising to send for Hyman when she is settled, she takes the baby and her savings to Grand Central Station. Choosing her destination on the basis of what she can afford, she buys a one-way ticket to Ansonia, Connecticut, a town with hills and trees where she hopes to start a new life. Although a *Bulletin of the Center for Children's Books* contributor felt that the "book is weakened" by Angell's focus on historical setting, Hanna B. Zeiger maintained in *Horn Book* that "Judie Angell has created a powerful, moving story rich in authentic images and characterization."

Angell's 1989 work, *Leave the Cooking to Me*, concerns a modern-day young woman who, like *One-Way to Ansonia*'s Rose, is determined to make her own way in the world. Fifteen-year-old Shirley Merton is seeking summer employment. Her mother, who runs her late husband's law firm, wants Shirley's work to be intellectually stimulating.

However, the only jobs available involve bagging groceries or shelving library books. Then Shirley's friend Mary Kay's mother needs last-minute help preparing for a dinner party. Cooking has been Shirley's forte since she began fixing meals for her mother and younger sister several years earlier, so she agrees to lend her assistance and winds up doing most of the work. At the party, one of the guests is so impressed with the food that she assumes it was prepared by a professional. When she asks Shirley for the name of the caterer for whom she works, Shirley invents the name "Vanessa" and supplies her own phone number. Soon, the woman calls to ask Vanessa to cater a party, and Shirley makes the arrangements. She tells her mother she has found a job, but refuses to disclose any information about it.

Shirley hires Mary Kay and a few other friends as kitchen help and a charming boy to wait tables in exchange for tutoring. Although the fictional Vanessa does not appear at the function, the caterers are so competent that no one doubts the company's legitimacy. As other guests sample Shirley's fare, she is hired to cater more and more functions, and the business becomes extremely lucrative. But when Mrs. Merton finds her daughter's stash of money, she suspects Shirley is involved in drug-dealing. Determined to learn the truth, Mrs. Merton goes to the local hangout, where she asks if anyone has done business with her daughter. But she gets a first-hand glimpse of Shirley's abilities when she is invited to a party catered by Vanessa. *Leave the Cooking to Me* was generally well received by reviewers, although one *Publishers Weekly* critic considered the dialogue to be "hokey and stilted." On the other hand, *School Library Journal* contributor Phyllis Graves felt readers would be interested in the characters, and called *Leave the Cooking to Me* "a light and amusing read."

On the Dark Side

In the late 1970s Angell adopted the pseudonym Fran Arrick and began producing novels about controversial topics for older teens. By depicting realistic family and community scenarios, the author brings prominent social issues such as suicide, prostitution, and Acquired Immunodeficiency Syndrome (AIDS) into a personal context. *Tunnel Vision*, Arrick's 1980 work, begins with the death of Anthony, a bright, athletic, well-liked fifteen-year-old who hangs himself with his father's neckties and leaves no note. The novel explores the reactions of Anthony's friends and relations, revealing the events that led up to the suicide through flashbacks. Anthony's family has been struggling for some time because his father's job requires him to be away from home for long periods. Although he was depressed, Anthony was attuned to the needs of his parents, rebellious sister, and rape-victim girlfriend. While none of these characters is certain of the reason for Anthony's suicide, each one blames someone different, and as they share their grief, they all gain new strength. A neighborhood police officer who has investigated a number of teen suicides describes the common element among the victims: "It's like each of them was caught inside a tunnel and they couldn't see any end to it or anything at all outside." Although one *Kirkus Reviews* critic judged the book to be "inoffensive but uninspired," others praised it as authentically and humanly presented. Laura Geringer stated in *School Library Journal* that the characters' "struggle to come to terms with [Anthony's decision] rings true, and should prompt some heated discus-

DELL-98579-X-U.S. $3.50
CAN. $4.50

Anthony never realized that
he had more than one choice.

TUNNEL
VISION
FRAN ARRICK

The suicide of a troubled teenager causes his family and friends to reexamine their lives in this 1980 work.

sions." *Publishers Weekly* contributor Jean F. Mercier declared that the "humanized cast grips the reader and can help, perhaps, to promote understanding of troubled teenagers."

In 1984 Arrick examined the impact of sudden unemployment on a well-off family in *Nice Girl from Good Home*. Brady Hewitt is a successful advertising executive whose wife, Deborah, and teenage children, Jeremy and Dory, are accustomed to country clubs and designer clothing. When Brady loses his job and takes to drinking, Deborah goes into denial and continues spending money as if nothing had happened. But then her husband puts their house up for sale, and she has a breakdown and is institutionalized. Echoing her mother's reaction, Dory buys an expensive dress, and Brady orders her to return it. She defies her father, making him furious, and then rebels by cutting school and spending time with troublemakers who help her plan a bomb threat. Jeremy, meanwhile, determines to ease the family's financial straits. Forgoing college to start a housepainting business, he suggests a job for his father that might help keep the family together. Audrey B. Eaglen remarked in *School Library Journal* that *Nice Girl from Good Home* "lacks the power of Arrick's *Tunnel Vision* ... because of a wildly unbelievable plot and flat characterization." However, a *Bulletin of the Center for Children's Books* contributor called the work "starkly realistic; the characters are convincing and their problems (and solutions) believable."

Arrick uses a quiet town setting to present the problem of handgun violence in her 1991 novel, *Where'd You Get the Gun, Billy?*. Billy, a high school student, shoots and kills his girlfriend, Lisa, and the entire community is deeply affected. One of Billy and Lisa's classmates, David, becomes intent on learning how Billy obtained the murder weapon. With Lisa's best friend Liz, David goes to the police station, where a lieutenant enumerates the ways in which guns are acquired, from permits to theft. The lieutenant then traces the revolver's hypothetical journey from legal owner to troubled teenager. His story implies that handguns are too readily available, but also points to the deeper societal ills that are the root causes of violence. While a *Publishers Weekly* reviewer decided that "the novel sacrifices verisimilitude for tabloid-style sensationalism," *School Library Journal*'s Ellen Ramsay praised Arrick's approach to the issue: "With its straightforward style and episodic plot, [the novel] effectively examines the problem."

In this 1984 novel, Dory's secure world is threatened when her father loses his job.

What You Don't Know Can Kill You, Arrick's 1992 novel, is narrated by thirteen-year-old Debra. Debra envies her attractive, intelligent eighteen-year-old sister, Ellen, who is dating Jack, a handsome college student. When a neighboring family is badly hurt in a car accident, Ellen volunteers to donate blood for a transfusion. When her blood is tested, however, Ellen learns that she has been infected with Human Immunodeficiency Virus (HIV). HIV antibodies can be transmitted through unprotected sexual contact, and eventually cause the deadly Acquired Immunodeficiency Syndrome (AIDS). Ellen did not practice safe sex because she believed her relationship with Jack to be monogamous, but Jack now confesses to having had an affair while at school. Ellen, Debra, and their parents are shocked and grief-stricken. Although Ellen remains healthy, the community soon learns about her condition and responds with hostility. Jack's guilt leads him to commit suicide, but Ellen's family is united by their struggle, and Debra vows never to engage in risky behavior. Reviewers responded favorably to the work, noting that the novel both reveals the ignorance and prejudice surrounding the AIDS virus and provides honest information. Susan R. Farber commented in *Voice of Youth Advocates*, "While the plot is not new, Debra's viewpoint and the family's deep grief make this an absorbing, emotional story." A *Publishers Weekly* critic found some of the dialogue unnatural, but added that *What You Don't Know Can Kill You* "should dispel notions of 'It can't happen to me' among careless, sexually active readers."

In contrast to the Arrick novels, which focus on harsh, serious topics for readers at the high school level, Angell's works under the pseudonym Maggie Twohill are lighter fare for middle school children. Twohill's protagonists encounter difficult obstacles, such as a parent's remarriage or the loss of a friend. But these works also function on a level of pure entertainment as the characters become involved in unusual adventures. In the 1985 work, *Jeeter, Mason and the Magic Headset*, Jeeter Huff receives a radio headset and a Cabbage Patch doll, which she names Mason, for her tenth birthday. As Jeeter is skateboarding and listening to music, she is surprised to hear Mason speaking over the headset, warning her of an oncoming bike. After that, Mason makes a series of predictions—including one about Jeeter's father's job—all of which come true. Trouble arises when Jeeter's older sister Carol-Ann wants Mason to supply advice on attracting boys and passing exams. Margaret Gross, writing in *School Library Journal*, referred to the work as a "clever, lively tale for pre-adolescents. Characters are believable, the dialogue and action on-target."

Valentine Frankenstein, which Twohill published in 1991, is a more realistic story about friendship and popularity. Walter is a shy but sweet fifth-grader whose low opinion of himself causes his classmates to dislike him. As Valentine's Day grows near, Amanda—Walter's only friend—decides to boost his self-esteem by stuffing the class Valentine box with unsigned cards addressed to him. When he receives them at their holiday celebration, Walter is surprised and overjoyed. The other children suddenly take an interest in him, and he soon becomes the most popular boy in the class. But when Walter begins ignoring Amanda, she is both jealous and concerned, and considers telling him the truth about the Valentines. Nancy P. Reeder maintained in *School Library Journal* that "Twohill has combined just the right amount of friendship and humor ... to create a readable, lighthearted story.''

While the novels written under the names Judie Angell, Fran Arrick, and Maggie Twohill differ in terms of the characters' ages, subject matter, and level of difficulty, they are unified by the respect for young people that their author exhibits. Angell reveals this through the strength and conviction of her protagonists as they come to terms with the changes involved in growing up. The author's frequent use of first-person narration allows her to tell stories through her young characters' insightful perceptions. Angell once reported that of all the rich childhood experience she brings to her writing, ''Most important to me are the feelings I recall so well.''

■ **Works Cited**

Angell, Judie, *Tunnel Vision*, Bradbury Press, 1980.

Eaglen, Audrey B., review of *Nice Girl from Good Home*, School Library Journal, December, 1984, p. 88.

Farber, Susan R., review of *What You Don't Know Can Kill You*, Voice of Youth Advocates, June, 1992, p. 91.

Geringer, Laura, review of *Tunnel Vision*, School Library Journal, April, 1980, pp. 119-20.

Graves, Phyllis, review of *Leave the Cooking to Me*, School Library Journal, January, 1990, p. 120.

Gross, Margaret, review of *Jeeter, Mason and the Magic Headset*, School Library Journal, September, 1985, p. 140.

Review of *Leave the Cooking to Me*, Publishers Weekly, December 22, 1989, p. 57.

Meet Judie Angell [publicity release], Bradbury Press, c. 1978.

Mercier, Jean F., review of *Dear Lola*, Publishers Weekly, November 7, 1980, p. 61.

Mercier, Jean F., review of *Tunnel Vision*, Publishers Weekly, June 20, 1980, p. 87.

Review of *Nice Girl from Good Home*, Bulletin of the Center for Children's Books, December, 1984.

Review of *One-Way to Ansonia*, Bulletin of the Center for Children's Books, November, 1985.

Ramsay, Ellen, review of *Where'd You Get the Gun, Billy?*, School Library Journal, March, 1991, p. 211.

Reeder, Nancy P., review of *Valentine Frankenstein*, School Library Journal, January, 1992, p. 117.

Sanhuber, Holly, review of *The Buffalo Nickel Blues Band*, School Library Journal, August, 1982, p. 110.

Review of *Secret Selves*, Booklist, November 1, 1979, p. 442.

Singer, Marilyn R., review of *Dear Lola*, School Library Journal, January, 1981, p. 56.

Review of *Tunnel Vision*, Kirkus Reviews, August 1, 1980, p. 983.

Weeks, Brigitte, review of *In Summertime It's Tuffy*, Washington Post Book World, August 14, 1977.

Review of *What You Don't Know Can Kill You*, Publishers Weekly, December 6, 1991, p. 74.

Review of *Where'd You Get the Gun, Billy?*, Publishers Weekly, December 21, 1990.

Zeiger, Hanna B., review of *One-Way to Ansonia*, Horn Book, March-April, 1986, pp. 205-6.

■ **For More Information See**

BOOKS

Gallo, Donald R., *Speaking for Ourselves: Autobiographical Sketches by Notable Authors of Books for Young Adults*, National Council of Teachers of English, 1990, pp. 8-9.

PERIODICALS

Bulletin of the Center for Children's Books, January, 1980; November, 1985.

Horn Book, April, 1978; February, 1980; February, 1981.

Kirkus Reviews, January 1, 1980, p. 8.

New York Times Book Review, October 9, 1977.

Publishers Weekly, February 28, 1977; April 23, 1982, p. 93; June 7, 1985, p. 81; December 22, 1989, p. 57; December 21, 1990, p. 57; November 15, 1991, p. 72; December 6, 1991, p. 74.

School Library Journal, May, 1977, p. 58; November, 1979, p. 73; April, 1993, p. 140.°

—Sketch by Joanna Brod

Piers Anthony

Member: Authors Guild, Authors League of America.

■ Awards, Honors

Nebula Award nomination, Science Fiction Writers of America, 1966, for short story "The Message"; Nebula Award nomination, 1967, and Hugo Award nomination, World Science Fiction Convention, 1968, both for *Chthon;* science fiction award, Pyramid Books/*Magazine of Fantasy and Science Fiction*/Kent Productions, 1967, and Hugo Award nomination, 1968, both for *Sos the Rope;* Hugo Award nomination, 1969, for novella "Getting through University," and 1970, for *Macroscope* and for best fan writer; Nebula Award nomination, 1970, for short story "The Bridge," and 1972, for novelette "In the Barn"; British Fantasy Award, 1977, and Hugo Award nomination, 1978, both for *A Spell for Chameleon.*

■ Writings

SCIENCE FICTION

Chthon, Ballantine, 1967.
(With Robert E. Margroff) *The Ring*, Ace Books, 1968.
Macroscope, Avon, 1969.
(With Margroff) *The E.S.P. Worm*, Paperback Library, 1970.
Prostho Plus, Berkley, 1973.
Race against Time, Hawthorne, 1973.
Rings of Ice, Avon, 1974.
Triple Detente, DAW Books, 1974.

■ Personal

Full name Piers Anthony Dillingham Jacob; has written as Piers A. D. Jacob and under joint pseudonym Robert Piers; born August 6, 1934, in Oxford, England; came to United States, 1940, naturalized, 1958; son of Alfred Bennis and Norma (Sherlock) Jacob; married Carol Marble, June 23, 1956; children: Penelope Carolyn, Cheryl. *Education:* Goddard College, B.A., 1956; University of South Florida, teaching certificate, 1964. *Politics:* Independent. *Religion:* "No preference." *Hobbies and other interests:* Tree farming.

■ Addresses

Office—c/o Tor Books, 175 Fifth Ave., New York, NY 10010.

■ Career

Electronic Communications, Inc., St. Petersburg, FL, technical writer, 1959-62; free-lance writer, 1962-63, 1966—; Admiral Farragut Academy, St. Petersburg, teacher of English, 1965-66; novelist, 1966—. *Military service:* U.S. Army, 1957-59.

Phthor (sequel to *Chthon*), Berkley Publishing, 1975.

(With Robert Coulson) *But What of Earth?*, Laser (Toronto), 1976, corrected edition, Tor Books, 1989.

(With Frances T. Hall) *The Pretender*, Borgo Press, 1979.

Mute, Avon, 1981.

Ghost, Tor Books, 1986.

Shade of the Tree, Tor Books, 1986.

(Editor with Barry Malzberg and Martin Greenberg) *Uncollected Stars* (short stories), Avon, 1986.

Total Recall, Morrow, 1989.

Balook, illustrated by Patrick Woodroffe, Underwood-Miller, 1989.

Hard Sell, Tafford, 1990.

(With Roberto Fuentes) *Dead Morn*, Tafford, 1990.

MerCycle, illustrated by Ron Lindhan, Tafford, 1991.

(With Philip Jose Farmer) *Caterpillar's Question*, Ace Books, 1992.

Killobyte, Putnam, 1993.

"OMNIVORE" SERIES; SCIENCE FICTION NOVELS

Omnivore, Ballantine, 1968.

Orn, Avon, 1971.

Ox, Avon, 1976.

"BATTLE CIRCLE" SERIES; SCIENCE FICTION NOVELS

Sos the Rope (also see below), Pyramid, 1968.

Var the Stick (also see below), Faber, 1972.

Neq the Sword (also see below), Corgi, 1975.

Battle Circle (omnibus volume; contains *Sos the Rope, Var the Stick,* and *Neq the Sword*), Avon, 1978.

"CLUSTER" SERIES; SCIENCE FICTION NOVELS

Cluster, Avon, 1977, published in England as *Vicinity Cluster*, Panther, 1979.

Chaining the Lady, Avon, 1978.

Kirlian Quest, Avon, 1978.

Thousandstar, Avon, 1980.

Viscous Circle, Avon, 1982.

"TAROT"; SCIENCE FICTION NOVEL PUBLISHED IN THREE PARTS

God of Tarot (also see below), Jove, 1979.

Vision of Tarot (also see below), Berkley Publishing, 1980.

Faith of Tarot (also see below), Berkley Publishing, 1980.

Tarot (contains *God of Tarot, Vision of Tarot,* and *Faith of Tarot*), Ace Books, 1988.

"BIO OF A SPACE TYRANT" SERIES; SCIENCE FICTION NOVELS

Refugee, Avon, 1983.

Mercenary, Avon, 1984.

Politician, Avon, 1985.

Executive, Avon, 1985.

Statesman, Avon, 1986.

FANTASY

Hasan, Borgo Press, 1977.

(With Robert Kornwise) *Through the Ice*, illustrated by D. Horne, Underwood-Miller, 1990.

(With Mercedes Lackey) *If I Pay Thee Not in Gold*, Baen, 1993.

"MAGIC OF XANTH" SERIES; FANTASY NOVELS

A Spell for Chameleon (also see below), Del Rey, 1977.

The Source of Magic (also see below), Del Rey, 1979.

Castle Roogna (also see below), Del Rey, 1979.

The Magic of Xanth (omnibus volume; contains *A Spell for Chameleon, The Source of Magic,* and *Castle Roogna*), Doubleday, 1981.

Centaur Aisle, Del Rey, 1982.

Ogre, Ogre, Del Rey, 1982.

Night Mare, Del Rey, 1983.

Dragon on a Pedestal, Del Rey, 1983.

Crewel Lye: A Caustic Yarn, Del Rey, 1985.

Golem in the Gears, Del Rey, 1985.

Vale of the Vole, Avon, 1987.

Heaven Cent, Avon, 1988.

Man from Mundania, Avon, 1989.

(With Jody Lynn Nye) *Piers Anthony's Visual Guide to Xanth*, illustrated by Todd Cameron Hamilton and James Clouse, Avon, 1989.

Isle of View, Morrow, 1990.

Question Quest, Morrow, 1991.

The Color of Her Panties, Avon, 1992.

Demons Don't Dream, Tor Books, 1993.

Harpy Thyme, Tor Books, in press.

"INCARNATIONS OF IMMORTALITY" SERIES; FANTASY NOVELS

On a Pale Horse, Del Rey, 1983.

Bearing an Hourglass, Del Rey, 1984.

With a Tangled Skein, Del Rey, 1985.

Wielding a Red Sword, Del Rey, 1987.

Being a Green Mother, Del Rey, 1987.

For Love of Evil, Morrow, 1988.

And Eternity, Morrow, 1990.

"DRAGON'S GOLD" SERIES; FANTASY NOVELS

(With Margroff) *Dragon's Gold*, Tor Books, 1987.

(With Margroff) *Serpent's Silver*, Tor Books, 1988.
(With Margroff) *Chimaera's Copper*, Tor Books, 1990.
Orc's Opal, Tor Books, 1990.
(With Margroff) *Mouvar's Magic*, Tor Books, 1992.

"APPRENTICE ADEPT" SERIES; SCIENCE FICTION/FANTASY NOVELS

Split Infinity (also see below), Del Rey, 1980.
Blue Adept (also see below), Del Rey, 1981.
Juxtaposition (also see below), Del Rey, 1982.
Double Exposure (omnibus volume; contains *Split Infinity, Blue Adept,* and *Juxtaposition*), Doubleday, 1982.
Out of Phaze, Ace Books, 1987.
Robot Adept, Ace Books, 1988.
Unicorn Point, Ace Books, 1989.
Phaze Doubt, Ace Books, 1990.

"MODE" SERIES; SCIENCE FICTION/FANTASY NOVELS

Virtual Mode, Putnam, 1991.
Fractal Mode, Putnam, 1992.
Chaos Mode, Putnam, in press.

"JASON STRIKER" SERIES; WITH ROBERTO FUENTES; MARTIAL ARTS NOVELS

Kiai!, Berkley Publishing, 1974.
Mistress of Death, Berkley Publishing, 1974.
The Bamboo Bloodbath, Berkley Publishing, 1975.
Ninja's Revenge, Berkley Publishing, 1975.
Amazon Slaughter, Berkley Publishing, 1976.

OTHER

Steppe (science fiction/history), Millington, 1976, Tor Books, 1985.
Anthonology (short stories), Tor Books, 1985.
Bio of an Ogre: The Autobiography of Piers Anthony to Age 50, Ace Books, 1988.
Pornucopia (erotic fantasy), Tafford, 1989.
Firefly (novel), Morrow, 1990, Avon, 1992.
Tatham Mound (historical fiction), Morrow, 1991.
Alien Plot (short stories), Tor Books, 1992.
Isle of Woman (historical fiction), Tor Books, 1993.
Letters to Jenny (nonfiction), Tor Books, 1993.

Contributor to *Science against Man*, edited by Anthony Cheetham, Avon 1970; *Nova One: An Anthology of Original Science Fiction*, edited by Harry Harrison, Delacorte Press, 1970; *Again, Dangerous Visions*, edited by Harlan Ellison, Doubleday, 1972; *Generation*, edited by David Gerrold, Dell, 1972; and *The Berkley Showcase*, edited by Victoria Schochet and John Silbersack, Berkley Publishing, 1981. Also contributor, with Robert Margroff, under joint pseudonym Robert Piers, of a short story to *Adam Bedside Reader*. Also contribu-tor of short stories to periodicals, including *Analog, Fantastic, Worlds of If, Worlds of Tomorrow, Amazing, Magazine of Fantasy and Science Fiction, SF Age, Vegetarian Times, Twilight Zone, Books and Bookmen, Writer, Gauntlet, Chic, Far Point, Starburst, Vertex,* and *Pandora*.

■ **Adaptations**

Macroscope, A Spell for Chameleon, The Source of Magic, Castle Roogna, Through the Ice, Virtual Mode, and *Fractal Mode* have been adapted to audio cassette.

■ **Work in Progress**

Two "Xanth" novels, *Geis of the Gargoyle* and *Roc and a Hard Place*, for Tor Books; *Tales from the Great Turtle*, for Tor; and *Spider Legs*, a science fiction novel.

■ **Sidelights**

Within a childhood scarred by illness, death, and isolation, prolific science fiction and fantasy author Piers Anthony escaped by immersing himself in books. "From the time I was 13, I had been hooked on science fiction," Anthony recalled in an interview with the *Science Fiction Radio Show (SFRS)* published in *The Sound of Wonder*. "It's what I did for entertainment. It was a whole different world, multiple worlds, each one of them better than the one I knew. And so when I thought about writing [science fiction], I thought I could be original because I had read everything in the field." He began to write at age twenty, finally deciding in college to make writing his career. As an adult, Anthony's therapy became his livelihood. His many popular series, including the "Magic of Xanth" with sixteen volumes published and more in progress, and his various novels and collections add up to almost one hundred books since 1967. "I am an SF writer today," he told Cliff Biggers in a *Science Fiction* interview, "because without SF and writing I would be nothing at all today."

Among the traumatic events of Anthony's youth were his family's moves to Spain when he was five and to the United States the next year, the loss of his cousin to cancer at fifteen, and his parents' divorce at eighteen. The effects of these occurrences are detectable throughout his writings. In *Piers Anthony*, Michael R. Collings points out several instances where Anthony's stories mirror his early life: the psychological turmoil suffered by many of his characters, including Brother Paul in

Tarot, which often parallels his own as a child; the vegetarianism he advocates in *Omnivore,* a result of his overwhelming aversion to death; the strength and health of his heroes, as in the illness-free world of *Chthon,* representing Anthony's personal ideal.

First Short Story Published

After years of submitting stories to magazines, Anthony sold his first piece, "Possible to Rue," to *Fantastic* in 1962. In the next several years, he worked variously as a free-lance writer and English teacher, but finally decided to devote all of his time to writing. *Chthon,* Anthony's first novel, was published in 1967, received numerous award nominations, and caught the attention of both critics and readers in the science fiction genre. The next year brought a prize from a contest jointly sponsored by Pyramid Books, Kent Productions, and the *Magazine of Fantasy and Science Fiction* for *Sos the Rope,* the first entry in the "Battle Circle" series.

Chthon traces the escape efforts of Aton Five, imprisoned on the planet Chthon and forced to work in its garnet mines. A *Publishers Weekly* reviewer commented on the many elements of the book, including language, myth, suspense, and symbolism, "a bursting package, almost too much for one book, but literate, original and entertaining." Those elements and Anthony's liberal use of them would become his trademark. In a detailed analysis of *Chthon* and its sequel, *Phthor,* Collings noted Anthony's liberal references to mythological symbols. Anthony's minionettes, women whose sons kill their fathers and then bear sons of their own with their mothers, are modeled after the Sirens, female creatures who lured sailors to their deaths. Aton's Oedipal struggle, another reference to myth, is apparent when he encounters his mother, a minionette. Literary references are present as well, exemplified by the resemblance of the prison caverns of Chthon to Dante's depiction of Hell in *The Inferno.* In *Chthon,* "Anthony has created a whole new world, a dream universe which you find yourself living in and, after a while, understanding," Leo Harris declared in *Books and Bookmen.* "Very poetic and tough and allegorical it all is, and it will rapidly have thee in thrall." While *Chthon* focuses on Aton's life, *Phthor* follows Aton's son, Arlo, who symbolizes Thor of Norse mythology. "The mythologies embedded in *Chthon* and *Phthor* go far beyond mere ornamentation or surface symbolism," Collings noted. "They define the thematic content of the novels. Initially, there is a clear demarcation between myth and reali-

Anthony's debut novel, published in 1967, incorporates elements of mythology into the story of Aton Five, a prisoner on the planet Chthon.

ty.... Yet early in *Chthon* Anthony throws that clear demarcation into question."

Trilogies Begin with "Battle Circle"

Anthony's first trilogy begins with *Sos the Rope,* based on a chapter of his 1956 B.A. thesis entitled "The Unstilled World." The first installment of the "Battle Circle" books, *Sos the Rope* explores the efforts of a group of radiation survivors led by Sos as they attempt to rebuild their society after the Blast. Yet the resulting Empire soon becomes a destructive force and Sos sets out to destroy it. The novel speaks against the dangers of centralized civilization and overpopulation: millions of shrews, like the Biblical plague of locusts, invade the area and consume every living creature within their reach. Eventually the horde destroys itself with its enormity and its wholesale pillaging. The shrews' rampage and ultimate demise serve as a metaphor for man's overcrowding and abuse of the environment. Humankind, like the shrews, will be decimated when it outgrows the Earth's ability to sustain it. In *Var the Stick* and *Neq the Sword*, the "Battle Circle" story is completed. The books' titles are actually characters' names; the trilogy's warriors are named after their weapons. Collings observed similarities to the epic works of Homer, Virgil, and John Milton in "Battle Circle," which "investigates the viability of three fundamental forms of epic: the Achilean epic of martial prowess; the Odyssean epic of wandering; and the Virgillian/Miltonic epic of self-sacrifice and restoration."

The "Omnivore" trilogy provided a forum for Anthony to further his exploration of the dangers humankind continues to inflict upon itself, and introduced his support of vegetarianism. "Like *Battle Circle, Chthon*, and *Phthor*," Collings observed, "*Omnivore* deals with control—specifically, with controlling the most dangerous omnivore of all, man." Three interplanetary explorers, the herbivorous Veg, carnivorous Cal, and omnivorous Aquilon, play out Anthony's views. The three journey to the planet Nacre, reporting back to investigator Subble and subsequently revealing to readers their adventures and clues to the secret threatening to destroy Earth. In the sequel, *Orn*, the three explorers venture to the planet Paleo, which resembles the Earth of 65 million years past, and encounter Orn, a creature whose racial memory endows it with the knowledge of its ancestors and enables it to survive the changes bombarding its planet. In *Ox*, the final volume of the trilogy, Veg, Cal, and Aquilon gradually uncover the existence of a sentient super-computer while exploring alternate worlds. As with other Anthony books, reviewers noted that the "Omnivore" volumes contain substantial discussions of technical and scientific issues. A *Publishers Weekly* reviewer described *Ox* as "a book for readers willing to put a lot of concentration into reading it." The similarly complex *Macroscope*, described by Collings as "one of Anthony's most ambitious and complex novels," seeks to place man in his proper context within the galaxy. The book increased Anthony's reputation but, due to a publisher's error, was not submitted for consideration for the important Nebula Award and lost one crucial source of publicity. Nevertheless, *Macroscope* was a milestone in Anthony's career. In a *Luna Monthly* review, Samuel Mines declared, "*Macroscope* recaptures the tremendous glamour and excitement

of science fiction, pounding the reader into submission with the sheer weight of its ideas which seem to pour out in an inexhaustible flood."

Beginning with the "Cluster" series, Anthony began writing "trilogies" of more than three books. "Cluster" became a series of five, and the still-active "Magic of Xanth" stands at sixteen novels plus the companion book *Piers Anthony's Visual Guide to Xanth* and the omnibus volume *The Magic of Xanth*. The "Apprentice Adept" series, with seven entries and an omnibus volume published between 1980 and 1990, was also originally planned as a trilogy. In the case of the "Xanth" books, Anthony attributed his decision to continue the series to reader response. "We did a third [Xanth novel], and said, 'Let's wrap it up as a trilogy and not do any more,'" Anthony remarked to *SFRS*. "Then the readers started demanding

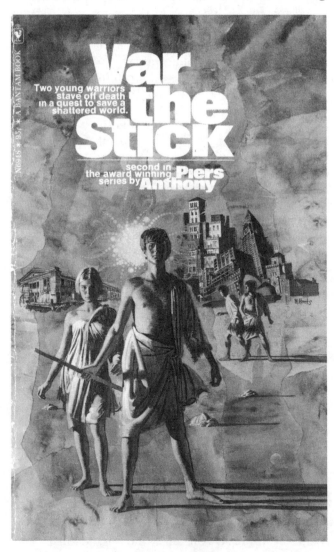

A warrior fights for the survival of his world in this 1972 work, part of the epic "Battle Circle" trilogy.

more, and more, and more, and finally both the publisher and the author were convinced. It's hard to say 'No' when the readers are begging for more."

Dispute Triggers Genre Switch

Anthony branched out from science fiction into fantasy writing with *A Spell for Chameleon*, the first of the "Xanth" books, published in 1977. Although one early work, *Hasan*, was fantasy, it was his second fantasy novel, *Chameleon*, that established Anthony in the genre. The switch to fantasy came as a result of Anthony's much-publicized split with his first publisher, Ballantine Books. As the author related to *SFRS*, Ballantine "was sending me statements-of-account that were simply not true.... I sent a letter demanding a correct statement and correct payments. Rather than do that, they blacklisted me for six years." Anthony moved to Avon Books; six years later, with a new administration at Ballantine, the author found himself invited back and wanted to give Ballantine another chance. His contract at Avon, however, prohibited him from writing science fiction for another publisher, so he decided to try fantasy. Luckily, Anthony knew and liked the fantasy editor at Ballantine, Lester del Rey; Ballantine's Del Rey imprint went on to publish the first nine "Xanth" novels as well as the early "Apprentice Adept" and "Incarnations of Immortality" entries. Anthony differentiates between his science fiction and fantasy works in their content as well as their popularity. "For the challenge and sheer joy of getting in and tackling a difficult problem and surmounting it, science fiction is better," Anthony remarked to *SFRS*. "But if I need money, fantasy is better." He later added, "I talk about writing fantasy in the sense of doing it for the money, but I also enjoy it. If I didn't enjoy it, I wouldn't do it for the money."

Anthony is best known for the "Xanth" books. An omnibus volume containing the first three "Xanth" novels—the trilogy originally planned—was published in 1981, but the series continues over a decade later. The "Xanth" stories are generally less complex and easier to read than Anthony's earlier works, appealing to younger readers as well as adults. In fact, the books are often referred to as "juvenile fiction."

A Spell for Chameleon, a 1978 Hugo Award nominee, introduced Bink, who tackles another recurring topic in Anthony's novels: maturity and control. The first "Xanth" installment chronicles Bink's growing-up; later volumes feature his son,

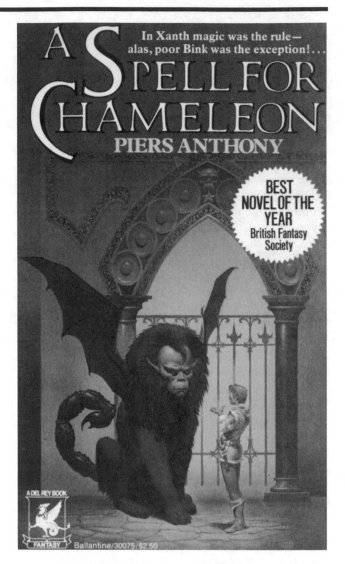

Courageous young Bink, whose quests for magic and adventure are chronicled in the "Magic of Xanth" series, was introduced in this award-winning 1977 fantasy novel.

Dor. In the land of Xanth, everyone and everything—even a rock or tree—has a magical talent, except Bink. *Chameleon* follows Bink on his quest to discover his talent or face exile to the boring, powerless land of Mundania. In the process, Bink gains not only knowledge of his talent but emotional maturity as well. Bink sets out on another adventure in *The Source of Magic*, assigned to discover the source of all magic in Xanth. In *Castle Roogna*, Bink's son Dor travels eight hundred years back in time to rescue his nurse's boyfriend. Throughout each book, Bink and Dor encounter innumerable illusions and feats of magic. "Piers Anthony ... apparently decided to invest his magical land of Xanth with every fantastical conception ever invented," a reviewer for *Isaac Asimov's Science Fiction Magazine* remarked. "It has

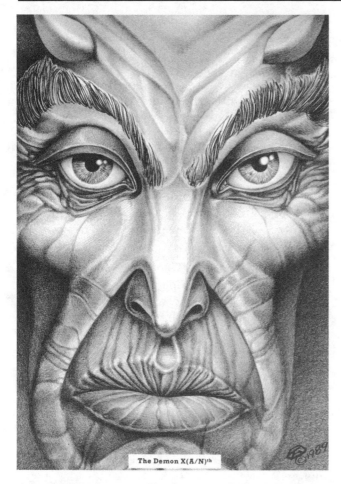

The Demon X(A/N)ᵗʰ

This illustration from *Piers Anthony's Visual Guide to Xanth* depicts the demon god who is the source of all magic in the fantasy world of Xanth.

quests, enchanted castles, riddles, unicorns, griffins, mermaids, giants (not to mention invisible giants), zombies, ghosts, elves, magicians, man-eating trees, enchantresses, and a host of inventions from Anthony's own fertile mind.''

"The Magic of Xanth" continued with *Centaur Aisle*, *Ogre, Ogre*, and *Night Mare*, the next "trilogy" of "Xanth" books. The first of these finds Dor filling in for Xanth's King Trent while he and Queen Iris take a trip to Mundania, good experience for Dor since he will one day become king. When the King and Queen fail to return, Dor sets out on another adventure. Anthony once again explores the process of maturing, as Dor leads a search party through Xanth and into Mundania, and falls in love with Princess Irene. In *Ogre, Ogre*, the half-human, half-ogre Smash must protect the half-human, half-nymph Tandy. A stupid, insensitive creature at the beginning of the tale, Smash gradually acquires more human traits until he finally realizes that he is in love with Tandy.

Later entries in the series added to Anthony's portrait of the fantastic land of Xanth, with story-lines including the rescue of the kingdom by a creature responsible for delivering bad dreams (*Night Mare*), the adventures of three-year-old Princess Ivy, lost and wandering in the forest with newfound friends Hugo and the Gap Dragon (*Dragon on a Pedestal*), the diminutive Golem's quest to rescue a lost baby dragon and prove himself worthy of attention (*Golem in the Gears*), Prince Dolph's protest against the Adult Conspiracy that keeps children ignorant of adult matters (*Heaven Cent*), and Princess Ivy's trip to Mundania in search of Good Magician Humphrey (*Man from Mundania*). Richard Mathews applauded the "Xanth" series in *Fantasy Review*, asserting that it "ranks with the best of American and classic fantasy literature."

Such a Punny Guy

Anthony's use of puns and other language tricks is a hallmark of the "Xanth" novels. "In Xanth," Collings noted, Anthony "incorporates much of this interest in language in furthering the plot and in establishing the essence of his fantasy universe. In Xanth, language is literal, especially what in Mundania would be called metaphors. Thus bread-fruit bears loaves of bread; shoetrees bear shoes in varying sizes and styles; nickelpedes are like centipedes, only five times larger and more vicious; and sunflowers are flowers whose blossoms are tiny suns blazing at the top of the stalk—a potent weapon if an enemy looks directly at them." In a *Voice of Youth Advocates* review of *Ogre, Ogre*, Peggy Murray found that Anthony's stories, "full of sophomoric humor and bad puns, have tremendous appeal with **YA** fantasy readers."

Cluster, the first novel in the series of the same name, was published in the same year as the first "Xanth" book. The original "Cluster trilogy" led to *Tarot*, published in three volumes as *God of Tarot*, *Vision of Tarot*, and *Faith of Tarot*. Intergalactic travel and adventure are again the subjects in the "Cluster" books, in which Anthony introduces the concept of Kirlian transfer, a type of out-of-body travel that requires much less energy than the outmoded "mattermission." The Kirlian transfer and other innovations are fundamental to the outcomes of the First and Second Wars of Energy, described in the first two volumes, and to the battle of an intergalactic force against the space amoeba in *Kirlian Quest*. "More than anything, the Cluster series is an exercise in enjoyment" for Anthony, Collings remarked. The author relishes the opportunity to create bizarre beings and situations unlike any the reader has experienced, such as a race with three sexes and the resulting differences in sexual practices.

Publication Hobbles 250,000-Word Novel

From the ending of *Kirlian Quest*, Anthony created *Tarot*, which he had intended for publication as one volume. Anthony emphasized in his interview with *SFRS* that *Tarot* is not a trilogy, but "a quarter-million-word novel." The novel was published, not only in three parts, but in two different years. "It bothered me because I feel that this is the major novel of my career," Anthony remarked in the *SFRS* interview published in 1985. "Split into three parts and published in two years—it washed me out totally. I had no chance to make a run for any awards or anything like that. It was simply gone." He resents referrals to the book as a trilogy because they imply that each volume is a full novel, when in fact they are each one-third of a novel.

Brother Paul, a character introduced in the "Cluster" trilogy and featured in *But What of Earth?*, is the central figure in *Tarot*, in which Anthony attempts to develop a definition of God. Collings acknowledged that the "brutality, horror, and disgust" present in the book were not unlike those of many other Anthony novels, but combined with religious references proved controversial and offensive to many readers. *Tarot* "is certainly not for the squeamish, nor is it altogether for those who enjoyed the first installment of Tarot civilization in the Cluster novels. Anthony himself admits this," Collings noted.

While continuing to add novels to the "Xanth" series, Anthony introduced three more series: the science fiction/fantasy novels of "Apprentice Adept," science fiction of "Bio of a Space Tyrant," and fantasy of "Incarnations of Immortality." Several single works followed as well, including *Anthonology*, a collection of his previously published short stories, *Bio of an Ogre: The Autobiography of Piers Anthony to Age 50*, and the mainstream novel *Firefly*. The "Apprentice Adept" books are set on the twin planets of Proton, dependent on technology for survival, and Phaze, where magic is the most valuable resource. In *Split Infinity*, Stile, hoping to avoid exile from Proton, enters the Game but is injured by an unknown enemy. His discovery of Phaze restores his hero status. In *Blue Adept*, Stile discovers that he once had an alternate self, a resident of Phaze, who was murdered. Stile's quest

to win the Game on Proton continues as he searches for "his" murderers and develops his own magical powers on Phaze. Along the way he meets his alter ego's widow, Lady Blue, and other enticing female characters, including a beautiful female robot and a half unicorn/half woman. In *Juxtaposition* Stile works to avert a disaster as the time approaches for the two worlds to temporarily merge and then separate forever. "Although this all sounds too confusing, it somehow fits together and it's a lot of fun," Paul Granahan commented in *Best Sellers*. Noting that he has hoped for "deeper endeavors" from Anthony, Granahan nevertheless remarked, "I highly recommend this imaginative series."

The five volumes of "Bio of a Space Tyrant" chronicle the life of Hope Hubris, the Tyrant of Jupiter, whose crimes include mass murder, cannibalism, rape, and prostitution of his sister and mother. In the first volume, *Refugee*, Anthony explores Hubris's childhood, uncovering the reasons for his incorrigibility. *Library Journal* reviewer Susan R. Nickerson noted that Anthony "manages to inject telling social comment along the way." In a review of *Mercenary* for *Fantasy Review*, Mary S. Weinkauf found, "Anthony combines political/social allegory with the kind of blood and sex adventure that lures readers to buy the next volume."

Incarnation of a New Fantasy Series

Anthony returns to pure fantasy in the "Incarnations of Immortality" series, which begins with *On a Pale Horse* and is set in "a world very much like ours, except that magic has been systematized and is as influential as science," a *Publishers Weekly* reviewer commented. The abstract concepts of Time, War, Nature, Fate, and Death are all real people—the Incarnations—and all are involved in the battle of Satan against God. In *Bearing an Hourglass*, a grief-stricken man agrees to take on the role of Chronos, the Incarnation of Time, and soon finds himself locked in a battle with Satan. *Booklist* reviewer Roland Green noted the religious and ethical content of the series that "even people who may disagree with [Anthony's] ideas will recognize as intelligently rendered." Subsequent volumes feature the Incarnations of Fate (*With a Tangled Skein*), War (*Wielding a Red Sword*), Nature (*Being a Green Mother*), Evil (*For Love of Evil*), and finally, Good (*And Eternity*). "This grand finale ... showcases Anthony's multiple strengths" including his humor, characterizations, and themes, a *Library Journal* reviewer declared.

Anthony explored a new genre in *Firefly*, a novel with science-fiction elements. Anthony told *AAYA* that he objected to the marketing of *Firefly* as a horror novel. "It is a mainstream novel dealing with sexual abuse, and I don't want teen readers picking it up with the notion that it's another vampire or werewolf novel," he commented. "It has a horror element, but that is incidental to its formidable social thrust." Set in Anthony's home state of Florida (as are the "Xanth" books and others), *Firefly* is an account of the hunt for a monster capable of desiccating its victims, leaving only skin and bones with no signs of entry. The monster uses pheromones, powerful sexual hormones, to attract and subdue its prey, earning it the name Firefly after that insect's mating—and killing—practices. In the end it is the pheromones

This 1983 work began Anthony's "Incarnations of Immortality" fantasy series in which the abstract concepts of Time, Fate, and Nature take on human form to battle Satan.

that enable the hunters to find the monster: they become severely sexually aroused for no apparent reason and recognize that the monster must be near. The book's explicit sexual content prompted a *Publishers Weekly* reviewer to conclude, "While some readers may find his ideas intriguing, many will be put off by a narrative that verges on the pornographic." Descriptions of consensual sex between the child Nymph and an adult, Mad, are particularly disturbing. Anthony employed a favorite method of communicating with his readers, the Author's Note at the end of the book, to discuss the issue. "This novel addresses more than peripherally the problem of abuse," Anthony wrote. "It occurs in many forms, physical and emotional, and is exacerbated by the insensitivity, ignorance, or downright malice of others.... The games five-year-old Nymph played with Mad were a joy to her at the time, but it was nevertheless abuse by our society's definition ..., and her life was significantly colored by the experience thirty years later." When Mad is convicted and dies in prison, Nymph believes she is responsible for his death; for the rest of her life she remains convinced that any man she loves is destined to die.

Despite Anthony's explanation, many readers wrote to complain. "Some seemed to think I was espousing sexual abuse," he said in an addendum to the Author's Note published in the paperback edition of *Firefly*. "I thought the context made it clear that I was not, but it seems that many folk see only what they wish to see.... Readers generally don't like being lectured, but will respond to material presented in an interesting manner. So I showed more than one type of sexual abuse in action, and showed the long-term consequences. I felt that this would make the problem clear without lecturing, and for many readers it did." The consequences presented included Nymph's psychological problems, manifested in her use of distinct personalities, each with its own name, to cope with her pain—a situation similar to the multiple personalities often developed by victims of violent sexual abuse during childhood. Another character, May, has a history of sadistic sexual abuse at the hands of her husband. After escaping from him and starting a new life, May finds just enough courage and strength to break away when he captures her again, but must rely on another man to help her. Addressing the elusive solution to the problem of abuse, Anthony recommended less lenience for offenders and more education for everyone. "Certain fundamental attitudes need to be revised," Anthony continued, "such as the

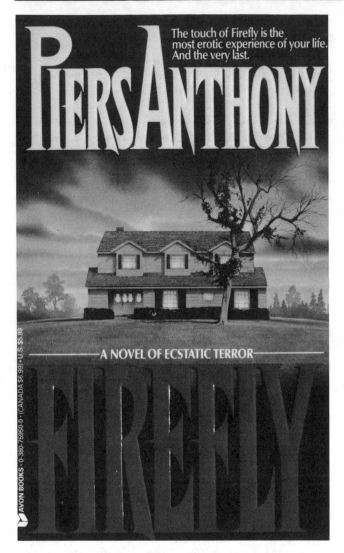

The touch of Firefly is the most erotic experience of your life. And the very last.

PIERS ANTHONY

—A NOVEL OF ECSTATIC TERROR—

FIREFLY

AVON BOOKS · 0-380-75950-0 · (CANADA $6.99) · U.S. $5.99

This 1990 novel about the hunt for a deadly creature generated controversy due to its explicit sexual content.

notion that women are inherently inferior to men, or that might makes right, or that sex is sinful, and because these may be embedded in religion the problem of reform is monstrous. But the alternative is to continue with the horrors this novel suggests.''

Virtual Mode also addresses ''some similar concerns in a less provocative manner,'' and is a novel ''to which teens relate well,'' Anthony remarked to *AAYA*. Published in 1991, *Virtual Mode* introduced the ''Mode'' series, in which characters traverse the universe through the use of ''skew paths'' anchored by other people. As the anchors change, the paths and destinies of the travelers are affected and new stories are presented. In *Virtual Mode*, Darius of Hlahtar ventures to Earth to bring the girl he loves, the suicidal Colene, back to his universe. Together Darius and Colene discover that they must build a skew path to complete the journey. *Publishers Weekly*'s Sybil Steinberg described Colene as ''a clearly defined character, virtues, flaws and all'' who is ''brought fully to life in this skillful, enjoyable book.''

Anthony told *AAYA* that *Tatham Mound* is among his works most likely to appeal to young adults. The story of fifteen-year-old Throat Shot, a sixteenth-century Florida Indian, *Tatham Mound* is based on an actual Indian burial mound discovered in North Florida and features historically accurate reconstructions of Spanish explorer Hernando de Soto's march across Florida and his battles with the Indian tribes of the area. A *Library Journal* reviewer described *Tatham Mound* as a ''heartfelt tribute to a lost culture'' and a ''labor of both love and talent.''

Firefly, *Virtual Mode* and *Tatham Mound* exemplify Anthony's desire to produce works of lasting value along with those written simply for entertainment. While he wants readers to enjoy his work, the author hopes also to provoke contemplation of the serious issues he presents. ''I'd like to think I'm on Earth for some purpose other than just to feed my face,'' Anthony remarked to *SFRS*. ''I want to do something and try to leave the universe a better place than it was when I came into it.''

■ Works Cited

Review of *And Eternity*, *Library Journal*, December, 1989, p. 176.

Anthony, Piers, *Firefly*, Morrow, 1990, Avon, 1992.

Biggers, Cliff, ''An Interview with Piers Anthony,'' *Science Fiction*, November, 1977, p. 60.

Review of *Chthon*, *Publishers Weekly*, June 5, 1967, p. 180.

Collings, Michael R., *Piers Anthony*, Starmont House, 1983.

Easton, Tom, review of *Bio of an Ogre: The Autobiography of Piers Anthony to Age 50*, *Analog*, January, 1989, p. 182.

Review of *Firefly*, *Publishers Weekly*, August 10, 1990, p. 431.

Granahan, Paul, review of *Juxtaposition*, *Best Sellers*, July, 1982, p. 135.

Green, Roland, review of *Bearing an Hourglass*, *Booklist*, July, 1984, p. 1497.

Harris, Leo, review of *Chthon*, *Books and Bookmen*, April, 1970, pp. 26-27.

Lane, Daryl, William Vernon, and David Carson, *The Sound of Wonder: Interviews from "The Science Fiction Radio Show,"* Volume 2, Oryx, 1985.

Mathews, Richard, "Xanth Series Extolled," *Fantasy Review,* March, 1984, pp. 24-25.

Mines, Samuel, review of *Macroscope, Luna Monthly,* September, 1970, p. 22.

Murray, Peggy, review of *Ogre, Ogre, Voice of Youth Advocates,* April, 1983, p. 44.

Nickerson, Susan R., review of *Refugee, Library Journal,* September 15, 1983, p. 1811.

Review of *On a Pale Horse, Publishers Weekly,* September 2, 1983, p. 72.

Review of *Ox, Publishers Weekly,* July 26, 1976, p. 78.

Review of *A Spell for Chameleon, Isaac Asimov's Science Fiction Magazine,* September, 1979, p. 18.

Steinberg, Sybil, review of *Virtual Mode, Publishers Weekly,* January 4, 1991, p. 61.

Review of *Tatham Mound, Library Journal,* August, 1991, p. 150.

Weinkauf, Mary S., "Space Foreign Legion," in *Fantasy Review,* August, 1984, p. 7.

■ For More Information See

BOOKS

Contemporary Literary Criticism, Volume 35, Gale, 1985, pp. 34-41.

PERIODICALS

Analog, August, 1992, pp. 167-168.
Fantasy and Science Fiction, August, 1986, pp. 37-40.
Horn Book, October 6, 1989, p. 84.
Library Journal, August, 1991, p. 150.
New York Times Book Review, April 20, 1986, p. 27.
Publishers Weekly, July 25, 1986, p. 174; August 29, 1986, p. 388; May 29, 1987, p. 73; February 10, 1989, p. 58; August 11, 1989, p. 444; August 25, 1989, p. 58; April 20, 1990, p. 61; May 11, 1990, p. 251; November 2, 1990, p. 58; December 21, 1990, p. 57; January 4, 1991, p. 61; October 18, 1991, p. 55; July 20, 1992, p. 237.
The Writer, August, 1989, pp. 11-13, 35.
Writer's Digest, January, 1991, p. 32.

—*Sketch by Deborah A. Stanley*

Steven Bochco

■ Personal

Full name, Steven Ronald Bochco; born December 16, 1943, in New York, NY; son of Rudolph (a concert violinist) and Mimi (an artist) Bochco; married in the 1960s; wife's surname, Blau (divorced); married Barbara Bosson (an actress), February 14, 1969; children: (second marriage) Melissa, Jesse. *Education:* Graduated from New York City High School of Music and Art; attended New York University; Carnegie Institute of Technology (now part of Carnegie-Mellon University), B.F.A., 1966. *Politics:* Liberal. *Hobbies and other interests:* Racquetball.

■ Addresses

Home—Pacific Palisades, CA; and Santa Fe, NM. *Office*—Steven Bochco Productions, Twentieth Century-Fox, 10201 West Pico Blvd., Los Angeles, CA 90035.

■ Career

Universal Studios, Los Angeles, CA, overseer of internship program, summer, 1960s, scriptwriter, editor, and producer for television and film, 1966- 78; MTM Enterprises, Studio City, CA, writer-producer, 1978-85; Twentieth Century-Fox, Los Angeles, writer-producer, 1985-87; affiliated with Steven Bochco Productions, Los Angeles, 1987—. Producer and executive producer for television, including the movies *Lieutenant Schuster's Wife,* 1972, and *Vampire,* 1979, the series *Griff,* 1973-74, *The Invisible Man,* 1975-76, *Richie Brockelman, Private Eye,* 1978, *Paris,* 1979-80, *Hill Street Blues,* 1981-85, *Bay City Blues,* 1983-84, *L.A. Law,* 1986-89, *Hooperman,* 1987-89, *Doogie Howser, M.D.,* 1989—, *Cop Rock,* 1990, *Civil Wars,* 1991—, and *Capitol Critters* (animated), 1992—, and the pilots *The Invisible Man,* 1975, *Richie Brockelman: Missing Twenty-four Hours,* 1976, and *Every Stray Dog and Kid,* 1981. Creator of series *Sarge,* 1971-72. *Member:* Academy of Television Arts and Sciences, Writers Guild of America.

■ Awards, Honors

Fellowship, William Morris Agency, 1960s; writing fellowship, MCA, 1960s; Emmy Award nominations for best writing in drama for a single program in a series, American Academy of Television Arts and Sciences, 1972 and 1973, both for *Columbo;* Emmy awards for best drama series, 1981, 1982, 1983, and 1984, all for *Hill Street Blues,* and 1987 and 1989, both for *L.A. Law;* Emmy awards for best writing in a drama series, 1981 and 1982 (and additional nominations, 1981 and 1982), both for *Hill Street Blues,* and 1987, for *L.A. Law;* Humanitas Prize for one-hour program, Human Family Institute, 1981, for *Hill Street Blues;* Edgar Allan Poe Award, Mystery Writers of America, 1981;

George Foster Peabody Broadcasting Award, University of Georgia—Henry W. Grady School of Journalism and Mass Communication, 1981; Writers Guild Award, Writers Guild of America, 1981; *Hill Street Blues* received People's Choice Award for new dramatic program, Proctor & Gamble Productions, 1982, People's Choice Other Award, 1982, Rockie awards for continuing series, Banff Television Festival, 1982, 1983, and 1985, Golden Globe awards for best drama series, Hollywood Foreign Press Association, 1982 and 1983, and People's Choice awards for dramatic program, 1983 and 1984; *L.A. Law* received People's Choice Award for new dramatic program, 1987, People's Choice awards for dramatic program, 1988 and 1989, and Golden Globe awards for best drama series, 1987 and 1988; *Doogie Howser, M.D.* received People's Choice Award for new comedy program, 1990; Image Award, National Association for the Advancement of Colored People.

■ Writings

SCREENPLAYS

(With Harold Clements) *The Counterfeit Killer* (based on television movie *The Faceless Man*), Universal, 1968.
(With Michael Cimino and Deric Washburn) *Silent Running*, Universal, 1971.

Also contributed to movie version of Rod Serling's television script *A Slow Fade to Black.*

SCRIPTS FOR TELEVISION SERIES; WITH OTHERS

The Name of the Game, National Broadcasting Company (NBC), 1968-72.
Columbo, NBC, 1971-78.
McMillan and Wife, NBC, 1971-76.
Griff, American Broadcasting Companies (ABC), 1973-74.
Delvecchio, Columbia Broadcasting System (CBS), 1976-77.
McMillan, NBC, 1977.
Turnabout, NBC, 1979.
Paris, CBS, 1979-80.
Hill Street Blues, NBC, 1981-85.
Bay City Blues, NBC, 1983-84.
L.A. Law, NBC, 1986—.
Hooperman, ABC, 1987-89.
Doogie Howser, M.D., ABC, 1989—.
Cop Rock, ABC, 1990.
Civil Wars, ABC, 1991-93.

Contributor of script material to *Ironside*, NBC, c. 1967.

OTHER TELEVISION WRITINGS

(With Bernie Kukoff) *Lieutenant Schuster's Wife* (movie), ABC, 1972.
Double Indemnity (movie), ABC, 1973.
The Invisible Man (pilot), NBC, 1975.
(With Stephen J. Cannell) *Richie Brockelman: Missing Twenty-four Hours* (pilot), NBC, 1976.
(With Michael Kozoll) *Vampire* (movie), ABC, 1979.
(With William Read Woodfield) *Columbo: Uneasy Lies the Crown* (movie), ABC, 1990.

■ Sidelights

"I want to do stuff that challenges folks and entertains folks, and I'm willing to take the risk that some people will not like what I do." That's an attitude that some say has changed the face of television, and it belongs to producer Steven Bochco, speaking to Robert Lindsey in the *New York Times Magazine.* As a maverick creator of acclaimed and sometimes controversial series such as *Hill Street Blues* and *L.A. Law*, he routinely defies network censors with racy dialogue and sexual content and tests viewers' concentration with layered action, sound, and plotting. Critics have commended his series for tackling difficult issues like incest, legal ethics, and police violence without oversimplifying or offering easy answers. Detractors argued that many of the so-called novelties in Bochco's shows had already appeared in programs such as *M°A°S°H*, *Lou Grant*, and *Barney Miller*, but that didn't prevent Bochco from gaining a reputation as "perhaps Hollywood's brightest and most innovative producer of television drama," noted Lindsey.

Bochco was not exactly born to success. From his childhood he was shadowed by financial worries, because his father, concert violinist Rudolph Bochco, "didn't have a knack for making money," the producer told Paula Span in *Esquire.* The family "held onto its ... apartment and never went without shoes, food, or a Steinway," Span reported, "but he could not provide them with financial stability." As Bochco's mother told Span, "One year was great, the next year was lousy." Rudolph urged his son toward a practical career, perhaps in engineering, but Bochco was more interested in sports, girls, and singing than studying. "My adviser informed me that I was not college material," he recalled in a 1988 *Rolling Stone* article by Mark Christensen. Despite that judgment, Bochco managed to win a scholarship to New York University.

The television series *Columbo*, which starred Peter Falk as a clever, disheveled detective, provided a springboard to Bochco's later success.

When Bochco transferred to Carnegie Institute of Technology, the idea of a writing career began to take root. "I'd always written stuff," Bochco told Christensen. "And even in high school, teachers had told me I was talented, encouraged me. Now, all of a sudden, I was surrounded by people with whom I shared common interests." A summer internship got his foot in the door at Universal Studios, and when he graduated he landed a full-time job there. According to Bochco's wife, Barbara Bosson, his work priorities reflected his uncertain upbringing. "Steven . . . didn't use[d] to say 'I'm going to go into TV and win a bunch of Emmys,'" Span quoted. "He used to say, 'I'm gonna be a millionaire.'"

Millions were still just a dream while Bochco worked for Universal, which at that time was regarded as something of a television factory for the way it churned out shows. "What I did when I first started there—and it was tremendous hands-on training—was take unsold pilots and episodes of 'Chrysler Theatre' and write an additional hour's material for them," Bochco explained in *American Film*. "It would be filmed, spliced in, and the whole thing released as an overseas movie package for television. Really, it was very smart business."

It was also a reasonably good living for Bochco. "I ended up pulling down $15,000 my very first year," he told Christensen. Bochco said his father was "happy, excited and nervous" about the job—nervous that Bochco would make a wrong move. "Because I don't think he'd ever made $15,000 a year in his whole life."

Eventually Bochco advanced to story editor of the detective series *Columbo*, which he assessed in *American Film* as "probably the single most fortunate thing that ever happened to me." The period was memorable to him for several reasons. For one thing, Bochco worked with director Steven Spielberg years before the latter made history with blockbuster films such as *Jaws, Close Encounters of the Third Kind, Raiders of the Lost Ark,* and *E.T. The Extraterrestrial.* As Bochco recalled, "The episode of 'Columbo' that Steven directed was the first one I ever wrote. And the two of us were really the baby boys at Universal. . . . I was twenty-six and Steven was twenty-two." Also, he noted, "because of 'Columbo''s success, I gained a degree of professional recognition in the business that I hadn't had before." That recognition included his first two Emmy Award nominations for writing.

During his years at Universal, Bochco also got a taste of filmmaking, helping to write the screenplays for *The Counterfeit Killer* and *Silent Running.* The latter, a 1972 film about a spaceborne botanist's efforts to preserve Earth's last vegetation after a nuclear war, helped push Bochco into producing. "I watched them make this thing, and I hated it," he complained in *American Film.* "I was so disturbed, as I guess most writers are, at seeing the terrible disparity between what was in my head and what they were putting on the screen, that I thought: I've got to be able to do something about this. . . . I started producing the next year." Bochco confessed that in the beginning he was an "awful producer," and his first several television projects lasted only a season or two. By 1978 he was ready to move on.

A New Kind of Cop Show

A few years after leaving Universal for MTM Enterprises, home of successful series such as *The Mary Tyler Moore Show* and its spin-off series *Lou Grant* and *Rhoda*, Bochco got an assignment to create a new police drama. He had already written for a number of crime shows, including *Columbo, McMillan and Wife,* and *Delvecchio,* and neither he nor his collaborator, Michael Kozoll, relished another. But Fred Silverman, the president of NBC

Bochco wrote the screenplay for *Silent Running*, a 1971 film that featured Bruce Dern as a spaceborne botanist determined to save Earth's last remaining plant life after a nuclear war.

Entertainment, put a different twist on the idea. He thought the series should have "an emphasis on personal lives. That put a bulb over my head," Bochco told Christensen in a 1986 *Rolling Stone* article. After that flash of inspiration, the show was "a genuine ensemble invention," he remarked in *American Film*. Bochco ultimately received much of the credit for its success, but as he put it, "I just wound up having the mouth."

Bochco and Kozoll began shaping *Hill Street Blues* around an ensemble cast rather than the traditional one or two leading characters, recognizing fairly soon that they would need a great deal of freedom to realize their vision. Discussing the situation with Lindsey, Bochco elaborated: "We agreed to do the show on the condition that they really leave us alone, give us genuine creative autonomy and a substantially greater degree of leniency from broadcast standards." The writers were surprised when NBC agreed to their terms, but the network "needed a pilot desperately," Bochco conceded in *American Film*. "There was very little time."

The pair started with eight regular characters and a style borrowed from *The Police Tapes*, a documen-tary program filmed in black-and-white with hand-held cameras. Aware that developing so many characters complicated the plot structure, they "began to think of it more in terms of a tapestry," Bochco noted in *American Film*. Plots and subplots could then overflow from one episode to the next instead of being tied up neatly at the end of each hour. Conventional series plot resolutions didn't satisfy Bochco anyway. "If you have neatness in 48 minutes, you've got to end up earnest, pedantic, didactic, and finally arrogant," he told Tony Schwartz in *New York*. Overlapping dialogue, a freer use of idiom, and camera angles that took in a broad picture, with characters moving through scenes from all sides, added to the illusion of reality. Unexpected and sometimes shocking plot twists created tension and held viewers' attention.

Hill Street Blues premiered mid-season, in January 1981. Reviews were mixed and ratings low, at least at first. Some writers criticized it for the charac-ters' many eccentricities, the way the show com-bined serious and comic elements, and what they considered gimmicky production techniques. Oth-ers, like *Film Comment* reviewer Richard T. Jameson, welcomed it as "one of the best series ever developed for television." Marveling at its free-flowing structure, Jameson remarked, "I have never encountered another TV program that betrayed less sign of anticipating commercial breaks or straining to tie off tonight's episode." John J. O'Connor, writing in the *New York Times*, liked that it "takes chances." He admitted that it sometimes "falls on its face, but its attempts to break the shackles of standard formats are rarely uninteresting."

Judging by ratings alone, the gritty police drama fell on its face for most of 1981; as Christensen reported in 1988, it was "the lowest-rated series ever to be renewed at the end of its first season." But Bochco and his colleagues proved ratings weren't everything in the fall of that year, when *Hill Street* captured an unprecedented eight Emmy awards. Crowning the honors were the Emmys for best drama series and best writing in a drama series, which Bochco shared as coproducer and coauthor. Emmys, however, were no guarantee of *Hill Street*'s survival, as Richard Corliss warned in a 1981 *Time* article. Corliss hoped that at least the exposure from the awards might convince viewers to tune in to the "ferociously intelligent" series, which he considered "very much its own show."

Censorship versus Creative Freedom

From the outset, *Hill Street* battled more than low ratings. Among Bochco's chief adversaries—despite NBC's creative autonomy pledge—were censors in the network "standards and practices" department. In Bochco's view, television should reflect real life, so sexual innuendo, vulgarity, nudity, violence, and so forth were legitimate parts of any show interested in realism. Censors, arguing that a television program is a guest in the viewer's home, complained that such elements required discretion. In his *New York Times Magazine* interview, Bochco explored the fundamental difference between television's aims and his own: "Television is not an art medium. . . . It is really a commercial sales medium. It does not want to do anything to encourage controversy or distress. The ideal piece of programming for selling things, I suppose, lulls you into a pleasant sense of well-being. . . . There's nothing wrong with that, but . . . that's not what I want to do."

An important issue in Bochco's disputes with censors was control of one's own work. Bochco explained to Lindsey: "If you accept their fiddling, you are giving away your adulthood. You have

accepted the role of precocious, mischievous child and they are the parent. Well, I'm not a child. And I've succeeded in spite of this business, not because of it." In Bochco's opinion, the audience alone should determine television standards. "If you have young kids, it's your responsibility as a parent to monitor what they see," he observed in *American Film*. "There's a button there. Turn it on; turn it off. That's a big thing of mine. But I am actually against any kind of broadcast standards. If you eliminated them tomorrow, there would be some excesses . . . but the pressures of the marketplace would ultimately determine what is acceptable fare for a substantial number of viewers."

Hill Street's high price tag caused strife between Bochco and MTM. "We were the most responsibly produced series on television," he insisted in a 1986 *Rolling Stone* article. As he told Christensen, "When you figure a very modest feature film comes in today at about $8 million, we were delivering comparable production values for about $1 million." But that was still well over the cost of more traditional police shows. Part of the trouble was that to achieve such a high degree of realism, the producers frequently filmed on the streets

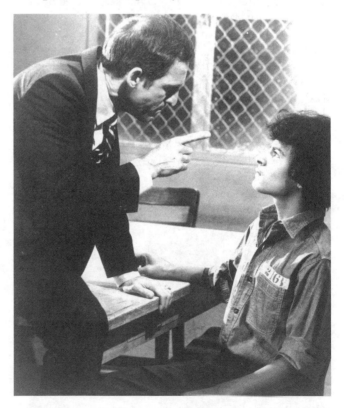

Captain Frank Furillo (Daniel J. Travanti) interrogates a suspect in an episode from the Emmy Award-winning *Hill Street Blues*, a gritty, realistic look at the lives of police officers.

instead of in a manufactured set. Multiple characters and complicated plotting also drove costs up. Recalled Bochco, "Money was a subject I fought with MTM about from the second year on." He maintained that "there are only two ways to make a cheaper *Hill Street*. One, reduce the number of characters—which leads to the second, reduce the number of stories." Either tactic, Bochco argued, would damage the series. "Like it or not, all of us . . . were in the position of having created a monster. Either you honor the monster, or you kill the monster. . . . You don't turn the monster into a pussycat." Because the show improved its ratings and continued to win awards, MTM stuck with it, however reluctantly.

Bochco's next project for MTM, *Bay City Blues*, caused even more headaches. Launched in 1983, the series about a minor-league baseball team was more costly than *Hill Street*; Bochco's expenses included the construction of an entire baseball stadium and eighty-five dollars a head per day for spectators to fill it. Worse, the series couldn't find an audience. "*Bay City* had great writing, great production values, great acting, and it bombed," Christensen reported in his 1986 *Rolling Stone* article. Bochco told him: "That's when I discovered how adrenaline addictive TV really is. It's as bad as heroin. People take their television very seriously. If you can't tell stories that generate an adrenaline rush, you're in trouble." Reviewing the show for *Time*, Richard Stengel described it as "a wry, funny, poignant and surprisingly grownup show about men who play a boys' game"; he thought the "rookie series appears to have the goods to make it in the majors." NBC disagreed, canceling *Bay City* after airing four episodes. According to David Milch, who wrote for the short-lived series, "*Bay City Blues* was one of the most expensive fiascos in television history," quoted Christensen in 1988.

By 1985 Bochco's rocky relationship with MTM had become unsalvageable. Quipped Christensen in 1986, "It's not every day that the best producer in dramatic television is fired from the best TV production house in Hollywood for the high crime of having the best show in prime time." The split reportedly had several causes. The cost of *Hill Street* had been a long-standing issue, but Bochco told Christensen: "I was not asked to leave MTM because I produced an expensive show that I refused to make less costly. . . . No, it was personal. They didn't want me. . . . Some people consider me difficult. I guess some people consider me arrogant." Milch, in Christensen's 1988 *Rolling Stone*

profile, acknowledged that "Steven was always a very confrontational producer." As he observed, that kind of approach "only works if you are the irreplaceable man." Once *Hill Street Blues* reached the golden moment for a series—enough episodes to go into syndication, where it might make as much as one million dollars per episode—MTM could afford to let Bochco go.

Looking back on his work with the celebrated police drama, Bochco admitted in *American Film* that "even though the rewards of doing 'Hill Street' were enormous, creatively and professionally, it wasn't a fun show to make. We were at war every single day. We were doing something we had no business trying to do, making forty-eight-minute movies in seven, eight days." The normal grind of script writing, arduous enough in a traditional series, became exhausting for *Hill Street*'s writers. As Bochco remarked in a 1989 *People* article, "We kept chewing up more story lines in a season than most shows do in five years." The show's various challenges brought Bochco to call the series "a runaway train" in *American Film*.

For a number of critics, *Hill Street* was worth the effort it took to produce. At its best, wrote Todd Gitlin in his book *Inside Prime Time*, it was "a mature and even brilliant show that violated many conventions, pleased critics, caught the undertow of cultural change, and ran away with the Emmys." Span in *Esquire* contended that *Hill Street* "transformed the lives of everyone associated with it; it also changed television itself. Into the conventional few-good-men police plot, it wove the stuff of aching, infuriating, ridiculous reality, too much to shoehorn into an hour." In its breadth, its exuberant blend of drama and humor, and its attention to characters, it reminded some reviewers of the Victorian novels of Charles Dickens. It was "as intellectually and emotionally provocative as a good book," claimed author Joyce Carol Oates in *TV Guide*. "In fact, from the very first, *Hill Street Blues* struck me as Dickensian in its superb character studies, its energy, its variety; above all, its audacity." Recognizing that sometimes its humor is "rather slap-dash and broad, even outrageous," she remarked that "this, too, is in the solid Dickensian tradition."

Though ousted from the show that had brought him fame, Bochco had no lack of options when he left MTM. With numerous Emmys to his credit and a fifteen-million-dollar commitment from NBC for another series, he was welcome at all of the major Hollywood studios. Bochco chose Twentieth Century-Fox, where he dealt frankly with his big-spender reputation. Quoted Christensen in 1988: "The only thing I said was, 'Look, if you'd like me to build you a Rolls-Royce, I'll build you a Rolls-Royce. If you'd like me to build you a Chevrolet, I'll build you a Chevrolet. But please do not ask me to build you a Rolls for the price of a Chevy.'"

Lucrative *Law*

Bochco's first project for his new employer was the upscale legal drama *L.A. Law*. Like *Hill Street*, it was an ensemble series with a documentary flavor, interwoven stories, and a taste for controversy. This time, however, Bochco and his colleagues intended to keep costs under control. On-location filming gave way to a studio set, and the number of recurring characters dropped from *Hill Street*'s twelve to thirty to a more manageable nine or ten. Striving as ever for authenticity, Bochco got help with legal details and scripts from lawyer/writer Terry Louise Fisher, who had previously been a producer for another successful police show, *Cag-*

ney and Lacey. Together they created a series that "moves the profession into the litigious real world," as Richard Zoglin put it in a 1986 *Time* review.

For Bochco, the subject of law was both timely and interesting. "This is the most litigious society, I think, in the history of mankind," he told Lindsey. To make the most of the American penchant for lawsuits, he and Fisher set *L.A. Law* in a full-service law firm, handling everything from criminal cases to contract disputes to divorces. They were thinking long-range, preparing for a run that could make it to syndication. "If you work on a show for five years," Bochco explained to *New York* writer Tony Schwartz, "it better be about something. I find the law endlessly interesting. It's about morality, right and wrong, good and evil." The tough issues inherent in the subject—including injustice and lawyers' ethics—just increased its appeal for Bochco. "Do your research, make sure you have good technical advisers to make sure you don't

Lawyers in Love? Bochco won several more Emmy awards for his work as a writer and producer of the acclaimed legal drama *L.A. Law*, which has included such stars as Harry Hamlin and Susan Dey in its cast.

make any grievous errors," he said in the *New York Times Magazine.* "But more important is not to run from the aspects of the law which are the most intimidating."

Characterization proved one of the show's most distinctive aspects to critics. Whereas previous law series had featured sleuths like Perry Mason or high-minded crusaders as in *The Defenders,* Bochco and Fisher's attorneys often appeared as "unprincipled hired guns who, uninterested in truth or justice, go for the jugular to win a case and make a buck," observed Lindsey. Bochco felt that this portrait struck closer to reality and public opinion. As he remarked to Lindsey: "I think the general impression that a lot of lawyers are jerks is not without some validity. They say power corrupts and absolute power corrupts absolutely.... I saw a survey showing that the two least-respected professions were lawyers and politicians." For Zoglin, however, the series countered that cynical view too obviously with a self-righteous one: "For every cold-blooded attorney obsessed with money and position, there is a principled white knight who speaks up for integrity." Other critics focused on gender and race. Writing in *Ms.,* Michele Kort pointed out the show's dearth of non-white lawyers, which she felt left it somewhat vulnerable to criticism, even though "women judges of all races turn up all the time." And some of the male characters seemed "the product of a female's wish-fulfilled fantasy of the perfect man—loving, flexible, strong but not macho." Kort also mused, however, that they "almost certainly . . . represent alter egos of Bochco."

Like *Hill Street Blues, L.A. Law* impressed award-givers, repeating the earlier series's feat of capturing the Emmy awards for best dramatic series and best writing for a dramatic series, among others. And like the earlier show, it received a mixed critical response. Kort deemed *L.A. Law* "the best new show of this television season" and described it as "video drama that feels as real (or surreal) as the evening news—and is as addictive." On viewing the pilot in 1986, Zoglin tempered his appreciation of its fresh slant with reservations about its messages. "*L.A. Law*'s gavel too often hits like a sledgehammer," he grumbled. By 1988 he had come to see the series as "TV's savviest courtroom drama." In a *Time* article assessing Bochco's influence, Zoglin quipped: "Bochco's sly accomplishment is to have concocted a show that, while styling itself as a no-holds-barred look at the legal profession, manages to reaffirm a host of romantic

Hooperman, starring John Ritter as a San Francisco detective who also serves as the landlord of his apartment building, blended elements of comedy and drama into its stories.

illusions about lawyers.... The show says you can have your ideals and your BMW too."

Critical quibbles aside, *L.A. Law* became an even bigger hit with viewers than *Hill Street Blues.* Two months into its first season it took over *Hill Street*'s long-standing Thursday evening time slot, and by the end of that season the six-year-old police drama was finished. *L.A. Law* continued to win awards and settled in for a run of more than seven years, although it wasn't all smooth sailing. In its second season, a conflict developed between Bochco and Fisher over her salary and job title, resulting in Fisher's firing, a lawsuit against Bochco and Fox, and an out-of-court settlement.

Bochco followed *L.A. Law* in 1987 with the half-hour comedy-drama *Hooperman,* which he had created with Fisher. Touted by Zoglin in the spring of 1988 as "one of the season's top-rated new series and an ambitious pioneer of TV's newest form, the 'dramedy,'" it featured John Ritter as a plainclothes detective who added landlord-tenant relations to his responsibilities after his apartment building's owner was murdered. "I'm very, very juiced about this," Bochco told Christensen in a pre-premiere conversation, published in *Rolling*

Stone in 1988. "I think John Ritter is one of those people who radiates so much talent that if you just put his name in the phone book someplace, it would jump right out at you. And I think we've been able to bring some really great new characters to life." Others, unfortunately, seemed less enthusiastic. Zoglin called the series "provocative but overly congested" in a 1988 article and commented that it "has yet to hit its creative stride." Some viewers reportedly found its combination of humor and action confusing. Almost exactly two years after the series's debut, ABC canceled it.

Around the time *Hooperman* premiered, Bochco took the industry by storm with "one of the best deals ever made in television," as Christensen reported in 1988. Bochco agreed to create seven new series for ABC to distribute over the next six years, with three more to follow sometime thereafter. In return, ABC guaranteed Bochco approximately fifty million dollars, along with unprecedented extras such as a fee of $1.5 million in the event that the network rejected a Bochco series. Further, Bochco would retain ownership of his shows, standing to pocket additional millions for any that made it to syndication. It was, as Span put it, "a deal that set car phones warbling all over town."

Doctor Doogie, the Kid Kildare

Bochco launched the first of his ten contracted ABC series in 1989. *Doogie Howser, M.D.* details the personal and professional trials of a boy who earns a medical degree at age fourteen and is a second-year hospital resident at sixteen. It was inspired in part by Bochco's father, who at age nine was already a professional violinist. When Bochco was a child, "*prodigy* didn't mean anything to me," he confessed to Diane Haithman in the *Los Angeles Times*. "All I knew was I had a dad who was a violinist—that's what he did professionally. But he was also a guy who was a gifted portrait painter, self-taught, a wonderful architect, self-taught, a wonderful designer and master-builder, a voracious reader.... He audited medical school when he was a 20-year-old kid, because he had a bunch of friends who were medical students." *Doogie Howser, M.D.* became something of a tribute to Bochco's dad, right down to the computer-animated violinist that ran as the logo for Steven Bochco Productions at the end of each episode.

"Every kid's fantasy is of being empowered, like an adult," Bochco told *Detroit Free Press* writer Marc

Gunther. "That's what adolescents rail against. Their parents are collaring them, yanking on that leash. They want to have what seems to be the unbridled fun and freedom and mobility of an adult." For Bochco, Doogie Howser is "a kid who is living that fantasy and discovering, in many, many, many ways, every day of his life, hopefully with some fun attached to it, that it's an awesome responsibility, being free." The pilot episode focused on Doogie's sixteenth birthday, for which his colleagues stage a prank seduction that proves decidedly less funny to the sixteen-year-old than to the adult staff. "Although later episodes might be lighter," Bochco explained to Haithman, "my choice was to do something that aches, so you could see what is fundamental to the concept—the compelling complexity and difficulty of being a boy in an adult world." Reviewing the new series for the *Detroit Free Press*, Susan Stewart pronounced it "flawed-yet-interesting.... There is nothing here to criticize, and nothing to compel anybody to keep watching. Unless we are 14-year-old girls." Stewart acknowledged the appeal of teenage star Neil Patrick Harris and likened Doogie to television's much-loved Dr. Kildare, with the added charm of being "young enough to take you to the prom." Young viewers reportedly flocked to the show.

Already well known for innovation, Bochco took his biggest creative leap yet with his next ABC series, a mixture of police action and music that aired in 1990 under the title *Cop Rock*. *Newsweek*'s Harry F. Waters called it "the season's most-touted entry" and Bochco's "farthest-out concept." In a seemingly standard courtroom scene, for example, the show would suddenly have a jury singing out its verdict like a gospel choir. Some viewers were uneasy with the combination. Skeptical critics like Zoglin, assessing *Cop Rock* in 1991, contended that "the gritty cop scenes were so compelling that the musical numbers (which rarely measured up) seemed like rude interruptions." Suggested Waters, "Even a Bochco can botch one." The show lasted three months.

During the 1991 season, Bochco retreated to safer territory with the drama *Civil Wars*. Like *L.A. Law*, the new series centered on lawyers, but this time Bochco focused on just one of America's legal arenas: divorce court. Waters reported it as "the season's most anticipated show" in a 1991 review. To Zoglin, it was "bleaker and more brutal than anything Bochco has done before"; the critic observed that ABC had found the premier episode so grim that they had Bochco add some lighter

The trials and triumphs of a teenage doctor form the basis of the Bochco-produced series *Doogie Howser, M.D.*, starring Neil Patrick Harris.

moments. Along with a callous husband divorcing over his wife's weight gain, then, the show presented a wackier subplot about a husband who thinks he is the reincarnation of singer Elvis Presley. Waters pronounced the results successful: "It's the smartest, tangiest and most appealing drama series ever to undergo involuntary cosmetic surgery."

In *Civil Wars*, "as in any Bochco production," related John Leonard in *New York*, "we expect and get a fine supporting cast . . . excellent guest stars . . . gritty scripts, with gallows humor [and] characters who'll surprise us with their pathos *and* their bounce." Acknowledging the presence of such Bochco trademarks, Zoglin expressed reservations about other aspects of the series, which he felt had "too little of interest going on outside the courtroom," for instance. Still, he dubbed it "a canny compendium of every relationship issue the '90s has to offer," adding that "it feeds one of TV's most enduring myths: that the cold legal system has a human face." The emotional angle of *Civil Wars* also struck Waters. The show, he wrote, "never goes preachy on us and, at times, turns poignantly affecting."

Critical response to Bochco's work has long been mixed. Reviewers have described it variously as ground-breaking and old hat, fresh and gimmicky, mature and adolescent. When some lauded Bochco's use of ensemble casts, others pointed out their use in earlier shows, such as the Korean War sitcom *M°A°S°H;* those hailing his treatment of serious modern issues faced off against others who decried his use of humor as juvenile. At their best, Span asserted, Bochco's shows "radiate intelligence and irreverence, achieving oddly effective amalgams of absurd humor and grim drama, and they reflect an adult appreciation of life's ambiguities. Few network offerings are as well written, performed, or produced."

Pursuit of the new, daring, or even outrageous is a key element of Bochco's style. Said former NBC chair Grant Tinker to Zoglin in 1988, "He rocks the boat as a hobby." Since first obtaining a measure of artistic freedom with *Hill Street Blues*, Bochco has constantly pushed at the limits of network propriety. Of course, "as a decade of R-rated movies has shown, freedom does not guarantee quality," noted Corliss in September 1981. But in Bochco's case, he suggested, "talent and ambition, pumping at high octane, can achieve it." The boldness and idiosyncrasies of his shows have occasionally drawn criticism, but as Bochco told Christensen in 1988, "I don't feel I have a responsibility to present a balanced point of view. That's propaganda, not entertainment."

Integral to Bochco's view of his work is his role as a writer. "More than anything else," Lindsey revealed, "Bochco considers himself a storyteller." According to the journalist, Bochco's method is to write "in what he calls a 'stream of conscience.' Then he rewrites—sometimes four and five revisions." In an industry obsessed with images, Bochco has the distinction of being a man of words. "In twenty-plus years of working in this business and writing continually," he told *American Film*, "I don't really see what I write. I *hear* it." That affinity for language was apparent to reviewers, who observed that Bochco's characters often sport dialogue more complicated than the norm.

Life as a Leader

For all his vaunted power and influence in television production, Bochco long saw himself "as more of a chorus member than a soloist," he told Zoglin in 1988. Elaborating on his emergence as a leader, he confessed to Span that "it's taken me twenty years, half my life, all that length of time to get okay with the fact that I am a boss.... It's not a natural gear." An incident during a Writers Guild strike in 1988 betrayed how oblivious he was of his managerial image. Bochco urged the Guild to accept an offer from the studios and was surprised to earn the hostility of writers he considered peers, but who saw him as an executive—the opposition.

Bochco's considerable influence in the television industry has enabled him to give friends and family members a career break. He has been known to hire his wife, in-laws, children, and school buddies, a practice he defended in a 1981 *People* article by David Gritten: "The only rule I have about working with friends and loved ones is that I'm not going to penalize them for [the relationship], but if they're not better than the next person on the list, I'm not going to hire them, either. I've never been very sensitive about charges of nepotism because I've turned Barbara down for parts before. We've had a few words about that."

Inevitably, achievement brought pressure. As Bochco told Zoglin in a 1988 *Time* article: "I never imagined the tyranny of success—the way you have to deal with a new standard of excellence....

Do you play the game not to lose? Or do you keep going for a win—pushing it a bit or doing it better or different?" Instead of playing it safe, Bochco continues to take chances, likening television to baseball, where succeeding in three out of ten attempts is something to celebrate. He doesn't think too far ahead. "I think the most amazing thing about my career," Bochco told Christensen in 1988, "is that I've never had any specific goals and ambitions. I like the process. I like the work. I have no idea what I'll do next."

Goals or no goals, the man Christensen called in 1988 "the prototypical Eighties TV producer, a schizophrenic combination of writer and businessman, equal parts sensitive soul and mako shark" has shown no sign of throwing in the towel. Bochco continues to conjure up hits "for people who don't watch much TV," as Gunther phrased it. He knows the kind of odds that are stacked against him. In a *U.S. News and World Report* article, Bochco described the massive amount of creative work that goes into each season and declared that a major reason for television's failings is that "there simply are not enough talented people to go around." He knows about fickle viewers, who "bemoan the fact that there is not generally a higher level of programming" while "some of the finest things on the air die for lack of an audience." But Bochco has managed to keep a balanced view of his work. As Milch told Zoglin in 1988, "What keeps him fresh is that he's not obsessive.... Family life is important to him." In an industry notorious for burning out talent, Bochco has maintained his standing as "the most influential, the most highly paid, and by far the most visible television producer in the business," as Span described him, "a man who has made the Emmy telecast a kind of personal promenade."

■ Works Cited

Bochco, Steven, "Too Many People Use TV 'As a Tranquilizing Presence,'" *U.S. News and World Report*, June 20, 1983, p. 68.

Bochco, Steven, "On Playing to Win by Producing and Plotting *Hill Street Blues*," *People*, summer, 1989, p. 153.

Christensen, Mark, "Lawyers, Guns and Money," *Rolling Stone*, March 13, 1986, pp. 27-28.

Christensen, Mark, "Bochco's Law," *Rolling Stone*, April 21, 1988, pp. 75-76, 81-82.

Corliss, Richard, "Midwinter Night's Dreams: 'Hill Street Blues,'" *Time*, January 26, 1981, p. 72.

Corliss, Richard, "Too Good for Television? *Hill Street Blues* Has Everything Going for It— Except Ratings," *Time*, September 14, 1981, p. 88.

"Dialogue on Film: Steven Bochco," *American Film*, July-August, 1988, pp. 14, 16-18.

Gitlin, Todd, *Inside Prime Time*, Pantheon, 1983.

Gritten, David, "'Hill Street' to Easy Street? Eight Emmys Clear the Way for Bochco & Bosson," *People*, September 28, 1981, pp. 55-56.

Gunther, Marc, "A Legacy of Excellence: TV's Steven Bochco Ignores Dad's Advice, Wins Honors, Riches," *Detroit Free Press*, September 19, 1989, pp. 1B, 6B.

Haithman, Diane, "Bochco on His Own: Veteran Producer's New Firm Bows with 'Doogie Howser,'" *Los Angeles Times*, September 14, 1989, Section 6, pp. 1, 12.

Jameson, Richard T., "Quality up the Wazoo," *Film Comment*, March-April, 1981, pp. 78-79.

Kort, Michele, "Terry Louise Fisher: Her Own Background as a D.A. Shows up in Plot, Character, and Grit in the Season's Hottest Series," *Ms.*, June, 1987, pp. 38, 42, 44.

Leonard, John, "Divorce Bochco-Style," *New York*, November 25, 1991, p. 94.

Lindsey, Robert, "From 'Hill Street' to 'L.A. Law,'" *New York Times Magazine*, August 24, 1986, Section 6, p. 30.

Oates, Joyce Carol, "For Its Audacity, Its Defiantly Bad Taste and Its Superb Character Studies," *TV Guide*, June 1, 1985, pp. 4-7.

O'Connor, John J., "The 'Hill Street Blues' Lesson," *New York Times*, December 13, 1981, p. 33.

Schwartz, Tony, "Steven Bochco Goes from 'Hill Street' to the Taut Glitz of 'L.A. Law,'" *New York*, September 15, 1986.

Span, Paula, "Bochco on the Edge," *Esquire*, May, 1990, pp. 158, 160, 162, 164, 166-68.

Stengel, Richard, "Good Field, Good Hit: A New NBC Series, *Bay City Blues*, Looks Like an All-Star," *Time*, October 31, 1983, p. 117.

Stewart, Susan, "Two Medical Entries: One Frail, One DOA," *Detroit Free Press*, September 19, 1989.

Waters, Harry F., "A Season on the Brink: Desperate to Outrun Fox, the Big Three Launch Lineups That Are Rocking, Ribald, Real . . . and Risky," *Newsweek*, September 3, 1990, p. 70.

Waters, Harry F., "War and Pieces: From Steven Bochco, a Tangy Take on Divorce," *Newsweek*, November 25, 1991, p. 62.

Zoglin, Richard, "Sue, Sue! Bang, Bang! New Shows from the Creators of *Hill Street* and *Miami Vice*," *Time*, September 22, 1986, pp. 88-89.

Zoglin, Richard, "Changing the Face of Prime Time: Trendsetting Producer Steven Bochco Turns out Hits by Rocking the Boat," *Time*, May 2, 1988, pp. 75-76.

Zoglin, Richard, "Divorce, Bochco-Style," *Time*, November 25, 1991, p. 85.

■ For More Information See

BOOKS

Contemporary Literary Criticism, Volume 35, Gale, 1985, pp. 47-61.

Contemporary Theatre, Film, and Television, Volume 6, Gale, 1989, p. 40.

Newsmakers 89, Gale, 1989, pp. 5-8.

PERIODICALS

New Republic, July 18, 1981, pp. 27-29.°

—*Sketch by Polly A. Vedder*

Edgar Rice Burroughs

■ Personal

Also wrote as Normal or Norman Bean, and as John Tyler McCulloch. Born September 1, 1875, in Chicago, IL; died after several heart attacks while suffering from Parkinson's Disease, March 19, 1950, in Encino, CA; son of George Tyler (a distiller and battery manufacturer) and Mary Evaline (Zeiger) Burroughs; married Emma Centennia Hulbert, January 1, 1900 (divorced, 1934); married Florence Dearholt, 1935 (divorced, 1942); children: (first marriage) Joan Burroughs Pierce, Hulbert, John Coleman; stepchildren: (second marriage) Lee, Caryl Lee. *Education:* Michigan Military Academy, Orchard Lake, graduate, 1895.

■ Career

Writer, 1912-50. Michigan Military Academy, Orchard Lake, MI, instructor and assistant commandant, 1895-96; owner of a stationery store, Pocatello, ID, 1898; associated with American Battery Company, Chicago, IL, 1899-1903; associated with Sweetser-Burroughs Mining Company in Idaho, 1903-04; Oregon Short Line Railroad Company, Salt Lake City, UT, railroad policeman, 1904; worked at a variety of temporary jobs, 1904-08; Sears, Roebuck and Company, Chicago, manager of stenographic department, 1908; Burroughs and Dentzer (advertising agency), Chicago, partner, 1908-09; Physicians Co-Operative Association, Chicago, office manager, 1909; State-Burroughs Company (sales firm), Chicago, partner, 1910-11; System Service Bureau, Chicago, manager, 1912-13. Mayor, Malibu Beach, CA, 1933; United Press war correspondent in the Pacific during Second World War. Founder of Edgar Rice Burroughs, Inc. (publishing house), Burroughs-Tarzan Enterprises, and Burroughs-Tarzan Pictures. *Military service:* U.S. Army, 7th U.S. Cavalry, 1896-97, discharged; Illinois Reserve militia, became major.

■ Writings

"MARTIAN" SERIES

A Princess of Mars (originally serialized under pseudonym Norman Bean as *Under the Moons of Mars* in *All-Story,* February-July, 1912), McClurg, 1917.

The Gods of Mars (originally serialized in *All-Story,* January-May, 1913), McClurg, 1918.

The Warlord of Mars (originally serialized in *All-Story,* December, 1913-March, 1914), McClurg, 1919.

Thuvia, Maid of Mars (originally serialized in *All Story Weekly,* April, 1916), McClurg, 1920.

The Chessmen of Mars (originally serialized in *Argosy All Story Weekly,* February-April, 1922), McClurg, 1922.

The Master Mind of Mars (originally published in *Amazing Stories Annual*, Volume 1, number 1, July 15, 1927), McClurg, 1928.

A *Fighting Man of Mars* (originally serialized in *Blue Book*, April-September, 1930), Metropolitan, 1931.

Swords of Mars (originally serialized in *Blue Book*, November, 1934-April, 1935), Burroughs, 1936.

Synthetic Men of Mars (originally serialized in *Argosy*, January 7-February 11, 1939), Burroughs, 1940.

Llana of Gathol (four short stories: "The City of Mummies" originally published in *Amazing Stories*, March, 1941; "Black Pirates of Barsoom" originally published in *Amazing Stories*, June, 1941; "Yellow Men of Mars" originally published in *Amazing Stories*, August, 1941; "Invisible Men of Mars" originally published in *Amazing Stories*, October, 1941), Burroughs, 1948.

John Carter of Mars (two short stories: "John Carter and the Giant of Mars" originally published in *Amazing Stories*, January, 1941; "Skeleton Men of Jupiter" originally published in *Amazing Stories*, February, 1943), Canaveral Press, 1964.

"TARZAN" SERIES

Tarzan of the Apes (originally published in *All-Story Magazine*, October, 1912), McClurg, 1914.

The Return of Tarzan (originally serialized in *New Story*, June-November, 1913), McClurg, 1915.

The Beasts of Tarzan (originally serialized in *All-Story Cavalier*, May 16-June 13, 1914), McClurg, 1916.

The Son of Tarzan (originally serialized in *All-Story Cavalier*, December 4-25, 1914), McClurg, 1917.

Tarzan and the Jewels of Opar (originally serialized in *All-Story Cavalier*, November 18-December 16, 1916), McClurg, 1918.

Jungle Tales of Tarzan (six short stories published individually under collective title *The New Stories of Tarzan* in *Blue Book*, August, 1916-September, 1917), McClurg, 1919.

Tarzan the Untamed (seven short stories published individually in *Red Book* and *All-Story Weekly*, March, 1919-April, 1920), McClurg, 1920.

Tarzan the Terrible (originally serialized in *All-Story*, February 12-March 27, 1921), McClurg, 1921.

Tarzan and the Golden Lion (originally serialized in *All-Story*, December 9, 1922-January 20, 1923), McClurg, 1923.

Tarzan and the Ant Men (originally serialized in *All-Story*, February 2-March 17, 1924), McClurg, 1924.

The Tarzan Twins (juvenile; also see below), Volland, 1927.

Tarzan, Lord of the Jungle (originally serialized in *Blue Book*, December, 1927-May, 1928), McClurg, 1928.

Tarzan and the Lost Empire (originally serialized in *Blue Book*, October, 1928-February, 1929), Metropolitan, 1929.

Tarzan at the Earth's Core (originally serialized in *Blue Book*, September, 1929-March, 1930), Metropolitan, 1930.

Tarzan the Invincible (originally serialized under title *Tarzan, Guard of the Jungle* in *Blue Book*, October, 1930-April, 1931), Burroughs, 1931.

Tarzan the Triumphant (originally serialized under title *The Triumph of Tarzan* in *Blue Book*, October, 1931-March, 1932), Burroughs, 1931.

Tarzan and the City of Gold (originally serialized in *Argosy*, March 12-April 16, 1932), Burroughs, 1933.

Tarzan and the Lion-Man (originally serialized in *Liberty*, November, 1933-January, 1934), Burroughs, 1934.

Tarzan and the Leopard Men (originally serialized in *Blue Book*, August, 1932-January, 1933), Burroughs, 1935.

Tarzan's Quest (originally serialized under title *Tarzan and the Immortal Men* in *Blue Book*, October, 1935-March, 1936), Burroughs, 1936.

Tarzan and the Tarzan Twins, with Jad-Bal-Ja, the Golden Lion (juvenile; sequel to *The Tarzan Twins*; also see below), Whitman Publishing, 1936.

Tarzan and the Forbidden City (originally serialized under title *The Red Star of Tarzan* in *Argosy*, March 19-April 23, 1938), Burroughs, 1938.

Tarzan the Magnificent (two short stories: "Tarzan and the Magic Men" serialized in *Argosy*, September 19-October 3, 1936; "Tarzan and the Elephant Men" serialized in *Blue Book*, November, 1937-January, 1938), Burroughs, 1939.

Official Guide of the Tarzan Clans of America, privately printed, 1939.

Tarzan and the Foreign Legion, Burroughs, 1947.

Tarzan and the Tarzan Twins (juvenile; contains *The Tarzan Twins* and *Tarzan and the Tarzan Twins, with Jad-Bal-Ja, the Golden Lion*), Canaveral Press, 1963.

Tarzan and the Madman, Canaveral Press, 1964.

Tarzan and the Castaways (three short stories: "Tarzan and the Champion" originally published in *Blue Book*, April, 1940; "Tarzan and the Jungle Murders" originally published in *Thrilling Adventures*, June, 1940; "The Quest of Tarzan" originally serialized in *Argosy*, August 23-September 6, 1941), Canaveral Press, 1964.

Also author of *Tarzan and Jane: A Junglelogue*, *Tarzan's Good Deed Today*, a short play, and an unpublished Tarzan novel left unfinished at his death.

"INNER WORLD" SERIES

At the Earth's Core (originally serialized in *All-Story Magazine*, April 4-April 25, 1914), McClurg, 1922.

Pellucidar (originally serialized in *All-Story Cavalier*, May 1-29, 1915), McClurg, 1923.

Tanar of Pellucidar (originally serialized in *Blue Book*, March-August, 1929), Metropolitan, 1930.

Back to the Stone Age (originally serialized in *Argosy*, January 9-February 13, 1937), Burroughs, 1937.

Land of Terror, Burroughs, 1944.

Savage Pellucidar (four short stories: "The Return to Pellucidar" originally published in *Amazing Stories*, February, 1942; "Men of the Bronze Age" originally published in *Amazing Stories*, March, 1942; "Tiger Girl" originally published in *Amazing Stories*, April, 1942; "Savage Pellucidar" originally published in *Amazing Stories*, November, 1963), Canaveral Press, 1963.

"VENUS" SERIES

Pirates of Venus (originally serialized in *Argosy*, September 17-October 22, 1932), Burroughs, 1934.

Lost on Venus (originally serialized in *Argosy*, March 4-April 18, 1933), Burroughs, 1935.

Carson of Venus (originally serialized in *Argosy*, January 8-February 12, 1938), Burroughs, 1939.

Escape on Venus (four short stories: "Slaves of the Fishmen" originally published in *Fantastic Adventures*, March, 1941; "Goddess of Fire" originally published in *Fantastic Adventures*, July, 1941; "The Living Dead" originally published in *Fantastic Adventures*, November, 1941; "War on Venus" originally published in *Fantastic Adventures*, March, 1942), Burroughs, 1946.

The Wizard of Venus, Ace Books, 1970.

OTHER

The Mucker (two stories: "The Mucker" originally serialized in *All-Story Cavalier*, October 24-November, 1914; "The Return of the Mucker" originally serialized in *All-Story Cavalier*, June 17-July 15, 1917), McClurg, 1921, published in England as *The Man without a Soul*, two volumes, Methuen, 1921-22.

The Girl from Hollywood (originally serialized in *Munsey*, June-November, 1922), Macaulay, 1923.

The Land That Time Forgot (three short stories: "The Land That Time Forgot" originally published in *Blue Book*, August, 1918; "The People That Time Forgot" originally published in *Blue Book*, October, 1918; "Out of Time's Abyss" originally published in *Blue Book*, December, 1918), McClurg, 1924.

The Eternal Lover (two short stories: "The Eternal Lover" originally published in *All-Story*, March 7, 1914; "Sweetheart Primeval" originally serialized in *All-Story Cavalier*, January 23-February 13, 1915), McClurg, 1925, published as *The Eternal Savage*, Ace Books, 1963.

The Bandit of Hell's Bend (originally serialized in *All-Story*, September 13-October 18, 1924), McClurg, 1925.

The War Chief (originally serialized in *All-Story*, April 16-May 14, 1927), McClurg, 1927.

The Outlaw of Torn (originally published in *New Story*, January, 1914), McClurg, 1927.

The Cave Girl (two short stories: "The Cave Girl" originally serialized in *All-Story*, July-September, 1913; "The Cave Man" originally serialized in *All-Story Cavalier*, March 31-April 21, 1917), McClurg, 1925.

The Moon Maid (three short stories: "The Moon Men" originally serialized in *All-Story*, February 21-March 15, 1925; "The Moon Maid" originally serialized in *All-Story*, May 5-June 2, 1925; "The Red Hawk" originally serialized in *All-Story*, September 5-19, 1925), McClurg, 1926, abridged edition published as *The Moon Men*, Canaveral Press, 1962.

The Mad King (two short stories: "The Mad King" originally published in *All-Story*, March 31, 1914; "Barney Custer of Beatrice" originally serialized in *All-Story Cavalier*, August 7-21, 1915), McClurg, 1926.

The Monster Men (originally published under title *A Man without a Soul* in *All-Story Magazine*, November, 1913), McClurg, 1929.

Jungle Girl (originally serialized under title *The Land of Hidden Men* in *Blue Book*, May-September, 1931), Burroughs, 1932, published as *The Land of Hidden Men*, Ace Books, 1963.

Apache Devil (sequel to *The War Chief*; originally serialized in *All-Story*, May 19-June 23, 1928), Burroughs, 1933.

The Oakdale Affair (originally published in *Blue Book*, March, 1918) [and] *The Rider* (originally serialized under title "H.R.H. the Rider" in *All-Story*, December 14-28, 1918), Burroughs, 1937.

The Lad and the Lion (originally serialized in *All-Story Cavalier*, June 30-July 14, 1917), Burroughs, 1938.

The Deputy Sheriff of Comanche County (originally serialized under title *The Terrible Tenderfoot* in *Thrilling Adventures*, March-May, 1939), Burroughs, 1940.

The Man-Eater (originally serialized in *New York Evening World*, November, 1915; also see below), privately printed, 1955.

Beyond Thirty (title story originally published in *All Around*, February, 1916 [also see below]; includes "The Man-Eater"), privately printed, 1955.

The People That Time Forgot, Ace Books, 1963.

The Lost Continent (contains "Beyond Thirty"), Ace Books, 1963.

Tales of Three Planets (short stories: "The Resurrection of Jimber-Jaw" originally published in *Argosy*, February 20, 1937; "Beyond the Farthest Star" originally published in *Blue Book*, January, 1942; "Tangor Returns"; and "The Wizard of Venus"), Canaveral Press, 1964.

Beyond the Farthest Star, Ace Books, 1964.

The Girl from Farris's (originally serialized in *All-Story Cavalier*, September 23-October 14, 1916), House of Greystoke, 1965.

The Efficiency Expert (originally serialized in *All-Story*, October 8-29, 1921), House of Greystoke, 1966.

I Am a Barbarian, Burroughs, 1967.

(Under pseudonym John Tyler McCulloch) *Pirate Blood*, Ace Books, 1970.

Also author of unpublished, unproduced play *You Lucky Girl!*, c. 1927. Author of column "Laugh It Off," *Honolulu Advertiser*, 1941-42 and 1945. Contributor, sometimes under pseudonym Norman Bean, to *All-Story*, *Writer's Digest*, *New York World*, and other publications.

■ Adaptations

FILMS

The Lad and the Lion, Selig Polyscope Co., 1917.

Tarzan of the Apes, starring Elmo Lincoln and Enid Markey, National Film Corp., 1918.

The Romance of Tarzan, starring Elmo Lincoln and Enid Markey, National Film Corp., 1918.

Revenge of Tarzan, starring Gene Pollar and Karla Schramm, Samuel Goldwyn, 1920.

The Adventures of Tarzan, starring Elmo Lincoln and Louise Lorraine, Weiss Bros., 1920.

Tarzan and the Golden Lion, starring James H. Pierce, Dorothy Dunbar, and Edna Murphy, RKO Pictures Corp., 1927.

The New Adventures of Tarzan, starring Herman Brix and Ula Holt, Burroughs-Tarzan Enterprises, 1935.

Tarzan and the Green Goddess, starring Herman Brix and Ula Holt, Burroughs-Tarzan Enterprises, 1936.

Tarzan's Revenge, starring Glenn Morris and Eleanor Holm, Twentieth Century-Fox, 1938.

Tarzan, the Ape Man, starring Denny Miller, Metro-Goldwyn-Mayer, 1959.

Tarzan Goes to India, starring Jock Mahoney, Metro-Goldwyn-Mayer, 1962.

Tarzan's Three Challenges, starring Jock Mahoney, Metro-Goldwyn-Mayer, 1963.

Tarzan and the Valley of Gold, starring Mike Henry, American International Pictures, 1965.

Tarzan and the Great River, starring Mike Henry, Paramount, 1967.

Tarzan and the Jungle Boy, starring Mike Henry, Paramount, 1968.

The Land That Time Forgot, starring Douglas McClure and John McEnery, American International Pictures, 1975.

At the Earth's Core, American International Pictures, 1976.

The People That Time Forgot, starring Patrick Wayne and Sarah Douglas, American International Pictures, 1977.

Tarzan, the Ape Man, starring Miles O'Keefe and Bo Derek, Metro-Goldwyn-Mayer/United Artists, 1981.

Greystoke: The Legend of Tarzan, Lord of the Apes, starring Christopher Lambert, Warner Bros., 1984.

TARZAN PICTURES STARRING JOHNNY WEISMULLER

Tarzan, the Ape Man, with Maureen O'Sullivan, Metro-Goldwyn-Mayer, 1932.

Tarzan and His Mate, with Maureen O'Sullivan, Metro-Goldwyn-Mayer, 1934.

Tarzan Escapes, with Maureen O'Sullivan, Metro-Goldwyn-Mayer, 1936.

Tarzan Finds a Son, with Maureen O'Sullivan, Johnny Sheffield, and "Cheeta," Metro-Goldwyn-Mayer, 1939.

Tarzan's Secret Treasure, with Maureen O'Sullivan, Metro-Goldwyn-Mayer, 1941.

Tarzan's New York Adventure, with Maureen O'Sullivan, Metro-Goldwyn-Mayer, 1942.

Tarzan's Desert Mystery, with Johnny Sheffield, RKO Radio Pictures, 1943.

Tarzan Triumphs, with Nancy Kelly, RKO Radio Pictures, 1943.

Tarzan and the Amazons, with Johnny Sheffield and Brenda Joyce, RKO Radio Pictures, 1945.

Tarzan and the Leopard Women, with Johnny Sheffield and Brenda Joyce, RKO Radio Pictures, 1945.

Tarzan and the Huntress, with Brenda Joyce, RKO Radio Pictures, 1947.

Tarzan and the Mermaids, with Brenda Joyce, RKO Radio Pictures, 1947.

TARZAN PICTURES STARRING LEX BARKER

Tarzan's Magic Fountain, with Brenda Joyce, RKO Radio Pictures, 1949.

Tarzan and the Slave Girl, with Vanessa Brown, RKO Radio Pictures, 1950.

Tarzan's Peril, with Virginia Huston, RKO Radio Pictures, 1951.

Tarzan's Savage Fury, with Dorothy Hart, RKO Radio Pictures, 1952.

Tarzan and the She-Devil, with Joyce McKenzie and Raymond Burr, RKO Radio Pictures, 1953.

TARZAN PICTURES STARRING GORDON SCOTT

Tarzan's Hidden Jungle, with Vera Miles and Jack Elam, RKO Radio Pictures, 1955.

Tarzan and the Lost Safari, Metro-Goldwyn-Mayer, 1957.

Tarzan's Fight for Life, Metro-Goldwyn-Mayer, 1958.

Tarzan and the Trappers, Metro-Goldwyn-Mayer, 1958.

Tarzan's Greatest Adventure, Metro-Goldwyn-Mayer, 1959.

Tarzan the Magnificent, Paramount, 1960.

SERIALS

The Son of Tarzan (fifteen episodes), National Film Corp., 1920-21.

The Adventures of Tarzan (fifteen episodes), Great Western Producing Co., 1921.

Tarzan the Mighty (fifteen episodes), starring Frank Merrill and Natalie Kingston, Universal, 1928.

Tarzan the Tiger (fifteen episodes), starring Frank Merrill and Natalie Kingston, Universal, 1929.

Tarzan the Fearless, starring Buster Crabbe and Jacqueline Wells, Principal Productions, 1933.

Jungle Girl (fifteen episodes), Republic Pictures, 1941.

Tarzan (television series), starring Ron Ely, NBC-TV/Banner Productions, 1966-68.

Tarzan, Lord of the Jungle (animated series), featuring the voice of Robert Ridgely, Filmation, broadcast on CBS-TV, September 1, 1976-77 (16 episodes); later broadcast as part of "The Batman/Tarzan Hour," 1977-78 (6 new episodes), and "Tarzan and the Super Seven," 1978 (6 new episodes).

Tarzan (television series), starring Wolf Larson, WorldVision, 1991—.

Tarzan first appeared on the radio (featuring the voices of Joan Burroughs Pierce as Jane and her husband James H. Pierce as Tarzan from 1932-34; continued with Carlton Kadell as Tarzan in 1934), produced by American Radio Features; another radio show—half-hour episodes—began in 1951, sponsored by General Foods and featuring Lamont Johnson as Tarzan.

OTHER

Tarzan of the Apes (stage presentation), adapted by Herbert Woodgate, produced in England, 1920; produced on Broadway at Broadhurst Theatre, September 1, 1921.

Fritz Leiber, *Tarzan and the Valley of Gold* (novel), Ballantine, 1966.

Philip Jose Farmer, *A Feast Unknown* (novel), Essex House, 1969.

Philip Jose Farmer, *Lord of the Trees* [and] *The Mad Goblin* (two novels), Ace, 1970.

Philip Jose Farmer, *Lord Tyger* (novel), Doubleday, 1970.

John Carter of Mars (collection of comic strips that ran from 1941-43), illustrated by John Coleman Burroughs, House of Greystoke, 1970.

Philip Jose Farmer, *Tarzan Alive: A Definitive Biography of Lord Greystoke*, Doubleday, 1972.

Philip Jose Farmer, *Time's Last Gift* (novel), Ballantine, 1972.

Burne Hogarth's The Golden Age of Tarzan, 1939-1942 (comic strip collection), edited by Maurice Horn, Chelsea House, 1977.

Tarzan has also appeared in a long-running newspaper comic strip, as well as in a series of comic books. Currently he is appearing in a high-quality format series produced in Europe. John Carter was also featured in a Marvel Comics series during the

1970s. The film rights to *A Princess of Mars* have been purchased by Walt Disney.

A large number of fanzines are devoted to Edgar Rice Burroughs' work; these include *Barsoomian, Burroughs Bulletin, Burroughs Newsbeat, Burroughs Reader & Thuria, Burroughsiana, Edgar Rice Burroughs News Dateline, Edgar Rice Burroughs Quarterly, ERBania, ERB-Apa, ERB-Collector, ERB Digest, ERB-Dom, ERB-Fan, ERBivore, Fantastic Worlds of ERB, Gridley Wave, Jasoomian, Odwar, Oparian, Tarzan Drum Beat, Tarzine,* and *La Tribune des Amis d'Edgar Rice Burroughs.*

■ Sidelights

On December 1, 1911, at about eight o'clock in the evening, a thirty-six-year-old man picked up a pen and began to write a story. This man had lived out almost half his life and was, by his own standards, a failure. He had tried many different occupations—serving as a cavalryman in Arizona, working for his family's battery concern, punching cattle on his brothers' ranch in Pocatello, Idaho, managing a department for Sears, Roebuck & Co. in Chicago, prospecting for gold in Idaho and Oregon—and had failed at all of them. Recently, however, he had achieved a small success; a serialized fantasy story he had written for a pulp magazine had been accepted for publication and brought him $400. He had completed another story, a pseudo-historical romance, but it alone would not provide for his wife and little children. That night he would try to duplicate his first success. He wrote: "*I had this story from one who had no business to tell it to me, or any other.... The yellow, mildewed pages of a man long dead, and the records of the Colonial Office dovetail perfectly with the narrative of my convivial host, and so I give you the story as I painstakingly pieced it out from these several various agencies.*"

The man was Edgar Rice Burroughs; the story was *Tarzan of the Apes.* Since that December evening, Burroughs' Tarzan has become one of the most celebrated fictional characters of all time. He achieved his greatest popularity through scores of motion pictures based on his adventures, ranging from the 1918 silent film *Tarzan of the Apes* through the 1984 *Greystoke.* He has also appeared in television programs, comic books, and related media, and currently ranks with Sherlock Holmes, Superman, Mickey Mouse, and Dracula in recognition and archetypal power. "Estimates of the sales of the Tarzan series," wrote Russel B. Nye in his 1970 work *The Unembarrassed Muse: The Popular*

Arts in America, "vary from twenty to fifty millions—and as Alva Johnson once wrote, the nation's trees resounded for years with Tarzan cries and the snapping of youthful collarbones. The apeman has never been absent from at least one of the popular entertainment media since."

Burroughs himself became something of a media star when Tarzan was at the height of his popularity. In 1932, in response to a query from a publisher for personal information about himself, he wrote a humorous short sketch detailing his life and career (later published as *Edgar Rice Burroughs Tells All*). Wildly fictional, the article followed the author's life from birth in China's Forbidden City, where his father was military advisor to the Empress. The fictional "Burroughs" was kidnapped by gypsies, graduated summa cum laude from Yale, and served with Custer at the Little Big Horn. "After wandering for six weeks," the writer explained, "... I reached an army post, but when I attempted to rejoin my regiment, I was told that I was dead. Insistence upon my rights resulted in my being arrested for impersonating an officer." "Burroughs" later joined Stanley's expedition to Africa in search of Dr. Livingston, was captured by Arabs, escaped to fall into the hands of cannibals, escaped once again, travelled to Russia where he served in the Czar's guard, and ended up inheriting some eight million dollars and marrying the Czarina's lady-in-waiting. "I am sorry," "Burroughs" stated, "that I have not led a more interesting existence ... but I am one of those fellows who has few adventures and always gets to the fire after it is out."

"I Was Born in Peking"

Burroughs' own life, although not quite as exciting as his fictional account, nonetheless had its moments. He was born in Chicago, Illinois, the fourth and youngest son—two other children having died in infancy—of a well-to-do battery manufacturer and his wife. Mr. George Tyler Burroughs had served in the Army of the Potomac during the Civil War, resigning in 1865 with a commission as brevet major. Mary Evaline Burroughs worked as a schoolteacher in Iowa until she married George Tyler in 1863. The couple settled in Chicago, on the city's middle-class west side. Edgar "was a sensitive child, observant, and eagerly attentive," explained Irwin Porges in *Edgar Rice Burroughs: The Man Who Created Tarzan.* "An impression of lightness—pale skin and golden-brown hair—conveyed also the image of delicate health that concerned his parents."

Health problems made Burroughs' early education somewhat uneven. Edgar (called "Ed" by his family and friends) began his studies at Brown School, the local public institution, which his brothers had attended. He made many friends there, including Emma Centennia Hulbert, a neighbor and the girl who would later become his wife. However, when Chicago was threatened by an epidemic of diphtheria during his sixth-grade year, Burroughs' parents removed him from Brown and enrolled him in a private school. "The only one available on the West Side," wrote Porges, "was Mrs. K. S. Colley's School for Girls. To a twelve-year-old boy the prospect was appalling."

Despite the onus of attending a girls' school, Ed managed rather well at Mrs. Colley's institute. His lowest mark, according to Porges, was an 80, received in composition. Nonetheless, he was very unhappy there and so, in the fall of 1888, he was enrolled in the Harvard School in Chicago, some distance from his home. At this school, however, Ed let his academic marks slip. His delicate health, which had caused his parents so much concern, was improving, thanks to his intense interest in outdoor activities. By 1891, he had departed the Harvard School, probably because of the threat of an epidemic, but he carried no fond memories of his days there. "The typical school studies, the lessons in Greek and Latin, he found dreary tasks," explained Porges. "Highly imaginative, he could discover in these subjects nothing to motivate him." "'I was never a student'" at the Harvard School, Porges cited Burroughs as saying many years later; "'I just went to school there.'"

"Shortly After ... I Was Kidnapped by Gypsies"

Ed received a break from schooling in 1890, in the summer of his fifteenth year. George and Harry Burroughs, Ed's oldest brothers, had recently moved west to develop some ranch land owned by Major Burroughs in the new state of Idaho, and on July 3rd Ed travelled out to join them. Although he was an experienced rider, the streets of Chicago had not prepared him for the rigors of Idaho cowboy life. "The greenest of ranch hands, young Burroughs began to gain his experience in the most painful ways," declared Porges. "His brothers George and Harry were hard put to find some tasks he could do." Eventually Ed became a sort of jack-of-all-trades, removing sagebrush, picking up the mail, driving horses—in short, becoming a true cowhand. He stayed at the Idaho ranch until the

fall of 1891, when his father summoned him to return to school.

"This brief Idaho period in 1891 had given Ed freedom and a touch of the kind of carefree, adventurous life he would seek again," wrote Porges. "A restlessness and a need to express his masculinity remained with him, governing some of his future actions." It was planned that Ed should attend prestigious Phillips Academy in Andover, Massachusetts, where his brother Frank had been for the past two years. Although the young man from Chicago by way of Idaho made friends easily—he was elected president of his class—he was not interested in maintaining the academic standards required by the school. On January 15, 1892, the principal requested that Major George Burroughs withdraw his son from the academy. "Ed's stay at Phillips terminated as abruptly as it began," declared Porges. "It appears that his election as president and his dismissal from the school occurred close enough in date almost to coincide. Obviously, at the class graduation in 1894 President Burroughs would not officiate."

The education of young Mr. Burroughs was becoming a serious issue with his family. "Retired Major Burroughs," Porges explained, "turned to a popular solution, often adopted by parents of problem sons: Ed would be sent to a military academy." Accordingly, in the spring of 1892 Ed entered the Michigan Military Academy in Orchard Lake, some miles northwest of Detroit. The discipline required of him there, coupled with threats of hazing by upperclassmen (sanctioned by some of the staff) proved to be quite a shock, and by April, Ed had had enough. He fled the academy, returning home to Chicago. A terse telegram from the Commandant addressed to Major Burroughs followed, reporting Ed's desertion; it was followed by a tactful letter explaining the situation, and within a few days Ed was back at the academy of his own free will. This time he was there to stay.

By the fall of 1892, Ed had settled into the routine of the academy. He participated in sports, including football and baseball, drilled with the cadets, played practical jokes, worked on the school paper as artist and contributor, and was both promoted and reduced to the ranks on several occasions. He developed his riding skills to a great degree, participating in exhibitions with other cadets. Even his grades improved. By the time he graduated in June, 1895, he considered himself ready for a career in the military. He requested a commission to West Point from an Idaho congressman through his brother George. "Unfortunately," wrote

Porges, "as far as candidate Edgar R. Burroughs was concerned, the hopes of Congressman Wilson and the dreams of the state of Idaho were not to be realized." He failed the entrance examination.

"I ... Was Attached to the 7th Cavalry"

Burroughs did not quite know what to do with himself once his dreams of attending West Point were squelched. Finally he accepted a post at the Michigan Military Academy, his alma mater, as assistant commandant, serving as instructor in subjects ranging from cavalry and Gatling gun techniques to professor of geology. "Ironically, Ed, who had taken delight in breaking many of the rules when he was a cadet, now turned into a strict disciplinarian," Porges declared. He lost the popularity he had gained when he was himself a cadet, and his enthusiasm for the post rapidly dimmed. "By the spring of 1896," explained Porges, "Ed's impatience with his confining duties, the routine of school schedules, of supervisory tasks, reached a climax." He resigned his position and travelled to Detroit to enlist in the U.S. Army.

On May 24, 1896, Edgar Rice Burroughs was sworn in as a private in the U.S. 7th Cavalry at Fort Grant, Arizona Territory. "His dream now," stated Porges, "was to be a commissioned officer in the regular army; and with the experience and training he had acquired at the academy, the appointment might be possible. But if it could not be obtained, he was prepared to serve an apprenticeship as an enlisted man and was planning for the commission that was bound to come." However, he had not reckoned with the hardships he was to face at Fort Grant—which was, according to the recruiting sergeant in Detroit, the worst possible assignment. The commanding officer was, according to Ed, both lazy and inept, while the men, usually drunk, were subjected to hard, prison-like labor and uneven discipline. In addition, Ed contracted dysentery within a few weeks of his arrival and was diagnosed by the camp doctors as having a heart condition that threatened his military career.

Weakened by disease and bored with the monotony of camp life, Ed sought diversion whenever he could find it. "A dangerous outlaw, the Apache Kid, was roaming the countryside with his band of cutthroats," wrote Porges, "while there were reports of towns being raided by another bandit called Black Jack. To Ed these depredations became a source of hope rather than fear; he wrote, 'We were always expecting boots and saddles and praying for it, for war would have been better than

camp life at Fort Grant.'" Still very sick with dysentery, Burroughs lied about his condition and obtained permission to go on patrol with his company in search of the Apache Kid. They returned to camp empty-handed, after a fruitless series of maneuvers. Ed had once again had enough. On March 23, 1897, thanks to the efforts of his father, he received his discharge on the basis of poor health.

At the age of twenty-one, Ed was without an occupation. He worked for a brief period for his father's battery company, then headed back to Idaho to join his brothers at the ranch. When the Spanish-American War broke out early in 1898, he tried to get a post with Teddy Roosevelt's "Rough Riders," but met with no success. Later that same year he borrowed money from his brother Harry and purchased a stationery store in Pocatello, Idaho, which he ran for about six months until the original owner returned and bought it back. In 1899 he participated in the spring roundup on the ranch, but it appeared that a cowboy's life was not for him. Other urges called him back to Chicago. On Wednesday, January 31, 1900, Ed and his childhood friend Emma Hulbert were married.

Married Life

"Throughout the years," Porges related, "Ed's unchanging devotion to Emma proved to be an element of constancy in his erratic life." Thoughts of Emma had soothed Burroughs in his army days, and his childhood affection had gradually deepened. Emma even had a positive influence on Ed's behavior. "During the years 1901-2," Porges continued, "Ed made a serious attempt to adjust to his work and to assume the responsibilities of a married man." He took a position with his father's firm, the American Battery Company, but working under his father's supervision proved too much for him to handle. In 1903, the couple moved out to Idaho, where the Burroughs brothers were now dredging gold from the Snake River.

But married life had not really settled Burroughs' restless nature. The gold-dredging enterprise lasted only a year; by 1904 Ed and Emma were in Salt Lake City, where Ed found work as a railroad policeman. This too grew disagreeable, and the two returned to Chicago to start over. "From 1904 to 1910," declared George T. McWhorter in *Edgar Rice Burroughs: A Biographical Sketch*, "there followed a succession of temporary jobs which included that of time-keeper for a construction company, selling light-bulbs to janitors and candy to drugstores, peddling Stoddard's lectures from door to door, working as an accountant for the E. S. Winslow Company, and, at an emotional nadir, offering his services as a commissioned officer in the Chinese Army, a venture mercifully aborted." He spent some time at the headquarters of Sears, Roebuck in Chicago, managing the company's correspondence. In addition, his family was growing. A daughter, Joan, was born in January, 1908, followed by a son, Hulbert, in August of 1909.

In July, 1911 Burroughs, now thirty-five, was still searching for his niche in life. At the time, he was running an unsuccessful business, trying to sell pencil sharpeners using door-to-door salesmen paid on commission. Time hung heavy on his hands as he waited for the salesmen to report, and to pass away the hours he began to write. "Since he would seldom draw upon real-life experiences," asked Porges, "where would he find the story plots that he needed? His search for excitement, for high adventure in his early years had ended in disappointment. Whatever he found fell far short of his expectations." Instead, Burroughs drew on his dreams—dreams of exotic places, strange planets, beautiful women, and brave heroes. "As he wrote," Porges declared, "the real world of the commonplace became the unreal one; it vanished, and in its place he conjured up a strange fierce civilization set in the midst of a dying planet. The new world closed around him, all sounds of the old were gone, and he was a man lost in a perilous land where science battled against savagery, beauty against ugliness."

The Incomparable Dejah Thoris

Burroughs started his story—tentatively entitled "Dejah Thoris, Martian Princess," but originally published as "Under the Moons of Mars" and known in book form as *A Princess of Mars*—with a device common to much of his fiction, a "framing sequence" explaining how he came upon the tale. The sequence relates how the narrator's beloved uncle John Carter, formerly of the Army of Northern Virginia, travelled to Arizona in 1866 to prospect for gold. He disappeared for ten years, then returned, giving no explanation for his long absence. One day some years after his return, the narrator (another fictional Burroughs) discovers his uncle's body outside Carter's home. The manuscript—the text of the story itself—is willed to Burroughs, and it tells the true story of the ten-year absence and Carter's strange and wonderful exploits on the surface of Mars.

Strange creatures, exotic women, and terrifying monsters abound in this 1927 story, the sixth installment of the popular Martian series.

As John Carter tells the story, he is cornered by Apaches in an ancient cave somewhere in the Arizona mountains. Gases suddenly released from the cavern overcome him; he is separated from his body and travels, through a form of astral projection, to Mars. Landing naked and alone on the Red Planet, he finds that his earthly muscles give him phenomenal strength and jumping powers. He is discovered and taken prisoner shortly afterwards by fifteen-foot-tall green Martians—fierce, six-limbed, fanged warriors. He learns the history and language of Mars, or Barsoom as the natives call it, and is gradually introduced to the exotic flora, fauna, and technology. So great is Carter's fighting prowess that he rises from captivity to the rank of chieftain among the Tharks, the tribe in whose company he fell. He also befriends the greatest and fiercest of their warriors, the noble Tars Tarkas.

However, the true action of the story, and its sequels *The Gods of Mars* and *The Warlord of Mars*, begins with the introduction of the Princess of Helium, who falls captive to the Tharks. Dejah Thoris is the most beautiful woman on two worlds, and her description serves as a prototype for every beautiful woman Burroughs ever created: "Her face was oval and beautiful in the extreme, her every feature was finely chiseled and exquisite, her eyes large and lustrous and her head surmounted by a mass of coal black, waving hair, caught loosely into a strange yet becoming coiffure. Her skin was of a light reddish copper color, against which the crimson glow of her cheeks and the ruby of her beautifully molded lips shone with a strangely enhancing effect." "She was as destitute of clothes as the green Martians who accompanied her," he continued. "Indeed save for her highly wrought ornaments, she was entirely naked, nor could any apparel have enhanced the beauty of her perfect and symmetrical figure."

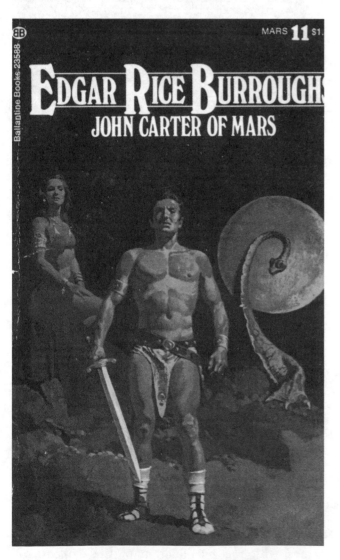

This 1964 reprint contains two short stories about Burroughs' space-traveling adventurer, John Carter.

The World of Barsoom

So begins the first segment in a cycle that, according to John Flint Roy in *A Guide to Barsoom*, "is undoubtedly one of the greatest science fiction series of all time." In fifteen magazine stories published between 1912 and 1943, Burroughs created a fully-realized fantastic world. "Taking the planet Mars as a basis," Roy explained, "Burroughs created a world of dead seabeds, towering mountains, polar ice caps, underground rivers, weird plants, beautiful flowers, and strange beasts. He peopled it with four different human races and one semi-human. He gave it a history, several phases of civilization, and an assortment of religions. He added dauntless heroes, beautiful maidens, evil villains, and fearful monsters—all the ingredients necessary for a series of thrilling adventures on any world." His wonderful creations, which have enchanted several generations of readers, include the eight-legged beasts of burden and transport called *thoats*; the vicious yet loyal ten-legged *calot*, equivalent to an earthly dog; the egg-laying females of the Martians; marvelous fliers held aloft by a special "eighth ray"; and special rifles and pistols with ranges of about 300 miles.

Without denigrating his vivid imagination and story-telling ability, some critics have concluded that Burroughs may have drawn inspiration for some of his ideas from contemporary sources. These include the theories of turn-of-the-century astronomer Percival Lowell, who believed that the scars in the Martian landscape, visible through earthly telescopes, were canals meant to carry water to dry parts of the planet and were therefore signs of intelligent life. "That Burroughs read and made use of Percival Lowell's books *Mars and Its Canals* and *Mars as the Abode of Life* cannot be denied," Roy stated; "and definitely he perused newspaper articles and Sunday supplements dealing with the Red Planet. Thus it was that he wrote of a Mars patterned on the facts and theories of the day." Richard A. Lupoff, writing in *Edgar Rice Burroughs: Master of Adventure*, suggested that two late nineteenth-century works of fiction, *Lieut. Gullivar Jones: His Vacation* and *The Wonderful Adventures of Phra the Phoenician*, both by Edwin Lester Arnold, may have provided prototypes for John Carter. The late science fiction Grand Master Fritz Leiber, in an essay entitled "John Carter, Sword of Theosophy," found similarities between some of Burroughs' Martian ideas and the doctrines of the late nineteenth-century religious cult of Theosophy; "It seems to me very plausible," he wrote, "that Burroughs' writing . . . in the early

The bizarre alien world of Burroughs' imagination is captured by artist Michael Whelan in his depiction of Thuvia, Maid of Mars.

part of this century, should have found background material in the cults flourishing right around him.''

Although Ed had demonstrated a writing talent before—while working in Idaho in 1903, for instance, he had put together the manuscript of a fairy tale entitled "Minidoka 937th Earl of One Mile Series M"—"Under the Moons of Mars" was his first attempt at writing for commercial publication. He submitted it to Thomas N. Metcalf, editor of *All-Story*, a pulp fiction magazine, using the pseudonym "Normal Bean" to indicate that although the story was fantastic in the extreme, the author himself was merely an average person. Metcalf, or one of his proofreaders, later changed Burroughs' pseudonym to "Norma*n*," believing the author's original choice to be a misprint. "Metcalf paid Burroughs $400 for magazine rights to the story," explained Lupoff, "and ran it as a six-part serial from February through July, 1912." Through his acceptance of Burroughs' Martian fantasy, Lupoff continued, "Metcalf gave first

public exposure to a science fiction classic, a story which . . . is still read as vivid high adventure . . . purely on its own merits as an engrossing story." "The world," declared Lin Carter in *Imaginary Worlds: The Art of Fantasy*, "was never quite the same again."

"The publication of *Under the Moons of Mars*," wrote Sam Moskowitz in *Under the Moons of Mars: A History and Anthology of the Scientific Romance in the Munsey Magazines, 1912-1920*, ". . . brought onto the magazine scene a writer whose instantaneous and phenomenal popularity shaped the policies of the early pulp magazines, making them the focal center of science fiction and inspiring a school of writers who made the scientific romance he wrote the most accepted form for more than twenty years." Yet the story held equal, if not greater, significance for Burroughs himself, stated Porges: "He had attained an insight, a vision of his suppressed creativity. A fuller confidence and understanding were not far away. He was on the verge of finding himself." It marked his entrance into maturity. Never again would he be without work.

The Ape-Man

After the successful sale of *Under the Moons of Mars*, Burroughs immediately began work on a second project, one suggested by Thomas Metcalf: a pseudohistorical romance set in thirteenth-century England, called *The Outlaw of Torn*. However, the story as Burroughs first constructed it did not suit Metcalf's needs. "To a critical reader," declared Porges, "'The Outlaw of Torn' was nothing more than a ragged patchwork of assorted characters and incidents, hastily conceived and ineffectively bundled together. Even as a picaresque romance with the customary string of loosely related adventures, which Ed attempted to create through brief descriptions and bits of historical reference, it was completely unconvincing." Ed was not as comfortable in a historical setting as he was in one of his own making, and he did not sell *Outlaw* until the summer of 1913, after many reworkings.

In the meantime Ed still had a family to feed, so he fell back on his imagination, which had served him so well in his Martian story. On March 6, 1912, according to Porges, he wrote to Metcalf about his latest effort—about "the scion of a noble English house—of the present time—who was born in tropical Africa where his parents died when he was about a year old. The infant was found and adopted by a huge she-ape, and was brought up among a band of fierce anthropoids." "The mental development of this ape-man in spite of every handicap, of how he learned to read English without knowledge of the spoken language, of the way in which his inherent reasoning faculties lifted him high above his savage jungle friends and enemies, of his meeting with a white girl, how he came at last to civilization and to his own," Burroughs continued, "makes most fascinating writing and I think will prove interesting reading, as I seem especially adapted to the building of the 'damphool' species of narrative."

Burroughs called his 'damphool' story *Tarzan of the Apes*. Like *Under the Moons of Mars*, *Tarzan* began with a framing sequence telling how an unnamed narrator came across the story through the indiscretions of a British colonial officer. Since its first publication in October of 1912, the general story has become familiar to thousands, and its characters—Tarzan's tragically-fated parents, John

and Alice Clayton; Kala, the she-ape who took the infant in place of her own dead child and raised it to adulthood; D'Arnot, the French lieutenant whom Tarzan rescues from cannibals and who in turn teaches him French, his first spoken human language; and Jane Porter, the first white girl the young Tarzan had ever seen, who was to become the great love of his life—are recognized by many more through the many films loosely based on Burroughs' work. The original story, however, differs in many respects from the image propagated by the Tarzan films. Perhaps the greatest of these is that Tarzan does not speak a broken English; in fact, he teaches himself to read English and speaks it fluently by the end of the novel.

Although primarily the product of the author's fertile imagination, *Tarzan of the Apes* shared ideas and themes with myths, legends, and other previously published works. One of the latter, many critics claimed, was Rudyard Kipling's *Jungle Books*. Kipling himself wrote in his autobiography *Something of Myself* that the work "begot Zoos of [imitators]. But the genius of all genii was ... *Tarzan of the Apes*." The image of the man raised in the wild—the feral man—however, is very ancient. Burroughs himself cited the legend of Romulus and Remus, the twins who were suckled by a wolf and grew up to found the city of Rome, as a direct inspiration. Kipling drew his own ideas from ancient Indian sources. Another author frequently cited as a possible Burroughs inspiration was H. Rider Haggard, who composed romantic adventure novels set in Africa in the late 19th century, and whose work was very popular both in his native England and in America.

Tarzan's exploits proved even more popular than had John Carter's Martian adventures, and Burroughs was quick to capitalize on his success. The ape-man's first adventure ran in *All-Story* for October of 1912; that same month, Burroughs began marketing both the book rights for the story and rights for newspaper syndication. By the end of the month, according to Porges, he had a rough outline of the first of many sequels, entitled *The Return of Tarzan*, which he completed on January 8, 1913.

The Return chronicles Tarzan's reversion to the wilderness; rejected by Jane Porter in favor of his titled cousin whom he rescued from a forest fire in the Wisconsin wilderness, he returns to France and D'Arnot, and indulges in the debauchery of pre-World War I Paris. Caught in a compromising situation with Countess Olga de Coude, a married lady (he was lured to her house by a false note and

Tarzan, the King of the Jungle—Burroughs' most famous creation—first appeared in this 1912 pulp magazine.

broke in because he thought she was being attacked), Tarzan is challenged to a duel by the lady's husband. To prevent further injury, D'Arnot arranges an appointment for his friend in Africa. Bound for Capetown, however, Tarzan is attacked by the same villains whom he had bested in Countess Olga's chambers, and is tossed overboard. He reaches shore, rejects western civilization, and tries briefly to take up his life again among the great apes. That, too, proves unsatisfying; Tarzan joins a band of natives, the Waziri, becomes their chief, and travels with them to the city of Opar, a treasure trove still inhabited by the remnants of an ancient race. Jane, in the meantime, has been marooned (again) on the coast of Africa with her father, her fiancee William Clayton, and a few companions. "Eventually," Lupoff explained, ". . . William Clayton conveniently dies, D'Arnot turns up with another French rescue party, and in a double wedding ceremony officiated over by Professor Porter (who is a clergyman as well as a scholar), Tarzan marries Jane and Lord Tennington marries Hazel, Jane's best friend."

The Return of Tarzan set patterns that Burroughs repeated in many of his later Tarzan books: the lost city inhabited by the remnants of an ancient race, the lost castaways threatened by wild animals and human villains, and beautiful, scantily-clad women—"Burroughs," declared Arthur Prager in *Rascals at Large; or, The Clue in the Old Nostalgia*, "loved to undress his characters"—who fall in love with either Tarzan himself or one of his comrades from the outside world. It also introduced one of the best-remembered of Tarzan's recurring characters: La, High Priestess of Opar. Unlike the rather prim Jane, La was a true sex goddess who openly lusted after the ape-man. Burroughs describes her in *Tarzan the Invincible* as "an almost naked woman, whose gorgeous beauty was her first and most striking characteristic. Two golden discs covered her firm breasts, and a narrow stomacher of gold and precious stones encircled her hips, supporting in front and behind a broad strip of soft leather studded with gold and jewels." "La ('a priestess but yet a woman') was the genuine article," wrote Prager. "She only wanted one thing—to Do It with Tarzan and she kept trying through twenty-two books, unsuccessfully but with unflagging enthusiasm. Tarzan (to our disappointment) stayed faithful to Jane but we know what *we* would have done, if the opportunity had arisen, and if we had known how."

The Inner World

With the Tarzan series well underway, Burroughs turned his attention to other projects. In February, 1913, he completed a story that would form the basis of a third series, ranked with his Martian and Tarzan books. Like *Tarzan* and *Under the Moons of Mars*, *At the Earth's Core* begins with a framing sequence, in which the hero of the tale actually narrates his story to an unnamed listener. The protagonist's name is David Innes, heir of a Connecticut fortune. David goes on an experimental trip with inventor Abner Perry, who has just developed a subterranean prospector, a machine for burrowing through the earth's crust in search of valuable minerals. Due to an oversight on Perry's part, however, the machine proves unsteerable and burrows straight down into the earth. David and Abner resign themselves to certain death, but at the last moment they break into a new world in the center of the earth, a world called Pellucidar. Pellucidar is illuminated by a single unchanging

This 1923 novel explores the land of Pellucidar, a stone-age world located at the Earth's core.

light source—it is a land without night, inhabited by many strange creatures, including the wolf-like hyaenadons, the Sagoths, semi-intelligent ape-like creatures, the Mahars, super-intelligent winged reptiles, and human men and women with a stone-age technology, including David Innes' love Dian the Beautiful.

Burroughs returned to Pellucidar in a sequel published the following year—called simply *Pellucidar*—and followed that story with others spread, like the Martian and Tarzan stories, over a series of years. Between writing the adventures of David Innes, John Carter, and Tarzan, he produced stories that did not develop into full series. In *The Mucker,* Burroughs attempted a story about an immoral man who is transformed through exposure to the outdoors and the love of a good woman. *The Girl from Farris's* is a social novel about the perils of Chicago life. *The Mad King* and its sequel *Barney Custer of Beatrice* are romances about mistaken identity in a small European kingdom in the vein of Anthony Hope's *The Prisoner of Zenda.*

Burroughs had greater success with stories in a more fantastic vein, such as *Nu of the Neocene* and *Sweetheart Primeval,* which tell of Barney Custer's sister Victoria and her trip back to prehistoric Africa, where she finds her soul-mate, the neolithic hunter Nu. *The Cave Girl* and its sequel *The Cave Man* form sort of a Tarzan-in-reverse story, in which Eastern wimp Waldo Emerson Smith-Jones, scion of an ancient Bostonian family, is marooned on a savage island. In order to survive, he "overcomes his weakness and timidity," Lupoff stated, "and is gradually transformed into a powerful giant who lives in the island jungle, stalks game with craft and courage, and in general adapts himself totally to his new surroundings." He also meets a tribe of primitive people and falls in love with one of them—Nandara, the cave girl of the first story's title, who rechristens Waldo "Thandar, the Brave One."

Among the best of Burroughs' non-series titles is the trilogy of stories published together in book form under the title *The Land That Time Forgot.* Written during the early months of America's involvement in the First World War and fuelled by Burroughs' strong anti-German prejudices, the stories tell how a German submarine and the English boat crew that captures it are drawn by a magnetic force to a mysterious uncharted island, which they call Caspak. There they find prehistoric monsters like those that haunt Pellucidar but, unlike Burroughs' Inner World explorers, they also discover no less than seven types of hominids.

These range from the ape-like Ho-lu to the Galu, who are identical with modern man. Burroughs also creates a special relationship between the different hominids through a unique concept of evolution: "In Caspak," explained Lupoff, "evolution is not a titanic, eons-long process in which each individual member of each species plays but a tiny role. Rather, each individual undergoes the full development of his species." Inhabitants of Caspak begin as primitive life forms at the southern end of the island and, as they move northwards, evolve slowly into different types. Those that can survive the entire trip end up as Galus. "If *The Land That Time Forgot* had been published as a treatise in imaginary biology," wrote Lupoff, "it might have been regarded as a piece of fascinating fantasy. As the science-fiction novel that it is, it is no less a fascinating fantasy while also being a thrilling adventure story of the finest sort produced by its author."

Success at Last

Edgar Rice Burroughs had found his true occupation. With the birth of his third child, John Coleman, he decided to devote himself to writing full-time, and he began producing an incredible amount of manuscript. Between 1913, when he began his writing career, and 1919, Burroughs wrote and published more than thirty stories, including six Tarzan stories, four Martian stories, two stories in the Pellucidar series, two-thirds of *The Land That Time Forgot* trilogy, and a variety of shorter works. In addition, by the same date he had seen seven of these published in book form.

Burroughs' prolificacy, however, was only one factor in his success. "A powerful influence," stated Porges, "was his conditioning in the business world, an emphasis on dollars-and-cents practicality that had been started in his childhood and reinforced during his later employment experiences." Early in his career Burroughs learned the value of selling only the original serial rights to a story, retaining future serial rights and book rights. He had surrendered all serial rights to "Under the Moons of Mars" and "Tarzan of the Apes"; this meant that any money gained from future magazine publication of the stories would go to the company that originally published them, and not to the author. By mid-1913, Burroughs had contracted with an agency to distribute *The Return of Tarzan* and his story "The Cave Girl" to newspapers, bringing that money into his own pocket. He set up competitive bidding between editors who wanted his stories, and insisted on being paid top per-word rates, keeping careful record of the number of words in his stories. Years later, he broke with established publishers, choosing to publish his books himself.

These business practices helped stabilize Burroughs' economic future, but in many ways he remained as impulsive as ever. In 1913, he suddenly moved his family from Chicago to California, settling in Coronado, and entering one of his most productive periods. "His earnings, collected during the summer of 1913 before he left California," wrote Porges, "totaled more than $4,600 from sales of stories and from the *Evening World* [newspaper] syndication. In California payments . . . had brought him approximately $6,000. He had written approximately 413,000 words." Yet he returned to Chicago in March of 1914, staying for another two years before leaving on a cross-country automobile tour that again landed him in California. He came back to Illinois in 1916 largely because of wartime duties—he held a major's commission in the Illinois Reserve militia and combed the area enthusiastically for recruits—but by 1919 Burroughs had made up his mind to relocate permanently to the San Fernando Valley. He purchased an estate in the foothills of the Santa Monica mountains, christened it Tarzana, and planned to become a gentleman farmer, raising Angora goats, Berkshire hogs, beans, corn, apricots, and alfalfa.

Burroughs also continued his Tarzan series with a set of linked stories that reflected his wartime anti-German feelings (collected in *Tarzan the Untamed* and *Tarzan the Terrible*). In these tales, a group of German troops attack Tarzan's African estates while the owner is away, slaughter the servants, burn the estate, and leave behind a charred corpse wearing Jane Clayton's rings. Tarzan returns, buries the remains, and sets out on a vendetta against all Germans. He unleashes lions in the trenches, stalks German officers, and in general wreaks havoc among the enemy. After many adventures, he discovers that Jane was merely abducted by the Germans, and he sets off to find her. Tarzan's travels take him to the land of Pal-ul-don, "the strangest of all the lands of the Africa which Burroughs described," according to Lupoff. There he finds a species of tailed hominids with two separate races—black and white—called the Wazdon and the Ho-don, who share a land with descendants of dinosaurs (called *Gryffs*). Eventually Tarzan and Jane are reunited and the last of Jane's kidnappers is killed by a timely bullet from their son Jack. In a decision that rather parallels

Burroughs' decision to remain in California, Tarzan and Jane surrender their option to return to England, preferring to rebuild their plantation and to commit themselves to a life in the wilds of Africa.

"Ah*AAAAH*ah-*AH*ah*AH*ah-*AH*ah*AH*ah"

With his move to California, Burroughs seemed to think that he had left Tarzan behind. He stated in a letter to a friend—cited by Porges—that "I think that I can never write another Tarzan story and I am not posing when I say that I do not see how the reading public can stand for any more of them if they are as fed up on Tarzan as I am. . . . I feel that I have said and re-said a dozen times everything that there is to say about Tarzan." But his ape-man was yet to reach his greatest popularity in a new genre—the infant motion picture industry.

Actually, as early as 1914, Burroughs had tried to interest the motion picture industry in his material. At the time he wrote the above letter, however, he was in the midst of a bitter struggle between two rival producers over the rights to two of the earliest Tarzan films: *The Return of Tarzan* and *The Revenge of Tarzan*. The process, which ended only after one of the producers died suddenly, soured Burroughs on working with people in the industry. He commented in another letter, written in 1922 and cited by Porges: "The producers never read the stories, and it is only occasionally, I imagine, that the director reads them. In fact, in the making of Tarzan of the Apes, it was forbidden that anyone connected with it read the story, for fear it might influence their work and make it more difficult for the director. Little wonder then that such asinine methods produce such asinine results. As far as I know, no one connected with the making of a single Tarzan picture has had the remotest conception of either the story or the character, as I conceived it."

Certainly the yodelling cry and the "Me Tarzan—you Jane" exchange that became identified with Johnny Weismuller's portrayal of the ape-man was never part of Burroughs' original conception of the character. "The original Tarzan—Burroughs' fantasy—is so cultivated," wrote Edward Said in an article in *Interview*, "whereas the movie Tarzan is a barely human creature, monosyllabic, primitive, simple." Gabe Essoe, in his *Tarzan of the Movies: A Pictorial History of More Than Fifty Years of Edgar Rice Burroughs' Legendary Hero*, cited an anecdote told by Weismuller about his portrayal of the jungle hero: "I remember once (as Tarzan) I was

Johnny Weismuller, the best known of the Hollywood Tarzans, courageously confronts a ferocious rhinoceros in the 1932 MGM feature *Tarzan, the Ape Man.*

supposed to point somewhere and say, 'You go.' I must've felt talkative that day because I pointed and said, 'You go quick.' 'Cut,' the director yelled. 'What's the matter, Johnny? We don't want to load this scene with any long speeches. Just do it like it's written.'"

For a time in the 1920s Burroughs tried producing his own Tarzan pictures. Eventually, however, he resigned himself to Hollywood's tendency to change his works; he added in the 1922 letter cited above, "the pictures paid well in box office receipts, and really that is all that counts." His daughter, Joan, even married James Pierce, one of the early Tarzans, and later the two of them together portrayed Tarzan and Jane on the radio. Yet despite his seeming acceptance, Burroughs did manage his own small revenge on the film industry. In *Tarzan and the Lion-Man*, first published in 1933, Burroughs told the story of a film crew on location in Africa who run into difficulties and are rescued by Tarzan. In the final chapter, entitled

"Hello, Hollywood," John Clayton visits America to see what Hollywood has done to the people he rescued in Africa the year before. He is spotted by a casting director who thinks he would make a good Tarzan. Then the casting director introduces Clayton to Mr. Goldeen, the production manager: "Goldeen's eyes surveyed Clayton critically for an instant; then the production manager made a gesture with his palm as though waving them away. He shook his head. 'Not the type,' he snapped. 'Not the type, at all.'" "As Clayton followed the casting director from the room," Burroughs continued, "the shadow of a smile touched his lips."

Instead, Clayton is cast as the white hunter Tarzan rescues from a lion, while a professional dancer is given the role of Tarzan. During filming of Clayton's scene, the lion goes berserk—the actor playing Tarzan bolts, and Clayton leaps on the beast and stabs it to death. "Clayton leaped erect," Burroughs related; "he placed one foot upon his kill and raised his face to the heavens; then he checked himself and that same slow smile touched his lips." "An excited man rushed onto the set," Burroughs concluded. "It was Benny Goldeen, the production manager. 'My God!' he cried. 'You've killed our best lion. He was worth ten thousand dollars if he was worth a cent. You're fired!'"

"I Have Tasted Fame—It Is Nothing"

Burroughs cultivated a similar sense of irony in other works. In *Tarzan and the Ant Men*, he depicts a primitive tribe of people, the Alali, who are weak male slaves totally dominated by physically powerful females (in this story, Tarzan introduces one of the males to the use of weaponry, beginning a reversal of the situation). In the same volume Burroughs satirically uses a civilization of tiny humans in much the same way that Jonathan Swift used the Lilliputians in *Gulliver's Travels*. *Tarzan, Lord of the Jungle* shows two warring cities peopled by the descendants of English crusaders. The

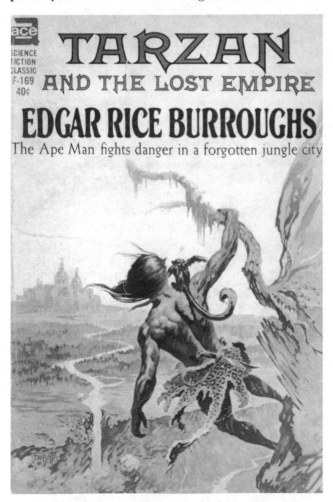

ace SCIENCE FICTION CLASSIC F-169 40¢

TARZAN
AND THE LOST EMPIRE
EDGAR RICE BURROUGHS
The Ape Man fights danger in a forgotten jungle city

Tarzan—Burroughs' ideal man—encounters the denizens of a lost jungle city in this thriller, originally published in 1929.

inhabitants of the City of the Sepulchre believe they have completed their mission, and that they can therefore return to England. The inhabitants of the City of Nimmr believe that they have not completed their mission and must press on. Both groups are not so much concerned with fulfilling their own mission as with preventing the other group from fulfilling its mission.

In *The Moon Maid*, Burroughs presents an indictment of communism, told as a "future history" story. In 2025 an expedition from the earth led by Commander Julian and Lieutenant Commander Orthis arrives at the moon and discovers that it is inhabited by three human or semi-human races: the Va-gas, a race of centaurs; the Kalkars, barbaric humans; and the U-gas, a relatively advanced race of humans. Thanks to the treachery of the jealous Orthis, the Kalkars seize control of the moon, exterminate the U-gas, and in 2050 invade and conquer the earth. The Americans, stripped of their rights, revert to a Plains Indian style of life. The families of Julian and Orthis continue the struggle over centuries, until the Kalkars are reduced to small enclaves on the coasts of North America and are finally driven into the seas. "Burroughs' obvious deep feeling about communism, his revulsion at its tyranny and terror in the name of justice," wrote Lupoff, "is a powerful force in making [the book] an outstanding example of that form of imaginative literature dubbed 'social science fiction' by [Isaac] Asimov."

Burroughs continued in this satiric vein with his last series, set on the planet Venus and begun in the early 1930s. Like the Martian series, the Venusian books feature an American hero—Carson Napier—a beautiful girl whom he loves—Duare, *janjong* (princess) of the city of Kooaad in the kingdom of Vepaja—and a wild, exotic planet to adventure in, which the natives call Amtor. Burroughs' Venusian stories, however, are far more satiric than those set on Mars. In the first novel, Duare is captured by raiding Thorists, who practice the Amtorian equivalent of communism. Carson sets off to rescue her and, in the course of their adventures, they find the city-states of Havatoo, run by a scientific council which determines the length of a person's life according to his usefulness to society, and Korva, where society is threatened by the dictator Mephis and his Zanis (a version of Hitler and his Nazis).

The many different worlds of Edgar Rice Burroughs often were linked through the introductory framing sequences of his stories. Burroughs used a first-person narrator, linking the action directly with the author. Barsoom/Mars also serves as the destination for Julian and Orthis in *The Moon Maid*, and for Carson Napier in *Pirates of Venus*. The Gridley Wave is the discovery of Jason Gridley, who uses it to pick up messages from both Barsoom and Pellucidar. Gridley's contact with Abner Perry in Pellucidar leads him into the Inner World with the assistance of Tarzan in *Tarzan at the Earth's Core*. Victoria Custer's adventures in *Nu of the Neocene* and *Sweetheart Primeval* take place in Africa, while she and her brother are guests on the Clayton's African estate. Occasionally Burroughs worked in details from real life. Jason Gridley is a fictional resident of Tarzana, a real town. When fictional Carson Napier, in *Pirates of Venus*, comes to Burroughs, seeking to use him as a psychic contact on his trip to Mars, he speaks not only with the author but also with his real-life secretary, Ralph Rothmund.

Burroughs expounded his own ideas about perfect societies in his fiction. In a series of newspaper columns written in 1928, he stated a theory of eugenics that he believed the United States should put into practice. Tarzan himself is perhaps the best example of this—a man, raised among apes, who, thanks to his genes, is able to stretch himself beyond his upbringing and to teach himself to read, write and reason. La, High Priestess of Opar, and her subjects are all products of thousands of years of controlled breeding, intended to produce stunningly beautiful women and ape-like men. Burroughs advocated sterilizing criminals and idiots in order to prevent their producing offspring that might share their undesirable characteristics. The council of Havatoo in the Venus stories has a function similar to this—as did the Nazi party in Germany at the time Burroughs was writing. Other causes that Burroughs championed—such as wildlife conservation and the healthful effects of exercise—are still popular today.

Perhaps the most pervasive of Burroughs' themes, however, is that of death and the struggle to avoid it. "Burroughs' original Martian trilogy," wrote John Hollow in the *Dictionary of Literary Biography*, "is a particularly fine instance of science fiction's attempt to cope with what Burroughs himself called 'the stern and unalterable cosmic laws,' the certainty that both individuals and whole races grow old and die." Yet nearly all of Burroughs' major heroes are provided with some antidote against aging and death. John Carter is deathless through some unexplained agency. He stated in *A Princess of Mars* that he cannot remember his childhood; as long as he can recall, he has

been a man about thirty years old in appearance, even though he believes that one day he will finally die. Tarzan is provided with an immortality drug by a dying witch doctor in one of his adventures. The Venusians have also developed an antidote to death, and they inoculate Carson Napier with it. Even the inhabitants of Pellucidar are spared the ravages of time, thanks to its peculiar form of daylight. Unlike Mars and the outer earth, which are illuminated by the sun, Pellucidar is lit by a single, unchanging light source. There is no night in Pellucidar, and as a result the humans living there have no concept of time. They therefore age at their own individual rates. In fact, Abner Perry seems to David Innes to regain some of his lost youth in Pellucidar.

"I Am Sorry That I Have Not Led a More Exciting Existence"

Eternal youthfulness, an important part of Burroughs' writing, was not the author's fate. Personal problems plagued him for the last sixteen years of his life. "After thirty-four years of marriage, he divorced his wife Emma in 1934," wrote Pastor Henry Hardy Heins in his preface to *Edgar Rice Burroughs: Master of Adventure.* "A later marriage also ended in divorce. By this time ERB was in Hawaii, where on December 7, 1941, he witnessed the actual bombing of Pearl Harbor, and where he spent the war years as the oldest accredited United Press correspondent in the Pacific theater. By the end of the war in 1945 he was 70 years old, and had been invalided home to California with a heart condition." "Here a final irony awaited the creator of Tarzan," Heins concluded. "There was no place in Tarzana for him to live."

Burroughs was acutely aware of his fading vitality. In the framing sequence that begins *Llana of Gathol*, the last of the Martian books published during his lifetime, Burroughs brings John Carter back to earth one last time, to visit the nephew to whom he had willed the manuscript of *A Princess of Mars* many years before. Carter, still youthful and vigorous, notes Burroughs' aging and the two comment sadly on the inevitability of death. "You are the last of my Earthly kin whom I know personally," Carter states, confessing his reasons for returning to Earth. "Every once in a while I feel an urge to see you and visit with you. . . . After you are dead, and it will not be long now, I shall have no Earthly ties—no reason to return to the scenes of my former life." Burroughs reminds Carter of his own children, who are Carter's blood relations, and requests, "After I am gone, see them occasionally.'' Carter nods. '''Perhaps I shall,' he half promised.''

Llana of Gathol appeared in 1948; two years later, Burroughs died. ''On Sunday, March 19, 1950,'' Porges related, ''Ed finished his breakfast and sat in bed, reading the comic pages. He was alone, and death came to him suddenly and quietly.'' ''Life's road,'' the biographer continued, ''had been a long one. He traveled from a Chicago childhood to frustrating schooldays, to danger and adventure in Arizona and Idaho, to the tedium of business offices, and to the strange, wild creation of fantastic characters and events on paper.'' However, Porges added, ''his greatest journey, forever to be appreciated by his host of readers, began in his imagination. It took him to the jungles of Africa and allowed him to soar through space and arrive, unconcerned with all boundaries and limitations, at his own teeming worlds. At first *his* worlds, they quickly became the pleasure and dream worlds of others—the eternal legacy of Edgar Rice Burroughs.''

''To attempt a final evaluation of the massive science-fiction output of Edgar Rice Burroughs is not an easy task,'' stated Lupoff. Burroughs had many limitations as a writer. ''Through his own experiences,'' wrote Porges, ''he viewed the best writer as the natural or untrained one. He rejected the concept of writing as a craft that required an apprenticeship period, like any other profession, a period in which the writer would develop through careful study, practice, and analysis of other authors' stories. This Burroughs, a natural storyteller, had never done.'' ''A conflict of goals was also involved,'' Porges continued. ''He could conceive only of writing to entertain. The subtler and more refined uses of language—those that he might regard as a kind of stylistic pretense—were of course integral to the story's aims and the demands it made upon the reader. If the challenge were intellectual and the goals included a psychological probing of the characters or a perception of social issues, the language and style of the story were not separable from its content. These goals, often associated with realistic or 'literary' stories, were beyond Burroughs' scope.''

Burroughs' work helped establish both science fiction and ''swords and sorcery'' fantasy as separate genres. Indeed, many of his original innovations were imitated to such an extent that they have become cliches. For instance, ''in the archetypal Burroughs novel . . .,'' declared Hollow, ''an incredibly strong man saves an incredibly beautiful woman from rape by incredible villains.'' His powerful imagination inspired such award-winning writers as Leigh Brackett and Ray Bradbury, Fritz Leiber and Philip Jose Farmer. ''A number of people changed my life forever in various ways,'' Bradbury wrote in his introduction to Porges' biography. ''Mr. Burroughs convinced me that I could talk with the animals, even if they didn't answer back.'' ''But then again,'' he concluded, ''his greatest gift was teaching me to look at Mars and ask to be taken home. . . . Because of him and men like him, one day in the next five centuries, we will commute forever, we will go away. . . And never come back. And so live forever.''

Several of Burroughs' characters have achieved literary immortality. John Carter remains an active property in Hollywood, and Tarzan of the Apes continues to appear (if only sporadically) on movie and television screens. But they exist most vividly in the minds of Burroughs' many readers. ''Tarzan lives on,'' concluded Prager. ''My contemporaries and I are thankful for the bright moments Burroughs gave us in the dreary Depression days. We will always be grateful for the jewels of Opar, for excursions through the trees, for La with her solid gold brassiere, for half-naked ingenues swooning in the arms of lust-crazed anthropoids, for hunting Numa's hot, fetid breath, for blood and poisoned arrows and cannibals and hidden treasures and murderous lascars and slave traders and burning kisses and elephants and innocent lust and violence and the inimitable Tarzan of the Apes. They just don't write them like that any more.''

■ Works Cited

Bradbury, Ray, introduction to *Edgar Rice Burroughs: The Man Who Created Tarzan* by Irwin Porges, Brigham Young University Press, 1975, pp. 17-21.

Burroughs, Edgar Rice, *A Princess of Mars*, McClurg, 1917.

Burroughs, Edgar Rice, *Tarzan the Invincible*, Burroughs, 1931.

Burroughs, Edgar Rice, *Tarzan and the Lion-Man*, Burroughs, 1934.

Burroughs, Edgar Rice, *Llana of Gathol*, Burroughs, 1948.

Burroughs, Edgar Rice, *Edgar Rice Burroughs Tells All: An Autobiographical Sketch*, Peking Press, 1989.

Carter, Lin, *Imaginary Worlds: The Art of Fantasy*, Ballantine, 1973.

Essoe, Gabe, *Tarzan of the Movies: A Pictorial History of More Than Fifty Years of Edgar Rice Burroughs' Legendary Hero*, Citadel, 1968.

Heins, Henry Hardy, preface to *Edgar Rice Burroughs: Master of Adventure* by Richard A. Lupoff, Canaveral Press, 1965, pp. 9-25.

Hollow, John, "Edgar Rice Burroughs," *Dictionary of Literary Biography*, Volume 8: *Twentieth Century American Science Fiction Writers*, Gale, 1981, pp. 87-92.

Kipling, Rudyard, *Something of Myself for My Friends Known and Unknown*, Doubleday, Doran, 1937.

Leiber, Fritz, "John Carter, Sword of Theosophy," *The Spell of Conan*, edited by L. Sprague de Camp, Ace, 1980, pp. 211-17.

Lupoff, Richard A., *Edgar Rice Burroughs: Master of Adventure*, Canaveral Press, 1965.

McWhorter, George T., *Edgar Rice Burroughs: A Biographical Sketch*, Bottleneck Blues Press, 1992.

Moskowitz, Sam, *Under the Moons of Mars: A History and Anthology of the Scientific Romance in the Munsey Magazines, 1912-1920*, Holt, 1970.

Nye, Russel B., "The Future as History: Science Fiction," *The Unembarrassed Muse*, Dial, 1970, pp. 270-79.

Porges, Irwin, *Edgar Rice Burroughs: The Man Who Created Tarzan*, Brigham Young University Press, 1975.

Prager, Arthur, "The Victory Cry of the Bull Ape," *Rascals at Large; or, The Clue in the Old Nostalgia*, pp. 17-43.

Roy, John Flint, compiler, *A Guide to Barsoom: The Mars of Edgar Rice Burroughs*, Ballantine, 1976.

Said, Edward, "Jungle Calling," *Interview*, June, 1989, pp. 60-65, 112.

■ **For More Information See**

BOOKS

Aldis, Brian W., "From Barsoom to Beyond the Borderlands: Swords, Sorceries and Zitidars," *Trillion Year Spree: The History of Science Fiction*, Atheneum, 1986, pp. 155-74.

Attebery, Brian, "Fantasy and Escape," *The Fantasy Tradition in American Literature: From Irving to Le Guin*, Indiana University Press, 1980, pp. 109-33.

Cochran, Russ, *The Edgar Rice Burroughs Library of Illustration*, privately printed, 1976.

Day, Bradford M., *Edgar Rice Burroughs Bibliography*, Science Fiction and Fantasy Publications, 1956.

Day, David, *The Burroughs Bestiary: An Encyclopaedia of Monsters and Imaginary Beings Created by Edgar Rice Burroughs*, New English Library, 1978.

Farmer, Philip Jose, *Tarzan Alive: A Definitive Biography of Lord Greystoke*, Doubleday, 1972.

Fenton, Robert, *The Big Swingers*, Prentice-Hall, 1967.

Harwood, John, *The Literature of Burroughsiana*, Camille Cazedessus, Jr. [Baton Rouge], 1963.

Heins, Henry Hardy, *A Golden Anniversary Bibliography of Edgar Rice Burroughs*, Donald M. Grant, 1964.

Holtzmark, Erling B., *Tarzan and Tradition: Classical Myth in Popular Literature*, Greenwood Press, 1981.

Holtzmark, Erling B., *Edgar Rice Burroughs*, Twayne, 1986.

Lenburg, Jeff, *The Encyclopedia of Animated Cartoon Series*, Arlington House, 1981.

Lupoff, Richard A., *Barsoom: Edgar Rice Burroughs and the Martian Vision*, Mirage Press, 1976.

McWhorter, George T., *Edgar Rice Burroughs Memorial Collection: A Catalog*, House of Greystoke, 1991.

Moskowitz, Sam, "To Barsoom and Back with Edgar Rice Burroughs," *Explorers of the Infinite: Shapers of Science Fiction*, World Publishing, 1963, pp. 172-88.

Twentieth-Century Literary Criticism, Gale, Volume 2, 1979; Volume 32, 1989.

Twentieth-Century Science Fiction Writers, 3rd edition, St. James, 1991.

PERIODICALS

Dalhousie Review, spring, 1976, pp. 83-92.
Esquire, December, 1963.
Extrapolation, fall, 1986, pp. 208-20, 221-33.
Hudson Review, autumn, 1959.

OBITUARIES

Illustrated London News, March 25, 1950.
Newsweek, March 27, 1950.
New York Times, March 20, 1950.
Publishers Weekly, April 1, 1950.
Time, March 27, 1950.
Wilson Library Bulletin, May, 1950.

[Sketch reviewed by George T. McWhorter, Director of the Burroughs Memorial Collection, University of Louisville Library]

—*Sketch by Kenneth R. Shepherd*

Orson Scott Card

■ Personal

Has also written under pseudonyms Brian Green and Byron Walley; born August 24, 1951, in Richland, WA; son of Willard Richards (a teacher) and Peggy Jane (a secretary and administrator; maiden name, Park) Card; married Kristine Allen, May 17, 1977; children: Michael Geoffrey, Emily Janice, Charles Benjamin. *Education:* Brigham Young University, B.A. (with distinction), 1975; University of Utah, M.A., 1981. *Politics:* Moderate Democrat. *Religion:* Church of Jesus Christ of Latter-day Saints (Mormon).

■ Addresses

Home—Greensboro, NC. *Agent*—Barbara Bova Literary Agency, 40 Seagate Dr., #1201, Naples, FL 33940.

■ Career

Volunteer Mormon missionary in Brazil, 1971-73; operated repertory theater in Provo, UT, 1974-75; Brigham Young University Press, Provo, proofreader, 1974, editor, 1974-76; *Ensign* magazine, Salt Lake City, UT, assistant editor, 1976-78; free-lance writer and editor, 1978—. Senior editor, Compute! Books, Greensboro, NC, 1983. Teacher at various writers workshops and universities, including University of Utah, 1979-80 and 1981, Brigham Young University, 1981, and Clarion Writers Workshop, East Lansing, MI, 1982. Local Democratic precinct election judge and Utah State Democratic Convention delegate. *Member:* Science Fiction Writers of America.

■ Awards, Honors

John W. Campbell Award, best new writer of 1977, World Science Fiction Convention, 1978, for "Ender's Game"; Hugo Award nominations, World Science Fiction Convention, 1978, 1979, and 1980, for short stories, and 1986, for novelette, *Hatrack River;* Nebula Award nominations, Science Fiction Writers of America, 1979 and 1980, for short stories; Utah State Institute of Fine Arts prize, 1980, for epic poem "Prentice Alvin and the No-Good Plow"; Nebula Award, 1985, and Hugo Award, 1986, both for *Ender's Game;* Nebula Award, 1986, Hugo Award, 1987, and Locus Award, 1987, all for *Speaker for the Dead;* World Fantasy Award, 1987, for novelette *Hatrack River;* Hugo Award, and Locus Award nomination, both 1988, both for novella *Eye for Eye;* Locus Award for best fantasy, Hugo Award nomination, and World Fantasy Award nomination, all 1988, all for *Seventh Son;* Mythopocic Fantasy Award, Mythopoeic Society, 1988, for *Seventh Son;* Locus Award, 1989, for *Red Prophet;* Hugo Award, 1991, for *How to Write Science Fiction and Fantasy.*

■ Writings

SCIENCE FICTION/FANTASY

Capitol: The Worthing Chronicle (short stories), Ace Books, 1978.

Hot Sleep: The Worthing Chronicle, Baronet, 1978.

A Planet Called Treason, St. Martin's, 1979, revised edition, Dell, 1980, published as *Treason*, St. Martin's, 1988.

Songmaster, Dial, 1980.

Unaccompanied Sonata and Other Stories, Dial, c. 1980.

Hart's Hope, Berkley Publishing, 1982.

The Worthing Chronicle, Ace Books, 1983.

Ender's Game (first novel in "Ender" series; also see below), Tor Books, 1985.

Speaker for the Dead (second novel in "Ender" series; also see below), Tor Books, 1986.

Ender's Game [and] *Speaker for the Dead*, Tor Books, 1987.

Wyrms, Arbor House, 1987.

(With others) *Free Lancers*, Baen Books, 1987.

Seventh Son (first novel in "The Tales of Alvin Maker" series; also see below), St. Martin's, 1987.

Red Prophet (second novel in "The Tales of Alvin Maker" series), Tor Books, 1988.

Prentice Alvin (third novel in "The Tales of Alvin Maker" series), Tor Books, 1989.

Folk of the Fringe (collection), Phantasia Press, 1989.

(With Lloyd Biggle) *Eye for Eye—The Tunesmith*, Tor Books, 1990.

(Some stories under pseudonym Byron Walley) *Maps in a Mirror: The Short Fiction of Orson Scott Card*, Tor Books, 1990.

Worthing Saga, Tor Books, 1990.

Xenocide (third novel in "Ender" series), Tor Books, 1991.

The Abyss (novelization of screenplay), Pocket Books, 1991.

Lost Boys, HarperCollins, 1992.

Flux, Tor Books, 1992.

Cruel Miracles, Tor Books, 1992.

The Changed Man, Tor Books, 1992.

The Memory of Earth (first novel in "Homecoming" series), Tor Books, 1992.

Monkey Sonatas, Tor Books, 1993.

The Ships of Earth, Tor Books, 1993.

The Call of Earth (second novel in "Homecoming" series), Tor Books, 1993.

Also author of novelette *Hatrack River*. Contributor to *The Bradbury Chronicles: Stories in Honor of Ray Bradbury*, edited by William F. Nolan and Martin H. Greenberg, New American Library, 1991. Contributor to numerous anthologies.

EDITOR

Dragons of Darkness, Ace Books, c. 1980.

Dragons of Light, Ace Books, 1983.

Future on Fire, Tor Books, 1991.

PLAYS

(And director) *Tell Me That You Love Me, Junie Moon* (adaptation of work by Majorie Kellogg), produced in Provo, UT, 1969.

The Apostate, produced in Provo, UT, 1970.

In Flight, produced in Provo, 1970.

Across Five Summers, produced in Provo, 1971.

Of Gideon, produced in Provo, 1971.

Stone Tables, produced in Provo at Brigham Young University, 1973.

(And director) *A Christmas Carol* (adapted from the story by Charles Dickens), produced in Provo, 1974.

Father, Mother, Mother, and Mom, produced in Provo, 1974, published in *Sunstone*, 1978.

Liberty Jail, produced in Provo, 1975.

Also author of *Rag Mission* (under pseudonym Brian Green), published in *Ensign*, July, 1977; *Fresh Courage Take* (and director), produced in 1978; *Elders and Sisters* (adapted from a work by Gladys Farmer), produced in 1979; and *Wings* (fragment), produced in 1982.

OTHER

"Listen, Mom and Dad ...": Young Adults Look Back on Their Upbringing, Bookcraft, 1977.

Saintspeak, the Mormon Dictionary, cartoons by Calvin Grondahl, Signature Books, 1981.

Ainge, Signature Books, 1982.

A Woman of Destiny (historical novel), Berkeley Publishing, 1983, published as *Saints*, Tor Books, 1988.

Compute's Guide to IBM PCjr Sound and Graphics, Compute, 1984.

Cardography, Hypatia Press, 1987.

Characters and Viewpoint, Writer's Digest Books, 1988.

How to Write Science Fiction and Fantasy, Writer's Digest Books, 1990.

Also author of introduction to *You're a Rock, Sister Lewis*, by Susan D. Smallwood, Hatrack River Publications. Living Scriptures, Ogden, UT, author of audio plays, beginning in 1978, coauthor of animated videotapes. Author of regular review columns "You Got No Friends in This World," *Science Fiction Review*, 1979-86, "Books to Look

For," *The Magazine of Fantasy and Science Fiction*, 1987—, and "Gameplay," *Compute!*, 1988—. Contributor of articles and reviews to periodicals, including *Washington Post Book World*, *Short Form*, *Science Fiction Review*, and *Destinies*.

Card's manuscripts are housed at Brigham Young University.

■ Adaptations

Ender's Game, *Seventh Son*, *Speaker for the Dead*, *Xenocide*, *The Memory of Earth*, *Lost Boys*, and *The Call of Earth* have all been adapted for audio cassette.

■ Work in Progress

The Redemption of Columbus, *Children of the Mind* (a new Ender book), *Alvin Journeyman*, *Master Alvin*, and books four and five of the "Homecoming" series.

■ Sidelights

"Ender turned seven. They weren't much for dates and calendars at the Battle School, but Ender had found out how to bring up the date on his desk, and he noticed his birthday. The school noticed it, too; they took his measurements and issued him a new Salamander uniform and a new flash suit for the battleroom. He went back to the barracks with the new clothing on. It felt strange and loose, like his skin no longer fit properly.

"He wanted to stop at Petra's bunk and tell her about his home, about what his birthdays were usually like, just tell her it was his birthday so she'd say something about it being a happy one. But nobody told birthdays. It was childish. It was what landsiders did. Cakes and silly customs. Valentine baked him his cake on his sixth birthday. It fell and it was terrible. Nobody knew how to cook anymore, it was the kind of crazy thing Valentine would do. Everybody teased Valentine about it, but Ender saved a little bit of it in his cupboard. Then they took out his monitor and he left and for all he knew, it was still there, a little piece of greasy yellow dust. Nobody talked about home, not among the soldiers; there had been no life before Battle School. Nobody got letters, and nobody wrote any. Everybody pretended that they didn't care.

"But I do care, thought Ender. The only reason I'm here is so that a bugger won't shoot out Valentine's eye, won't blast her head open like the soldiers in the videos of the first battles with the buggers.

Won't split her head with a beam so hot that her brains burst the skull and spill out like rising bread dough, the way it happens in my worst nightmares, in my worst nights, when I wake up trembling but silent, must keep silent or they'll hear that I miss my family, I want to go home."

With the creation of Andrew "Ender" Wiggin, the young genius of *Ender's Game*, Orson Scott Card launched a successful, award-winning career as a science fiction and fantasy writer. Since his debut in the field in 1977, when his short story "Ender's Game" appeared in *Analog* magazine, Card has penned more than twenty-four science fiction novels and has become the only writer to win two sets of Hugo and Nebula awards for consecutive novels in a series. In many of his works, Card focuses on the moral development of his young protagonists, whose abilities to act maturely and decisively while in challenging situations often determine the future of their communities. Card, a devout Mormon, is intrigued by the role of the individual in society, and credits his solid religious background with instilling in him both a strong sense of community and an affinity for storytelling. "I don't want to write about individuals in isolation," he told Graceanne A. Decandido and Keith R. A. Decandido in *Publishers Weekly*. "What I want to write about is people who are committed members of the community and therefore have a network of relationships that define who they are. I think if you're going to write about people, you have to write about storytelling." In his works Card is deeply concerned with his own unresolved moral and philosophical questions as well, and maintains that science fiction affords him the benefit of exploring these issues against a futuristic and imaginative backdrop. "In some of the best SF, you move into a universe where all moral bets are off, where you have a group of aliens, or humans in an alien setting, who live by different rules because some key aspect of life that we take for granted as human beings has been changed radically.... After a while we can see ourselves through their eyes and see how bizarre we are. Then you come back and you question everything."

Before science fiction captured the young Card's interest, the theater drew his attention. At the age of sixteen, he entered the Mormon-founded Brigham Young University (BYU) to study his craft and just a few years later was penning plays and seeing them produced. Though his education was delayed for a brief time when he served as a Mormon missionary in Brazil during the early 1970s, he founded a theater company upon his return to

Utah—in spite of having no "capital or common sense," as he admitted to the Decandidos.

Following his graduation with honors in 1975, he took a job as an editor for *Ensign* magazine, the official publication of the Mormon religion, and continued working for the BYU Press, a job he had begun while still a student. Facing a bleak financial situation, though, he realized he needed to make a vocational change. "I was supporting myself on the pathetic wages paid to an editor at a university press—and BYU's wages were even more pathetic than usual," he recounted to the Decandidos. "I knew that there was no hope of paying off my debts through my salary, so I made a serious effort to write fiction as a career."

With his experience as a dramatist, Card already possessed some basic techniques of storytelling: He

A six-year-old genius holds the fate of the Earth in his hands in this 1985 science fiction thriller, a Nebula and Hugo Award winner.

knew how to develop a scene, how to write dialogue, and how to create as well as resolve tension. Moreover, the idea for "Ender's Game" as well as notions for other science fiction works had been brewing in the back of his mind for a long while. "All the time that I was a playwright," he told Jean W. Ross in a *Contemporary Authors* interview, "these science fictional ideas that never showed up in my plays were dancing around in the back of my mind." The genre, he felt, offered him the most expedient way of getting published, since the field thrives on up-and-coming talent and fresh ideas. He also admitted that he chose science fiction because, as he told Ross, "I knew the genre. While it was never even half my reading, I had read enough to be aware of the possibilities within it. It allowed the possibility of the kind of high drama that I'd been doing with religious plays for the Mormon market.... In order to write the kind of intense romantic drama that I wanted to write, I needed the possibilities that science fiction and fantasy offered."

"Ender" Engenders Acclaim

Hoping to break into the field, Card sent "The Tinker," one of his first short stories, to Ben Bova, then editor of the leading science fiction magazine *Analog*. Bova in turn rejected the work, though he did not crush the aspirations of its author. "Apparently he [Bova] saw some reason to hope that I might have some talent," Card explained to the Decandidos. "His rejection letter urged me to submit a *real* science fiction story, because he liked the way I wrote." The *real* story became "Ender's Game," which, upon its publication, garnered Card the World Science Fiction Convention's John W. Campbell Award for best new writer.

Though Card was thrilled with his sudden success, he later admitted in *Publishers Weekly* that he was "not so stupid as to quit my job." He retained his position as editor for *Ensign* and in 1978 began composing audio plays for Living Scriptures. He also continued honing his writing skills and released his first book, *Capitol*, during that same year. A collection of short stories, the work follows the fall of the planet Capitol and revolves in part around the drug somec, which induces a state of suspended animation in its user and allows him to live for several thousand years. At least one reviewer remarked upon Card's literary skill in *Capitol*: The collection "demonstrates a fine talent for storytelling and characterization," decided a critic for *Publishers Weekly*. Card's 1980 novel *Songmaster* generated praise as well. The lyrical tale, set in a futuristic galactic society that reveres those who sing, focuses on Ansset, a "Songbird" who is summoned to serve the emperor. The work encompasses "personal growth and exploration melded into a tale of interplanetary politics and court intrigue," asserted Richard A. Lupoff in *Washington Post Book World.* "*Songmaster* is a first-class job." Some of Card's other early works, however, including *Hot Sleep* and *A Planet Called Treason,* encountered critical censure for employing standard science fiction elements like "brain-taping techniques," and for containing what some reviewers considered gratuitous violence. George R. R. Martin in the *Washington Post Book World* especially criticized Card's 1981 work, *Unaccompanied Sonata and Other Stories,* which he found filled "with death, pain, mutilation, dismemberment, all described in graphic detail." The volume includes such unfortunate characters as a malformed infant who is drowned in a toilet and whose body is sliced to pieces, and a woman whose breasts are chopped off and eaten. Apart from these negative evaluations, the general critical consensus of Card's early works was that they display imagination, intelligence, literary aptitude, and promise. "Card is a young, talented, and ambitious writer," conceded Martin.

That ambition and talent was both revealed and recognized in 1985, when Card released *Ender's Game* and garnered both a Hugo Award as well as a Nebula Award, science fiction's highest honors. *Ender's Game,* a full-length version of Card's first published short story, revolves around Andrew "Ender" Wiggin, a youngster of superior intellect who is selected—at the age of six—to train as a commander in an impending war against invading "bugger" aliens. Seen as humanity's sole hope for survival, Ender is sent to the brutal Battle School, where he is mercilessly practiced in physical and computer-aided "games" that teach leadership and military tactics. Card follows Ender throughout the novel as he is isolated from contact with his family and friends and is ultimately responsible for slaughtering almost the entire bugger race in what he later learns is an unnecessary battle.

Although some critics found the plot of *Ender's Game* formulaic and of the conventional "superhero saves world" variety, most commended Card for his ability to create a character who—though he commits almost total genocide—generates sympathy from readers. Card upholds Ender's youthful innocence and naivete throughout the work, reviewers noted, and allows him to experience remorse for his actions. The author "goes to great

pains to shield Ender's childish innocence from truth, to keep us from calling him one more brute of history," wrote Tom Easton in *Analog Science Fiction/Science Fact.* Commentators also pointed out that *Ender's Game* rises above standard science fiction fare since it ponders moral questions regarding the manipulation of children as well as the significance of compassion. *Ender's Game* "succeeds because of its stress on the value of empathy," emphasized Easton. Some of the characters "are ... guilty of despicable acts, but they are saved by their ability to bleed for the souls they mangle." *Washington Post Book World* reviewer Janrae Frank averred: "Card is a writer of compassion and his heart breaks for the individual men and women of good will who find themselves caught up and forced to participate in the race's homicidal crossfire."

An adult Ender seeks to reestablish a devastated race of alien beings—a race he helped to destroy—in this 1986 sequel to *Ender's Game.*

Ironically, *Ender's Game* was not a book Card consciously set out to write. Under contract for *Speaker for the Dead* (which ultimately became the sequel to *Ender's Game*), Card noticed that Ender was emerging as the book's protagonist. "That made it [*Speaker for the Dead*] a kind of sequel," Card revealed to Ross, "although its plot had nothing to do with the original plot; it was just using a character." Card also realized he was expending a great deal of creative energy trying to move readers from the conclusion of "Ender's Game" to the beginning of *Speaker for the Dead*. "It wasn't working," Card finally admitted. "I needed to do a novel version of 'Ender's Game' just to set up *Speaker for the Dead*. That's the only reason 'Ender's Game' ever became a novel."

Ender as an Elder

Shortly after the publication of *Ender's Game*, Card released its sequel, *Speaker for the Dead*. Winner of Hugo and Nebula awards, the work opens three thousand years after the first volume and follows the adult Ender as he roams the galaxy attempting to atone for the massacre of the buggers. He has turned himself into a "Speaker for the Dead"—a sort of historical apologist who responds to calls for information on the lives of deceased members of any race. Additionally, he has vowed to find a home for the one surviving bugger queen so she can reestablish her species. In the course of the novel Ender's duties as Speaker take him to the planet Lusitania, where the "piggies," a native alien species, pose a viral threat to humanity's existence.

Speaker for the Dead generally met with an enthusiastic reception. Many critics considered the work proof of Card's maturing literary strength and praised the author for crafting compelling characters who face issues of acceptance, guilt, fear, empathy, and redemption. Easton in *Analog Science Fiction/Science Fact* particularly commended the character of Ender, emphasizing that Card endows him with "clear vision" and "insight into the human soul, drawn from his own hell of guilt." Richard E. Geis in *Science Fiction Review* proclaimed that in this character Card "has created . . . a giant of compassion and intelligence and perspective." The reviewer added: "Card is a fine writer, with great insight, great idealism and love." Both "*Ender's Game* and *Speaker for the Dead*," remarked *Fantasy Review* commentator Michael R. Collings, "succeed equally as straightforward SF adventure and as allegorical, analogical disquisitions on humanity, morality, salvation, and re-

Set in an alternate pioneer America, this 1987 work introduces Alvin Maker, who, as the seventh son of a seventh son, is endowed with mystical powers.

demption." However, Elaine Radford of *Fantasy Review* found fault with Card, professing that "the character of Ender Wiggin, the near messianic superhero, is based on that of Adolf Hitler." Card, in what he admitted was an uncharacteristic rebuttal of a negative review, wrote in the same periodical that "there is no justification whatever in the text of *Ender's Game* or *Speaker for the Dead* for calling me a fascist, a racist, a genocide, or a sexist; on the contrary, in both books I spoke as eloquently and powerfully as I could in favor of compassion and empathy."

Card continued Ender's story five years later in 1991's *Xenocide*, which opens as the protagonist works feverishly with his adopted Lusitanian family to neutralize the piggies's deadly virus. Many critics ventured that with *Xenocide* Card relies more on the scientific ruminations of a multitude of contemplative characters rather than on a plot. "The real action is philosophical: long, passionate debates about ends and means among people who are fully aware that they may be deciding the fate of entire species, entire worlds," observed Gerald Jonas in the *New York Times Book Review.*

America, "Alvin Maker" Style

In 1987, while not yet finished with his "Ender" series, Card released *Seventh Son,* the first volume in his "Tales of Alvin Maker" series. A revision and expansion of an epic poem he wrote during graduate studies at the University of Utah, the series is set in an alternate, pioneer America, a nation of inchoate states to which witches have been exiled by the Puritans. *Seventh Son* details the early years of the series' protagonist, Alvin Miller, a "Maker," or one endowed with magical powers because of his distinctive status as the seventh son of a seventh son. Though many people possess mystical powers in Card's America—such as dowsing, hexing, and healing—Alvin owns the supreme talent of being able to control reality. *Red Prophet,* the second novel in the series, shifts the focus away from Alvin to the issue of the interfacing between colonists and Native Americans. Three individuals are featured in the work: Ta-Kumsaw, a Shawnee who wishes to reserve all land east of the Mississippi River for the whites, who have "despoiled" it with their presence, and keep all land west for the Indians; William Henry Harrison ("White Murderer Harrison"), who desires to slaughter all Native Americans; and Lolla-Wossiky, Ta-Kumsaw's brother and the "Red Prophet," who preaches of a land where both peoples can live in harmony. In the course of the work, Alvin is drawn into the struggle. "His hands heal and bring together these seemingly disparate elements into a force to be reckoned with," contended Sue Martin in the *Los Angeles Times Book Review. Prentice Alvin,* the third volume in the series, follows Alvin as he matures to nineteen years of age under the watch of his guardian "torch," one who can see into the future.

In reviews of the "Alvin Maker" books, many critics likened the character of Alvin to the biblical figure of Christ, and equated the Unmaker, Alvin's vile adversary who is intent on destroying the protagonist, with the devil. As Easton wrote in his review of *Prentice Alvin:* "The Great Enemy, whom we too easily identify as the devil, is the Unmaker, the foe of Making, of creation, of god. Because the Unmaker (often in the form of flowing water) is so

set on destroying Alvin, the boy is clearly Christ come again."

In 1992 Card introduced his "Homecoming" series with *The Memory of Earth,* a novel many critics found to be a mixture of philosophy, futuristic technology, and biblical lore. *Memory* opens on the planet Harmony, where for forty million years humans have been controlled by Oversoul, a powerful, global computer programmed to prevent humanity from destroying itself through needless wars. As the novel progresses, Oversoul falls into disrepair and requires restoration from Earth, a planet out of the reach of the citizens of Harmony, who have become technologically stagnant and possess no concept of space travel. To save itself as well as Harmony, Oversoul engages the aid of Wetchik and his son Nafai, members of an exten-

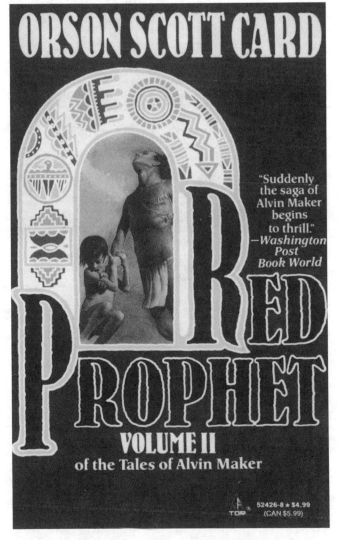

In this 1988 sequel to *Seventh Son,* Alvin, with the help of the preacher Lolla-Wossiky, must heal a growing rift between colonists and Native Americans.

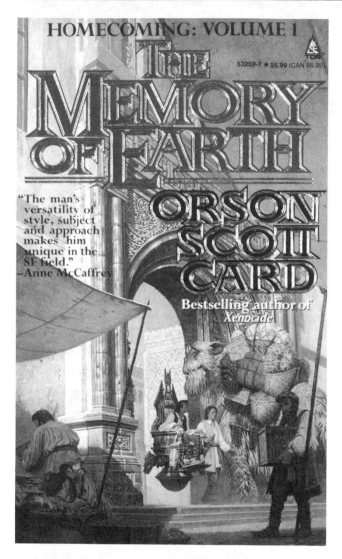

HOMECOMING: VOLUME 1

THE MEMORY OF EARTH

ORSON SCOTT CARD

"The man's versatility of style, subject and approach makes him unique in the SF field." —Anne McCaffrey

Bestselling author of Xenocide

53259-7 ★ $5.99 (CAN $6.99)

The inhabitants of the planet Harmony join with Oversoul, a supercomputer, to ensure the survival of humankind in this 1992 novel.

ded family that "most closely resembles Biblical tribesmen," contended Faren Miller in *Locus*. "They are herders, small traders, semi-nomadic men." David E. Jones, in his Chicago *Tribune Books* appraisal of *Memory*, decided that "what Card gives us is an interaction between supreme intelligence and human mental capability that is at once an intellectual exercise, a Biblical parable and a thoroughly enjoyable piece of storytelling." "Card has recaptured the originality and grace that so enthralled readers of *Ender's Game*," opined reviewer Joel Singer in *Voice of Youth Advocates*. "He expertly weaves Biblical imagery, modern science, philosophy, and emotion in a tale of a young man, Nafai, growing and maturing."

A Shift from Sci-Fi

Though Card has established himself firmly as a writer of science fiction and fantasy, he has not limited himself to the genre. Throughout his career he has forged into nonfiction, adaptations, and, most notably, historical fiction. *A Woman of Destiny*, his 1983 novel (published as *Saints* in 1988) set in the nineteenth century and revolving around the Mormon religion, is generally viewed by critics as his most significant work outside the field of science fiction. The volume turns on Dinah Kirkham, a courageous English woman who is converted to Mormonism by Joseph Smith, the founder of the religion, and then follows him to a Mormon community in Illinois where she becomes his "secret" second wife. (Polygamy, currently practiced by the Mormons, was not sanctioned at the time that the book is set.) When Smith is murdered in 1844, Kirkham escapes with her fellow Mormons to Utah, becoming a staunch leader as well as one of the many wives of Brigham Young, Smith's successor as president. *Los Angeles Times Book Review* critic Kristiana Gregory pronounced *A Woman of Destiny* an "engrossing epic," stressing that Card "is a powerful storyteller."

In a critique of the author's 1990 short story collection, *Maps in a Mirror*, *Analog Science Fiction/Science Fact* reviewer Easton characterized Card "as an intensely thoughtful, self-conscious, religious, and community-oriented writer." For example, inspired by a 1990 visit to Brazil for a science fiction convention, Card is attempting—at some personal monetary risk—to organize the translation of such authors as Roberto de Souza Causo, Braulio Tavares, and Hector Flory for release in the country. In spite of this undertaking and his many teaching positions, Card prefers a simple description of himself. As he told the Decandidos in *Publishers Weekly*, "I'm Kristine's husband, Geoffrey and Emily and Charlie's dad, I'm a Mormon, and I am a science fiction writer."

■ Works Cited

Review of *Capitol*, *Publishers Weekly*, December 4, 1978, p. 62.

Card, Orson Scott, *Ender's Game*, Tor Books, 1985.

Card, Orson Scott, in an interview with Jean W. Ross, *Contemporary Authors New Revision Series*, Volume 27, Gale, 1989, pp. 79-85.

Collings, Michael R., "Adventure and Allegory," *Fantasy Review*, April, 1986, p. 20.

Decandido, Graceanne A., and Keith R. A. Decandido, "*PW* Interview: Orson Scott Card," *Publishers Weekly*, November 30, 1990, pp. 54-55.

Easton, Tom, review of *Ender's Game, Analog Science Fiction/Science Fact*, July, 1985, pp. 180-81.

Easton, Tom, review of *Maps in a Mirror, Analog Science Fiction/Science Fact*, March, 1991, p. 184.

Easton, Tom, review of *Prentice Alvin, Analog Science Fiction/Science Fact*, August, 1989, pp. 175-76.

Easton, Tom, review of *Speaker for the Dead, Analog Science Fiction/Science Fact*, June, 1986, pp. 183-84.

Frank, Janrae, "Wars of the Worlds," *Washington Post Book World*, February 23, 1986, p. 10.

Geis, Richard E., review of *Ender's Game* and *Speaker for the Dead, Science Fiction Review*, February, 1986, pp. 14-15.

Gregory, Kristiana, review of *A Woman of Destiny, Los Angeles Times Book Review*, July 22, 1984, p. 8.

Jonas, Gerald, review of *Xenocide, New York Times Book Review*, September 1, 1991.

Jones, David E., "Trapped in a Serial Universe, Where Some Writers Manage to Thrive," *Tribune Books* (Chicago), March 1, 1992.

Lupoff, Richard A., "Beasts, Songbirds and Wizards," *Washington Post Book World*, August 24, 1980, p. 6.

Martin, George R. R., "Scanning the Stars of the Short Story," *Washington Post Book World*, January 25, 1981, pp. 9, 11.

Martin, Sue, "Battling the Natives Along the Mississippi," *Los Angeles Times Book Review*, February 14, 1988.

Miller, Faren, review of *The Memory of Earth, Locus*, February, 1992, pp. 17, 57.

Radford, Elaine, "Ender and Hitler: Sympathy for the Superman," *Fantasy Review*, June, 1987, pp. 11-12, 48-49.

Singer, Joel, review of *The Memory of Earth, Voice of Youth Advocates*, October, 1992, p. 236.

■ For More Information See

BOOKS

Contemporary Literary Criticism, Gale, Volume 44, 1987, pp. 163-65; Volume 47, 1988, pp. 66-69; Volume 50, 1988, pp. 142-51.

PERIODICALS

Analog Science Fiction/Science Fact, July, 1983, p. 103; September, 1988, p. 179; January, 1990, p. 305; December, 1991, pp. 159-60.

Booklist, December 15, 1985, p. 594.

Kirkus Reviews, December 1, 1980, p. 1542; November 1, 1984, p. 1021.

Kliatt, April, 1992, p. 56.

Library Journal, September 1, 1991, p. 252.

Locus, April, 1991, p. 15.

Magazine of Fantasy and Science Fiction, January, 1980, p. 35.

New York Times Book Review, June 16, 1985, p. 18; March 15, 1992.

Publishers Weekly, January 2, 1981, p. 49; January 24, 1986, p. 64; December 25, 1987, p. 65; September 16, 1988; December 23, 1988, p. 70; May 19, 1989, p. 72; August 17, 1990, p. 55; June 14, 1991, p. 48.

Science Fiction and Fantasy Book Review, April, 1979, p. 27; December, 1979, p. 155; June, 1983, pp. 21-22.

School Library Journal, January, 1991, p. 123; November, 1991.

Washington Post Book World, February 28, 1988; March 29, 1992.

Writer's Digest, October, 1986, pp. 26-28; November, 1986, pp. 37-38; December, 1986, pp. 32-36; May, 1989, pp. 31-33.

—Sketch by Denise Kasinec

Paul Fleischman

■ Personal

Born September 5, 1952, in Monterey, CA; son of Albert Sidney (a children's author) and Beth (a homemaker; maiden name, Taylor) Fleischman; married Becky Mojica (a nurse), December 15, 1978; children: Seth, Dana. *Education:* Attended University of California, Berkeley, 1970-72; University of New Mexico, B.A., 1977.

■ Addresses

Home—855 Marino Pines, Pacific Grove, CA 93950.

■ Career

Author. Has worked variously as a bagel baker, bookstore clerk, and proofreader. *Member:* Authors Guild, Authors League of America, Society of Children's Book Writers.

■ Awards, Honors

Silver Medal, Commonwealth Club of California, Golden Kite honor book, Society of Children's Book Writers, *New York Times* outstanding book citation, all 1980, all for *The Half-a-Moon Inn;* Newbery honor book, American Library Association (ALA), 1983, for *Graven Images: Three Stories;* Golden Kite honor book, Society of Children's Book Writers, and Parents' Choice Award, Parents' Choice Foundation, both 1983, both for *Path of the Pale Horse; Boston Globe-Horn Book* Award honor book, best book for young adults nomination, ALA, both 1988, and Newbery Medal, ALA, 1989, all for *Joyful Noise: Poems for Two Voices; Boston Globe-Horn Book* Award honor book, 1990, and ALA notable book, 1991, both for *Saturnalia;* ALA notable book, 1992, for *The Borning Room.*

■ Writings

FOR YOUNG READERS

The Birthday Tree, illustrated by Marcia Sewall, Harper, 1979.

The Half-a-Moon Inn, illustrated by Kathy Jacobi, Harper, 1980.

Graven Images: Three Stories (includes "The Binnacle Boy," "St. Crispin's Follower," and "The Man of Influence"), illustrated by Andrew Glass, Harper, 1982.

The Animal Hedge (picture book), illustrated by Lydia Dabkovich, Dutton, 1983.

Path of the Pale Horse, Harper, 1983.

Phoebe Danger, Detective, in the Case of the Two-Minute Cough, illustrated by Margot Apple, Houghton, 1983.

Finzel the Farsighted, illustrated by Sewall, Dutton, 1983.

Coming-and-Going Men: Four Tales, illustrated by Randy Gaul, Harper, 1985.

I Am Phoenix: Poems for Two Voices, illustrated by Ken Nutt, Harper, 1985.

Rear-View Mirrors, Harper, 1986.

Joyful Noise: Poems for Two Voices, illustrated by Eric Beddows, Harper, 1988.

Rondo in C, illustrated by Janet Wentworth, Harper, 1988.

Saturnalia, Harper, 1990.

Shadow Play (picture book), illustrated by Beddows, Harper, 1990.

The Borning Room, HarperCollins, 1991.

Time Train, illustrated by Claire Ewart, HarperCollins, 1991.

Townsend's Warbler, HarperCollins, 1992.

Bull Run, HarperCollins, 1993.

Copier Creations, HarperCollins, 1993.

OTHER

Contributor to various journals and magazines.

■ Sidelights

In 1977 Paul Fleischman was twenty-five years old, about to graduate from college, and he still wasn't sure what he wanted to be. Though he would soon receive a degree in history, Fleischman had given up on his original plan of being a teacher and was searching for another profession. When he returned to his parents' home at Christmas break that year, he was still undecided. Then one day Paul sat down at the typewriter his father had given him and began to type a story. His career had begun.

Twelve years later, when he accepted the prestigious Newbery Medal for one of his books, Fleischman recalled his decision to pursue a literary career. "Writing . . . seemed a possibility," he said in his acceptance speech (later published in *Horn Book*). "And as I was on the brink of graduation, needing to earn a living, it was time to reach for the possible." Fleischman's choice of careers was not as arbitrary as it might seem. His father, Sid Fleischman, is a noted author of books for young readers. For this reason, the author told *Something about the Author* (SATA), "writing for children always seemed an honorable and possible profession." What was extraordinary was Fleischman's quick success once he began to write. Even his father was amazed by the quality of the book Paul began in his bedroom that December, a work that was soon published as *The Birthday Tree*. "This was not a story written with the telltale creaks and groans of the beginner," Sid Fleischman wrote in

Horn Book. "It was the skilled handling of a difficult subject, the uncanny relationship between a boy and an apple tree planted in celebration of his birth. It was a bravura performance." In Sid Fleischman's opinion, Paul's lifelong exposure to the writing profession later contributed to his sudden literary achievements. "There have always been writers in and out of the house, talking story," Sid Fleischman wrote. "We forget that kids are listening. Paul was a lightning-quick study." Fleischman's contact with literature was also enhanced by the way his father involved the entire family in the writing process. The elder Fleischman often read passages of his work aloud to his children and sometimes incorporated their suggestions. "At the dinner table I'd often ask the kids for help with some balky story problems," he wrote, "and ideas would come bubbling up."

Whatever the source of his abilities, Paul Fleischman has earned an admirable reputation in the field of children's literature. His books display a close attention to the sound and rhythm of words. They are also noted for their diverse subjects and styles. He sets his stories in many different locations and historical periods; he writes both haunting supernatural mysteries and joyous celebrations of the natural world, and he produces inventive books of poetry as well as fictional stories and novels. This diversity has resulted in a unique body of work which moves beyond the subjects and styles traditionally reserved for young readers.

Haunted History

After publishing *The Birthday Tree* in 1979, Fleischman began to develop the style that would mark much of his later work. His next two books, *The Half-a-Moon Inn* and *Graven Images: Three Stories,* explored eerie situations and strange, haunting characters. *The Half-a-Moon Inn*'s hero Aaron is a twelve-year-old boy who is unable to speak. Aaron's mother leaves him alone in order to go to town to buy his birthday gift, making him promise that he will remain in the house. A sudden blizzard prevents his mother from returning, however, and after two days on his own, Aaron sets off to find her. Alone in the snow, Aaron becomes lost, eventually encountering a rag seller and then ending up at the Half-a-Moon Inn. There his real trouble begins as he is held captive by Miss Grackle, the owner of the inn, and forced to work for her. Miss Grackle has the ability to read Aaron's dreams, and can therefore anticipate his attempts to escape. She also beats the boy's feet, hoping that he will be unable to run away.

An illustration by Marcia Sewall for Fleischman's first book, *The Birthday Tree*, the story of an apple tree planted to commemorate a boy's birth.

Critics were quick to note *The Half-a-Moon Inn*'s change in tone as compared with *The Birthday Tree*. Virginia Haviland, writing in *Horn Book*, termed *The Half-a-Moon Inn* "a story of grisly threats, daring, and foul play," and several reviewers, among them *Booklist*'s Barbara Elleman, remarked on the book's "haunting atmosphere." Fleischman's examination of darker themes continued in his next book, *Graven Images*, a collection of three stories. "The Binnacle Boy" focuses on the mysterious death of a ship's crew, and features a deaf girl who, like Miss Grackle in *The Half-a-Moon Inn*, has the ability to divine people's thoughts. In "St. Crispin's Follower," the lightest of the book's three tales, an apprentice shoemaker falls in love

with a servant girl. Desperate for a means of winning her heart, he finds guidance from an unusual source: the figure of a saint on a broken weather vane. "The Man of Influence" tells the story of a starving sculptor who finds work only when he is hired by a ghost. In the end, the sculptor completes the statue, but he finds his contact with the ghost so unpleasant that he throws his payment into the sea.

As several critics noted, the chilling tales in both *Graven Images* and *The Half-a-Moon Inn* required careful handling by the author. The stories were intended to be spooky and mysterious, even a little frightening, but if they were too scary they could upset young readers. Ann Cameron's review of

A mute boy becomes lost and is taken captive by a creepy inn caretaker who can read the boy's dreams in this 1980 thriller.

Graven Images in the *New York Times Book Review* raised this question, but she was pleased by Fleischman's handling of his eerie material. "It emerges as a safe and satisfying tale," Cameron concluded. "Mr. Fleischman's darker tales will prickle the back of the neck without leaving nightmares behind."

As Fleischman noted in his Newbery acceptance speech, one of his greatest joys in writing is that it allows him to "scavenge among the past." A history student in college, it was not surprising that he would turn to writing books that examined specific periods from the past. His 1983 novel, *Path of the Pale Horse*, transports readers to the year 1793, when the novel's young protagonist, Lep, is studying medicine under the tutelage of Dr. Poole. When the doctor travels to Philadelphia to obtain medicine, Lep accompanies him. Once in the city, however, they are recruited to help battle a deadly epidemic of yellow fever. Lep's early efforts in aiding victims of the fever meet with success, but later, when Dr. Poole contracts the

sickness, Lep faces a more difficult challenge. A subplot involves Lep's sister who is living in Philadelphia, working for a man who sells magic rings that he claims will ward off the fever. In an attempt to get his sister to return home, Lep tries to convince her that the rings are a fraud. Lep, meanwhile, has to struggle with his own superstitious beliefs while upholding the validity of his medical knowledge.

Washington Post Book World reviewer Richard Slotkin found that *Path of the Pale Horse* dealt with "an unusual but exceptionally interesting historical event," but he was critical of Fleischman's writing on several points. "The setting seems flat and empty," Slotkin wrote, also noting an "inauthenticity of language" caused by the characters' unrealistic dialogue. Slotkin's criticism was balanced, however, by more positive notices. A *Kirkus Reviews* writer recommended the book, citing Fleischman's ability to "keep the plot perking." The critic also noted the unique writing style employed in *Path of the Pale Horse*. "Fleischman's period tone and narrative artifice," the reviewer wrote, "assure the comforts of a well-told tale."

Musical Words

Critics have frequently noted Fleischman's ability to produce graceful, musical language that fits well with the historical material in his books. This style has led some reviewers to compare Fleischman to prominent writers from the past. Ethel L. Heins, reviewing *Graven Images* in *Horn Book*, compared Fleischman to nineteenth-century authors Edgar Allan Poe and Nathaniel Hawthorne, noting that "the young author's timeless, elegant, figurative prose is fashioned with fluency and skill." The beauty of Fleischman's writing is no accident. In order to achieve a pleasing sound, the author takes painstaking care when constructing his stories. "I write only a page or so a day," Fleischman explained in his Newbery acceptance speech. "After several books it dawned on me that this was because I was writing prose that scanned, something that makes for slow progress." By saying that his writing "scanned," Fleischman meant that each sentence has a certain number of syllables, and that the words are chosen so that a certain rhythm is achieved. The pattern of the rhythm is known as its meter, and a consistent meter creates a steady beat, much like that found in a piece of music. "All my prose is written in 4/4 time," Fleischman explained, "though I never let the meter become so obvious as to attract attention." The musical sound of the writing is further enhanced through the use of rhyme and the repetition of particular sounds. "I work out my books in detail before starting," the author continued, "so that most of my writing time is devoted not to sense but to sound: to rhythm, to the rhyme of *so* and *below.*"

Fleischman's ability to create musical sounds in his writing is drawn from his lifelong interest in music itself. "I was never much of a reader as a child and have always been more attracted to music than books," he once told *SATA*. He studied piano at an early age, and when in high school he spent much of his time at the library listening to classical music. He later took up the recorder and the saxophone and performed with amateur musical ensembles. "Had I the talent to write music," Fleischman related, "I'd be doing that instead [of writing books]." Feeling that he didn't possess the skill to be a composer, Fleischman applied his musical knowledge to literature. "Writing prose [has] much in common with writing music," he explained in

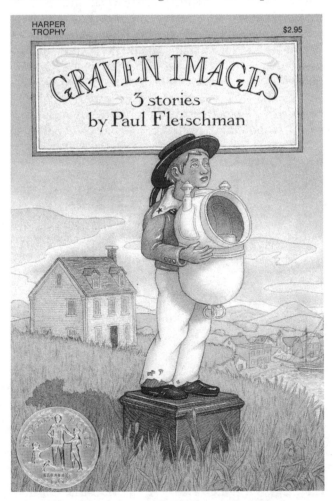

Three tales of the supernatural, including the story of a young girl with psychic powers, make up this 1982 collection.

his Newbery Medal acceptance speech. "Every chapter, every paragraph, every sentence, I discovered, has an arc to it, like a musical phrase. Every word has both a meaning and a music."

Though Fleischman's first eight books were all prose fiction, his emphasis on sound and rhythm eventually led him to poetry, a genre which makes greater use of musical language. The author's first poetry publication, *I Am Phoenix: Poems for Two Voices*, was published in 1985, and a second book of verse, *Joyful Noise: Poems for Two Voices*, followed two years later. This second collection received an enthusiastic response from reviewers and readers and soon became one of Fleischman's most popular books. *Joyful Noise* is made up of fourteen poems, each of which is about a different insect. Bees, mayflies, book lice—all are transformed into characters who relate many details about their lives and behavior. Fleischman's words echo the sound and movements of the insects; fireflies, for instance, are described as "flicking, flitting, flashing." These sounds are made more striking because the poems are designed to be read aloud. As the title suggests, these are "poems for two voices," requiring two readers to recite the poems together. Sometimes the two readers alternate, first one reading a line, then the other. At other times they speak in unison, sounding much like a singing choir.

Fleischman had pioneered the two-voice approach in *I Am Phoenix*, but most critics felt that he had perfected the style in *Joyful Noise*. A *Kirkus Reviews* writer remarked on the book's "vivid language, strong images, and the masterful use of two voices in musical duet." The critic summed up *Joyful Noise* as "a splendid collection of poems in many moods." *Voice of Youth Advocates* reviewer Donna Houser announced that "every library should have a copy of this book," and this praise was seconded by Mary M. Burns in *Horn Book*. "Every so often a book is published which demands accolades," Burns wrote. "This marvelous, lyrical evocation of the insect world belongs in that category." The critic noted the book's appeal for children of several different age groups and proclaimed that "each selection is a gem, polished perfection. If Paul Fleischman never wrote another book, his reputation would remain secure with this one." Fleischman received further acclaim for *Joyful Noise* when the book was awarded the 1989 Newbery Medal from the American Library Association, one of the highest honors in children's literature.

JOYFUL NOISE

Poems for Two Voices

PAUL FLEISCHMAN

illustrated by Eric Beddows

Designed to be read aloud by a pair of voices, Fleischman's innovative 1988 poetry collection recreates the sounds and movements of insect life.

Return to the Past

Despite the success of his poetry, Fleischman soon returned to writing historical novels. *Saturnalia* focuses on the Roman festival that was held in honor of the god Saturn, a celebration in which, for one day, masters and servants traded places. *The Borning Room* presents sixty-seven years of American history as it is perceived by one character: Georgina Carolina Lott. The book centers on the room where Georgina is born in 1851 and in which she dies in 1918. In between, Georgina experiences many important events. As a child she absorbs the anti-slavery beliefs of her Ohio family, shelters a runaway slave, and witnesses the death and destruction of the Civil War. Later she becomes active as a suffragette, working to give women the right to vote. These historical events are balanced by smaller experiences in Georgina's life: the joy of a family sing-along, the danger of life-threatening diseases, the demands and rewards of raising her own family. Fleischman's mix of the historical and the personal created a multilayered story which impressed many critics. "The two themes are so skillfully intertwined," wrote Burns, "that they are mutually supporting elements in an exquisite narrative." The critic also praised Fleischman's ability to condense a lifetime's worth of events into a short book. "He has mastered the art of compression without sacrificing content," the reviewer wrote. "Thus, the dimensions of one small room expand to become a universal setting for the grand drama that is life."

Though his career has been marked by several distinct types of writing—haunting horror stories, historical dramas, evocative poetry—Paul Fleischman's work contains several unifying elements. His books often feature dramatic situations in which lives are very much on the line. As *New York Times Book Review* contributor Susan Bolotin wrote in her review of *The Borning Room*, "his characters always experience a nitty-gritty relationship with life and death that most middle-class children today know only through television or newspaper headlines." Fleischman's books are also distinguished by their finely crafted prose. As Bolotin noted, "children need to hear what lyrical writing sounds like." Fleischman's young readers are treated to the elegance of carefully written words, and to the compelling stories those words can tell.

■ Works Cited

Bolotin, Susan, review of *The Borning Room*, *New York Times Book Review*, November 10, 1991, p. 54.

Burns, Mary M., review of *Joyful Noise: Poems for Two Voices*, *Horn Book*, May-June, 1988, pp. 366-67.

Burns, Mary M., review of *The Borning Room*, *Horn Book*, November-December, 1991, p. 744.

Cameron, Ann, review of *Graven Images: Three Stories*, *New York Times Book Review*, November 28, 1982, p. 24.

Elleman, Barbara, review of *The Half-a-Moon Inn*, *Booklist*, June 15, 1980, p. 1531.

Fleischman, Paul, *Joyful Noise: Poems for Two Voices*, Harper, 1988.

Fleischman, Paul, "Newbery Medal Acceptance," *Horn Book*, July-August, 1989, p. 442.

Fleischman, Sid, "Paul Fleischman," *Horn Book*, July-August, 1989, p. 452.

Haviland, Virginia, review of *The Half-a-Moon Inn*, *Horn Book*, June, 1980, p. 294.

Heins, Ethel L., review of *Graven Images: Three Stories*, *Horn Book*, December, 1982, p. 656.

Houser, Donna, review of *Joyful Noise: Poems for Two Voices, Voice of Youth Advocates,* August, 1988, p. 145.

Review of *Joyful Noise: Poems for Two Voices, Kirkus Reviews,* December 15, 1987, p. 1732.

Review of *Path of the Pale Horse, Kirkus Reviews,* April 1, 1983, pp. 375-76.

Slotkin, Richard, "Tales of Two Cities," *Washington Post Book World,* May 8, 1983, pp. 15-18.

Something about the Author, Volume 39, Gale, 1985, pp. 72-73.

■ For More Information See

BOOKS

Children's Literature Review, Volume 20, Gale, 1990, pp. 63-70.

PERIODICALS

Bulletin of the Center for Children's Books, March, 1983, pp. 125-26; October, 1985, p. 26.

Horn Book, June, 1983, p. 289; May-June 1986, pp. 329-30; September-October, 1986, p. 551; September-October, 1988, p. 614; May-June, 1990, p. 337; January-February, 1991, p. 63; March-April, 1993, pp. 187-89.

New Yorker, November 26, 1990, p. 144; November 25, 1991, p. 146, 148.

New York Times Book Review, April 27, 1980, pp. 45, 67; March 4, 1984, p. 31; September 8, 1985, p. 35; March 26, 1989, p. 18; September 30, 1990, p. 39; November 11, 1990, p. 52; May 31, 1992, p. 38.

Publishers Weekly, February 25, 1983, p. 88; November 22, 1985, p. 53; June 27, 1986, p. 94; January 29, 1988, p. 432; September 30, 1988, pp. 67-68; February 23, 1990, p. 126; March 16, 1990, p. 72; September 28, 1990, p. 102; July 12, 1991, p. 66; July 19, 1991, p. 57; June 1, 1992, p. 64.

School Library Journal, September, 1979, p. 110; May, 1983, p. 92; December, 1983, p. 65; November, 1985, p. 84; May, 1986, pp. 102-03; February, 1988, p. 79; November, 1988, p. 86; February, 1989, p. 8; May, 1990, p. 122; September, 1990, p. 226; December, 1990, pp. 21-22; August, 1991, p. 145; September, 1991, p. 278; October, 1991, p. 74; December, 1991, p. 29; August, 1992, p. 162.

Voice of Youth Advocates, June, 1986, p. 78.

—Sketch by Jeff Hill

Sue Grafton

■ Personal

Full name, Sue Taylor Grafton; born April 24, 1940, in Louisville, KY; daughter of Chip W. (an attorney and writer) and Vivian (a high school chemistry teacher; maiden name, Harnsberger) Grafton; married third husband, Steven F. Humphrey, October 1, 1978; children: (first marriage) Leslie; (second marriage) Jay, Jamie. *Education:* University of Louisville, B.A., 1961. *Hobbies and other interests:* Jogging, walking, reading, cooking, bridge.

■ Addresses

Office—P.O. Box 41447, Santa Barbara, CA 93140.

■ Career

Screenwriter, lecturer, and novelist. Has also worked in the medical field as an admissions clerk, cashier, and clinical/medical secretary. Story editor, with Stephen F. Humphrey, *Seven Brides for Seven Brothers* (television series), Columbia Broadcasting System, Inc. (CBS-TV), 1982-83. Speaker at numerous conferences, including Midwest Writ-ers Conference, Southwest Writers Conference, and Smithsonian Campus on the Mall. *Member:* International Association of Crime Writers, Writers Guild of America (West), Mystery Writers of America, Private Eye Writers of America (president, 1989-90).

■ Awards, Honors

Christopher Award, 1979, for *Walking through the Fire;* Mysterious Stranger Award, Cloak and Clue Society, 1982-83, for *A Is for Alibi;* Shamus Award, best hardcover private eye novel, Private Eye Writers of America, and Anthony Award, both 1986, both for *B Is for Burglar;* Macavity Award, best short story, and Anthony Award, both 1986, both for "The Parker Shotgun"; Anthony Award, 1987, for *C Is for Corpse;* Doubleday Mystery Guild Award, 1989, for *E Is for Evidence;* American Mystery Award, best short story, 1990, for "A Poison That Leaves No Trace"; Falcon Award, best mystery novel, Maltese Falcon Society of Japan, and Doubleday Mystery Guild Award, both 1990, both for *F Is for Fugitive;* Doubleday Mystery Guild Award, Shamus Award, and Anthony Award, all 1991, all for *G Is for Gumshoe;* Doubleday Mystery Guild Award, and American Mystery Award, both 1992, both for *H Is for Homicide.*

■ Writings

"KINSEY MILLHONE" MYSTERIES

A Is for Alibi, Holt, 1982.
B Is for Burglar, Holt, 1985.
C Is for Corpse, Holt, 1986.

D Is for Deadbeat, Holt, 1987.
E Is for Evidence, Holt, 1988.
F Is for Fugitive, Holt, 1989.
G Is for Gumshoe, Holt, 1990.
H Is for Homicide, Holt, 1991.
I Is for Innocent, Holt, 1992.
J Is for Judgment, Holt, 1993.

NOVELS

Keziah Dane, Macmillan, 1967.
The Lolly-Madonna War (also see below), P. Owen, 1969.

TELEPLAYS

Walking through the Fire, CBS-TV, 1979.
Sex and the Single Parent, CBS-TV, 1979.
Nurse, CBS-TV, 1980.
Mark, I Love You, CBS-TV, 1980.

TELEPLAYS; WITH HUSBAND, STEPHEN F. HUMPHREY

Seven Brides for Seven Brothers (pilot), CBS-TV, 1982.
A Caribbean Mystery, CBS-TV, 1983.
A Killer in the Family, American Broadcasting Company, Inc. (ABC-TV), 1983.
Sparkling Cyanide, CBS-TV, 1983.
Love On the Run, National Broadcasting Company, Inc., 1985.
Tonight's the Night, ABC-TV, 1987.

OTHER

Lolly-Madonna XXX (screen adaptation of *The Lolly-Madonna War*), Metro-Goldwyn-Mayer, 1973.

Contributor of "Kinsey Millhone" short stories to anthologies, including *Mean Streets: The Second Private Eye Writers of America Anthology,* edited by Robert J. Randisi, 1986; *Sisters in Crime,* edited by Marilyn Wallace, 1989; and *A Woman's Eye,* edited by Sara Paretsky and Martin H. Greenburg, 1991. Contributor to periodicals, including *California Review* and *Redbook.* The "Kinsey Millhone" novels have been translated into numerous languages, including Dutch, Russian, Polish, Spanish, and French.

■ **Adaptations**

Some of Grafton's novels are available on audio cassette.

■ **Sidelights**

"My name is Kinsey Millhone. I'm a private investigator, licensed by the state of California. I'm thirty-two years old, twice divorced, no kids. The day before yesterday I killed someone and the fact weighs heavily on my mind. I'm a nice person and I have a lot of friends. My apartment is small but I like living in a cramped space. I've lived in trailers most of my life, but lately they've been getting too elaborate for my taste, so now I live in one room, a 'bachelorette.' I don't have pets. I don't have houseplants. I spend a lot of time on the road and I don't like leaving things behind. Aside from the hazards of my profession, my life has been ordinary, uneventful, and good. Killing someone feels odd to me and I haven't quite sorted it through. I've given a statement to the police, which I initialed page by page and then signed. I filled out a similar report for the office files. The language in both is neutral, oblique, and neither says quite enough."

With this brief description, readers were introduced to Sue Grafton's popular "female dick," a private eye with what Susan Morgan of *Interview* described as "a smart mouth, a bad attitude, and the most appalling eating habits." Since her introduction in *A Is for Alibi,* Millhone's independent nature and common-sense style have made her a favorite with readers and critics alike. In many ways, the character is very similar to her creator. "Kinsey Millhone is my alter-ego ... the person I might have been had I not married young and had children," Grafton once commented. "Kinsey and I have different biographies, different life lines ... but our observations of the world, our attitudes, and many (though not all) of our opinions are the same.... She can only 'know' what I know so I consider it my responsibility to make sure she knows the right stuff. The trick is doing it so smoothly that the reader doesn't spot the effort. To the reader it should feel like 'Well, of course she'd know that—any good detective would.'"

Grafton: The Background Report

Like that of her fictional heroine, Grafton's early life was a bittersweet period. "Both sets of my grandparents were Presbyterian missionaries in China," the author recalled in an interview with *Authors and Artists for Young Adults* (*AAYA*). "My father was born there; my mother was born in West Virginia and moved to China when she was three or so.... I don't recall all the details, but I know that my parents knew each other. What generally happened in those days was that the children would be educated in China, then come to the United States for college. So my parents met again when they came to the States, fell in love and eventually got married." While the senior Graftons' unique upbringing offered some benefits (they could, for example, speak Chinese when they wanted to keep their conversations private), it also posed problems for their two daughters. Grafton noted: "Both of my parents were alcoholics, but they were also lovely, educated, smart, caring people. I think in part because they were raised in such a restrictive environment that when they got to the United States and met the demon rum, they just didn't know how to cope with it."

Grafton inherited her parents' love for reading; she did not, however, inherit a deep love for school. "As a child, I was a very earnest and dutiful student who had constant stomachaches," she told *AAYA*. "I remember being very frightened of school (and I give a lot of that to Kinsey, so that when she talks about her early school days, you can trust that it's my biography we are dealing with)." Because Grafton was so concerned with being a "perfect" student, school held little joy or interest for her: "By the time I got out of high school, I was one of those students whose report cards always read 'Does not live up to her potential.'... I always made Bs—I just didn't work very hard at school. I was more interested in escaping criticism."

Grafton's early writing efforts involved articles for her junior and senior high school papers; she also wrote a lot of poetry. "I started out like many kids writing poetry because of the hormone storms that most teenagers go through. You know, you have all of these melancholy emotions and this great engulfing sense of tragedy at fifteen," she reminisced in her interview. Despite these early efforts, Grafton never seriously considered writing as a future career. She remembered that "you were told early on that writers just never made any money, that they all starved to death. I didn't think that was particularly appealing; besides, at the time, all the popular novels were about two men on the road, having great adventures—and I wasn't allowed to hitchhike."

Grafton adapted one of her first novels, *The Lolly-Madonna War*, for the screen as *Lolly-Madonna XXX*, a 1973 film starring Rod Steiger and Robert Ryan.

Around age eighteen, Grafton started writing short stories and drafting book-length ideas. Eventually, she took a creative writing extension course at UCLA. "It was taught by Robert Kirsh, who was then the book editor for the *Los Angeles Times*. He encouraged me to write my first novel," Grafton told *AAYA*. Although she was not happy with the final result, Grafton kept working on new ideas. "From the age of twenty-two on, I wrote at night, every night, while I was working full time and raising a family," she once commented. "I wrote because I couldn't help it, because the writing interested, amused, and satisfied me. I wrote in the face of rejection, frustration, hardship, weariness, and stress. The very act of doing what I loved gave me energy."

Grafton wrote four book-length manuscripts before publishing her first novel, *Keziah Dane*. The book revolves around the efforts of a family matriarch to keep her clan together despite natural disasters and a greedy interloper. A reviewer for the *Times Literary Supplement* concluded that, despite some flaws, *Keziah Dane* was an "impressive first novel. . . . The talent here is certainly original, but not yet organized." Grafton followed *Keziah Dane* with *The Lolly-Madonna War*, a novel about two feuding mountain families. Even with the publication of this second work, however, the author felt that something was missing. She told *AAYA:* "I think I understood then that it was not going to be my place in life to do mainstream fiction. Had I stayed with it, I would probably have become a regional eccentric writer—which would have been fine had it felt right to me, if that had been my ambition and my passion."

Mysterious Inspiration

Grafton's move into the realm of mystery was motivated, in part, by her father's work in the genre. In her interview, the author noted that her father was "very passionate about mystery novels, which he wrote at the office in the evenings." Two of his efforts—including the Mary Roberts Rhinehart award-winning *The Rat Began to Gnaw the Rope*—were published. Unfortunately, while Grafton's father talked a lot about the writing process in general, he never discussed his technique for composing mysteries. "I greatly regret that," Grafton related, "because at this point I would love to sit down and talk to him about plotting, which to me is the great 'bug-a-boo' of mystery." She added, however, that she did find some of her father's unfinished notes regarding a third book in progress. "It's in the kind of code an author uses

when they're just jotting notes down quickly. . . . I have often thought about completing the book. My husband has suggested that maybe there would be a way for Kinsey to discover a manuscript that I could, in essence, coauthor with my father."

Along with feeding his daughter's love for the mystery genre, C. W. Grafton also helped inspire the framework for the "Kinsey Millhone" series. "I was always interested in mysteries with linking or related titles," Grafton reported to *AAYA*, "largely because my father based the only two books of his unfinished series on a children's nursery rhyme. I also knew about John D. MacDonald, whose titles were linked by color, and Harry Kemmelman, whose works were linked by the days of the week. One day I was reading a book of cartoons by Edward Gorey, who had done a series of pen-and-ink drawings about little Victorian children 'done in' by various means, like 'B is for Basil, eaten by bears.' A cartoon lightbulb formed over my head, and I thought to myself, 'Gee, why couldn't you do a series of books based on the alphabet?' So here I am, one book a year until 2008."

Grafton's decision to feature a female protagonist seemed a logical one. "I elected to write about a female because I'm female (hot news, huh?) and I figured that it was my one area of expertise," she once explained. In order to learn more about what a private eye's job actually entailed, Grafton "hit the books." The author confessed: "When I started work on *A Is for Alibi*, I wasn't even sure what a private investigator did. In the process of writing that first book, I began the long (and continuing) task of educating myself. I studied forensics, toxicology, books on burglary and theft, homicide, arson, anatomy, poisonous plants—you name it."

Shooting from the Lip and the Hip

A Is for Alibi introduced Grafton's Kinsey Millhone as both a principled P.I. and wise-cracking loner. For the author, Millhone became an alter-ego able to do many of the things her creator could not. "We're one soul in two bodies, and Kinsey got the good one," Grafton told *AAYA*. "We both jog, although I've had to cut back. For awhile, I used to lift weights, but it was so boring that now I have Kinsey do the lifting; in exchange, I let her have all the junk food she wants—I can't eat junk food anymore or I'd be as wide as a horse, so I think it's a fair trade. What I envy about her is her eternal youth. . . . When she turns forty, I'll be a haggard old woman. She'll never have to grow old, and she will never suffer the indignities the rest of us are going to have to suffer—she doesn't even have to diet!"

One of Millhone's most endearing qualities is her idiosyncratic nature. She cuts her own hair, has no interest in the latest fashions, and takes pride in her tart tongue. According to Grafton, "Kinsey just doesn't get it about being female. Nobody ever taught her the rules about make-up and all that, so she really lives a very liberated life—I mean, if your heroine is chasing bad guys, you don't want her to have to stop and adjust her mascara." Grafton's detective is also famous for her unsentimental regard for conventional emotional ties. The author told Morgan that Millhone "is the ideal dispassionate observer of domestic life—she's an orphan. She's been divorced twice, she lives alone.... Kinsey tells the truth about what's going down; she says things that other people think and repress."

Millhone's ability to "cut to the chase" has often come in handy, especially when: a) her clients' motives are not always what they seem, b) new suspects start to come out of the woodwork, and c) people try to kill her. In *A Is for Alibi*, the detective is hired by accused murderer Nikki Fife, recently released from prison and seeking to prove her innocence in the death of her husband Laurence. After accepting the case, Millhone is confronted with a number of colorful alternative suspects, a romantic interest, and a new killing. The backdrop for *B Is for Burglar* ranges from California to Florida, as Millhone tries to track down a missing wealthy widow whose mysterious disappearance soon begins to look like murder. Car accident victim Bobby Callahan, Millhone's client in *C Is for Corpse*, hires the P.I. to find out who—if anyone—has tried to kill him by running his car off the road, while Kinsey's search for a deadbeat client turns ugly in *D Is for Deadbeat*.

Critical reaction to Millhone's first cases emphasized Grafton's ability to balance an interesting character with exciting plot twists. Nick B. Williams, writing in the *Los Angeles Times Book Review*, cheered *B Is for Burglar* for having "plenty of surprises." "Kinsey Millhone . . . is an admirable creation. Study Kinsey closely and you'll find a thoroughly up-to-date, feminine version of Philip Marlowe, Raymond Chandler's hard-boiled hero," wrote David Lehman in a review of *C Is for Corpse* for *Newsweek*. And a reviewer for *Publishers Weekly* summed up *D Is for Deadbeat* by claiming that "the pleasure of this story comes through. Let's give it 'D' for Dandy."

Idiosyncratic California detective Kinsey Millhone is introduced in this 1982 thriller in which an accused murderess tries to clear her name—with deadly results.

E Is for Evidence marked a change for Grafton's sleuth. In an interesting shift, Millhone becomes one of the prime suspects in an "arson for hire" scheme. The detective finds the process of clearing her name hampered not only by planted evidence and evasive clues, but by the sudden reappearance of her ex-husband as well. *New York Times Book Review* contributor Vincent Patrick was particularly impressed by this entry in the series: "The plot is just fine and does what a plot ought to do in a good detective novel: it keeps us turning pages and serves as a vehicle for the *really* interesting stuff, an unveiling of the characters' foibles by the worldly-wise but uncorrupt private eye." Katrine Ames, writing in *Newsweek*, was equally laudatory, noting that Grafton "is a funny writer; her movements are crisp, her dialogue snappy, and (though Kinsey denies it) her heroine has class."

In *F Is for Fugitive*, Kinsey gets back to chasing bad guys. In this case, her target is Bailey Fowler, whose checkered past includes a murder conviction and a prison escape. After seventeen years on the run, Fowler has run afoul of the law once again; he has also managed to escape from a medium-security penal institution. Hired by Fowler's family, Kinsey's job is two-fold: to find the man and help clear his name. "Ms. Grafton's work surpasses what limps along as detective fiction these days," claimed Ed Weiner in a review of *F Is for Fugitive* for the *New York Times Book Review*. "She is consistent in accomplishing two extremely difficult tasks. First, she has successfully replaced the raw, masculine brutality and gore of the Parkers and Valins and Leonards with heart-pounding, totally mesmerizing suspense.... Tougher yet, she has made Kinsey Millhone real, somebody we actually believe exists."

Millhone is again faced with some tough personal dilemmas in both *G Is for Gumshoe* and *H Is for Homicide*. In the former, the investigator celebrates a birthday, moves into a new apartment, takes on what should be a simple missing persons case, and finds herself on a hit list; she also gets *very* involved with the man she hires to act as her bodyguard. The death of a workplace pal puts Millhone in the middle of a particularly nasty insurance fraud investigation—an investigation that requires some hair-raising undercover tasks— in *H Is for Homicide*. Reviewing the latter book for *Publishers Weekly*, a contributor noted that Millhone "remains a star supported by a lively cast."

Marilyn Stasio, writing in the *New York Times Book Review*, called *I Is for Innocent* "a true challenge for the private eye.... The dirty work rejuvenates Kinsey, who never loses her sense of humor but who doesn't play cute for a minute." In this entry, Millhone searches for evidence against a high-living architect, a man many people suspect of shooting his wife. As her investigation continues, the P.I. gets the chance to see just "how different" the rich can really be—with deadly results.

Plots and Plans

Finding new and interesting challenges for her fictional sleuth has sometimes proved difficult for Grafton. One of her biggest tasks is coming up with good—and believable—plots. "What I'm learning is incredible patience," she disclosed to *AAYA*. "I'm learning not to panic, not to make judgments about the work. I'm learning not to beat myself up if an idea doesn't occur to me." She added that coming up with fresh inspiration is "a lot like picking knots apart. I just sit here everyday with my little piece of string and pick at the knots.... Sometimes the inspiration for a book might come quickly, but often there is that first flash and then you have to sit down and do the hard work—which is the nuts and bolts and determination of exactly how it's actually going to lay out."

While working on the plot of each book, Grafton has to take into consideration the not-so-pleasant aspects of Millhone's job, such as having to shoot someone or taking a bullet herself. While admitting that she is "fascinated by violence in a strange sort of way," Grafton does not think her books are especially brutal. "I don't generally do graphic violence," she informed *AAYA*. "I'm so horrified

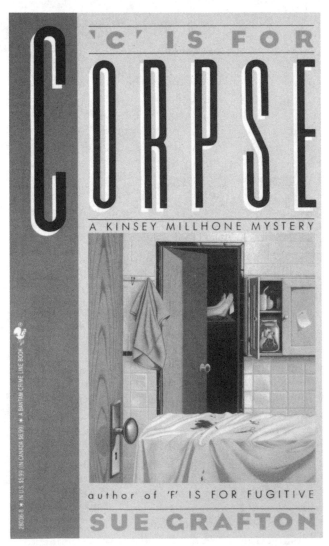

Millhone tries to discover who wants accident victim Bobby Callahan dead in this 1986 entry.

In this 1992 mystery, Kinsey must use all her wits to uncover the culprit behind a very bizarre murder scheme.

by it, so baffled and perplexed, that what I'm trying to do from book to book is understand what's going on in the world. I try to keep myself as far away from violence as possible, although I think violence needs to be looked at—[after all] it is the stuff of our nightmares."

Even though her years as a television writer exposed Grafton to a certain level of celebrity, the author does not see herself as "famous"; in fact, it is readers' devotion to Millhone that continues to amaze the author. "They are just avid about her. That's faintly mystifying to me, but also gratifying," Grafton mused in her interview, adding that she has "learned not to take it very seriously, because I think it's death to a writer to start thinking of yourself as hot shit.... I'm sort of tickled by the fascination, because it seems so unlikely, coming on the basis of a character who owns only one dress."

While Grafton does not rule out the possibility of exploring new mystery characters or other types of

novels in the future, she is unwilling to do so until she is "done with Kinsey." The author noted for *AAYA*: "Kinsey is very possessive—we'll see what happens when she is done with me. In the meantime, every day that passes, a little of my life is siphoned off to her.... If I felt that I was getting bored or burned out or if I needed to take a break, I might consider writing another kind of fiction as a way to refresh myself.... I did other kinds of writing before I got to her, so it isn't that appealing to me." With regard to Millhone's future, Grafton remarked: "By the time I get to 'Z,' I will owe her so much money that I will buy her off by letting her have her own book. I'd like to think that I invented her, but she assures me that she invented me, that I am just in her thrall. My life belongs to her and who knows what will happen to us."

■ Works Cited

Ames, Katrine, review of *E Is for Evidence*, *Newsweek*, July 18, 1988, p. 55.
Review of *D Is for Deadbeat*, *Publishers Weekly*, March 27, 1987, p. 38.
Grafton, Sue, *A Is for Alibi*, Holt, 1982, p. 1.
Grafton, Sue, interview with Elizabeth A. Des Chenes for *Authors and Artists for Young Adults*, January 27, 1993.
Review of *H Is for Homicide*, *Publishers Weekly*, March 15, 1991, p. 48.
Review of *Keziah Dane, Times Literary Supplement*, June 13, 1968, p. 13.
Lehman, David, review of *C Is for Corpse*, *Newsweek*, June 9, 1986, p. 77.
Morgan, Susan, interview with Sue Grafton in *Interview*, May, 1990, pp. 152-53.
Patrick, Vincent, "Lifestyles of the Rich and Quirky," *New York Times Book Review*, May 1, 1988, pp. 11-12.
Stasio, Marilyn, review of *I Is for Innocent*, *New York Times Book Review*, May 24, 1992, p. 25.
Weiner, Ed, "Who Killed the Town Lolita?," *New York Times Book Review*, May 21, 1989, p. 17.
Williams, Nick B., "Bloody Sunday," *Los Angeles Times Book Review*, August 4, 1985, p. 9.

■ For More Information See

PERIODICALS

Newsweek, May 14, 1990, pp. 66-67.
New York Times Book Review, May 5, 1982, p. 41; May 14, 1989, p. 34; July 28, 1991, p. 8.
People, July 10, 1989, pp. 81-82.
School Library Journal, September, 1990, p. 266.

—*Sketch by Elizabeth A. Des Chenes*

Isabelle Holland

Personal

Born June 16, 1920, in Basel, Switzerland; daughter of Philip (a U.S. Foreign Service officer) and Corabelle (Anderson) Holland. *Education:* Attended University of Liverpool; Tulane University of Louisiana, B.A., 1942. *Hobbies and other interests:* "All things Spanish—music, fiestas, the sound of the language; cats."

Addresses

Home—1199 Park Ave., New York, NY 10028. *Agent*—JCA Literary Agency Inc., 242 West 27th St., New York, NY 10001.

Career

Free-lance author of novels and short stories for adults, young adults, and children. Worked for various publications, including *McCull's*, New York City, until 1956; Crown Publishers, Inc., New York City, publicity director, 1956-60; J. B. Lippincott Co., New York City, publicity director, 1960-66; *Harper's*, New York City, assistant to publisher, 1967-68; G. P. Putnam's Sons, New York City, publicity director, 1968-69. *Member:* Authors Guild, Authors League of America, PEN.

Awards, Honors

National Book Award nomination, 1976, for *Of Love and Death and Other Journeys*; Church and Synagogue Library Association Ott Award, 1983, for *Abbie's God Book* and *God, Mrs. Muskrat, and Aunt Dot.*

Writings

BOOKS FOR CHILDREN AND YOUNG ADULTS

Cecily, Lippincott, 1967.
Amanda's Choice, Lippincott, 1970.
The Man without a Face, Lippincott, 1972.
The Mystery of Castle Rinaldi, American Educational Publications, 1972.
Heads You Win, Tails I Lose, Lippincott, 1973.
Journey for Three, illustrated by Charles Robinson, Xerox Family Education Services, 1974, Houghton, 1975.
Of Love and Death and Other Journeys, Lippincott, 1975, published in England as *Ask No Questions*, Macdonald and Jane's, 1978.
Alan and the Animal Kingdom, Lippincott, 1977.
Hitchhike, Lippincott, 1977.
Dinah and the Green Fat Kingdom, Lippincott, 1978.
Now Is Not Too Late, Lothrop, 1980.
Summer of My First Love, Fawcett, 1981.
Abbie's God Book, illustrated by James McLaughlin, Westminster, 1982.
A Horse Named Peaceable, Lothrop, 1982.

After the First Love, Fawcett, 1983.
The Empty House, Lippincott, 1983.
God, Mrs. Muskrat, and Aunt Dot, illustrated by Beth and Joe Krush, Westminster, 1983.
Perdita, Little, Brown, 1983.
Kevin's Hat, illustrated by Leonard Lubin, Lothrop, 1984.
Green Andrew Green, Westminster, 1984.
The Island, Little, Brown, 1984.
Jennie Kiss'd Me, Fawcett, 1985.
Henry and Grudge, illustrated by Lisa Chauncy Guida, Walker & Co., 1986.
The Christmas Cat, illustrated by Kathy Mitchell, Western Publishing, 1987.
Love and the Genetic Factor, Fawcett, 1987.
Toby the Splendid, Walker & Co., 1987.
Thief, Fawcett, 1988.
The Easter Donkey, Golden, 1989.
The Journey Home, Scholastic, 1990.
The Unfrightened Dark, Little, Brown, 1990.
The House in the Woods, Little, Brown, 1991.

NOVELS FOR ADULTS

Kilgaren, Weybright, 1974.
Trelawny, Weybright, 1974.
Moncrieff, Weybright, 1975.
Darcourt, Weybright, 1976.
Grenelle, Rawson Wade, 1976.
The deMaury Papers, Rawson Wade, 1977.
Tower Abbey, Rawson Wade, 1978.
The Marchington Papers, Rawson Wade, 1980.
Counterpoint, Rawson Wade, 1980.
The Lost Madonna, Rawson Wade, 1981.
A Death at St. Anselm's, Doubleday, 1984.
Flight of the Archangel, Doubleday, 1985.
A Lover Scorned, Doubleday, 1986.
Bump in the Night, Doubleday, 1988.
A Fatal Advent, Fawcett, 1989.
The Long Search, Thorndike, 1990.
Love and Inheritance, Thorndike, 1991.

OTHER

Contributor of short stories to periodicals, including *Collier's* and *Country Gentleman*. Holland's papers are kept in the Kerlan Collection at the University of Minnesota, Minneapolis, and in the deGrummond Collection at the University of Southern Mississippi, Hattiesburg.

■ Sidelights

Isabelle Holland is a respected author of books for a wide range of readers. Her work for children and young adults is known internationally and is cited for its realism. In this genre, she deals with topics that, while common to the average teenager, are often seen by critics as controversial. Characters in these books deal with social ostracization, parental neglect, and sexual awakenings. As a mystery writer, Holland has also created more than fifteen books that have been described as well written gothic fiction. Despite the inclusion of often sensational material—haunted houses, murder, and drugs—these volumes for adults, like Holland's young adult fiction, have been praised for their realistic characters. Some reviewers of her books have speculated that the author's primary concern is with creating believable protagonists. Holland affirmed this in *Speaking for Ourselves*, stating that "all my books, whatever the category or form, deal, most importantly, with the inner journey of the central character."

The daughter of a United States Foreign Service officer, Holland spent much of her childhood abroad. She was born in Switzerland, eventually moved to Guatemala, and later lived in northern England. When Holland was a teenager, the impending threat of World War II prompted her father to send his wife and daughter to the United States. It was the first time Holland had lived in her native country. The experience was awkward, but as with much of her childhood, it did provide fertile material for her future writings.

While Holland draws upon her geographically varied childhood as a resource for her writing, she credits her inspiration for crafting fiction to another source. "I think of myself as a storyteller," Holland wrote in *Speaking for Ourselves*, "and for this I am indebted to my mother." Holland's mother was often faced with the task of keeping her daughter entertained. To this end she turned to storytelling, creating tales that held Holland in rapt attention. As she grew older, Holland discovered that many of her mother's stories had roots in history and legend. She also found that in addition to being exciting and entertaining, these stories provided insight regarding real life situations. Holland was attracted to the idea of creating stories that could address genuine problems while simultaneously regaling a reader. This became an important goal in her writing. As she declared in *Speaking for Ourselves*, "stories, however long . . . should above all be interesting."

Holland's initial foray into professional writing came when she was thirteen years old. She sold her first story, "Naughty Betty," to *Tiger Tim*, a British children's magazine. The Betty named in the title is a little girl who hates to practice the piano—as did a young Isabelle Holland. This was an early example of the author using facets of her own life to infuse her fiction. For a time, Holland toyed with an epic-style narrative along the lines of Margaret Mitchell's *Gone with the Wind*. Her story revolved around a gambler in New Orleans, but the book was never completed because Holland could not conceive a conclusion. Abandoning her riverboat romance, Holland turned to subjects on which she was more closely informed. She began drawing on complex events from her childhood—the ones beyond annoying piano practices—modifying situations and emotions to create characters and events. She frequently utilized her background as an American abroad—an outsider—to inform her characters with a sense of alienation and estrangement. Holland also had extensive education in boarding schools and often used them as backdrops for her characters.

Publishes First Novel, *Cecily*

Using her experiences in English boarding schools, Holland created her first novel, 1967's *Cecily*. One of the two key characters is Elizabeth, a young woman who teaches at the Langley School, a prestigious English boarding academy. A product of England's public school system herself, Elizabeth is confident and proud, and she deals with her students in a smooth and efficient manner. While the emphasis at Langley is academics, proper feminine etiquette is also a priority, and there is an unspoken ideal that determines a student's success. The most accomplished girls at the school are the ones who are tall, good-looking, and cheerful. Into this environment comes thirteen-year-old Cecily. Cecily is awkward, overweight, and miserable; the opposite of the perfect Langley girl. This unhappy young girl's presence has a devastating effect on Elizabeth. Seeing Cecily as a disruption to her well-balanced teaching environment, Elizabeth fails to address the girl's problems sympathetically. The teacher's lack of compassion eventually backfires and her own personal life is ruined. Cecily meanwhile manages to divine some dignity from her experience at the school and emerges the stronger of the two women.

At the time *Cecily* appeared, most publishers did not have a separate category for young adults, the genre with which the book is most closely identified. As a result, the semi-autobiographical tale was published as an adult novel. Critics, however, had no trouble discerning the book as a valuable addition to the growing library of literature for young adults. *Horn Book* reviewer Ruth Hill Viguers described *Cecily* as "a beautifully polished gem of a novel." Edith C. Howley wrote in *Best Sellers* that the book is "tightly knit and plausible," cited the characters as clearly defined, and appraised the book overall as "well done." Critical attention for *Cecily* also focused on Holland's sharp characterization and her ability to present realistic young adult situations in an entertaining manner. With many young adult books built around superficial plots and stereotypical themes, the arrival of *Cecily* was viewed by critics as a refreshing change. Viguers stated in her review that Holland's book is "a relief from tired stories written especially for teen-agers."

Holland's next book, *Amanda's Choice*, was written for children but addresses problems that are universal to people in relationships. Amanda is an unhappy young girl whose father has recently remarried. Preoccupied with his new wife and other matters, her father does not pay enough attention to her. In an attempt to amend this

In Holland's first novel, published in 1967, the arrival of misfit teenager Cecily disrupts the environment at a stuffy boarding school.

situation, Amanda adopts vulgar language and mischievous behavior. This tactic earns her father's attention, but it is not the positive recognition that she craves. Amanda's relationship with Manuel, a young Cuban boy, helps her to realize that her life is not as bad as she perceives, and she is eventually able to reconcile her relationship with her father and stepmother. Alice Low wrote in the *New York Times Book Review* that Holland "understands child-rearing, psychological nuances and social problems, but she uses her characters to carry messages rather than to tell their flesh and blood stories." Reviewing *Amanda's Choice* in the *Bulletin of the Center for Children's Books*, Zena Sutherland lauded the book for its "memorable characterization" and "good style."

The Man without a Face

Holland's third novel, 1972's *The Man without a Face*, was appraised as "deeply affecting" by *Children's Literature in Education* contributor Corine Hirsch, who called the book Holland's "most interesting novel to date." The book is one of Holland's best known, primarily because of its controversial subject matter. Charles is a fourteen-year-old whose father has died. Since that time, his mother has remarried and divorced four times. He lives with her and his sisters. Viewing his mother's marriages as a betrayal to his father, Charles's attitude toward women in general is misogynistic—a term that signifies feelings of hate or distrust toward the feminine gender. Having loved and lost his father, he is also fearful of close relationships. In a misguided attempt to alleviate her son's unhappiness, Charles's mother is overly permissive and allows him to do as he pleases. As a result, Charles is insubordinate around authority figures, heedless of others' feelings, and unwilling to face his own emotions.

As the story begins, Charles and his family are spending their summer on an upper-class resort island. Because his grades have slipped considerably, Charles must enlist the aid of a tutor to gain entrance to an exclusive boarding school. He seeks the help of Justin McLeod, a reclusive native of the island. Years earlier Justin was responsible for the accidental death of a young boy and now spends most of his time alone on his ranch. When Charles and Justin first meet, there is a considerable personality clash. Justin is stern and reserved, a firm believer in a disciplined life. Charles is wary of Justin's authoritative posture and is also repulsed by the large scar on the tutor's face. As their relationship progresses, however, Charles finds

that Justin is filling much of the void left by his father. Justin's restrained manner poses little threat to Charles's fear of close emotional ties. With the tutor's positive influence, Charles begins to face his own feelings and becomes sensitive to the needs of others. He gains some understanding for his mother's numerous marriages and relates more openly with his family. The crucial and controversial event in the story, however, comes when Charles's cat is kicked to death by the delinquent boyfriend of one of his sisters. He goes to Justin for comfort and ends up spending the night in his tutor's bed. Holland implies that an act of homosexual love occurs between Charles and Justin. Soon after, Justin dies of a heart attack, leaving all of his possessions to Charles. Charles grieves his mentor's passing, but he realizes that

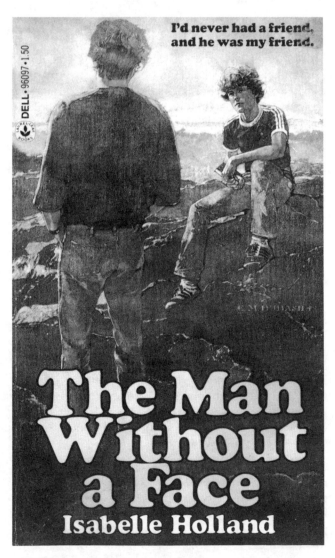

Rebellious teenager Charles develops an intense emotional relationship with Justin, his adult tutor, in Holland's controversial 1972 novel.

his relationship with Justin has helped him face his life and has enabled him to be open with others.

The inclusion of the homosexual element in *The Man without a Face* often sparked more discussion among critics than the novel's narrative quality. Many reviewers commented on Holland's motives, speculating on the novel's moral lessons. Sheryl B. Andrews wrote in *Horn Book* that "the author handles the homosexual experience with taste and discretion; the act of love between Justin and Charles is a necessary emotional catharsis for the boy within the context of his story, and is developed with perception and restraint." In an adverse response to the book, Frances Hanckel and John Cunningham, writing in the *Wilson Library Bulletin*, complained of potential anti-gay sentiment. Hanckel and Cunningham felt that "in light of such limited coverage of the gay experience in YA [young adult] fiction, the possible identification of such a major character as a corrupter of children is grossly unfair." Hirsch's reaction was mixed. While the reviewer disagreed with Holland's stance on parenting, complaining that "character and plot are manipulated in order to illustrate the dangers of permissiveness and the value of discipline," she did praise the author's use of homosexual themes, writing that "the novel's strength lies ... in the development of [Justin and Charles's] intense emotional relationship and the corresponding enrichment of Charles' sensibilities." *The Lion and the Unicorn* contributor Kate Fincke saw a deeper meaning in *The Man without a Face:* "Holland seems to have a twofold purpose. One is to speak some psychological truth on the matter of homosexuality; the other is to alleviate anxiety and to absolve guilt in the young adolescent reader about his own homosexual inclinations or acts." Comparing the fates of Justin and Charles at the novel's end, Fincke further interpreted that "what Holland implies is that the transient adolescent homosexual is acceptable, but the mature homosexual is doomed."

Holland stated in the *Horn Book* that she "didn't set out to write about homosexuality" in *The Man without a Face.* "I started this book with only the idea of a fatherless boy who experiences with a man some of the forms of companionship and love that have been nonexistent in his life." Holland wrote that the character of Justin possesses "qualities that mythologically as well as psychologically have always been the archetypes of fatherhood." These qualities, which include masculinity and kindness, filled a void in Charles and eventually helped the boy lead a better life. This, Holland

stated, was more important "than the almost incidental fact that the book is about love between two people of the same sex."

Teenage Insecurities, Adult Mysteries

Holland published another young adult novel in 1973, *Heads You Win, Tails I Lose*, about an obese girl who desperately tries to lose weight amidst her parents' marital problems. The novel was praised as well written, but many reviewers felt it was not as powerful as *The Man without a Face*. In 1974 Holland wrote what she considers her first novel for adults, *Kilgaren*, a gothic tale about a wealthy family and the dark secrets they keep. Nora E. Taylor, a contributor to the *Christian Science Monitor*, wrote that with *Kilgaren* Holland created "a rippling story that unfolds skin after onionskin of the unexpected, until the core is reached. It is worth the peeling."

Following *Kilgaren* Holland wrote the mystery *Trelawny*. The novel's protagonist, Kit Trelawny, lives in Trelawny Fell, a sprawling estate that may be haunted. As strange problems plague the estate, Kit learns that the solution may lie in confronting her past. Diane A. Parente, reviewing the novel in *Best Sellers*, assessed, "*Trelawny* is a novel for a summer afternoon, a winter evening.... [It] provides a temporary diversion from life's weightier problems." In 1975 Holland wrote another adult novel, *Moncrieff*, which has been described as a combination of realistic fiction and gothic suspense. In this novel, the protagonist, Antonia, and her son live in an old house that has a mysterious past. Faced with a failed marriage and the prospect of raising her son alone, Antonia has enough domestic problems with which to contend. To complicate matters, she is drawn into a mysterious web that involves her ex-husband. Joseph J. Feeney wrote in *Best Sellers* that "*Moncrieff* is almost unfailingly interesting. Its exposition is smooth and natural."

Holland returned to writing novels for young adults in 1975, producing the National Book Award nominee *Of Love and Death and Other Journeys*. The central character, Meg Grant, is a teenager who is coming to a crossroads in her life. She is at an age where the adulthood she so desperately craves is within her reach, but she is also repeatedly reminded of her proximity to childhood. Her priorities change significantly when she learns that her mother has cancer. When her mother dies, Meg must learn how to deal with her grief. She falls in love with a boy named Cotton

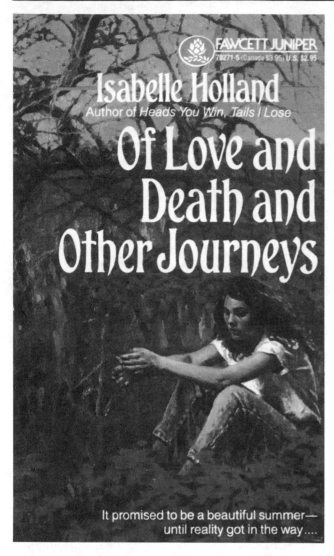

FAWCETT JUNIPER
70271-5 (Canada $3.95) U.S. $2.95

Isabelle Holland
Author of *Heads You Win, Tails I Lose*

Of Love and
Death and
Other Journeys

It promised to be a beautiful summer—
until reality got in the way....

Holland earned a National Book Award nomination
for this 1975 work depicting a teenage girl's struggle to
cope with the death of her mother.

but is rejected by him. Oddly, Cotton's rejection
triggers a realization in Meg that, although her
mother is gone, she can survive on her own and
lead a happy life.

Holland was praised for accurately evoking teenage emotion in *Of Love and Death*. "What makes
the book really entertaining is Isabelle Holland's
ability to capture all the precarious qualities of
teenhood," lauded Anne Marie Stamford in *Best
Sellers*. Stamford also admired Holland's skill in
depicting real life. She concluded her review by
stating that "the author's straightforward sense of
humor when describing people and situations
made me laugh out loud, a response rare indeed to
novels these days." A critic for *Kirkus Reviews*
praised the novel as "genuinely moving," and

assessed *Of Love and Death* as containing "real
emotion . . . that can't be ignored."

Holland returned to writing adult novels in 1976,
producing two new works, *Darcourt* and *Grenelle*.
In 1977 she wrote the young adult novel *Hitchhike*
about a young girl and her plans to get even with
her father. Pud is a sixteen-year-old at a boarding
school. Her father had promised to take her
camping at the end of the term but now tells her
that he cannot make the trip. Furious with him for
going back on his word, Pud decides to do something that she knows will upset her father: she
hitchhikes home. Her journey turns into a frightening realization of her father's admonitions against
hitchhiking. In an incident that leaves her badly
shaken, Pud is picked up by four young boys and
nearly raped. At the story's conclusion, Pud has
learned that although adults can be wrong about
some things, much of what they try to teach young
people has merit.

Reaction to *Hitchhike* was mixed, with some reviewers finding Holland's approach too heavy-
handed. Joyce Milton, writing in the *New York
Times Book Review*, felt that the author's writing
too often descended to tedious lectures against
subjects such as marijuana use and excessive
teenage freedom. Milton wrote: "Perhaps it's the
strain of handling potentially explicit material in a
manner suitable to the age group, but Holland
gives the impression of being out of sympathy with
youth." While *School Library Journal* contributor
Shirley Wilton agreed with Milton about the
author's excessive didacticism, she did state that
"the messages about the caring side of parental
discipline and about learning responsibility come
through, and Holland avoids the familiar teen
novel trap of damning the older generation."

Writes Realistic Fantasy for Children

Holland also wrote *Alan and the Animal Kingdom*
in 1977, an addition to her list of children's books
that already included *Amanda's Choice*, *The Mystery of Castle Rinaldi*, and *Journey for Three*. In this
story a young orphan, Alan, lives with his aunt and
a host of pets. In the years since losing his parents,
Alan has isolated himself from contact with the
outside world and people other than his aunt. He
lives as the only human in a fantasy kingdom
populated by his pets. When his aunt dies, Alan is
fearful of being sent to a place where he will not be
allowed to keep his animals. He decides to hide her
death, so as to protect both the animals and
himself. Trouble arises when Alan realizes that

participating in the society he loathes will be necessary to maintain his kingdom. Being only twelve years old, he finds that he cannot cash his aunt's checks, and with no money he cannot buy food or provide care for his pets. As his solitary existence becomes more difficult, Alan is forced to admit that he needs—and even craves—contact with other people. As Alan's kingdom crumbles, he learns that surrendering to humanity is not necessarily defeat, and that he and his beloved pets can survive the world together.

Critics again praised Holland for creating realistic characters, situations, and problems to entertain her readers. Reviews for *Alan and the Animal Kingdom* often cited Alan's conflict as authentic. Faith McNulty wrote in *Washington Post Book World* that "Isabelle Holland tells Alan's story the way fantasies are best told: with simplicity and convincing detail. Alan's problems are entirely credible." McNulty also appraised, "This is an 'orphan story' with an interesting twist." In *Kirkus Reviews*, Holland was commended for presenting a story with important themes that, with the inclusion of the animals, also appeals to children: "For most kids ... Alan's is an eminently sympathetic cause, and the added interest of coping alone enhances his likely appeal." A *Junior Bookshelf* reviewer commented that Alan "commands our sympathy," and concluded that the book's "final solution is neither sentimental nor engineered."

In 1977 Holland also published another mystery for adults, *The deMaury Papers*. In this tale, a female sleuth unravels a mystery set in an English country house. Reviewer Joe Vinson, writing in *Best Sellers*, felt that Holland left too many obvious clues and then concluded the novel too abruptly. He wrote, "The end of the story is both unexpected and ironic." Taylor was more impressed with *The deMaury Papers*, writing in another *Christian Science Monitor* review that "as always, it is next to impossible to put down a Holland mystery until the last thread has been untangled."

Holland wrote the suspense thriller *The Tower Abbey* in 1978, as well as another book for juveniles, *Dinah and the Green Fat Kingdom*. Exploring themes similar to Holland's previous books about young people, this novel tells the story of Dinah, an overweight girl just entering her teen years. Dinah's weight problem has created self-esteem problems for her. The story's moral is that Dinah must learn to love herself for the person inside, not the exterior ideal commanded by the majority of society. *Best Sellers* reviewer Eugenia E. Schmitz praised Holland's down-to-earth ap-

In this 1980 work, a motherless eleven-year-old turns to her grandmother for comfort and wisdom.

proach, commenting that "it is refreshing to find a well-written, humorous juvenile [book] about normal people. The characters are three-dimensional, the plot simple, credible and fast moving." Sutherland also found the book worthy, as she wrote in *Bulletin of the Center for Children's Books*, "The writing style is smooth, with good dialogue and excellent characterization."

In 1980 Holland published *Now Is Not Too Late*, which centers around the discoveries eleven-year-old Cathy makes while spending a summer with her grandmother. As with other Holland characters, Cathy is often at odds with the world. Similar to the fatherless Charles in *The Man without a Face*, Cathy has no mother. She is, however, fortunate enough to have her grandmother, a wise woman who shows Cathy that compromise does not always mean forsaking one's principles. During her summer, she also encounters a variety of other people, including an artist who asks the young girl to pose for her. In the episodes between the two, Holland indicates that this artist may indeed be Cathy's long-lost mother.

"Holland writes with polish and perception," appraised Sutherland in her review of *Now Is Not Too Late* in the *Bulletin of the Center for Children's Books*. Marilyn Kaye, a contributor to *Booklist*, was impressed with the author's characterizations, stating, "Cathy comes across as a very real and substantial figure whose hopes and fears are as vivid to the reader as they are to herself." And Mary M. Burns wrote in *Horn Book* that *Now Is Not Too Late* is "elegantly crafted" and "offers palpable descriptions of setting and characters as well as wonderfully pungent and wise observations on the human condition."

The 1980s proved to be just as busy a decade for Holland as the 1970s were. In 1980 she also published the suspense thriller *Counterpoint*, which was followed in 1981 by the young adult novel *The Summer of My First Love* and another thriller, *The Lost Madonna*. In 1982 she published the children's book *A Horse Named Peaceable*, about a young girl who is placed in a boarding school against her will and then discovers that her father has sold her beloved horse.

There's a Muskrat in My Book!

Holland wrote another children's book in 1982, *Abbie's God Book*, in which twelve-year-old Abbie conveys her thoughts on God, her family, and friends. In 1983 Holland published a related volume, *God, Mrs. Muskrat, and Aunt Dot*. The story centers around young Rebecca, a recent orphan. After the loss of her parents, Rebecca has come to live with her aunt and uncle. Told through a letter to God, Rebecca relates how her relationship with her imaginary friend, Mrs. Muskrat, has helped her adjust to her new life and surroundings. *Abbie's God Book* and *God, Mrs. Muskrat, and Aunt Dot* were jointly honored with the Church and Synagogue Library Association Ott Award in 1983.

Holland had a busy year in 1983. In addition to *God, Mrs. Muskrat, and Aunt Dot* and the young adult novel *After the First Love,*, she published *Perdita*, the story of a seventeen-year-old girl with amnesia. Perdita takes a job on a horse farm and, in a possible clue to her forgotten past, learns that she is an excellent rider. She also becomes aware, however, of a persistent fear that is plaguing her. In another 1983 book, *The Empty House*, a girl and her younger brother are outraged when their father is jailed for tax fraud. Against a majority of people who believe in their father's guilt, the youngsters set out to prove his innocence.

In 1984 Holland published two books for children, *Green Andrew Green* and *Kevin's Hat*, which is about a young crocodile who is teased by the other animals for wearing a new hat. She also published the young adult novel *The Island* in 1984. This book is a thriller about a teenager who visits a relative on a Caribbean island only to encounter life-threatening events. The mystery *A Death at St. Anselm's* rounded out Holland's writing activity for the year.

In the latter half of the 1980s, Holland continued to write prolifically, producing such mystery thrillers as *A Lover Scorned* in 1986, *A Fatal Advent* in 1989, and *Love and Inheritance* in 1991. She also returned to religious writing for children in 1987, when she published *The Christmas Cat*. In the story three homeless animals—a cat, a dog, and a donkey—are following a star in the hopes that it

Holland has produced several mystery thrillers, like this 1989 work.

will lead them to a king. As they travel, they find that their lives are changing in a wonderful way. Writing about another Christian holiday, Holland published *The Easter Donkey* in 1989.

Holland added three more novels to her lengthy resume in 1990. In addition to the adult novel *The Long Search*, she published a historical novel titled *The Journey Home*. Set in New York at the end of the nineteenth century, the story concerns two sisters who have become orphans. Seeking a new home, they board the orphan train bound for the new territories in the American West. Holland's third book published in 1990 is *The Unfrightened Dark*, a mystery for young adults. The novel centers on Jocelyn, a young orphan who is blind. Crooks have kidnapped her beloved seeing-eye dog, and it is up to Jocelyn to unravel the mystery of his abduction.

Sees Writing as Instructional

Holland's career as a writer spans more than twenty-five years. Beginning with the publication of *Cecily* in 1967, she has received considerable praise from critics, teachers, librarians, and readers. She has gained success in three distinct genres, and those familiar with her work have repeatedly remarked on the high quality evident in all three areas. While her mysteries have garnered significant reviews and sales, however, it is her work in the field of juvenile literature for which she is most highly regarded. Holland's handling of often sensitive material has been continually praised, as has her distinct portrayals of young people. As Sutherland appraised in the *Bulletin of the Center for Children's Books*, "it is . . . in insight into motivations and relationships that the author excels." Kaye echoed this sentiment in *Booklist*, opining that "Holland writes with compassion and a sensitive understanding of human nature and its idiosyncracies." "My books have always dealt with the relationship between the child or adolescent and the adult or adults who live in and dominate the young person's portrait of self," Holland stated in *Literature for Today's Young Adults*. She continued that "it is that struggle between the child and the adult in the creating of that self-portrait, that often preoccupies my writing." Holland assessed that parents or other adults will often unintentionally inflict mental damage on a young person, damage that can scar the child for many years. While Holland's books criticize the mistreatment of young people, she also views them as a means to make people aware of, and hopefully address and correct, these problems. She summarized by stating, "if my books are about the wounds given . . . they are also about the healing that can take place, given the right adult at the right time."

■ Works Cited

Review of *Alan and the Animal Kingdom, Junior Bookshelf,* June, 1980, pp. 143-44.

Review of *Alan and the Animal Kingdom, Kirkus Reviews,* March 15, 1977, p. 285.

Andrews, Sheryl B., "*The Man without a Face,*" *Horn Book,* August, 1972, pp. 375-76.

Burns, Mary M., "*Now Is Not Too Late,*" *Horn Book,* June, 1980, p. 297.

Feeney, Joseph J., "*Moncrieff,*" *Best Sellers,* January, 1976, pp. 306-07.

Fincke, Kate, "The Breakdown of the Family: Fictional Case Studies in Contemporary Novels for Young People," *The Lion and the Unicorn,* winter, 1979-80, pp. 86-95.

Hanckel, Frances, and John Cunningham, "Can Young Gays Find Happiness in YA Books?," *Wilson Library Bulletin,* March, 1976.

Hirsch, Corinne, "Isabelle Holland: Realism and Its Evasions in *The Man without a Face,*" *Children's Literature in Education,* spring, 1979, pp. 25-34.

Holland, Isabelle, "The People behind the Books: Isabelle Holland," *Literature for Today's Young Adults,* Scott, Foresman, 1980, p. 434.

Holland, Isabelle, *Speaking for Ourselves,* compiled and edited by Donald R. Gallo, National Council of Teachers of English, 1990, pp. 97-98.

Holland, Isabelle, "Tilting at Taboos," *Horn Book,* June, 1973, pp. 299-305.

Howley, Edith C., "Fiction: *Cecily,*" *Best Sellers,* April 1, 1967, p. 7.

Kaye, Marilyn, "Children's Books: *Now Is Not Too Late,*" *Booklist,* January 1, 1980, p. 667.

Low, Alice, "For Young Readers: *Amanda's Choice,*" *New York Times Book Review,* May 3, 1970, p. 23.

McNulty, Faith, "Flying Solo in Adult Skies," *Washington Post Book World,* June 12, 1977, p. E4.

Milton, Joyce, "Children's Books: *Hitchhike,*" *New York Times Book Review,* October 30, 1977, pp. 34, 36.

Review of *Of Love and Death and Other Journeys, Kirkus Reviews,* April 1, 1975, pp. 383-84.

Parente, Diane A., "*Trelawny,*" *Best Sellers,* December 1, 1974, pp. 382-83.

Schmitz, Eugenia E., "Young People's Books: *Dinah and the Green Fat Kingdom,*" *Best Sellers,* June, 1979, pp. 111-12.

Stamford, Anne Marie, "*Of Love and Death and Other Journeys*," *Best Sellers*, May, 1975, p. 33.

Sutherland, Zena, "New Titles for Children and Young People: *Amanda's Choice*," *Bulletin of the Center for Children's Books*, September, 1970, pp. 9-10.

Sutherland, Zena, "New Titles for Children and Young People: *Dinah and the Green Fat Kingdom*," *Bulletin of the Center for Children's Books*, April, 1979, p. 138.

Sutherland, Zena, "New Titles for Children and Young People: *Now Is Not Too Late*," *Bulletin of the Center for Children's Books*, March, 1980, p. 135.

Taylor, Nora E., "Escapism," *Christian Science Monitor*, June 12, 1974, p. F5.

Taylor, Nora E., "Isabelle Holland's Latest," *Christian Science Monitor*, August 3, 1977, p. 23.

Viguers, Ruth Hill, "*Cecily*," *Horn Book*, June, 1967, p. 353.

Vinson, Joe, "Sleuths and Spies: *The deMaury Papers*," *Best Sellers*, September, 1977, p. 174.

Wilton, Shirley, "*Hitchhike*," *School Library Journal*, September, 1977, p. 145.

■ For More Information See

BOOKS

Contemporary Literary Criticism, Volume 21, Gale, 1982, pp. 147-54.°

—*Sketch by David M. Galens*

H. M. Hoover

■ Personal

Full name, Helen Mary Hoover; born April 5, 1935, in Stark County, OH; daughter of Edward Lehr (a teacher) and Sadie (a teacher; maiden name, Schandel) Hoover. *Education:* Attended Mount Union College, Los Angeles School of Nursing, c. 1956, and Los Angeles City College. *Religion:* Protestant. *Hobbies and other interests:* Reading, long walks, rock hounding, gardening, music, cars (especially antique vehicles), ancient history, natural history.

■ Addresses

Home—9405 Ulysses Court, Burke, VA 22015.

■ Career

Worked in a clerical position at a steel company in Canton, OH; worked for a manufacturing company, an ad agency, and a chemical consulting firm in New York City; writer. *Member:* Authors Guild, Authors League of America, Society of Children's Book Writers and Illustrators, Children's Book Guild of Washington, D.C.

■ Awards, Honors

Children's Book of the Year designation, Child Study Association of America, and Best Book for Young Adults designation, American Library Association (ALA), both 1974, both for *The Lion's Cub;* Best Book for Young Adults designation, ALA, 1981, for *Another Heaven, Another Earth;* Central Missouri State College Award, 1984, for outstanding contribution to children's literature; Parent's Choice Honor Award, 1987, for *Orvis;* Best Book for Young Adults designation, ALA, and Parent's Choice Honor Award, both 1988, and Best Books for Children list, Library of Congress, 1989, all for *The Dawn Palace.*

■ Writings

SCIENCE FICTION NOVELS

Children of Morrow, Four Winds Press, 1973.
Treasures of Morrow (sequel to *Children of Morrow*), Four Winds Press, 1976.
The Delikon, Viking, 1977.
The Rains of Eridan, Viking, 1977.
The Lost Star, Viking, 1979.
Return to Earth: A Novel of the Future, Viking, 1980.
This Time of Darkness, Viking, 1980.
Another Heaven, Another Earth, Viking, 1981.
The Bell Tree, Viking, 1982.
The Shepherd Moon: A Novel of the Future, Viking, 1984.
Orvis, Viking, 1987.
Away Is a Strange Place to Be, Dutton, 1990.
Only Child (novella), Scott, Foresman, 1992.

NOVELS

The Lion's Cub (historical fiction), Four Winds Press, 1974.
The Dawn Palace: The Story of Medea (mythology), Dutton, 1988.

OTHER

Contributor to textbooks, including *Literature for Today's Young Adults,* edited by Aileen Pace Nilsen and Kenneth L. Donelson, Scott, Foresman, 1985; *Innocence and Experience: Essays and Conversations on Children's Literature,* Lothrop, 1987. Contributor to *Language Arts.* Hoover's manuscripts are included in the Kerlan Collection, University of Minnesota.

■ Work in Progress

A mythology book for young adults for the National Gallery of Art, and a science fiction manuscript waiting to be revised.

■ Sidelights

"It's always seemed to me that there is more lasting truth in fantasy than in fiction," futuristic writer H. M. Hoover notes in *Top of the News.* "Legend or myth, fairy tale or fable, all contain truth we sometimes can't articulate, but intuitively understand. We have all lived or worked on *Animal Farm* and know pigs who feel 'some animals are more equal than others.' We can see the great Oz in any humbugging politician. . . . The Dark Lord of Mordor is still with us and orcs do stalk suburban malls." M. Jean Greenlaw in *Twentieth-Century Children's Writers* praises Hoover's "detailed descriptions of the lanscape of any world she has created" in her many books of science fiction for young adults, including her futuristic vision of planet Earth.

Growing up in Rural Ohio

Hoover was born in the northeastern corner of Ohio in 1935, in the same house where many previous generations of her father's family had been both born and raised. The country house, "old by Ohio standards," was surrounded by woods, fields, ponds, creeks, and orchards. "Jefferson was president when the cellar hole was dug," she explains in an essay for the *Something about the Author Autobiography Series (SAAS).* "Begun as a large cabin, rooms were added through the years until it became L-shaped, then T-shaped, and

finally rectangular again, with dormer windows in the attic and a large front porch."

Hoover's childhood home was filled with books. Her parents, both schoolteachers, were well read and, as Hoover notes in an essay for *Fifth Book of Junior Authors and Illustrators,* "so were their four children, either by choice or in self-defense. I don't really remember a time when I couldn't read or was not read to." Coming from a family where books and reading were commonplace, the reading textbooks that she encountered when she started school came as a shock. "I couldn't believe I was being asked to waste my time with Dick and Jane after reading 'The Relief of Lucknow' in the *McGuffey's Fifth [Reader]* in our attic. It had always struck me as odd that few of our friends or neighbors had any books in their houses, while ours was overrun with reading material. I slowly decided that if people's first exposure to reading was Dick and Jane, it was probable that for the rest of their lives the very sight of a book might induce anxiety and the mad urge to cry 'Run, Self! Run! Run!'"

Hoover's first year of public school coincided with World War II, and, along with her fellow students, she participated in the war effort. "Patriotism demanded that students lug tons of newspapers to school on the school bus for paper drives and spend summer days picking milkweed pods so that their silky interiors could be used in place of kapok," Hoover recalls for *SAAS.* "Tinfoil was saved and wrapped into huge silver balls. Gas, sugar, and meat were rationed. . . . Little flags with gold stars in the center appeared in the front windows of houses and I realized dimly that the 'big kid' who lived there wouldn't be coming home again."

Public school was to become what Hoover calls "a mixed pleasure." Having spent much of her time growing up either by herself or in the company of her parents, the young Hoover found most of her schoolmates difficult to relate to. "The girls seemed given to jacks and jump rope at recess and thought softball—which I wanted to play—unladylike and rowdy, besides hurting their hands. Little boys, who did play softball, would not play with girls. Young children are arch conservatives." However, she soon made friends among her twenty-eight fellow classmates. Hoover kept the same friends and went to school with the same students until the end of junior high school.

By the time Hoover reached high school she was faced with many typical adolescent challenges. High school meant a twenty-six-mile bus trip that carried her from her comfortable farming community to a large consolidated high school in the nearby town of Louisville. Along with the new school came the establishment of a new "pecking order" among the many first-year students thrown together for the first time. "Being fat in one's teenage years was as much a source of misery then as now," she admits. "I survived socially by use of a wicked wit, including an unfortunate talent for nicknames that stuck to their victims, and my cruelty earned me a few lasting enemies." Another change for Hoover was that she now found it necessary to study to achieve the same grades she had once taken for granted. The days of being able to sit in class furtively reading a favorite book during a lecture on a subject she already knew were over. Hoover decided to meet the challenge of the larger, more competitive school by applying herself to such new subjects as biology, chemistry, Latin, algebra, and geometry. Although she found the sciences fascinating, math, she recalls, "remained a mystery."

Out in the Real World

Right after graduation, Hoover began work in the office of a steel company in Canton, Ohio, where she did stock inventory and other clerical duties. Always used to having lots of freedom, even within the constrains of school, she found it exhausting to be confined for an eight-hour stretch, and her job made her feel imprisoned. The opportunity to see what many of the steel mill workers had to sacrifice to earn a living and support their families—"they daily risked permanent disability and certain loss of hearing, without hope of a better job"—quickly made Hoover realize that such a life was not for her. She found another job near the campus of Mount Union College and enrolled in evening classes towards a degree so that she could somehow avoid finding herself in a similar situation.

But this inspiration was quickly overtaken by another. Influenced by a friend whom she greatly respected, Hoover decided to become a nurse. In the fall of 1956, she sold her car and moved to California where she began taking courses at the Los Angeles County Nursing School. "That I quit nursing school within six months was not the school's fault," she admits, adding that "the education I received was well worth the trip, having quickly taught me my total unsuitability for the profession." Finding herself in California with no place to live outside of the hospital dormitory, the twenty-year-old Hoover shifted gears. She quickly located an apartment and a job. She also enrolled

in night classes at nearby Los Angeles City College. "Palm trees and hibiscus to me seemed exotic, and to be so close to the Pacific Ocean was a thrill after living landlocked all my life," she recalls of this period. "Yucca grew wild in the mountains. The HOLLYWOOD sign was framed by my kitchen window. I relaxed, enjoyed, and drifted."

Despite the palm trees and the yucca dotting the California mountainsides, after two years Hoover and a friend left for the opposite coast, lured by the promise of New York City. Working at a series of clerical jobs, including copywriter and office manager for a small advertising agency, Hoover found that the routine of office work still proved to be less than inspiring. However, it was while living in New York City's energetic environment that she gained the impetus to begin writing. With the encouragement of close friends to support her, Hoover made a firm commitment to her writing career—if she was not able to at least partially support herself by writing within four years, she would find another career to pursue. She quit her job and "lived on savings and hope."

Fortunately, Hoover's strong determination and hard work paid off before her savings ran out. Her first success as a "writer" was to sell two short stories to *Scholastic*. "It then occurred to me that I was spending six weeks to write a story that paid $150," Hoover recalls. Confronted with anxiety over how she was going to pay the bills, her energy drained by the temporary jobs needed to supplement her small income, and fighting many nagging doubts about her ability to be successful as an author, Hoover nevertheless kept going and began her first novel. Within a few years, she had completed three novel-length manuscripts that she submitted to publishers under her full name, Helen Hoover. She soon discovered, however, that there was another children's author writing under the same name; she decided to write as H. M. Hoover to uncomplicate matters. Suddenly, the rejections she received were not quite as abrupt. "*Mr. Hoover* got more serious consideration than Helen ever did," she notes wryly in *SAAS*. "*He* got letters, not preprinted rejection slips. He even got a note expressing interest in a book, with a luncheon invitation to discuss the same, from a young woman editor who rather awkwardly, but quickly, lost interest when I called to confirm the date."

"Savings and Hope" Are Rewarded

Finally, at the close of the fourth year, *Children of Morrow* was accepted for publication by Four

THE LION'S CUB
H. M. HOOVER

Set in nineteenth-century Russia, Hoover's acclaimed 1974 historical story describes the ordeal of a Muslim boy who is captured by the enemy during a holy war.

Winds Press. Hoover's first published work, the novel had its beginnings in a walk that Hoover once took on a beach near a Manhattan landfill. As she describes it in *SAAS:* "Rain oozed through garbage and leached into the ocean. The snails, foul but alive, had swollen three to four times their normal size from feeding on the garbage. Instead of the polished beige with deeper brown 'eye,' their shells were gray, friable, completely lacking nacre. Nearby was a gull with three eyes, two on the right, one on the left; and a tern with an extra leg growing from its breast. Great flocks of gulls fed on the landfill, rising and swirling when trucks came to dump more garbage. The site was marked as a 'development area' and as I looked at that sign, I wondered if anyone in charge knew what they were truly developing and how the children of tomorrow would appreciate our stupidity, or if they would merely match it." *Children of Morrow,* along with its sequel, *Treasure of Morrow,* was the first of several of her books to explore Earth's future by depicting young people coping with the ecological consequences posed by its present.

Since *Children of Morrow* was published in 1973, Hoover has written other works of science fiction for young adults, including *The Delikon, The Lost Star, The Shepherd Moon,* and *Only Child. The Lion's Cub,* her second novel, was one of only a handful of books in which she explores other genres. A foray into historical fiction, *The Lion's Cub* came about because of Hoover's interest in old diaries and journals. Taking place in the nineteenth century, it is the story of a Muslim boy named Jemal-Edin who lives with his father in the Caucasus Mountains of Southern Russia during his people's holy war with the Russians. Jemal becomes a hostage of the enemy and, through his captivity and exposure to the Russian court of Czar Nicholas I, learns to better understand and accept the differences of the Christian infidels. Receiving praise by a reviewer in *Bulletin of the Center for Children's Books* for its "impressive consistency of period detail, historical fact, and dialogue," *The Lion's Cub* contains a strong ending and features the individualistic young protagonists that Hoover's fiction is noted for.

Thomas P. Dunn states in *Twentieth-Century Science-Fiction Writers* that Hoover's work provides "a congenial and fertile ground for exploring those problems young people may face in less exotic environments: alienation from parents, feelings of isolation, feelings of being trapped or of being an anomalous creature out of sync with the Universe." The author's young protagonists possess or learn to acquire abilities and mature sensitivities sometimes overlooked by the adults around them. Dunn links this with Hoover's use of science fiction as a teaching tool—a vehicle to express ideas as images—since "imaging is the very thinking process Einstein and other great thinkers use to generate new ideas. In Hoover's fiction we find provocative images of scientific concepts and a liberating experience for the human spirit."

The Shepherd Moon, published in 1984, features a typical Hoover heroine: intelligent, independent young Meredith Ambrose. Merry is a member of forty-third-century Earth's elite ruling class, a group who is able to live in luxury and whose directives determine the life-course of those born to the lower social orders. Understanding of the technology in place on the planet has regressed to a level below that required to develop it—The Great Destruction had previously eliminated much of the earth's population. Both culture and technology are in a state of decay. The arrival of Mikel, a sinister youth from a space habitat Earth built centuries before and had long since forgotten—he lands in the ocean near Merry's home one night during a severe storm—makes her aware of the inequity of her life of freedom and affluence compared to that of the rest of society. As her warnings of Mikel's evil intentions continue to fall on deaf ears, Merry also recognizes that although she is ignored and considered troublesome by her frivolous parents, her thoughtfulness and intelligence are not the negative qualities she once believed. "She gave a little laugh as understanding struck," Hoover's protagonist realizes. "If you were of her class, it could all be ignored—anything unpleasant. Her parents did that; in his own way, so did her grandfather—he could mourn a bronze soldier but not a dead officer. Her ancestors had tried to ignore dying. Her great-grandmother had apparently decided to ignore the entire world. But the world went on, waiting to be dealt with, if not now, later. And if she cared about herself, she'd have to learn to deal with it. It was a question not of power but of responsibility; someone had to take it. Otherwise things went on coasting into ruin."

As with several of Hoover's other books, reviewers praised *The Shepherd Moon* as a good introduction to the science fiction genre for young readers. Allene Stuart describes the work in *Fantasy Review* as a "gracefully written narrative which is more nearly futuristic romance than science fiction," later adding, "The real interest is generated by the courageous, inquiring, and supremely humane heroine." By contrast, *Orvis*, the novel Hoover published three years later, contains a seemingly uncharacteristic protagonist—neither "humane" *nor* a heroine—or a hero, for that matter. Orvis is an outmoded robot that is found by Toby and her friend Thaddeus. Although robots are not supposed to have feelings, a relationship forms between the human children and the machine as Toby and Thaddeus save Orvis from the scrap heap. The robot returns the favor by rescuing them from several dangerous situations in the wilderness known as The Empty on their way to Toby's great-grandmother's home. *Orvis* has been praised by reviewers for, as Lyle Blake Smithers comments in *School Library Journal*, the "successful depiction of an artificial intelligence that is humorous, likable, and believable."

Entering the World of the Fantastic

"All fiction writers create singular worlds if they try," Hoover remarks in *Top of the News*, "but in some respects fantastic worlds must be more real, more logically detailed and specific than straight fiction. When one writes about an alien world, it is

An unlikely relationship develops between man and machine after two children rescue an outdated robot from the junkyard in this 1987 tale.

just that to the reader. He or she must be told how and why it functions, and the telling must have consistency or all is lost. It must also be part of the story and not an inventory of facts." *The Dawn Palace*, published in 1988, was her chance to mesh both the fantastic and the singular. Basing her novel on Medea, the witch of Greek mythology who aided Jason and the Argonauts in their quest for the Golden Fleece, Hoover spent almost ten years in contemplation of the legend before actually beginning to write. "What made me decide to start the story was learning that it would have been possible, in 1250 B.C. or earlier, to make a gown that burst into flames when worn. And since both Glauce and Hercules were given garments of that type, I suspect that it was not an unknown custom to so gift enemies," she writes in *SAAS*. Full of vivid imagery and detailed description, *The Dawn*

Palace allows readers to enter "that world of long ago and to participate in the pain and frustration that Medea felt throughout her life," Greenlaw writes. However, the book was criticized by some reviewers for its lack of a real hero or heroine. As one critic says in *Bulletin of the Center for Children's Books,* "Jason is so unappetizingly cruel . . . and Medea so ruthlessly and blindly faithful." Hoover herself feels that the story somehow corrects the reader's perception about these mythological figures. "I always thought Medea was the victim of bad press," she tells *SAAS,* "and could never understand why Jason, Hercules, and their ilk were called 'heroes' since, in reading their adventures, they seemed little more than psychotic killers to me. But then, I've always sided with Cyclops. It was, after all, his island."

This award-winning 1988 work retells the legend of Jason and the Argonauts from the perspective of Medea, the witch of Greek mythology.

Science in Fiction

Each of Hoover's books present the reader with strong-willed, lively young protagonists and a rousing adventure tale. Her novels also provoke curiosity about more serious topics relating to the world of science. Hoover notes in *Language Arts:* "There is currently a great deal called science fiction that includes no science. Chemistry, biology, and the most elementary physics are ignored. I like some science in my science fiction. I also like it tempered with characters one cares about. Technology, like slang, ages very quickly. What seems smart today will be *passe* tomorrow. The story that relies strictly on state-of-the-art technology is doomed to a very short shelf life—and to boring the bulk of its readers."

One example of the way science fiction can be used to make readers think beyond the end of the story is the novel *Only Child,* published in 1992. Twelve-year-old Cody has spent his entire life as the only child aboard a spaceship, but when the ship lands on the planet of Patma, his secluded existence comes to an end. The natives of the young world, insect-like creatures called Skippers, kidnap the boy and demand that the human settlers leave the planet in exchange for his return. Under the guard of the Skippers, Cody learns a sad truth: humans have been killing these intelligent, essentially non-violent natives in violation of interplanetary laws after keeping their existence a secret to ensure rights to colonize the planet. Cody's broadening understanding of the cruelty of his own species and the manner in which he faces the decision of whom to side with, his people or the ill-used Skippers, won the praise of reviewers. "Hoover's premise, the evils of colonization, is a familiar theme, but her version is fresh and powerful," observes Lucinda Snyder Whitehurst in *School Library Journal.* Readers find the parallels between the Skippers of Hoover's novel and the many endangered species of our own planet both clear and thought-provoking.

Hoover draws the world of science into her fiction mainly through the evolutionary processes she predicts for the planet Earth. In addition to being teachers, Hoover's parents were both amateur naturalists, and their interest in the environment was passed on to their daughter. In many of her books, Earth is depicted as a planet where technological skill is on the decline, where mankind is engaged in the task of battling a regenerating ecosystem, and where cultures must develop independently, cut off from each other by areas of

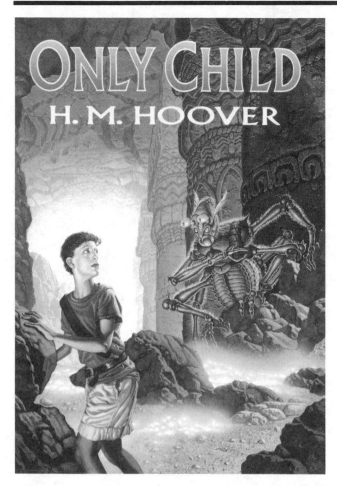

A boy must choose between his family and a race of aliens after he learns a disturbing secret in this 1992 work.

wilderness. "The reader never strains to enter those worlds because the land with its flora and fauna is so expressively presented," notes Greenlaw, who later adds: "The description is so much a part of the action that it does not become tedious. Indeed, it enhances the action of the story."

Advice for Young Writers

"One of the things that helps to create a writer is to be a lonely child—the younger the better—so that one learns to be alone and to amuse oneself in solitude," Hoover comments in *SAAS*, adding that "One of the benefits of solitude is that it allows time to think." Every job one takes, every new experience that one encounters, every person one gets to know help to fuel the writer's mind: "The mind constantly recycles data," she observes. Hoover combines the characteristics of many people she has known in real life to create the people in her books. "Real people are much too intricate— and self-contradictory—to be good or even believable characters. A writer uses one person's expression, or looks, or attitude toward life; or perhaps the way they walk, or talk, or even how their ears or hands may look. Characters in books are never whole, but if sketched successfully, give the illusion of completeness."

"Writing science fiction is far easier than writing historical fiction," she writes in *Horn Book*. "The author isn't limited to what really happened or is supposed, by reputable authority, to have happened. You can make up your own world, your own self-authenticated details, and so long as you stay true to yourself, no one can contradict you. It is the 'stay true to yourself' part that may give you problems—that and the telling detail that serves to fix the science or character or relationship in the mind. I am never sure if the detail will have the same weight for the reader as it does for me."

Hoover explains in *SAAS* that she has always viewed writing as hard work more than inspiration. "Books for me are a matter of discipline, of sitting down to work each day, of thinking about the story when not actually writing, of often drifting off to sleep plotting—although late-night ideas often turn out to be flaky when daylight comes again. Some days it is fun to write; other days very discouraging." Writers who claim to have never rewritten amaze Hoover: "Some writers claim that they can just sit down and the plot flows so smoothly that a book takes them less than a month. I consider myself lucky to complete a publishable page a day and, no matter how hard I try, can't seem to work much faster. Each sentence gets written a few times, and reworked, as does each paragraph, and each page. I write with a felt-tip pen on yellow legal pads and type it up later. There are times when I will write five pages only to realize afterward—never before—that I could have said all that more gracefully in one paragraph, or better still, one sentence. Brevity almost always improves a story. It is being brief that takes so much time."

Hoover has made her home in northern Virginia, where she continues to indulge in her love of reading and writing popular science fiction novels. "Every time there is any danger of getting pleased with myself, all that is necessary to bring me back to reality is a trip to any library," she tells *SAAS*. "There on the shelves are the hundreds and hundreds of books that have lived for fifty years, or a hundred, books so well written, so humane, that they are timeless and speak to each new generation of readers. Their authors teach me what to aim for, if not how to achieve it."

■ **Works Cited**

Review of *The Dawn Palace: The Story of Medea, Bulletin of the Center for Children's Books*, June, 1988, p. 207.

Dunn, Thomas P., "H(elen) M(ary) Hoover," in *Twentieth-Century Science-Fiction Writers*, St. James Press, 1991, pp. 384-85.

Greenlaw, M. Jean, "H(elen) M(ary) Hoover," in *Twentieth-Century Children's Writers*, St. James Press, 1989, pp. 465-66.

Hoover, H. M., essay in *Language Arts*, April, 1980.

Hoover, H. M., "Where Do You Get Your Ideas?," in *Top of the News*, fall, 1982.

Hoover, H. M., "Helen M. Hoover," in *Fifth Book of Junior Authors and Illustrators*, edited by Sally Holmes Holtze, H. W. Wilson, 1983.

Hoover, H. M., *The Shepherd Moon*, Viking, 1984.

Hoover, H. M., essay in *Something about the Author Autobiography Series*, Volume 8, Gale, 1989, pp. 119-30.

Horn Book, September, 1988, pp. 591-92.

Review of *The Lion's Cub, Bulletin of the Center for Children's Books*, January, 1975, p. 79.

Smithers, Lyle Blake, review of *Orvis, School Library Journal*, June 7, 1987, p. 96.

Stuart, Allene, review of *The Shepherd Moon, Fantasy Review*, September, 1984.

Whitehurst, Lucinda Snyder, review of *Only Child, School Library Journal*, July, 1992, p. 73.

■ **For More Information See**

BOOKS

Antczak, Janice, *Science Fiction: The Mythos of a New Romance*, Neal Schuman, 1985.

Gallo, Donald R., editor, *Speaking for Ourselves*, National Council of Teachers of English, 1990, pp. 100-01.

PERIODICALS

Horn Book, April, 1979, p. 199; June, 1984, p. 337.

Language Arts, September, 1982.

Times Literary Supplement, September 29, 1978, p. 1089; November 20, 1981, p. 1361.

Aldous Huxley

from the American Academy of Arts and Letters, 1959; D.Litt from the University of California, 1959; elected Companion of Literature, Royal Society of Literature, 1962.

■ Writings

NOVELS

Crome Yellow, Chatto & Windus, 1921, Doran, 1922.
Antic Hay, Doran, 1923.
Those Barren Leaves, Doran, 1925.
Point Counter Point, Doubleday, 1928.
Brave New World, Doubleday, 1932.
Eyeless in Gaza, Harper, 1936.
After Many a Summer Dies the Swan, Harper, 1939.
Time Must Have a Stop, Harper, 1944.
Ape and Essence, Harper, 1948.
The Genius and the Goddess (also see below), Harper, 1955.
Antic Hay and The Gioconda Smile, Harper, 1957.
Brave New World [and] *Brave New World Revisited*, Harper, 1960.
The Island, Harper, 1962.

POETRY

The Burning Wheel, B. H. Blackwell, 1916.
The Defeat of Youth and Other Poems, Longmans, Green, 1918.
Leda and Other Poems, Doran, 1920.
Selected Poems, Appleton, 1925.
Arabia Infelix and Other Poems, Fountain Press, 1929.
Apennine, Slide Mountain Press, 1930.
The Cicadas and Other Poems, Doubleday, 1931.

■ Personal

Full name Aldous Leonard Huxley; born July 26, 1894, in Godalming, Surrey, England; died November 22, 1963, in Los Angeles, CA; son of Leonard and Julia (Arnold) Huxley; married Maria Nys, 1919 (died, 1955); married Laura Archera (an author and psychotherapist), 1956; children: (first marriage) Matthew. *Education:* Balliol College, Oxford, B.A. (with high honors), 1916. *Hobbies and other interests:* Painting, walking, playing the piano, and "riding in fast cars."

■ Career

Author of novels, short stories, dramas, screenplays, and nonfiction. Worked for the British government during World War I; Schoolmaster at Eton College, Eton, England, 1917-19; staff member of *Athenaeum* and *Westminster Gazette*, and assistant at Chelsea Book Club, 1919-24. *Member:* Athenaeum Club.

■ Awards, Honors

Stanhope Historical Essay Prize, Balliol College, Oxford, c. 1915; Award of Merit and Gold Medal

The Collected Poetry of Aldous Huxley, edited by Donald Watt, Harper, 1971.

SHORT STORIES

Limbo: Six Stories and a Play, Doran, 1920.
Mortal Coils: Five Stories, Doran, 1922.
Little Mexican and Other Stories, Chatto & Windus, 1924.
Young Archimedes and Other Stories, Doran, 1924.
Two or Three Graces: Four Stories, Doran, 1925.
Brief Candles, Doubleday, 1930.
The Gioconda Smile (also see below), Chatto & Windus, 1938.
Collected Short Stories, Harper, 1957.
The Crows of Pearblossom, Random House, 1968.

PLAYS

Francis Sheridan's The Discovery, Adapted for the Modern Stage, Chatto & Windus, 1924, Doran, 1925.
The World of Light: A Comedy in Three Acts, Doubleday, 1931.
The Giaconda Smile (adapted from Huxley's short story), Harper, 1948, published as *Mortal Coils*, Harper, 1948.
The Genius and the Goddess (based on Huxley's novel), produced in New York City, 1957.

NONFICTION

On the Margin: Notes and Essays, Doran, 1923.
Along the Road: Notes and Essays of a Tourist, Doran, 1925.
Jesting Pilate: An Intellectual Holiday, Doran, 1926, published as *Jesting Pilate: The Diary of a Journey*, Chatto & Windus, 1957.
Essays New and Old, Chatto & Windus, 1926, Doran, 1927.
Proper Studies: The Proper Study of Mankind Is Man, Chatto & Windus, 1927, Doubleday, 1928.
Do What You Will (essays), Doubleday, 1929.
Holy Face and Other Essays, Fleuron, 1929.
Vulgarity in Literature: Digressions from a Theme, Chatto & Windus, 1930, Haskell House, 1966.
Music at Night and Other Essays, Chatto & Windus, 1930, Doubleday, 1931.
Beyond the Mexique Bay: A Traveller's Journal, Harper, 1934.
1936 ... Peace?, Friends Peace Committee (London), 1936.
The Olive Tree and Other Essays, Chatto & Windus, 1936, Harper, 1937.
What Are You Going to Do about It? The Case for Constructive Peace, Chatto & Windus, 1936.

Ends and Means: An Inquiry in the Nature of Ideals and into the Methods Employed for Their Realization, Harper, 1937.
The Most Agreeable Vice, [Los Angeles], 1938.
Words and Their Meaning, Ward Ritchie Press, 1940.
Grey Eminence: A Study in Religion and Politics, Harper, 1941.
The Art of Seeing, Harper, 1942.
The Perennial Philosophy, Harper, 1945.
Science, Liberty, and Peace, Harper, 1946.
(With Sir John Russell) *Food and People*, [London], 1949.
Prisons, with the "Carceri" Etchings by G. B. Piranesi, Grey Falcon Press, 1949.
Themes and Variations, Harper, 1950.
(With Stuart Gilbert) *Joyce, the Artificer: Two Studies of Joyce's Method*, Chiswick, 1952.
The Devils of Loudun, Harper, 1952.
(With J. A. Kings) *A Day in Windsor*, Britannicus Liber, 1953.
The French of Paris, Harper, 1954.
The Doors of Perception, Harper, 1954.
Heaven and Hell, Harper, 1956.
Tomorrow and Tomorrow and Tomorrow and Other Essays, Harper, 1956, published in England as *Adonis and the Alphabet and Other Essays*, Chatto & Windus, 1956.
A Writer's Prospect—III: Censorship and Spoken Literature, [London], 1956.
Brave New World Revisited, Harper, 1958.
Collected Essays, Harper, 1959.
On Art and Artists: Literature, Painting, Architecture, Music, Harper, 1960.
Selected Essays, Chatto & Windus, 1961.
The Politics of Ecology: The Question of Survival, Center for the Study of Democratic Institutions (Santa Barbara), 1963.
Literature and Science, Harper, 1963.
New Fashioned Christmas, Hart Press, 1968.
America and the Future, Pemberton Press, 1970.

COLLECTIONS

Rotunda: A Selection from the Works of Aldous Huxley, Chatto & Windus, 1932.
Texts and Pretexts: An Anthology with Commentaries, Chatto & Windus, 1932, Harper, 1933.
Retrospect: An Omnibus of His Fiction and Nonfiction over Three Decades, Harper, 1947.
Great Short Works of Aldous Huxley, Harper, 1969.
Collected Works, Chatto & Windus, 1970.
Science, Liberty, and Peace (includes *Literature and Science*), Chatto & Windus, 1970.

The Basic Philosophy of Aldous Huxley, American Institute of Psychology, 1984.

The Wisdom of the Ages, two volumes, Found Class Reprints, 1989.

SCREENPLAYS

(With Jane Murfin) *Pride and Prejudice* (based on the novel by Jane Austen), Metro-Goldwyn-Mayer, 1940.

(With others) *Madame Curie* (based on the book by Eve Curie), Metro-Goldwyn-Mayer, 1943.

(With John Houseman and Robert Stevenson) *Jane Eyre* (based on the novel by Charlotte Bronte), Twentieth Century-Fox, 1944.

Woman's Vengeance (based on Huxley's short story "The Gioconda Smile"), Universal, 1947.

AUTHOR OF INTRODUCTIONS, PREFACES, AND FOREWORDS

Pink, Maurice A., *A Realist Looks at Democracy,* Benn, 1930, Stokes, 1931.

Goldering, Douglas, *The Fortune,* Harmsworth, 1931.

(And editor) *The Letters of D. H. Lawrence,* Viking, 1932.

Butler, Samuel, *Erewhon,* Limited Editions Club, 1934.

Mendes, Alfred H., *Pitch Lake: A Story from Trinidad,* Duckworth, 1934.

Haire, Norman, *Birth Control Method (Contraception, Abortion, Sterilization),* Allen & Unwin, 1936.

de Ligt, Barthelemy, *The Conquest of Violence: An Essay on War and Revolution,* Dutton, 1938.

Merrild, Knud, *Knud Merrild, a Poet and Two Painters: A Memoir of D. H. Lawrence,* Routledge, 1938, Viking, 1939.

Gorky, Maksim, *A Book of Short Stories,* edited by Avram Yarmolinsky and Baroness Moura Budberg, Holt, 1939.

Unwin, Joseph Daniel, *Hopousia; or, The Sexual and Economic Foundations of a New Society,* Piest, 1940.

Montagu, Ashley, *Man's Most Dangerous Myth: The Fallacy of Race,* Columbia University Press, 1942.

Law, William, *Selected Mystical Writings,* edited by Stephen Hobhouse, Harper, 1948.

Krishanamurti, Jiddu, *The First and Last Freedom,* Harper, 1954.

Benoit, Hubert, *The Supreme Doctrine: Psychological Studies in Zen Thought,* Pantheon, 1955.

Mayer, Frederick, *New Directions for the American University,* Public Affairs Press, 1957.

Sulloway, Alvah W., *Birth Control and Catholic Doctrine,* Beacon, 1959.

Dolci, Danilo, *Report from Palermo,* Orion, 1959.

OTHER

(Translator) R. de Gourmont, *A Virgin Heart,* N. L. Brown, 1921.

(Editor) *An Encyclopedia of Pacifism,* Harper, 1937, Garland, 1972.

(Contributor) *This I Believe,* edited by Edward P. Morgan, Simon & Schuster, 1952.

The Letters of Aldous Huxley, Chatto & Windus, 1969, Harper, 1970.

Jonah, Gotham, 1977.

Contributor to periodicals, including *Life, Playboy, Encounter,* and *Daedalus.* The majority of Huxley's papers were destroyed in a house fire in 1961; the remaining papers are housed at the library of the University of California at Los Angeles. Additional material is kept at the Stanford University Library.

■ Adaptations

Point Counter Point (play), London, 1930.

Prelude to Fame (motion picture; based on Huxley's short story "Young Archimedes"), Universal, 1950.

Robert E. Thompson, adapter, *Brave New World* (television movie; based on Huxley's novel), National Broadcasting Company (NBC-TV), 1978, released as a cassette and as a filmstrip with cassette, Current Affairs and Mark Twain Media, 1978.

■ Sidelights

Novelist and essayist Aldous Huxley has been described by *New Statesman* contributor V. S. Pritchett as "that rare being—the prodigy, the educable young man, the perennial asker of unusual questions." Defining Huxley as a hybrid "artist-educator," Pritchett called the author "an extraordinary filler-in of the huge gaps in one's mind." Over the course of his long career, Huxley became known as a prolific author capable of provoking deep thought in his readers. He published more than thirty nonfiction pieces that ranged from travelogues to social criticism to examinations of literature. He wrote plays, short stories, poetry, and screenplays. Despite Huxley's facility and prolific output in these various genres, *Concise Dictionary of British Literary Biography* contributor Jerry W. Carlson assessed that "above all else, [Huxley] was a novelist." Novels such as *Crome Yellow, Point Counter Point,* and *Brave New*

World—the work with which he is most widely identified—earned Huxley his greatest fame and secured his place among the influential writers of the twentieth century.

Huxley was born on July 26, 1894, and was raised in one of England's most respected families. It is generally regarded that both his paternal and maternal ancestors were significant contributors to an ideological movement in nineteenth century England. This movement fostered the shift from religious mores to scientific thought among the British intellectual community. Huxley's father, Leonard, was highly active as an educator and a strong advocate for the teachings of his own father, the famed evolutionist Thomas Henry Huxley. His mother, the former Julia Arnold, was the granddaughter of Thomas Arnold, a notable reformer of the English public school system. Aware of their potent lineage, Huxley and his siblings were strongly encouraged to carry on the family tradition of intellectual pursuit. His brother Julian became a practical biologist who gained considerable fame for popularizing science. Huxley himself was pursuing a career in science when he was beset with an eye affliction that left him blind for over a year. The condition precluded him from the long hours of reading and research that the scientific field required. He never completely recovered, and the course of his life's work was forever changed.

The Education of Mr. Huxley

Huxley attended Balliol College at Oxford, where he completed his studies with high honors in English. While at Oxford, Huxley was introduced to Philip Morrell, a member of the British Parliament, and his wife, Lady Ottoline. Because of his family's reputation, Huxley was soon accepted into the Morrell's circle of friends. He began spending time at Garsington, the Morrell's country estate, where he met such influential literary figures as Virginia Woolf, T. S. Eliot, H. G. Wells, and D. H. Lawrence—with whom he would later forge a great friendship. Huxley's visits to the estate provided him with a view of modern life and thought that he could not obtain through academic study. He was fascinated by the fact that Garsington's guests could be both socially unconventional—often exceedingly ridiculous—and more intellectually stimulating than anyone he had yet encountered.

During his many stays at Garsington, Huxley met a young war refugee from Belgium named Maria

Nys. The two fell in love and married, prompting Huxley to move into the professional world. He briefly emulated his father's academic career, taking a teaching position at Eton College. His love of writing, however, soon influenced him to accept an assistant editor position with the periodical *Athenaeum*. Huxley's duties at the magazine included a good deal of flavorless tasks such as copy review and notice writing. It was his contribution of a weekly column—pieces then called middles because of their placement in the magazine—that held his interest at *Athenaeum* and allowed him to develop his literary voice. With the arrival of his son Matthew in 1920, Huxley supplemented his income with two more positions, those of drama critic for the *Westminster Gazette* and assistant at the Chelsea Book Club. Despite working long hours and writing lengthy columns for *Athenaeum*, Huxley found time during this period to begin writing fiction. In the same year that Matthew was born, Huxley published his first collection of short stories, *Limbo*. While he had previously published poetry volumes, including 1916's *The Burning Wheel* and *The Defeat of Youth* in 1918, *Limbo* marked his initial foray into his most popular writing style. The following year, Huxley published his first novel.

First Novel Impresses and Offends

Published in 1921, Huxley's debut novel, *Crome Yellow*, is viewed by many as a fictional parallel to the author's experiences at Morrell's Garsington. The Crome Yellow of the title refers to the country estate of one Henry Wimbush and his wife. Much as the actual estate of Garsington did, the fictional Crome Yellow serves as a gathering place for both intellectuals and intellectual poseurs. The Wimbushes surround themselves with famous faces and minds—not for edification, but for adornment and social status.

Into this environment comes a young poet, Denis Stone, who takes immediate note of the odd assortment of characters present. Denis observes the estate's various guests as they brag about pretentious achievements, misquote important figures, and misinterpret everything from modern art to each other's intentions. While Denis is a willing participant in this scholarly charade, he realizes that each of Crome Yellow's lodgers are little more than egotists who hold only their own knowledge and beliefs as true. Denis views these selfish people as a serious threat to the advancement of humanity. As he observes in the book, "One had a philosophy and tried to make life fit into it. One should have lived first and then made one's philosophy to fit life." Despairing later in the novel, Denis compares himself and his peers to parallel lines. While they seem alike and run alongside one another, they cannot touch or affect each other's life. As Denis laments, they will "meet only at infinity."

Crome Yellow marked the arrival of Huxley on the literary scene, and, with this novel of manners, many critics touted him as a champion of intellectual fiction. Carlson wrote that "for the young who had survived the war [World War I] or who had just come of age, Huxley was exhilarating; his work embodied the moral instability and the pretension that constituted the new era." Although Huxley's protagonist Denis Stone is often gloomy, the book is presented in a light manner that, as Carlson opined, "combines the grotesque and the beautiful." Despite *Crome Yellow*'s popularity with young educated people, many of Huxley's peers,

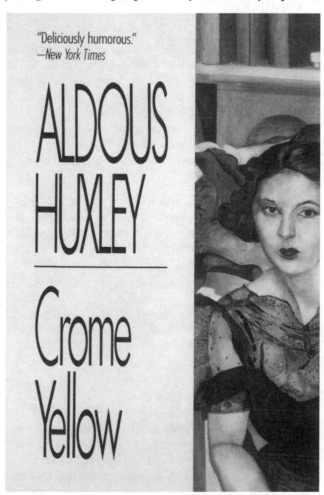

"Deliciously humorous."
—New York Times

ALDOUS HUXLEY

Crome Yellow

This 1921 social satire exposes the pretentiousness that pervaded the intellectual movement of post-World War I England.

notably Lady Ottoline Morrell, were upset by the novel. Lady Ottoline saw the estate of Crome Yellow as a thinly disguised version of Garsington and Huxley's characterizations as vicious parodies of his old friends. "Of course I base my characters partly on people I know," Huxley responded in *Writers at Work*. He denied any plausible connection to real people, however, stating that "fictional characters are oversimplified; they're much less complex than the people one knows." Carlson's assessment of the novel affirms the author's stance, assessing that "Huxley wrote to portray the characteristics of his era, not the characters of his friends."

Following the success of *Crome Yellow*, Huxley was able to negotiate a new contract with his British publisher, Chatto & Windus. Under the terms of the new agreement, Huxley would be responsible for delivering books under tight deadlines, but, as compensation, he would receive sizable royalties on the sales of his future books. This gave Huxley the financial stability to quit work as a journalist and completely devote himself to the writing of books. He made use of this new literary clout in 1923 and published *On the Margin,* a collection of the middles that he wrote for *Athenaeum* and a variety of new, longer pieces.

That same year, Huxley published his second novel, *Antic Hay*, which, in a vein similar to *Crome Yellow,* chronicles the self-centered behavior of post-World War I England. In a letter quoted by Carlson, Huxley explained that *Antic Hay* "is a book written by a member of what I may call the war-generation for others of his kind; and . . . it is intended to reflect . . . the life and opinions of an age which has seen the violent disruption of almost all the standards, conventions, and values current in the previous epoch." The novel further solidified Huxley's stature among the younger generation, selling five thousand copies in its first year of publication.

The following year, 1924, Huxley began work on his third novel, *Those Barren Leaves.* The book was published in 1925 and, similar to Huxley's publishing activity of 1923, was accompanied by a nonfiction volume, *Along the Road: Notes and Essays of a Tourist.* This book recounts the author's travels following the success of *Crome Yellow* and *Antic Hay,* and, as George Woodcock observed in the *Dictionary of Literary Biography,* "represents the period of Huxley's liberation from journalistic drudgery." In addition to recounting the time that Huxley and his family lived in Italy and travelled throughout Europe, the book also features essays on topics such as aesthetics and varying styles of painting. Although its title bills the book as a travelogue, *Along the Road* goes beyond scenic description. As Woodcock perceived it, *Along the Road* "is by no means entirely a book about physical travel.... Huxley is expanding his horizons mentally as well as territorially, and in the process developing a more discursive manner that enables him to pursue thoughts into their more elusive extremities."

The Turning Point of *Point Counter Point*

Huxley's pursuit of elusive thought drove him to spend the next three years creating a new novel. He described his intentions for the novel in a letter quoted by Carlson: "I am preparing for and doing bits of an ambitious novel, the aim of which will be to show a piece of life, not only from a good many individual points of view, but also under its various aspects such as scientific, emotional, economic, political, aesthetic, etc." Published in 1928, the novel *Point Counter Point* came to be viewed as a turning point in Huxley's fiction, a confluence of his essayist's ideals and his novelist's narrative technique.

Point Counter Point is designed to reflect a musical composition, in particular, composer Johann Sebastian Bach's B-minor suite. Huxley patterns relationships and dialogue after the intertwining melody and accompaniment lines evident in Bach's piece: as melodic phrases circle each other, then fuse into harmony, and then separate, so also do characters come together and part, each enacting their role in the passage. More than representing musical components, however, the characters in *Point Counter Point* are icons for various ideals and beliefs. Much as German novelist Thomas Mann did in his familial saga *Buddenbrooks*, Huxley attributes the success or failure of certain characters to the ideals they represent.

The book revolves around the lives and ideas of three key characters, Philip Quarles, Mark Rampion, and Maurice Spandrell. Quarles is a writer who longs to create a novel of ideas, much like the ones Huxley wrote. He wants his new book to give its readers a fresh perspective, "a new way of looking at things." A man of reason and a keen observer, Quarles serves as the reader's guidepost, providing explanation for some of Huxley's more complex concepts.

Rampion is a painter who detests modern society. His art depicts men as the monstrous creatures he perceives them to be. Depending on their affilia-

tion, Rampion bestows upon the objects of his revulsion such titles as "intellectual-aesthetic pervert" (a label he reserves for Quarles), "Jesus perverts," and "morality-philosophy perverts." His disgust is not limited to others, however, as he also refers to himself as a "pedagogue pervert." It is Quarles's opinion that because Rampion views society with such cynical caution—and plans his life and art accordingly—he "lives more satisfactorily."

On the negative side there is Spandrell, a nihilist. Spandrell believes that conscious human actions are inconsequential because a divine order has already been determined. Frustrated by his inability to comprehend the relationship between thought and action, and in an effort to discover if any act matters, Spandrell resorts to exploits calculated to provoke the intervention of God. He commits various acts of atrocity that include the murder of a fascist leader, not for political reasons, but for the forbidden pleasure of the crime. By the novel's end, none of the three men have achieved satisfactory results from their goals. Huxley indicates that, because of his brutal realism, Rampion may be the best off of the three. The artist is far from a happy man, however, for he is either ignored or avoided by the mainstream for his radical views. At the novel's end, he is left in a frustrating situation: how to save society, to make them live in an "integral" fashion when, from the majority's perspective, they see no flaw in their current patterns.

Point Counter Point continued the upward trend in Huxley's popularity, doubling the sales of his previous books. The novel's success established Huxley as a bestselling author and a definitive voice for a generation. Quoted by Carlson, Huxley appraised *Point Counter Point* as "a rather good, but rather frightful novel." Carlson termed the work as Huxley's "most panoramic, most ambitious, and most formally adventurous," calling it "the peak of Huxley's novelistic career."

Before beginning work on his next novel, Huxley once more renegotiated his contract with Chatto & Windus, securing a higher annual royalty rate and reducing the number of novels required of him. He also published a number of nonfiction pieces, including the essay collections *Do What You Will* and *Holy Face and Other Essays*. In 1930's *Music at Night*, the author examines popular culture and the rise of new entertainment forms. In discussing the book, Woodcock commented on "an interesting group of essays that seem to anticipate Huxley's own changing practices as a writer."

This 1932 novel, Huxley's most famous work, portrays a controlled utopia where free will and individual accomplishment have been replaced by programmed thought, feeling, and expression.

Up to and including *Point Counter Point*, Huxley's novels were categorized as carnivalesque, a literary form which Carlson defined as emphasizing "inclusion rather than selection.... Such works enact, celebrate, and ridicule, but do not resolve the conflicts among different characters, ideologies, literary genres, and forms of language." With the publication of *Brave New World* in 1932, most critics agreed that Huxley's fiction abandoned the carnivalesque discipline in favor of a more proactive stance. Carlson asserted that with *Brave New World* Huxley adopted the apologue as his primary form. Apologues, as specified by Carlson, are works of fiction that are "structured as persuasive arguments and subordinate character and plot to the development and exploration of certain ideas." As Huxley's first apologue, *Brave New World*

became his most popular novel and the work by which he is best known to a majority of readers.

Brave New World

Brave New World takes its title from a line in William Shakespeare's play *The Tempest:* "O, wonder / How many goodly creatures are there here! / How beauteous mankind is! / O brave new world / That has such people in't." The mankind in Huxley's brave new world is beautiful, although its splendor is of an engineered perfection and a carefully monitored class system. The time is the distant future, and advances in science and technology following Henry Ford's invention of the automobile have catapulted the human race to another level of existence. In the year 632 A.F. (After Ford, as in Henry), human beings no longer gestate in a human mother's womb; rather, they are conceived in laboratories and incubated in government controlled hatcheries. Through a process known as Bokanovsky Budding, ninety-three offspring can be derived from one egg. Once "born," a child is raised in a communal environment without a definite set of parents. Each child is assigned a social class at birth. They are subliminally instructed as to how to perform their duties, the requirements of their social standing, and the vital nature of human interaction.

Life in this utopian world is one of propagandized pleasure and happiness. Through various multimedia sources, the population is bombarded with information designed to convince them that they are incredibly content. Sex is strongly encouraged as a means of maintaining felicity, as is the consumption of Soma, an anxiety relieving drug that induces a dream-like state. Societal detriments such as stress, war, and unemployment have given way to blissed-out euphoria, subdued peace, and a simple, manageable job for everyone. In maintenance of this environment, individual achievement, personal opinion, and other elements contributing to strong identity have been all but eliminated. The effect is a near homogenous population in which the personality and ideas of one citizen is reflective of everyone else.

Bernard Marx is a member of this society's alpha class, the upper caste that is in charge of governing Western Europe. His life provides him with every gratification he can imagine, yet he is often bothered by a sensation of discontent. Rather than delight in the pleasure and guiltless noncommittment of group sex, Bernard would rather be alone with Lenina, the woman he loves. When he expresses his monogamous desires to others, he is ridiculed as abnormal and antisocial. As a high-ranking citizen, however, Bernard is afforded the luxury of travel, and he takes advantage of this privilege so that he may have Lenina to himself. The couple travels via rocketship to the New Mexican territory.

Years before, a sudden desert thunderstorm had swept a young girl away into this untamed land. During his visit to New Mexico, Bernard encounters this person, now an old woman. Over the course of her accidental exile, the woman has given birth—an unheard of organic birth—to a son. Named John but known as the Savage, the boy has grown into a man. Free from the rigid constraints of life in Western Europe, the Savage has grown up with freedom of choice, and he has developed a fierce intellect. Excited by this discovery, Bernard contacts His Fordship Mustapha Mond, the resident controller of Western Europe. Fordship Mond decides that the Savage and his mother would be of educational interest to the populace and arranges for them to come to England.

There is a considerable culture clash upon the Savage's arrival in Western Europe. He is amazed by the advanced technology available, and his intelligence is inspired with possibilities. The behavior of the people he encounters, however, convince him that this world is far from perfect. He is shocked by the even-handed complacency of the populace, the fact that no one expresses any extreme emotion. To him, it is a heinous crime that these people are not allowed to experience intense joy or tragedy, that they are denied the miracle of natural childbirth or the intellectual challenge of reading Shakespeare. The Savage's talk of freedom, of the empowerment of emotion pushes Bernard's glimmer of discontent into full disagreement with the method of life in the Fordship. While Huxley follows Bernard's attempts at reform, the centerpiece of the book is the moral debate between Mond and the Savage. In a verbal battle, each man espouses his theory of the meaning of life; the Savage passionately argues for concepts of free thought, religion, and monogamous romance, Mond advocates controlled equality, suppression of zealotry, and a median of emotion. The outcome of their debate leaves the Savage with the realization that, although he may be right, there is nothing he can do to change the brave new world. As Bernard and other rebels are exiled to Ireland, the Savage—too cultured for the wilds of New Mexico and too feral for the sterility of England—ends his own life.

"Brave New World was projected onto the screen of the future," stated Woodcock, "it was derived almost entirely from Huxley's alarmed observance of tendencies he saw in the world around him." Huxley's view of a doomed utopia preceded that of George Orwell's 1984 by some sixteen years (Orwell was, coincidentally, a student of Huxley's during his brief teaching stint at Eton). There are similarities in both books regarding an unsettling view of the future. But where Orwell's book deals with the oppressive qualities of an oligarchy, Huxley's novel is more concerned with emotional apathy fostered by advancing technology. Huxley later pointed to a key difference between the two novels, stating that because Orwell's novel was written after the rise of Stalinism and Hitlerism—two very strong and oppressive dictatorships—it reflected a paranoia of big government. Similar to the way Orwell's predictions regarding despotic, pervasive governments have come true, the modern world has seen many of Huxley's prophecies realized in the decades since his death. The Feelie, a kind of sensorial movie offered as diversion to the people of Brave New World, has evolved into the technology of virtual reality in which computer-generated images and sensations entertain the user. The widespread use of stress-relieving drugs like Soma—valium, seconal, and halcion—is now commonplace and are frequently used by people to escape the pressures of reality. Even the reliance on television for entertainment—an activity that reduces a person's pulse to a rate lower than that of slumber—has roots in Huxley's society where such passive forms of amusement are encouraged.

The numerous concepts suggested by Brave New World have made the novel a study centerpiece for social scientists, teachers, and technology mavens, and a favorite among readers for several generations. Carlson opined that the book's success can be attributed to Huxley's "mastery of the apologue form. Economical in structure and sure-handed in its treatment of scene and character, the novel is didactic but not essayistic." While critic Edward Cushing found Huxley's narrative technique of average strength, he did admire the author's intent and the novel's moral. Cushing wrote in the Saturday Review of Literature that "Mr. Huxley is eloquent in his declaration of an artist's faith in man, and it is his eloquence, bitter in attack, noble in defense, that, when one has closed his book, one remembers." New York Times Book Review contributor John Chamberlain found Huxley's novel a humorous attack on progressive global thought. In his review he contended that Brave New World satirizes "the imminent spiritual trustification of mankind, and has made rowdy and impertinent sport of the World State whose motto shall be Community, Identity, Stability."

Huxley Perfects His Craft, Goes Hollywood

Huxley did not publish his next novel until 1936. In between *Brave New World*'s appearance and the release of that novel, *Eyeless in Gaza*, he only produced one other work, the travelogue *Beyond the Mexique Bay* in 1934. As Woodcock expressed, "the travel books often assume the discrete form of brief essays on moral and aesthetic topics." Woodcock believed that books such as *Beyond the Mexique Bay* and *Jesting Pilate* serve as "bridges" between Huxley's essays and fiction, that in fact Huxley used these nonfiction works to perfect his transformation from carnivalesque novelist to apologist. In the four years between *Brave New World* and *Eyeless in Gaza* Huxley's generation came of age, and with this maturation, the novelist advanced in status from notorious fringe writer to outright celebrity. He became a revered luminary at numerous social occasions and was even the dinner guest of the king and queen of Belgium. This period also saw Huxley take action on behalf of his conscientious interests, becoming an active supporter and spokesperson for the Peace Pledge Union and other pacifist causes.

1936's *Eyeless in Gaza* tells the story of Anthony Beavis, an academic who is striving to organize his life and love. Beavis is involved with a woman named Helen, who has been his lover for seven years. As he approaches middle age, Beavis feels that he must make some sense of his relationship with Helen. According to Carlson, Huxley determined that the novel is about liberty. The author wrote, "What happens to someone who becomes really very free—materially free ... and then mentally and emotionally. The rather awful vacuum that such freedom turns out to be."

After the publication of *Eyeless in Gaza*, Huxley and his family travelled to America with the intention of continuing on to India as part of a series of lectures advocating peace. Ironically, World War II broke out and the Huxley's peace mission was grounded. Unable to return to England, he settled his family in California. His proximity to Hollywood later enticed Huxley to try his hand at writing screenplays, including adaptations of Jane Austen's *Pride and Prejudice* and his own short story "The Gioconda Smile." Before he undertook those projects, however, he was in-

Huxley's skills as an essayist are showcased in this 1934 travelogue.

spired to comment on the California lifestyle in a novel. *After Many a Summer Dies the Swan*, published in 1939, is a satirical novel that employs the character of a young Englishman, Jeremy Pordage, to, as Carlson described, "explore a world of eccentric characters who represent modern foibles." Pordage encounters people drunk on a lifestyle of too much money and too much leisure. Unable to find constructive activities, these hapless Californians spend their time in pursuit of pointlessly ridiculous goals such as finding the correct adornment for the elevator in one's mansion.

Huxley's foray into screenwriting provided the author with a diversion from the horrors of World War II, but he was convinced that it would not supplant the writing of books as his primary career. As he stated in *The Letters of Aldous Huxley*, "telling a story in purely pictorial terms doesn't allow any of the experimentation with words in their relation to things, events and ideas, which is *au fond* my business." While finding the movie industry artistically unsatisfying, Huxley did enjoy the financial rewards of the work, stating that "they have paid me a lot of money.... Always a pleasant state of affairs."

Huxley's next novel, *Time Must Have a Stop*, was published in 1944 and was preceded by a series of nonfiction works. Cited as Huxley's most tightly structured and conventional novel, *Time Must Have a Stop* is concerned with seventeen-year-old Sebastian Barnack and his modest goals. For Sebastian, the world has boiled down to two objectives: obtaining a new suit and finding himself a mistress. Unable to achieve his desires under the strict reign of his father, Sebastian travels to Italy, where he experiences a more aesthetic lifestyle—much as Huxley himself did upon his journey to that country.

Examines Dystopian Future

In 1948, Huxley published *Ape and Essence,* a novel that, like *Brave New World,* adopts its title from a Shakespearean play, in this case from *Measure for Measure*. Also like its predecessor, *Ape and Essence* is a vision of a dystopian future, this time set in Southern California in the year 2018. The novel is presented in the format of a screenplay that has been rescued from a studio's incinerator. As the narration explains, the world is in virtual ruin from an atomic blast. The only pocket of civilization to survive is in New Zealand, the rest of the world has reverted to primitivism.

As *Ape and Essence* begins, Alfred Poole, a young botanist from New Zealand, arrives in Los Angeles as part of an exploratory mission. Not long after Poole's party lands, however, they are attacked by a savage tribe and all but Poole are killed. Poole negotiates his survival by agreeing to teach these people how to scientifically grow food. He soon realizes the precarious nature of his bargain when he discovers how these people conduct their day to day lives. Existing as a brutal caste, these savages are subject to the zealous whims of the eunuch priests who act as their leaders. Traditional religion has been abandoned in favor of worship to Belial, a lord of hell. Common practices include human sacrifice, burying enemies alive, and exhuming corpses for clothes and jewelry.

Among the tribe is a dissenter named Loola who disapproves of her people's merciless tactics. She and Poole are drawn to each other and develop a relationship. Because the act of sexual intercourse is only allowed during a brief period once a year, Loola and Poole's liaison is viewed as illicit. The couple are branded as "hots," or sexual criminals, and are condemned to death. They manage to escape, however, and seek asylum within a community of other hots. In a break from traditional narrative technique, Huxley has his characters come face-to-face with their fictionality. During Loola and Poole's flight from persecution, they come upon a tree under which a man named William Tallis is buried. Tallis is the author of the screenplay that is the book *Ape and Essence*. In this brief interlude, fictional characters confront the corpse of their creator, himself a fictional concoction created by Aldous Huxley.

Critical reaction to this work—Huxley's ninth novel—was lukewarm. As Carlson appraised, "despite its clever form and economical presentation, [the novel] is a distinctly minor work." Alfred

THE DOORS OF PERCEPTION

aldous huxley

Huxley chronicles his experiences as the subject of a series of experiments with mescaline in this 1954 nonfiction work.

Kazin, writing in the *New York Herald Tribune Weekly Book Review*, held a more critical opinion of Huxley's work, stating that the author's "dryly moralistic vision of life ... is the burden of his novel." In a more positive notice, *Atlantic Monthly* reviewer Charles J. Rolo described Huxley as an author who "always has something important to say and says it entertainingly." While Rolo felt that *Ape and Essence* was not on a par with the author's previous work, he still rated the novel "in the upper bracket of the year's fiction."

Over the next fifteen years, Huxley would write only two more novels, his last works of fiction. During that time he produced a large quantity of nonfiction, much of which is considered among his best work. In 1952 he published *The Devils of Loudun*, a true account of a series of demonic possessions that beset a group of nuns in the French convent of Loudun. The book recounts the arrest, trial, and subsequent burning of Urbain Grandier, the supposed author of the possessions. It also follows the story of Father Surin, a priest who attempted to exorcise the Abbess of the convent only to succumb to the possessions as well. The book was extremely popular among college students and fans of paranormal activity. As Huxley saw it, however, the case was merely a depiction of the nature of religion. In Sybille Bedford's *Aldous Huxley: A Biography*, the author stated, "This is the whole message of this extraordinary episode—religion is infinitely ambivalent. It has these wonderful sides to it, and these appalling sides."

In the early 1950s, in an attempt to explore the further reaches of his own mind, Huxley submitted himself as a subject in a series of experiments. The experiments centered around the effects of the hallucinogen mescaline. Huxley underwent several doses of the narcotic and later wrote about his experience in the 1954 book *The Doors of Perception*. Once again his work struck a chord with college students. *The Doors of Perception*, however, was not only embraced by progressive academians, but by other social radicals, including members of the beatnik movement who sought mind-expanding experiences in the 1950s. Huxley's book is thought to be one of the contributing factors to the use of mescaline and other hallucinogens such as LSD for recreation, an activity that became widespread in the 1960s.

Return to Brave New World

In 1958, twenty-six years after the appearance of *Brave New World*, Huxley published *Brave New World Revisited*, a book that examines western life in the prosperous era following World War II. Contending that the society depicted in *Brave New World* will eventually come to be, Huxley calls for the human race to take note of, and reverse, its impending fate. While the author acknowledges that subliminal teaching and high tech entertainment such as the feelie are not yet evident in the world of 1958, he does call attention to existing conditions that indicate a pattern of propagated emotional control. Pointing to imagery evident in print, radio, and television, Huxley argues that the average person is subjected to repeated suggestions as to how to live the perfect, happy life. He further contends that people are led to believe that a lifestyle that differs from the idealized ones depicted in films, advertisements, and television programs is unsatisfactory. Huxley devotes the last two chapters of the book to possible solutions to these problems, claiming that it is still possible to divert the human race from a potentially adverse future. As he states in the book, "That we are being propelled in the direction of Brave New World is obvious. But no less obvious is the fact that we can, if we so desire, refuse to co-operate with the blind forces that are propelling us."

Brave New World Revisited received a substantial amount of attention upon its publication, partly due to the book's relation to Huxley's most famous novel. Many critics, however, felt that the book was an important work in its own right, one that related significant detail on modern society. "*Brave New World Revisited* is of the utmost importance for the knowledge of growing psychic pressures in a world in transition," appraised *New York Times Book Review* contributor Joost A. M. Meerloos. While lamentably viewing the book as a departure from Huxley's fiction, *Saturday Review* critic Granville Hicks commented that "if we have lost something in the way of entertainment, what we have gained is more important." Commenting on the author's talent for presenting invigorating arguments, Christopher Sykes wrote in the *Spectator* that "Mr. Huxley's writing remains as compelling and as brilliant as ever."

Huxley also used *Brave New World Revisited* to clarify the intentions of his 1932 novel. Whereas critics such as the *New York Times Book Review*'s Chamberlain saw *Brave New World* as a satirical take on complacency and conformity, the book's author clearly felt otherwise. As Huxley states in *Brave New World Revisited*: "Any culture which, in the interests of efficiency or in the name of some political or religious dogma, seeks to standardize the human individual, commits an outrage against man's biological nature."

The Best of All Possible Worlds

Following 1955's *The Genius and the Goddess,* Huxley's last novel, *The Island,* was published in 1962, one year before his death in 1963. The novel differs from Huxley's previous utopian and dystopian work in that it offers a positive depiction of a perfected world. Where novels like *Brave New World* and *Ape and Essence* point to major flaws in future societies, the community portrayed in *The Island* is a modern Eden of egalitarian, ecological, and economical virtue. The island of the title is a land mass named Pala that is situated in the Indian Ocean. The Palanese have developed a social system that utilizes the best concepts of western technology and eastern spirituality; a favorite Palanese maxim states "We must dream in a pragmatic way." Following this motto, every aspect of life on the island is a perfect fusion of aesthetics and practicality. Each function—education, agriculture, law enforcement—is carefully plotted to avoid friction.

Into this careful balance comes Will Farnaby, an embittered, world-weary journalist. As Will is educated in the ways of Palanese life, he notices a lightening of his spirit, that much of his cynicism is evaporating. Through his relationship with a native woman, he also learns to let go of the guilt dictated by prudish western mores. However, the island's paradise is threatened with the appearance of outside invaders. Greedy for the island's abundant natural resources, especially its oil reserves, western business overruns the delicate balance of Pala.

"Aldous Huxley's final novel, *Island,* marks the culmination of a lifetime of speculation on the problems of the modern world and on possible solutions for these problems," wrote Charles T. McMichaels in *Studies in the Literary Imagination.* McMichaels continued that "the novel also contains what must be considered as Huxley's final statement on the nature of mystical reality, a bringing together of the transcendent and immanent ideas that he had held at various times throughout his life." Concurring with this line of thinking, *New York Times Book Review* contributor Chad Walsh stated that "*Island* is a welcome and in many ways unique addition to the select company of books—from Plato to now—that have presented, in imaginary terms, a coherent view of what society is not but might be." Reviewer Richard S. Kennedy found the author's final book to be a fitting grace

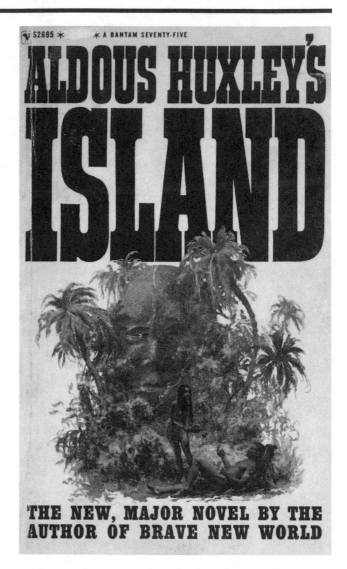

THE NEW, MAJOR NOVEL BY THE AUTHOR OF BRAVE NEW WORLD

The utopian society of Pala is threatened by outsiders in this 1962 book, Huxley's last published novel.

note to his profession. As Kennedy wrote in the *Southwest Review:* "Huxley has drawn together here the thought and experience of a lifetime. He has managed to synthesize religion and science, social order and individualism, and the cultural values of East and West. As a humanistic document, *Island* provides a worthy and fitting close to the career of a great intellectual of our time."

"The Last Victorian Man of Letters"

"Aldous Huxley had not one but several reputations," appraised Bernard Bergonzi in *Encounter,* "ranging from the witty iconoclast of the 'twenties to the expatriate guru of the California desert." Huxley was many things to a vast array of readers: a mysticist, a scientist, an aesthete, and a visionary. As Carlson commented, "Although conspicuously modern in intellect, he may have been, in his diversity of talents, the last Victorian man of letters." Carlson dissected Huxley's fiction into an early and a late period that ascribed a carnival-esque inclination to the former and an apologue format to the latter. Kennedy asserted that the author evolved from a sardonic novelist of manners "embittered over the flabbiness of values in the twentieth century," through an increasingly serious phase of social consciousness, to a period that reflected Huxley's interest in world religion, philosophy, and mysticism.

Through these discussions of Huxley's writing, it is generally agreed that the author's intentions for writing fiction went beyond the desire to craft a good yarn. As Huxley himself was quoted by Woodcock as saying: "I am not a born novelist but some other kind of man of letters possessing enough ingenuity to be able to simulate a novelist's behavior not too convincingly." To a number of critics, the membrane between Huxley the novelist and Huxley the didact became more nebulous with the author's foray into the apologue format. From *Brave New World* onward, Huxley's fiction is viewed as serving the master of ideology and education over that of entertainment.

The writing careers of Huxley and the Russian author Leo Tolstoy are often compared for their striking similarity in this respect. Tolstoy wrote what are considered fictional masterpieces such as *War and Peace* and *Anna Karenina* early in his career, and then used his literary clout to put forth his ideas of morality in such books as *Resurrection* and *The Kruetzer Sonata*. Nearly a century later, Huxley followed a similar path of early success and subsequent didactism. As Woodcock appraised: "Both men underwent a 'conversion' that resulted in a profound change in the kinds of books they wrote, and in both there was an evident rejection of certain aspects of their past." For Huxley this meant the creation of novels like *Brave New World* and *Ape and Essence* that stress that there is something wrong with the world and that it is up to the planet's inhabitants—if they wish to maintain their autonomy—to correct it. As Pritchett suggested, "for Huxley, perhaps the most accomplished educator of his generation, to shock was to ensure the course of intellectual freedom."

Huxley was diagnosed with cancer in 1960, five years after his first wife, Maria, had died of the disease. In the remaining three years of his life his health steadily declined. He died in his Los Angeles, California, home on November 22, 1963, at the age of sixty-nine. His work in both fiction and nonfiction is highly regarded for its social relevance and penetrating appraisal of modern society, people, and thought. While his work is often laced with pessimism, Huxley revealed in a 1957 issue of the *New York Times* that he held some optimism for the future of mankind. As he was quoted: "The most comforting lesson . . . is that the human race is tougher than we thought. Man has lived through two world wars, he can live at the poles and the equator. There is no reason to be boundlessly pessimistic although there's lots to be alarmed at, but we are not yet at the abyss. After all, it's amazing that only a small proportion of mankind breaks down and goes mad."

■ Works Cited

Bedford, Sybille, *Aldous Huxley: A Biography*, Carroll & Graf, 1973.

Bergonzi, Bernard, "Life's Divisions: The Continuing Debate on Aldous Huxley," *Encounter*, July, 1973, pp. 65-68.

Carlson, Jerry W., "Aldous Huxley," *Concise Dictionary of British Literary Biography*, Volume 6: *Modern Writers, 1914-1945*, Gale, 1991, pp. 186-209.

Chamberlain, John, "Aldous Huxley's Satirical Model T World," *New York Times Book Review*, February 7, 1932, p. 5.

Cushing, Edward, "Such People," *Saturday Review of Literature*, February 13, 1932, p. 521.

Hicks, Granville, "Huxley Revisited," *Saturday Review*, November 15, 1958, p. 12.

Huxley, Aldous, *Brave New World Revisited*, Harper, 1958.

Huxley, Aldous, *The Island*, Harper, 1962.

Huxley, Aldous, *Writers at Work: The "Paris Review" Interviews*, introduction by Van Wyck Brooks, Viking, 1963.

Huxley, Aldous, *Crome Yellow*, Harper, 1965.

Huxley, Aldous, *Point Counter Point*, Harper, 1969.

Huxley, Aldous, *The Letters of Aldous Huxley*, edited by Grover Smith, Harper, 1970.

Kazin, Alfred, "Fantastic Forecast of the Post-Atomic Age," *New York Herald Tribune Weekly Book Review*, August 22, 1948, p. 3.

Kennedy, Richard S., "Aldous Huxley: The Final Wisdom," *Southwest Review*, winter, 1965, pp. 37-47.

McMichaels, Charles T., "Aldous Huxley's *Island*: The Final Vision," *Studies in the Literary Imagination*, April, 1968, pp. 73-82.

Meerloos, Joost A. M., "How Will Man Behave?," *New York Times Book Review*, November 16, 1958, p. 22.

New York Times, August 25, 1957.

Pritchett, V. S., "Aldous Huxley," *New Statesman*, December 6, 1963, p. 834.

Rolo, Charles J., review of *Ape and Essence*, *Atlantic Monthly*, September, 1948, pp. 102, 104.

Shakespeare, William, *The Tempest*, Viking, 1959.

Sykes, Christopher, "Teacher without Faith," *Spectator*, February 20, 1959, p. 269.

Walsh, Chad, "Can Man Save Himself?," *New York Times Book Review*, April 1, 1962, pp. 4, 46.

Woodcock, George, "Aldous Huxley," *Dictionary of Literary Biography*, Volume 100: *Modern British Essayists, Second Series*, Gale, 1990, pp. 127-38.

■ For More Information See

BOOKS

Atkins, John, *Aldous Huxley: A Literary Study*, Orion, 1968.

Baker, Robert S., *The Dark Historic Page: Social Satire and Historicism in the Novels of Aldous Huxley 1921-1939*, University of Wisconsin Press, 1982.

Bedford, Sybille, *Aldous Huxley: A Biography*, two volumes, Chatto & Windus, 1973-74.

Birnbaum, Milton, *Aldous Huxley's Quest for Values*, University of Tennessee Press, 1971.

Bowering, Peter, *Aldous Huxley: A Study of the Major Novels*, Oxford University Press, 1969.

Brander, Laurence, *Aldous Huxley: A Critical Study*, Bucknell University Press, 1970.

Clark, Ronald W., *The Huxleys*, McGraw, 1968.

Dictionary of Literary Biography, Volume 36: *British Novelists, 1890-1929: Modernists*, Gale, 1985, pp. 46-70.

Firchow, Peter E., *Aldous Huxley, Satirist and Novelist*, University of Minnesota Press, 1972.

Greenblatt, Stephen Jay, *Three Modern Satirists: Waugh, Orwell, and Huxley*, Yale University Press, 1965.

Holmes, Charles M., *Aldous Huxley and the Way to Reality*, Indiana University Press, 1969.

Huxley, Julian, editor, *Aldous Huxley, 1894-1963: A Memorial Volume*, Harper & Row, 1965.

Huxley, Laura Archera, *This Timeless Moment: A Personal View of Aldous Huxley*, Farrar, Strauss, 1968.

Krisham, Bharathi, *Aspects of Structure, Technique, and Quest in Aldous Huxley's Major Novels*, Alquist & Wiksell, 1977.

Kuehn, Robert E., editor, *Aldous Huxley: A Collection of Critical Essays*, Prentice-Hall, 1974.

May, Keith M., *Aldous Huxley*, Elek, 1972.

Meckier, Jerome, *Aldous Huxley: Satire and Structure*, Barnes & Noble, 1971.

Thiel, Berthold, *Aldous Huxley's "Brave New World,"* Gruner, 1980.

Thody, Philip, *Aldous Huxley: A Bibliographical Introduction*, Studio Vista, 1973.

Watts, Harold H., *Aldous Huxley*, Twayne, 1969.

Woodcock, George, *Dawn and the Darkest Hour: A Study of Aldous Huxley*, Viking, 1972.

PERIODICALS

Kenyon Review, winter, 1965, pp. 49-93.

Partisan Review, March-April, 1943, pp. 143-58.°

—Sketch by David M. Galens

Akira Kurosawa

■ Personal

Born March 23, 1910, in Tokyo, Japan; son of Isamu (a physical education teacher) and Shima Kurosawa; married Yoko Yaguchi (an actress; real name, Kato Kiyo), 1945 (died February 1, 1985); children: Hisao (son), Kazuko (daughter). *Education:* Graduated from Keika High School, 1928. *Hobbies and other interests:* Collecting Japanese lacquerware and antique French and Dutch glassware; golf; American football games.

■ Addresses

Home—2-21-6 Seijo Setagaya-Ku, Tokyo, Japan. *Office*—c/o Kurosawa Production Inc., 3-2-1 Kirigaoka, Midori-Ku, Yokohama, Japan.

■ Career

Director, screenwriter, and producer of motion pictures. Photo Chemical Laboratory (PCL Studios; became Toho Films), Tokyo, Japan, assistant director to Yamamoto Kajiro, 1936-42; principle director, 1942-48 and 1952—; also director for Daiei Motion Picture Company, Chofu City, Japan, and for Shochiku studios. Assistant director on

films, including *Senman choja* (title means "The Millionaire"), 1936; *Chakkiri Kinta*, 1937; *Otto no teiso* (title means "A Husband's Chastity"), 1937; *Sengoku gunto den* (title means "The Saga of the Vagabonds"), 1937; *Nadare* (title means "Avalanche"), 1937; *Chinetsu* (title means "Subterranean Heat"), 1938; *Bikkuri jinsei* (title means "Life Is a Surprise"), 1938; *Tojuro no koi* (title means "Tojuro's Love"), 1938; *Tsuzurikata kyoshitsu* (title means "Composition Class"), 1938; *Chushingura,* 1939; and *Uma* (title means "Horses"), 1941. Cofounder of Film Art Association, 1948; founder of Kurosawa Production Inc., 1960; cofounder of Yonki no Kai (production company), c. 1970. Paintings exhibited at Proletarian Art Research Institute, beginning in 1928. Appeared in documentaries, including *75 Years of Cinema Museum,* Hershon-Guerra, 1972, and *Pacific Century,* Public Broadcasting Service (PBS-TV), 1992.

■ Awards, Honors

Named best director in Japan, 1947, for *Subarashiki nichiyobi;* Geijutsu Sai Grand Prize, Japan Ministry of Education, 1949, for *Stray Dog;* Grand Prix, Venice Film Festival, and Academy Award for best foreign-language film, Academy of Motion Picture Arts and Sciences, both 1951, for *Rashomon;* Silver Lion Award, Venice Film Festival, 1954, for *The Seven Samurai;* Director's Prize, Berlin Film Festival, and International Critics' Award, both 1959, for *The Hidden Fortress;* Moscow Film Festival Soviet Filmmakers' Association Prize, 1965, for *Red Beard;* Geijutsu Sai Prize for Excellence, Japan Ministry of Education, 1970, for

Dodesukaden; Academy Award for best foreign-language film, 1976, Donatello Prize [Italy], 1977, and Moscow Film Festival First Prize, all for *Dersu Uzala;* award for "humanistic contribution to society in film production," European Film Academy, 1978; cowinner of Golden Palm, Cannes Film Festival, and winner of Donatello Prize, both 1980, for *Kagemusha;* Academy Award nomination, best director, 1985, for *Ran;* Golden Jubilee Special Directorial Award, Directors Guild of America, 1986; Decorated Order of Yugoslav Flag; other film awards.

■ Writings

(With Michel Mesnil) *Kurosawa Presentation par Michel Mesnil,* Seghers, 1973.

Something Like an Autobiography, translated from the Japanese and prefaced by Audie E. Bock, Knopf, 1982.

(Author of foreword) Joseph L. Anderson and Donald Richie, *The Japanese Film: Art and Industry,* Princeton University Press, 1982.

(With Bertrand Raison and Serge Toubiana) *Le livre de Ran,* Cahiers du Cinema, 1985.

(With Michel Esteve) *Akira Kurosawa,* Lettres Modernes, 1990.

DIRECTOR; SCREENWRITER, EXCEPT AS NOTED

Sugata Sanshiro (title means "Judo Saga"; based on the novel by Tsueno Tomita), Toho Films, 1943.

Ichiban utsukushiku (title means "The Most Beautiful"), Toho Films, 1944.

Zoku Sugata Sanshiro (title means "Sanshiro Sugata, Part II"; based on the novel by Tsuneo Tomita), Toho Films, 1945.

Tora no o o fumo otokotachi (adapted from the Kabuki play *Kanjincho* ["The Subscription List"]; released in the United States as *The Men Who Tread on the Tiger's Tail*), Toho Films, 1945.

(Creator of scenario) *Asu o tsukuru hitobito* (title means "Those Who Make Tomorrow"), Toho Films, 1946.

(Written with Eijiro Hisaita) *Waga seishun ni kui nashi* (title means "No Regrets for Our Youth"), Toho Films, 1946.

(Written with Keinosuke Uekusa) *Subarashiki nichiyobi* (title means "One Wonderful Sunday"), Toho Films, 1947.

(Written with Uekusa) *Yoidore tenshi* (released in the United States as *Drunken Angel*), Toho Films, 1948.

(Written with Senkichi Taniguchi) *Shizuka naru ketto* (title means "The Quiet Duel"; based on the play by Kazuo Kikuta), Daiei Motion Picture Company, 1949.

(Written with Ryuzo Kikushima) *Nora inu* (released in the United States as *Stray Dog*), Shin Toho/Geijutsu Kyokai, 1949.

(Written with Kikushima) *Skyandaru* (released in the United States as *Scandal*), Shochiku, 1950.

(Written with Shinobu Hashimoto) *Rashomon* (adapted from the short stories "In the Grove" and "Rashomon" by Ryunosuke Akutagawa), Daiei Motion Picture Company, 1950, translated from the Japanese by Donald Richie, Grove, 1969, published in book form in English as *Rashomon and Other Stories,* translated from the Japanese by Takashi Kojimi, Liveright, 1952.

(Written with Hisaita) *Hakuchi* (title means "The Idiot"; adapted from the novel by Fyodor Dostoyevsky), Shochiku, 1951.

(Written with Hashimoto and Hideo Oguni) *Ikiru* (title means "Living"; released in the United States as *Doomed*), Toho Films, 1952, translated from the Japanese by Richie, Simon & Schuster, 1968.

(Written with Hashimoto and Oguni) *Shichinin no samurai* (released in the United States as *The Seven Samurai*), Toho Films, 1954, translated from the Japanese by Richie, Simon & Schuster, 1970, published in *The Seven Samurai and Other Screenplays,* Faber and Faber, 1992.

(Written with Hashimoto and Oguni) *Ikimono no kiroku* (released in the United States as *Record of a Living Being/I Live in Fear*), Toho Films, 1955.

(Written with Hashimoto, Kikushima, and Oguni) *Kumonosu-Jo* (title means "Castle of the Spider's Web"; adapted from the play *Macbeth* by William Shakespeare; released in the United States as *The Throne of Blood*), Toho Films, 1957.

(Written with Oguni) *Donzoko* (adapted from the play by Maxim Gorky; released in the United States as *The Lower Depths*), Toho Films, 1957.

(Written with Hashimoto, Kikushima, and Oguni) *Kakushi toride no san akunin* (released in the United States as *The Hidden Fortress*), Toho Films, 1958.

(Written with Hashimoto, Hisaita, Kikushima, and Oguni) *Warni yatsu hodo yoko nemuru* (released in the United States as *The Bad Sleep Well*), Kurosawa Productions/Toho, 1960.

(Written with Kikushima) *Yojimbo* (title means "The Bodyguard"), Kurosawa Productions/Toho, 1961.

(Written with Kikushima and Oguni) *Sanjuro* (adapted from the novel *Hibi Heian* by Shugoro Yamamoto), Kurosawa Productions/Toho, 1962.

(Written with Kikushima and Oguni) *Tengoku to Jigoku* (adapted from the novel *King's Ransom* by Ed McBain; released in the United States as *High and Low*), Kurosawa Productions/Toho, 1963.

(Written with Masato Ide, Kikushima, and Oguni) *Akahige* (based on the novel by Shugoro Yamamoto; released in the United States as *Red Beard*), Kurosawa Productions/Toho, 1965.

(Written with Hashimoto and Oguni) *Dodesukaden* (adapted from the novel *Shiki Ga Nai Machi* by Shugoro Yamamoto; also released as *Dodes'ka-den*), Yonki no Kai/Toho, 1970.

The Complete Works of Akira Kurosawa, nine parts, Kinema Juniposha, 1970.

Dersu Uzala (based on the novel *Dersu, the Trapper* by Vladimir Arseniev), translated by Malcolm Burr, Soviet MosFilm, 1975.

(Written with Ide) *Kagemusha* (title means "Shadow Warrior" or "The Double"), Kurosawa Productions/Toho, 1980.

(Written with Ide and Oguni) *Ran* (based on William Shakespeare's play *King Lear*), Kurosawa Productions/Herald Ace Inc./Greenwich Film Production/Nippon Herald Films/Sandrew Film and Teater, 1985, translated from the Japanese by Tadashi Shishido, Shambhala, 1986.

Dreams (also known as *Akira Kurosawa's Dreams*), Kurosawa Productions, 1990.

Hachigatsu No Kyohshikyoku (released in the United States as *Rhapsody in August*), Kurosawa Productions/Feature Film Enterprise No. 2/Shochiku, 1991.

Madadayo (title means "Not Ready Yet"), Kurosawa Productions, 1993.

OTHER

Also author of screenplays directed by others, including *Uma*, 1941; *Seishun no kiryu* (title means "Currents of Youth"), 1942; *Tsubasa no gaika* (title means "A Triumph of wings"), 1942; *Ginrei no hate* (title means "To the End of the Silver Mountains"), 1947; *Shozo*, 1948; *Jakoman to Tetsu* (title means "Jakoman and Tetsu"), 1949; *Akatsuki no dasso* (title means "Escape at Dawn"), 1950; *Tekichu odan sanbyakuri* (title means "Three Hundred Miles Through Enemy Lines"), filmed in 1957. Also author of other screenplays, including *Daruma-dera no doitsujin* (title means "A German at Daruma Temple"); *Dohyosai* (title means "Wrestling Ring Festival"); *Jajauma monogatari* (title means "Story of a Bad Horse"); *Dokkoi kono yari* (title means "The Lifted Spear"). Writer of one segment of *Yotsu no koi no monogatari* (title means "Four Love Stories"). Author of the one-act play *Shaberu* (title means "Talking"), c. 1945.

The 1985 film *Runaway Train* was adapted from a screenplay written by Kurosawa during the late 1960s. Some of Kurosawa's screenplays have been published in the periodical *Eiga Hyoron*. Film extracts from *Uma*, *Rashomon*, *The Seven Samurai*, *Throne of Blood*, *Kagemusha*, and *Ran* appeared in the documentary *A.K.* (also known as *Kurosawa Akira* and *A.K.: The Making of Ran*), Greenwich Film/Herald Ace Inc., 1985.

■ Adaptations

The Seven Samurai was adapted into the western film *The Magnificent Seven*, United Artists, 1960, and was loosely remade as the science fiction film *Battle Beyond the Stars*, New World, 1980; *Rashomon* was remade into *The Outrage*, Metro-Goldwyn-Mayer (MGM), 1964; and *Yojimbo* was adapted as *A Fistful of Dollars*, United Artists, 1964.

■ Sidelights

"I am not a special person. I am not especially strong; I am not especially gifted. I simply do not like to show my weakness, and I hate to lose, so I am a person who tries hard. That's all there is to me."

These humble words, voiced by Japanese filmmaker Akira Kurosawa in his *Something Like an Autobiography*, denote a vast understatement in the eyes of critics and film scholars. For Kurosawa, who has directed some thirty films during his prolific fifty-seven-year career, is regarded by many as the greatest Japanese filmmaker of all time, if not the most preeminent moviemaker alive today. A screenwriter as well as a director, Kurosawa has staked his reputation through award-winning films such as *Rashomon*, *The Throne of Blood*, *The Seven Samurai*, and *Ran*. His works, renowned for their depiction of the contrasting sides of humanity, frequently intermix strains of violence and compassion. Dabbling in a variety of genres, ranging from historical epics set in feudal Japan to modern-day detective stories and social commentaries, Kurosawa is credited with fashioning "some of the most vivid, physical-action sequences in the history of cinema," according to an *American Film* article by Gerald Peary. "No other filmmaker is so inspired as Kurosawa in finding visual analogues for emotional experience," relates James Bowman in *American Spectator*. Kurosawa "is, above everything else, an exact psychological observer," assessed Tony Richardson in *Sight and Sound*. He's "a keen analyst of behaviour—in a fundamentally detached way."

Known throughout the motion picture industry for his own bursts of intemperate behavior, Kurosawa is regarded as a perfectionist. He continually strives to craft films of superior quality, despite demands from studio executives to work faster and cheaper. This drive has caused him to go over budget on occasion, as he often slows production to wait for proper conditions, particularly in situations involving weather. The result is films with ideas and visuals that are carefully and methodically developed. "Kurosawa's imagery is often violent and extreme," observed Ian Buruma in an article for the *New York Times*. "He has said that he likes extreme weather conditions, and indeed many of his most memorable scenes take place in lashing rains, icy snowstorms or suffocating heat. His battle scenes are among the greatest ever put on film."

In addition to his use of vibrant imagery, Kurosawa often displays a penchant for sentimentality. The scope of his screenplays has run the gambit from death and brutality, to the influences of the nuclear age, to the struggle and demonstration of hope in a cruel world. "Kurosawa is fond of insisting that every artist has, ultimately, only one theme," related Akira Iwasaki in *Japan Quarterly*. "In his own case, he says, it is the question of why men cannot live together more happily and with greater good will than they do." The critic added, "Most of his films have a theme expressible in one line, or even one word: good, evil, happiness, unhappiness, the beauty of love—problems that boil down in essence to the problems of the existence of man, its meaning and its forms." Alan P. Barr in *Massachusetts Review* opined that "Kurosawa, as obsessively as any other artist, [explores] the nature and possibility of heroic action in a world that is basically corrupt, corrupt almost as a consequence of its human-ness." And in his *Films of Akira Kurosawa*, Donald Richie, who has translated some of the moviemaker's scripts into English, describes Kurosawa's central theme: "The world is illusion, you yourself make reality, but this reality undoes you if you submit to being limited by what you have made."

A Descendant of Samurai

The filmmaker's reality began on March 23, 1910, in Tokyo, Japan. Born to Isamu and Shima Kurosawa, he was the youngest of eight children and a descendant of samurai—dual sword-carrying war-

In 1986, Kurosawa accepted the Golden Jubilee Special Directorial Award from the Directors Guild of America.

riors who were part of the aristocratic class during Japan's Shogunate (feudal society). His father's ancestry can be traced to Abe Sadato, an eleventh-century samurai who lived in northern Japan. Isamu, who had earlier moved the family from the north to Tokyo, had been in the first graduating class of the Toyama Army Academy and had taught at the school before becoming a physical education instructor. In his *Something Like an Autobiography*, Kurosawa describes Isamu's love of sports, noting that he built the county's first swimming pool. His father's ardor for baseball was passed on to Kurosawa. Of his mother Shima he writes that she was "a typical woman of the Meiji era, Japan's age of swift modernization, during which women were still expected to make extreme sacrifices so that their fathers, husbands, brothers or sons could advance.... In such a way as to escape my father's notice, she would listen to all my complaints. Writing about her like this makes it sound as if I'm trying to set her up as a model for some moral tale.

But that is not the case. She simply had such a gentle soul that she did these things naturally."

In his autobiography the filmmaker illuminates other details about his family and early years. While he admits that the Kurosawas were very traditional in many ways, they did take a special interest in one form of modern technology—the motion picture. During Kurosawa's childhood, the film industry was in its infancy in its silent era. The family took the train to the nearest theater as movie houses were not yet commonplace. The youngster delighted in watching comedies, including the slapstick of Charlie Chaplin. Although he admits that his early movie-going experiences did not influence his later decision to become a film director, he writes: "I simply enjoyed the varied and pleasant stimulation added to ordinary everyday life by watching the motion-picture screen. I relished laughing, getting scared, feeling sad and being moved to tears." He adds, however, "Looking back and reflecting on it, I think my father's attitude toward films reinforced my own inclinations and encouraged me to become what I am today. He was a strict man of military background, but at a time when the idea of watching movies was hardly well received in educators' circles, he took his whole family to the movies regularly." His parents also took the family to hear master storytellers—an activity that Kurosawa particularly enjoyed.

Other memories of his early childhood are not as pleasant. Describing himself as physically weak and a slow learner, Kurosawa recalls feeling like his head was in a cloud—a condition that prohibited him from adequately responding to school lessons and games. As a result, his teachers and fellow students often belittled him. When Kurosawa was in his second year of primary school, his fog began to lift after the family moved to another district in Tokyo. He remembers that his new school, Kuroda, was more traditional, lending a militaristic atmosphere. "Imagine someone like me suddenly appearing among a group that lives by purely Japanese customs: a haircut like a sheltered little sissy's, a belted, double-breasted coat over short pants, red socks and low, buckled shoes," he relates in *Something Like an Autobiography*. "What's more, I was still in a wide-eyed daze and had a face as white as a girl's. I immediately became a laughingstock."

Kurosawa continued to be taunted at his new school. He notes: "[Other children] pulled my long hair, poked at my knapsack, rubbed snot on my clothes and made me cry a lot. I had always been a crybaby, but at this new school I immediately got a new nickname on account of it. They called me Konbeto-san ('Mr. Gumdrop') after a popular song that had a verse something like this: *Konbeto-san at our house, He's so much trouble, so much trouble. He's always in tears, in tears. Blubber blubber, blubber blubber.*" Apparently, the song equated the size of the crybaby's tears with gumdrops. "Even today I can't recall that name," Kurosawa adds, "without a feeling of severe humiliation." His Konbeto-san period lasted only about a year as Kurosawa began to overcome his difficulties, partially through the help (masked as bullying) of his older brother Heigo. Later, as he gained respect, he became known as "Kuro-chan."

Kurosawa remembers that the first time he felt any "confidence" was in an art class taught by Mr. Tachikawa. Devising an unusual picture in which he used his saliva to blend the colors, Kurosawa was mocked by other students when his teacher began to discuss the work in class. Tachikawa reprimanded the laughing pupils and lauded Kurosawa's picture, giving it the highest mark. Following the encouragement of his teacher, he developed an enthusiasm for art, especially drawing. Later, he would choose painting as his profession. His performance in his other studies improved as well, and he eventually became president of his class in primary school. His vice president was his friend Keinosuke Uekusa, who later worked on several filmscripts with him. Despite his successes, Kurosawa still had difficulties, especially with the teacher who succeeded Tachikawa. One day the instructor openly ridiculed his artwork in front of the other students. "I think this was the first time I ever experienced the savagery that lies in the human heart," Kurosawa recalled in *Something Like an Autobiography*. "But I acquired a determination to work so hard that this teacher would never be able to criticize me again."

Kurosawa's self-confidence continued to improve in the following years. When he was in the fifth grade he began to study *kendo* swordsmanship in school. Exhibiting prowess at the sport, he asked to be enrolled in private lessons, much to the delight of his father. During this time his daily schedule consisted of an eighty-minute walk to the fencing facility, more than thirty-minutes of *kendo* instruction, the lengthy walk back home for breakfast (including a stop at the Hachiman shrine for devotions), regular classwork at Kuroda, calligraphy lessons after school, and extra study at Tachikawa's house. Among Kurosawa's favorite subjects were history, composition, grammar, and art; he was not particularly fond of science and math.

The Great Kanto Earthquake, Depression, War

Following graduation from primary school, Kurosawa entered Keika High School. He became an avid reader, enjoying books by Japanese novelists such as Higuchi Ichiyo and Natsume Soseki and by Russians like Ivan Turgenev. He was interested in stories focusing on nature rather than humanity. But Kurosawa had to contend with the dark realities of these two worlds when they collided on September 1, 1923. On that day he experienced the Great Kanto Earthquake—an event that decimated buildings, altered the landscape, and brought death to thousands of Tokyo residents. Kurosawa, who had been in the city earlier that day, just missed being caught in the calamity and the fires that later ripped through Tokyo. Although Kurosawa and his family were unharmed in the disaster, he and Heigo did witness firsthand the effects of the catastrophe, which also led to untold lootings and killings. Once the aftershocks died down, the pair journeyed into the tumbled city. "At first we saw only an occasional burned body, but as we drew closer to the downtown area, the numbers increased," he recalls. "The burned landscape for as far as the eye could see had a brownish red color. In the conflagration everything made of wood had been turned to ashes, which now occasionally drifted upward in the breeze.... Amid this expanse of nauseating redness lay every kind of corpse imaginable. I saw corpses charred black, half-burned corpses, corpses in gutters,... and every manner of death possible to human beings displayed by corpses. When I involuntarily looked away, my brother scolded me, 'Akira, look carefully now.'"

Also during his high school days, he continued to have problems in matters concerning physical strength. In an effort to help his son overcome his weak constitution, Kurosawa's father sent him to the north of Japan one summer to live with relatives. Isamu hoped the demands of rural life would help his child's disposition. Back at school, Kurosawa began taking compulsory military training classes. Being a bit of a prankster, he ultimately failed the course. Despite his low military marks, he graduated from high school in 1928 and contemplated painting as a career. An enthusiast of French artist Paul Cezanne and Dutch impressionist Vincent Van Gogh, he set out to paint landscapes on Tokyo's periphery. But when his family encountered financial difficulties, Kurosawa considered getting a job with a more consistent income.

Rocked by the Great Depression, which began in 1929, he soon had no money for painting supplies. Nevertheless, he tried to continue his pursuit of the arts, increasing his reading as books were inexpensive and visiting the cinema on occasion. He also found himself moved by Japan's changing political climate, which included the suppression of communist activity and a rise in proletarian movements. Although not a member of the Communist Party himself, he did join the leftist Proletarian Artists League and edited one of the group's newsletters. In 1930 he was summoned by the army to determine his eligibility for the service. Suffering from hunger and exhaustion, he failed his physical examination. By 1932 disinterest and a serious illness led Kurosawa away from his political activities.

The ailing Kurosawa, who had been living on his own for several years in unheated boarder's rooms, was taken in by his brother Heigo while he recovered. Heigo had a steady job as the narrator of silent films at a local movie house. But Heigo soon faced losing his job with the advent of sound motion pictures and led a workers' strike in an effort to secure other employment opportunities. Meanwhile Kurosawa moved back with his parents. Some time after he was fired, Heigo committed suicide, and Kurosawa lost not only a brother but a role model. As Kurosawa toyed with the idea of painting, he took odd jobs preparing illustrations for periodicals. At the age of twenty-five, Kurosawa applied for a job at Photo Chemical Laboratory (PCL Studios) as an assistant director, never dreaming that the position would lead to some sixty years in the motion picture industry.

In order to obtain the job at PCL Studios (which later became Toho), Kurosawa had to convince his future employers that he was one of the five best candidates among the more than five hundred people who applied. The first part of the screening process was the composition of an essay about the problems inherent in the Japanese film industry. Despite his lack of formal studies in the film field, Kurosawa relied on his observations as a motion picture enthusiast. "In my answer I suggested, humorously, that if weakness were basic, there could be no cure," Kurosawa later said in *Show Business Illustrated*. "I also said that films could always be made better." After a couple of interviews, he was offered the position that paid $560 per month. Although he accepted, he planned on returning to painting one day. For Kurosawa, assuming the duties of an assistant director involved further education—hands-on training. His "teacher" throughout his introduction to the behind-the-scenes world of Japanese cinema was director Yamamoto "Yama-san" Kajiro.

Under Kajiro's tutelage, Kurosawa became familiar with all aspects of film production. "Management theory at P.C.L. regarded the assistant directors as cadets who would later become managers and directors," notes Kurosawa in his autobiography. "They were therefore required to gain a thorough mastery of every field necessary to the production of a film. We had to help in the developing laboratory, carry a bag of nails, a hammer and a level from our belts and help with scriptwriting and editing as well. We even had to appear as extras in place of actors and do the accounts for location shooting." Kajiro allowed his assistants to experiment in the various duties of the director. Kurosawa's mentor would include the unaltered work of his assistants in his films, even if the picture could be improved through his intervention. After several years, Kurosawa eagerly anticipated becoming a director.

Kurosawa struggled to make his dream a reality. Engulfed in World War II, the Japanese government began to exercise more censorship. Film scripts were reviewed by a board, which included army officials, and were rejected if deemed unpatriotic. For example, movies could not feature any symbols that looked like chrysanthemums—that was the emblem of the former imperial government. And since Japan was siding with Germany during the war, censors were eager to axe any film that used concepts or themes that could be associated with England or the United States. After several rejections, Kurosawa finally was permitted to take the helm on his first film. Like Kajiro, he adopted the tradition of writing or cowriting the screenplays of the pictures he directed.

Directs First Feature

Based on a story by Tsueno Tomita, Kurosawa's 1943 debut *Sugata Sanshiro* follows the adventures of a young man versed in martial arts. As the film progresses, the protagonist comes to understand that judo is a spiritual discipline, not a form of fancy fighting. Among the film's cast is Takashi Shimura, an actor who subsequently appeared in many of the director's films. During production of the movie, Kurosawa began to establish his reputation for filming under proper weather conditions. Seeking to film the picture's final battle scene under extremely windy conditions, Kurosawa took his crew to an area noted for its gales and waited for the breeze to turn gusty. The studio allowed three days for the location shooting, and Kurosawa finally got his violent winds on the third day. Winds would also figure prominently in some of his later films.

In his next feature, *Ichiban utsukushiku*, Kurosawa entered the world of workers in a military lens factory. Centering around the efforts of a group of teenaged, female volunteers, the picture depicts the struggle of one girl to maintain the same production speed as her male peers. Before bringing his screenplay to film, Kurosawa deemed that his actresses needed to shed their glamorous images, and he required them to institute a schedule consisting of running, volleyball, and marching. Representing the other actresses, Yoko Yaguchi approached Kurosawa to argue against some of these practices. Described by Kurosawa as both head-strong and stubborn, Yaguchi eventually married the director in 1945 amid the war. A day after the wedding, the shrine in which they were married was damaged when the U.S. Air Force led an air raid over Tokyo. Times were tough, especially for Yoko, who gave up her career for marriage (she had been receiving a salary three times that of Kurosawa's).

In 1945 Kurosawa also made a sequel to *Sugata Sanshiro*. Later he began work on his *Men Who Tread on the Tiger's Tail*. During production of the latter film, Japan was defeated by the Allied forces. Under the terms of Japan's surrender, the country was occupied by Allied soldiers, including Americans. Occasionally such personnel would visit Toho studios—some of the foreign servicemen enjoyed having their pictures taken. Unbeknownst to Kurosawa at the time, one of his favorite directors, American western master John Ford, toured the set with a group of officials.

Although the war and its aftermath had brought about a shortage of film stock in Japan, Kurosawa managed to finish *The Men Who Tread on the Tiger's Tail*. Based on the Kabuki play *Kanjincho*, otherwise known as "The Subscription List," the film centers on the life of a medieval warrior. Upon completion the picture was reviewed by a new censorship board consisting of Allied officials. The film was initially rejected due to its feudal setting, a theme that the occupying forces opposed. The movie was finally released some seven years later.

Despite the decision to ban the film, Kurosawa generally found Allied censors to be more progressive than the defunct, strict Japanese censors. His next project was *Asu o tsukuru hitobito* ("Those Who Make Tomorrow"). According to Audie Bock in *Japanese Film Directors*, "Kurosawa denies any responsibility for this film, which was a company command slapped together in one week." He then turned his energy to film *Waga seishun ni kui nashi* ("No Regrets for Our Youth"), cowritten by Eijiro Hisaita. The tale, beginning in the liberal 1930s, delves into the oppression that a leftist couple experiences during the war. Met with critical success, the picture achieved some international recognition. Kurosawa's next two pictures, *Subarashiki nichiyobi* ("One Wonderful Sunday") and *Drunken Angel*, were also social commentaries. Teaming with his former schoolmate Uekusa to write the former film, Kurosawa attempted to portray the plight of impoverished lovers who cannot afford to attend a concert. The picture concludes with the despondent sweethearts seeking solace in an empty amphitheater. In an unusual ending, the young woman tries to cheer her boyfriend, asking the audience to join in as her beau conducts an imaginary orchestra. The finale and the movie itself proved more successful with Parisian viewers than with those in Kurosawa's homeland. One elderly Japanese gentleman, however, did send a postcard describing the sobering effect of the movie and its impact. Kurosawa and Uekusa were delighted to see that the note was from their former teacher, Mr. Tachikawa.

The former classmates also cowrote *Drunken Angel*. Based on the rise of black marketeering and gangster activity as a result of Japan's defeat in the war, the story charts the efforts of an alcoholic doctor working in the urban slums, as well as the exploits of a brash, young mobster. The part of the racketeer was played by aspiring actor Toshiro Mifune, who continued to head the cast in many of Kurosawa's films. The movie, considered by many critics to be one of the director's most important early films, earned him national kudos. During his successes, however, Kurosawa was saddened by the death of his father. He also had to contend with several workers' strikes at Toho. Disgruntled with management's handling of the situation, he left Toho to work at other studios. His first picture outside of Toho was *Shizuka naru ketto* ("The Quiet Duel") for Daiei in 1949. Cowritten by Kurosawa, the story delves into the life of a young doctor who operates on a patient with syphilis during the war. As a result of the surgery, the physician contracts the disease himself and cancels his plans to wed his betrothed once he arrives back

home. The film met with little critical success as some reviewers found the tale overly sentimental.

Kurosawa's next picture, *Stray Dog*, was produced by Shin Toho and Geijutsu Kyokai. Also released in 1949, the film is set amid the chaos and corruption of the post-war underworld. The tale delineates the saga of a police officer whose gun is stolen on a crowded Tokyo bus. Attempting to catch the thief and recover the weapon, the detective follows a trail of robberies and killings involving the pistol. Soon the young officer, whose search takes him to both affluent and poverty-stricken areas, begins to understand that the criminal's impulses are not so unlike his own. A number of critics noted Kurosawa's use of strong imagery in the film, suggesting that the lawman's shame regarding his lost revolver is symbolic of the country's loss of face during the Second World War. In other instances, reviewers pointed out that Western music is prevalent in scenes depicting the unscrupulous activities of

Winner Of The Grand Prize 1951 Venice Film Festival

ACCLAIMED THE BEST PICTURE OF THE YEAR FROM ANY COUNTRY

"BEST foreign film of year" "Best directed film of year" —Nat'l B'd of Review

"A rare piece of film art" —N.Y. TIMES

Rasho-Mon

Four people offer very different accounts of the same brutal crime in *Rashomon*, Kurosawa's award-winning 1950 study of truth and human frailty.

black marketeers, while traditional Japanese music is heard when the villain is finally apprehended.

Rebels against Sensationalism

In 1950's *Scandal*, made for Shochiku studios, Kurosawa relates the tale of a singer and a painter who become the targets of sensationalizing journalists in need of a spicy story. Although the couple meet by chance, their innocent relationship is falsely presented as an impassioned, sordid love affair by the press. The duo team with an aging lawyer to take the fabricating reporters to court. But the attorney, who needs money to help his ailing daughter, accepts a bribe to lose the case. Eventually justice prevails as the lawyer confesses and the muckrakers are found guilty.

According to Kurosawa, the impetus for the project was a defamatory article he read in a tabloid about the alleged, scandalous sexual behavior of a woman he refers to as "X." In his autobiography, he recalls: "When I saw the sensationalistic way this headline article was presented, I couldn't help thinking about how helpless she must feel. Outraged, I reacted as if the thing had been written about me, and I couldn't remain silent. Such slander cannot be permitted. This was not freedom of expression, I felt, it was violence against a person on the part of those who possess the weapon of publicity." His anger and frustration with unjust journalism has remained with him ever since.

Despite Kurosawa's skeptical view of reporters, the foreign press voiced high praise for the director's next film, *Rashomon*, made for Daiei. Based on stories by Ryunosuke Akutagawa, the work is set in eleventh-century Japan and concerns the alleged murder of a nobleman and the rape of his wife. The couple, traveling through a forest, encounter the renowned bandit Tajomaru. Feeling a bit lethargic, the sleepy brigand initially opts to let the couple pass his resting spot, but changes his mind after a strong, cool breeze interrupts his nap. The disruptive wind not only awakens the dozing outlaw but causes the traveling woman's veil to flutter from her face, revealing her beauty to the thief. Deciding he must have the object of such radiance, the miscreant quickly plots to fool the couple and sets out after them.

Critics were particularly impressed with the innovative method Kurosawa used in recounting the *Rashomon* parable. As the details of the alleged assault and death unfold via flashbacks, the viewer is subjected to four very different versions of the events—the accounts of the bandit, the wife, the husband (through a medium), and a woodcutter who witnessed the occurrence. In courtroom scenes the oft-scratching villain claims he raped the wife and stabbed the husband at the woman's urging; she could not face life knowing that two living men had witnessed her defilement. The nobleman maintains that his wife enjoyed having sex with Tajomaru and pleaded with the bandit to kill him. Disgraced and dejected, he took his own life when the robber refused to carry out the murder. The woman asserts that her husband held her in such contempt after the rape that her intense feelings of shame overcame her and she killed him. Finally, the woodcutter recalls that the nobleman and bandit dueled, the latter defeating his cowardly foe.

Inquiring into the relativity of truth, *Rashomon* goes further in casting doubt about what actually happened in the forest. The audience learns that the woodcutter himself had an ulterior motive to lie about the happenings; he had stolen the dagger used in the husband's death. A priest who has heard all of the accounts—some in court and others via the woodcutter while they wait out a severe rainstorm under the dilapidating Rashomon gate—voices his disgust for and distrust of the dark nature of humankind. Kurosawa adds a glimmer of hope, however, as the storm dodgers hear the cries of an abandoned baby and the woodcutter volunteers to take the child into his family. When the story concludes, viewers are left to ponder which accounts constitute reality and if each participant truly believes his/her embellished version of the tale.

While *Rashomon* fared well in Japan, the film received a more enthusiastic recognition abroad. Its foreign debut signaled the introduction of Japanese cinema to many American audiences. The feature won best picture honors at the 1951 Venice Film Festival, won the Academy Award for best foreign-language film, and was the first Japanese film to receive a wide distribution in the West. "*Rashomon* is a symphony of sight, sound, light, and shadow, in celluloid," judged Jesse Zunser in *Cue* magazine. Calling the film "as brilliant in its multifaceted plot as a cut gem," the critic further deemed it "as fascinating in the variety of its engrossing complexities as a chess problem." Other reviewers lauded the film for showing the contrasting sides of good and bad in humanity. "[*Rashomon* is a] torpid, stylish Japanese study in human frailty," surmised Manny Farber in *Nation Associates*. Still others perceived that the players were perfectly cast, including Mifune as the bandit and Shimura as the woodcutter. Some years later Hollywood remade *Rashomon* as *The Outrage* starring Paul Newman, Claire Bloom, and William Shatner.

Hakuchi ("The Idiot"), Kurosawa's next feature after *Rashomon*, marked the director/writer's entry into adapting foreign tales into Japanese settings. Based on a story by Kurosawa's favorite novelist, nineteenth-century Russian Fyodor Dostoyevsky, *Hakuchi* features an epileptic, shell-shocked soldier who seeks to win the affections of another man's girlfriend. His rival, a wealthy businessman played by Mifune, intervenes, and passions surmount. Originally filmed at 245 minutes, the work was substantially cut by its studio, Shochiku, despite Kurosawa's protests. It was his contention that such alterations would make the film difficult to follow and ultimately would lead to the movie being synonymous with its title. In his *The Films of Akira Kurosawa*, Richie comments on the negative critical response toward the final version of the film: Kurosawa's "desire to 'preserve' Dostoyevsky weakens the film at every turn because Kurosawa's faith in his author was so strong, and so blind, that he seemed to feel that the mere act of photographing scenes from the novel would give the same effect on the screen as they do on the page. What occurs, however, is merely a devastating simplification."

Reviewers were much more laudatory about Kurosawa's next film, *Ikiru*, released as *Doomed* in the United States. Considered one of his best films, the contemporary social commentary concerns a Japanese civil servant who is diagnosed with terminal stomach cancer. Realizing that he has wasted his days by merely going through the motions of living, he decides to experience life. He attempts to cast off his conservative values by taking a wild, all-night trip to show clubs with a hack novelist he meets in a bar. Trying to cast off his nickname "Mummy," he determines to do something good for the world before he expires. He takes on a project to clean up an area tainted with sewage and turn it into a park for children. To achieve his goal he must bypass governmental red tape by pestering officials to act. Following the opening of the playground, for which all the stalling bureaucrats then claim credit, the ailing man dies in *his* park. Friends, family, coworkers, and bureaucrats gather at his wake and exchange compliments for the job *they* did building the park. Finally the funeral-goers find themselves acknowledging the deceased's achievements.

Written by Kurosawa, Shinobu Hashimoto, and Hideo Oguni, the central message of *Ikiru* is spoken by the novelist to the dying man in a bar: "Man finds truth in misfortune. Having cancer has opened your eyes to life. Men are such fools! They only realize how beautiful life is, when they're face to face with death. And even these people are rare. Some die without knowing what life is. . . . Man's duty is to enjoy life. It's against God's will not to do so. Man must have a lust for life. Lust is considered immoral, but it isn't. A lust for life is a virtue." Having found his purpose—to build the park—the ailing government employee has cast off despair and fought to make one part of the world better.

Films Japanese "Western," *The Seven Samurai*

Ikiru served to bring Kurosawa more recognition from Western audiences. The film also marked the director's return to Toho. His next film, considered by critics to be his most successful and polished work to that date, was 1954's *Seven Samurai*. He again teamed with Hashimoto and Oguni to create the script. Set in the sixteenth century, the film opens to a Japan with a class structure composed of samurai, farmers, craftsmen, and merchants. Amid widespread hunger, a group of farmers becomes enraged when its crops are again raided by ruthless brigands who leave a trail of death and destruction in their wake. Weak and defenseless, the agrarians send a few men into town to hire skilled samurai to defend their homes. The farmers have no means of payment, however, and only offer shelter and meals as compensation. While most samurai laugh at the farmers' request, one warrior accepts the challenge, believing that honor and justice must triumph. Played by Shimura, the leader recruits six others to assist in defending the farmers.

In *The Seven Samurai*, Kurosawa presents vivid characterizations of the warriors, including the farmer's son (Mifune) who tries to pass himself off as a samurai to join in the fight. Mifune's scene-stealing protagonist, who is accepted into the ranks of the true soldiers, adds an element of humor through his actions and expressions. The benevolent nature of the samurai is also depicted in segments that show the warriors training the farmers in combat tactics. The final battle footage, filmed in torrential rain and mud, features fancy horsemanship, fervent sword fights, and tragic deaths. When the would-be warrior Mifune is eventually killed, he dies a full-fledged samurai. The picture ends with the surviving soldiers realizing that they are indeed a dying breed, while the farmers begin planting anew.

A group of samurai warriors defend a village against raiding bandits in *The Seven Samurai*, which won the 1954 Silver Lion Award and was later adapted as the western film *The Magnificent Seven*.

Kurosawa's interest in making a film like *The Seven Samurai* was discussed by Lillian Ross in *New Yorker* magazine. She notes that the director's interest was fueled by "the desire to have modern Japanese learn that the great old powerful samurai left a rich cultural heritage, which means much more than the physical strength and swordsmanship depicted in many Japanese movies. He feels it's important to show the high level of education, the sense of beauty, the spiritual training, and the mental sharpness of the samurai class. That is the spirit of the Japanese heritage."

Critical and public response to the three-and-a-half-hour film was positive, especially in the West. The film won the Silver Lion Award at the Venice Film Festival. Some reviewers compared Kurosawa's work to that of American western veteran John Ford. Enthusiasm was so high in Hollywood, in fact, that the film was remade as the epic western *The Magnificent Seven*, starring Yul Brynner, Eli Wallach, Steve McQueen, Charles Bronson, James Colburn, and other future stars. The rights to *The Seven Samurai* were initially secured by Hollywood producer Lou Morheim for $250.

According to a reviewer in *Motion Picture Guide*, "When interviewed, Morheim stated that Kurosawa had been asked why he made *The Seven Samurai* and how it came to pass, and the Japanese master was quoted as having said, 'All I was doing was trying to make a Japanese western.' Morheim saw that and quickly nailed down the remake rights." The adapted storyline concerns a group of Mexican villagers who are frequently subjected to raiding parties led by Wallach. The desperate townspeople hire seven gunslingers to help them thwart their foes.

Continuing his work for Toho, Kurosawa made *Record of a Living Being/I Live in Fear* in 1955. The film revolves around an old man who, believing his homeland may be targeted for destruction via the atom bomb, seeks to move his family to South America. Kurosawa's next two projects, both released in 1957, were adaptations of earlier works. *The Throne of Blood*, a look at a Japanese warlord's demise due to greedy ambition, was based on British writer William Shakespeare's tragedy *Macbeth. The Lower Depths*, a view of how a priest inspires a group of insufferable land barons and seedy characters to change their ways, was adapted from Russian writer Maxim Gorky's story.

Kurosawa's 1958 film *The Hidden Fortress* was also set in feudal Japan. Compared to the western genre by various critics, the picture focuses on the adventures of a princess as she attempts to pass through battle-torn territory to reclaim her crown. A number of humorous situations arise as the royal youth, her protector, and two peasants try to outwit the enemy forces. American filmmaker George Lucas *Star Wars* cited *The Hidden Fortress* as the inspiration for his science-fiction/fantasy adventure. Lucas has said he modeled his Princess Leia after Kurosawa's Princess Yukihime and turned the Japanese director's peasants into robots R2-D2 and C-3PO. After the release of *Star Wars*, *Hidden Fortress*, which won an International Critics' Award and the Berlin Film Festival Director's Prize, saw a revival in the early 1980s.

Kurosawa followed *The Hidden Fortress* with *The Bad Sleep Well*, a modern-day suspense drama about a man who goes undercover to reveal the real reasons behind his father's suicide—the construction company for which he worked made him the scapegoat after its underhanded dealings were exposed. The son will not rest until he wreaks havoc within the firm, pitting the guilty executives against each other. During the course of his mission, he inadvertently falls in love with the boss's daughter. The film, according to a number of commentators, is said to borrow from Shakespeare's *Romeo and Juliet* and *Hamlet*. A number of critics, however, including American filmmaker Frances Ford Coppola, asserted that the work is superior to Shakespeare's.

With the filming of *The Bad Sleep Well*, the director debuted his own company, Kurosawa Production Inc., although the picture was also underwritten by Toho. In his subsequent features, *Yojimbo* and *Sanjuro*, Kurosawa returned to the samurai/western genre. In the former work, an itinerant, masterless samurai brings peace to a feuding village after conning both warring factions to hire him to defeat the other side. As the battle for control of the area ensues, the hero sits idle, watching the opposing forces eliminate each other. *Yojimbo* was sequeled by *Sanjuro*, which finds the title character helping a small group of men overcome a ruthless gang. Sensing the western potential in *Yojimbo*, Italian filmmaker Sergio Leone remade the picture into the classic "spaghetti western" *A Fistful of Dollars*, starring Clint Eastwood, in 1964. Noting this and other remakes, Audie Bock states in the preface of Kurosawa's

autobiography that "no other Japanese director has ever received such homage from the West."

From Failures to Comebacks

As Kurosawa continued filmmaking in the 1960s, he found it increasingly difficult to produce pictures of his renowned quality within budget. Although Japanese studios proffered a mere pittance compared to the sums expended by Hollywood, Kurosawa's insistence on filming under precise conditions often slowed production and required additional funding. In 1963 he saw the release of *High and Low*, the saga of a wealthy businessman who risks all to help free his chauffeur's kidnapped son. His next film, *Red Beard*, was some two years in the making. The winner of the Moscow Film Festival Soviet Filmmakers' Association Prize, the work concerns a young, arrogant doctor who discovers strength of character through the example of an old physician. However, the picture received a number of negative reviews—critics voiced concerned over the movie's length. The prolonged production time itself also cost Kurosawa as a frustrated Mifune announced he would not work with the director again.

Kurosawa's perfectionism led to further problems as the 1970s approached. He was hired to direct the Japanese portion of Hollywood's World War II epic *Tora, Tora, Tora*, which tells the saga of Japan's bombing of the U.S. naval base at Pearl Harbor, Hawaii, from the perspective of both military forces. Kurosawa, a man called "the emperor" by the Japanese press due to his directorial methods, was unaccustomed to working with American actors. And some of the performers allegedly complained that working for Kurosawa was no different than being in the confines of the army itself. Following some disagreements with the studio over scheduling and its right to edit his work, Kurosawa left the project and began working on *Dodesukaden*. His first color film, the feature delves into the lives of people in an urban slum. The picture, made for Toho, also received funding from Yonki no Kai, a production company Kurosawa founded with other Japanese directors. Critical reaction to the film was indifferent, although the production later received the Geijutsu Sai Prize for Excellence.

Discouraged, Kurosawa found himself facing increased financial difficulties. He was also physically ill, suffering from an undiagnosed gallbladder condition. In 1971 he attempted suicide. It would be several years before he returned to filmmaking.

Kurosawa demonstrated his fighting spirit by making a successful comeback with 1975's *Dersu Uzala*. The film marked a significant departure for Kurosawa as it was made outside his native Japan in Siberia with a Soviet cast. Kurosawa had been asked by officials in the Soviet Union to make the feature, and he wrote the screenplay based on a story by Vladimir Arseniev. The tale depicts the life of a turn-of-the-century wilderness man who assists and befriends an army captain on a surveying expedition. In the end the title character must come to terms with civilization when he finally encounters it. Lauded for its inclusion of scenes depicting man against severe nature, the work won an Academy Award for best foreign-language film and similar honors in Italy.

Through the achievement of *Dersu Uzala*, Kurosawa also confirmed that he was able to make quality films if given an adequate budget. However, the funding problems he had encountered with Toho in the past had caused a considerable rift, leading him to accept foreign financial support for his subsequent films. Offering to help Kurosawa obtain funding were various American admirers, including Coppola and Lucas. The latter, in fact, assisted Kurosawa in obtaining an advance for the international distribution rights for the director's next film, *Kagemusha*. At that point Toho, too, contributed monies, creating the largest budget for a Japanese picture to that date.

When filming 1980's *Kagemusha*, Kurosawa returned to the feudal Japan setting to render the plight of a condemned thief who tries to escape his sentence by impersonating a dead warlord. Delving into concepts such as loyalty and class structure, the picture was a cowinner of the Golden Palm Award at the Cannes Film Festival. Kurosawa's next film, 1985's *Ran*, is also a period piece, set in sixteenth-century Japan. Based on Shakespeare's *King Lear*, the project was the culmination of a ten-year dream that began when Kurosawa was having trouble finding funding. Through the assistance of French film producer Serge Silberman, the director was able to acquire an $11.5 million budget—then the highest in Japan. Reportedly, Kurosawa viewed *Kagemusha* as a dress rehearsal for *Ran*, a film requiring some 1,400 costumes that took three years to create.

Kurosawa received an Academy Award nomination in 1985 for *Ran*, a Japanese version of Shakespeare's *King Lear*.

Ran, a word meaning "chaos" or "madness," alters the Shakespearean story by chronicling the lives of a ruthless overlord and his three sons, rather than a king and his three daughters. The story begins as the ruler Hidetora announces plans to retire and redistribute his lands to his children Taro, Jiro, and Saburo. While the eldest siblings appear pleased with the decision, the youngest brother voices concern that the situation will lead to violence as the sons will surely battle each other for control of the empire. For his protestations, Saburo is banished and eventually marries the daughter of another warlord. As predicted, the remaining brothers begin preparations to fight, both exiling their father from their castles. Hidetora is left to wander the countryside with a few loyal samurai and his court jester, played by transvestite rock singer Peter. When Saburo hears of the mistreatment of Hidetora, he readies his army to defend his father.

In *Ran*, Taro is eventually killed by Jiro's men. The deceased's wife, Lady Kaede—a woman whose home was destroyed by the vicious and greedy Hidetora in his days of conquest—attacks her brother-in-law Jiro, cutting his neck. In a scene that critics lauded for its intensity, Lady Kaede turns from potential murderess to seductress as she sucks the blood from Jiro's wound and thrusts herself upon him sexually. She becomes Jiro's lover and uses him to exact her revenge on Hidetora's family; she will not rest until all are destroyed. As the tragedy continues, Saburo is reunited with his father, only to be shot by his brother's forces. As the son dies in Hidetora's arms, the old man is overcome with grief and succumbs to death as well. The stage is set for Saburo's awaiting army to begin combat with Jiro's troops.

Receiving widespread international distribution, *Ran* was a critical and box-office success. "There are moments in *Ran* ... when the screen throbs with so much life, so many soldiers on horseback, such extraordinary battles, that one thinks, this is what [Russian writer Leo] Tolstoy saw in his mind when he wrote about [French emperor] Napoleon's invasion of Russia in *War and Peace*," noted Gerald Peary in *American Film*. Kurosawa "can make 1,000 soldiers seem three times as strong and do the same for his $11.5 million budget," assessed Peter Travers in *People*. *Newsweek*'s David Ansen exclaimed, "At its best, this film reminds us of what

Eight surrealistic vignettes comprise Kurosawa's intensely personal 1990 release, *Dreams*.

movies can achieve." And Jan Kott assessed in *New York Review of Books*, "Kurosawa is a peerless master of battle scenes," adding, "even the cruelest of them makes you gasp in amazement. They are a vision of the apocalypse rendered with the highest artistic perfection."

Some two years after *Ran*, Kurosawa saw the release of his partial life story, *Something Like an Autobiography*. Describing events shaping his existence since "babyhood," the filmmaker concludes his work with the making of *Rashomon* in 1950. He writes: "*Rashomon* became the gateway for my entry into the international film world, and yet as an autobiographer it is impossible for me to pass through the Rashomon gate and on to the rest of my life. Perhaps someday I will be able to do so." He adds, "I am a maker of films; films are my true medium. I think that to learn what became of me after *Rashomon* the most reasonable procedure would be to look for me in the characters in the films I made after *Rashomon*. Although human beings are incapable of talking about themselves with total honesty, it is much harder to avoid the truth while pretending to be other people."

Autobiographical Portraits in *Dreams*

Three years later, in 1990, an eighty-year-old Kurosawa saw the release of his next film *Dreams*. Again the director turned to foreign investors for the picture's $12 million budget. Among those aiding in the production were American directors Martin Scorsese, who appears as painter Vincent Van Gogh in the feature, George Lucas, whose Industrial Light and Music studios lent some special effects work, and Steven Spielberg. Described by reviewers as one of Kurosawa's most personal productions, *Dreams* contains eight segments depicting a range of colors and images like that of a painting. In one sequence a youth sneaks away to watch a secret, magical wedding of foxes in the forest. In two other pieces, the horrors of nuclear destruction are observed. In another *Dreams* vignette, a child becomes upset after his family chops down a peach tree orchard. He watches as the distraught spirits come to life as dolls to bring their message of sorrow. Other segments deal with unrequited love, a mountain climber's brush with death, and the faceless ghosts that haunt a soldier. *Dreams* was deemed "a spiritual autobiography, a closing of worldly concerns," by Peter Rainer in *American Film*.

Kurosawa continued his exploration of nuclear devastation in his 1991 film, *Rhapsody in August*.

Centering on the bombing of Nagasaki during World War II by the U.S. Air Force, the anti-war story uses an elderly protagonist to reveal some of the effects of the nuclear blast that claimed the lives of thousands of Japanese. That character, a grandmother who lost her husband when the bomb decimated the area in August of 1945, tells her grandchildren about the explosion that occurred a short distance from her home. Her intent is not to encourage ill will, but to help the youths realize that without acknowledging the past, humankind is condemned to repeat its atrocities. She is concerned that the youngsters' parents have been caught up in materialism and have chosen to ignore their country's history. In turn, her grandchildren have come to regard the bombing as an ancient fairy tale. The film, which stars American romantic lead Richard Gere as the grandmother's nephew, faced some criticism from the U.S. press due to its subject matter. Other reviewers welcomed the picture, claiming it revealed a facet of World War II history that the cinema has virtually avoided.

Kurosawa relaxing with actor Akira Terao on the set of *Dreams*.

In 1993, Kurosawa completed work on a new film, titled *Madadayo* ("Not Ready Yet"). Mike Y. Inoue, director on the board of Kurosawa Production Inc., described the motion picture to *AAYA*: "This is a story about a heart-warming exchange between a professor and his former students." Noting that the film was invited to the year's Cannes Film Festival, Inoue added: "According to Kurosawa, there is something very precious in this film which has been forgotten these days. He hopes that the audience, after seeing this film, will leave the theater with broad smiles on their faces, feeling very refreshed."

During his later years, Kurosawa has had his share of confrontations with the Japanese press. An outspoken critic of his country's cinema, he often receives negative assessments for his work from Japanese reviewers and film students despite the popularity of his films at home and abroad. In Kurosawa's films, "his strong views are stated with a directness that many Japanese find disconcerting," explains *New York Times* reporter Ian Buruma. "His extraordinary talent, his directness, his egotism, make Kurosawa stick out in Japan. He has, at considerable personal cost, always resisted this maxim of mediocrity, as have the heroes in his films. He refuses to conform to a society that tends to celebrate the ordinary (*heibon*) as a virtue." Buruma adds: "Despite his zest for making films, paintings, sculptures, anything that will serve as an outlet for his prodigious energy, he seems a bit out of step with the society around him—a society which, in his mind, appears to have let him down. Young critics tend to regard him as an anachronism, an arrogant dinosaur trying in ever more grandiose fashion to recreate a forgotten and, today, irrelevant past. His humanistic concerns and worship of classical art seem out of place in post-modern Tokyo."

American critic Donald Richie suggests that the reason Kurosawa's films have not fared better in Japan is due to their success abroad. Richie told readers of *American Film*: "The Japanese have a very strong opinion that anyone who makes it in the West cannot be any good, and Kurosawa did make it. He has always had to pay for this appreciation from the West, although he himself has never wooed the West." Kurosawa, in fact, has stated that he is unsure why he has had such success with American audiences. Contending that his films are truly "Japanese" and not geared for American audiences, the director also acknowledges the universal message of his work.

As Kurosawa continues to direct, he has no plans to retire. He hopes that when death comes, he will be hard at work on the set. "There are people," quotes Richie in his *Films of Akira Kurosawa*, "who criticize my work . . . and say it is not realistic. But I feel that merely copying the outward appearance of the world would not result in anything real— that is only copying. I think that to find what is real one must look very closely at one's world, to search for those things which contribute to this reality which one feels under the surface. These are few and one uses them to create. . . . To be an artist means to search for, find, and look at these things; to be an artist means never to avert one's eyes."

■ Works Cited

Ansen, David, "A Japanese 'King Lear': Kurosawa's Shakespearean Epic," *Newsweek*, January 6, 1986, pp. 64-65.

Barr, Alan P., "Exquisite Comedy and the Dimensions of Heroism: Akira Kurosawa's *Yojimbo*," *Massachusetts Review*, winter, 1975, pp. 158-68.

Bock, Audie, *Japanese Films Directors*, Kodansha International, 1985, p. 182.

Bowman, James, "Going Down in History," *American Spectator*, April, 1992, pp. 63-64.

Buruma, Ian, "Japan's Emperor of Film," *New York Times*, October 29, 1989.

Farber, Manny, review of *Rashomon*, *Nation Associates*, January 19, 1952.

Iwasaki, Akira, "Kurosawa and His Work," translated by John Bester, *Japan Quarterly*, January-March, 1965, pp. 21-31.

Kott, Jan, "The Edo Lear," *New York Review of Books*, April 24, 1986.

Kurosawa, Akira, *Something Like an Autobiography*, translated and prefaced by Audie E. Bock, Vintage Books, 1983.

Kurosawa, Akira, Hideo Oguni, and Shinobu Hashimoto, *Ikiru*, Toho/Brando, 1960.

Nash, Jay Robert, and Stanley Ralph Ross, review of *The Seven Samurai*, *Motion Picture Guide: 1927-1983*, Cinebooks, 1986.

Peary, Gerald, "Akira Kurosawa: Japan's Existential Cowboy Looks West and Thinks East," *American Film*, April 4, 1989, pp. 80-82.

Rainer, Peter, review of *Dreams*, *American Film*. April, 1991.

Richardson, Tony, "Film Reviews: 'The Seven Samurai,'" *Sight and Sound*, spring, 1955, pp. 195-96.

Richie, Donald, "He's the Pure Artist," *American Film*, April, 1982, p. 50.

Richie, Donald, *The Films of Akira Kurosawa*, University of California Press, 1970.

Ross, Lillian, "Profiles: Kurosawa Frames," *New Yorker*, December 21, 1981.

Show Business Illustrated, April, 1962.

Travers, Peter, review of *Ran*, *People*, December 2, 1985.

Zunser, Jesse, "Reviews: *Rashomon*," *Cue*, December 29, 1951.

■ For More Information See

BOOKS

Anderson, Joseph L., and Donald Richie, *The Japanese Film: Art and Industry*, Tuttle, 1959.

Contemporary Literary Criticism, Volume 16, Gale, 1981, pp. 394-406.

Kurosawa, Akira, director, *Rashomon*, edited by Donald Richie, Rutgers University Press, 1987.

Kurosawa, Akira, *Seven Samurai and Other Screenplays*, Faber and Faber, 1992.

Newsmakers: The People behind Today's Headlines, 1991 Cumulation, Gale, 1992, pp. 235-39.

PERIODICALS

Film, January-February, 1958, pp. 22-23.

Film Comment, November-December, 1980.

Film Culture, Volume 2, number 4, 1956, pp. 3-7.

Hudson Review, summer, 1961, pp. 270-83.

Interview, September, 1990.

Library Journal, May 1, 1992, p. 131.

New York Times, October 6, 1971, p. 39.

People, September 10, 1990, p. 13; February 9, 1991.

Quarterly Review of Film Studies, spring, 1985, pp. 166-69.

Rolling Stone, September 20, 1990.

Time, September 10, 1990, p. 82; January 27, 1992, p. 67.

Village Voice, September 4, 1990.

Wilson Library Bulletin, June, 1989, p. 107.

[Sketch verified by Mike Y. Inoue, Director on the Board of Kurosawa Production Inc.]

—*Sketch by Kathleen J. Edgar*

Annie Leibovitz

■ Personal

Full name, Anna-Lou Leibovitz; born October 2, 1949, in Westbury, CT; daughter of Sam (a U.S. Air Force colonel) and Marilyn (a modern-dance instructor) Leibovitz. *Education:* San Francisco Art Institute, B.F.A., 1971; studied photography with Ralph Gibson. *Hobbies and other interests:* Bicycling, hiking.

■ Addresses

Home—New York, NY. *Office*—Annie Leibovitz Studio, 55 Vandam St., New York, NY 10013. *Agent*—Jim Moffat, Art & Commerce, 108 West 18th St., New York, NY 10011.

■ Career

Kibbutz Amir, Israel, member of archaeological team excavating King Solomon's temple, 1969; *Rolling Stone* (magazine), San Francisco, CA, and New York City, photographer, 1970-73, chief photographer, 1973-83; *Vanity Fair* (magazine), New York City, contributing photographer, 1983—; Annie Leibovitz Studio, New York City, owner. Tour photographer for rock band the

Rolling Stones, 1975; World Cup Games, Mexico, poster photographer, 1986; American Ballet Theater, portrait photographer for fiftieth anniversary tour book, 1989; White Oak Dance Project, documentary photographer, 1990; Mary Boone Gallery, portrait photographer, 1990; advertising photographer for American Express, Arrow, Beef Industry Council, Christian Brothers, the Gap, Honda, Rose's Lime Juice, and *U.S. News and World Report;* photographer for movie posters, record album covers, and book covers. *Exhibitions:* Sidney Janis Gallery, New York City, 1983, and tour of U.S. and European cities, 1983-85; Sidney Janis Gallery, 1986, and tour, 1986-89; Arles Festival, France, 1986; James Danziger Gallery, New York City, 1991; National Portrait Gallery, Washington, DC, 1991, then International Center of Photography, New York City, 1991, and tour of U.S., European, and Far East cities, 1991-93.

■ Awards, Honors

Photographer of the Year, American Society of Magazine Photographers, 1984; Innovation in Photography Award, American Society of Magazine Photographers, 1987; Clio Award, Clio Enterprises, and Campaign of the Decade, *Advertising Age,* both 1987, and Infinity Award for applied photography, International Center of Photography, 1990, all for photography for American Express "Portraits" advertising campaign.

■ **Writings**

(Editor) *Shooting Stars*, Straight Arrow Books, 1973.

Photographs, Pantheon, 1983.

(With others) *Visual Aid*, edited by James Danziger, foreword by Cornell Capa, Pantheon, 1986.

(Photographer) Alan Olshan, editor, *American Ballet Theatre: The First Fifty Years*, Dewynters PLC, 1989.

(Photographer) Jim Henke, *Human Rights Now!*, Amnesty International, 1989.

Photographs—Annie Leibovitz, 1970-1990, HarperCollins, 1991.

Misha and Others: Photographs, Smithsonian Institution Press, 1992.

Contributor of photographs to periodicals, including *Bunte, Cambio 16, El Europeo, Elle, Epocha, Esquire, Interview, Le Nouvel Observateur, Life, Ms., Newsweek, New York Times Magazine*, London *Observer, Paris Match, Stern*, London *Sunday Times, Switch, Time, Vogue*, and *Zeit*.

■ **Sidelights**

Best known for her bold, colorful photographs for the cover of *Rolling Stone* magazine, Annie Leibovitz is "the portraitist of the rock generation," wrote Mary Ann Tighe in the *Washington Post Book World*. Her famous subjects have ranged from rock legend Chuck Berry to former U.S. President Richard Nixon. Often her portraits capture the essence of her subjects' images or dig beneath the veneer of fame to reveal unexpected vulnerability. Some pictures, notably nudes such as her 1991 *Vanity Fair* cover shot of pregnant actress Demi Moore, have sparked controversy. Leibovitz's subjects have appeared smeared with mud or covered with roses, naked or swathed in yards of cloth, impeccably made-up or wildly disheveled. Through hundreds of attention-getting images, Leibovitz "has helped define the nature of stardom in a star-struck age," asserted Charles Hagen in *ARTnews*.

When she entered the San Francisco Art Institute in 1967, Leibovitz had no plans for a career in photography. Halfway through her painting studies, however, she went on a vacation in Japan and the Philippines and bought a camera. Photography hooked her interest immediately. As she remarked in *ARTnews*, "I was totally seduced by the wonderment of it all.... To see something that afternoon and have it materialize before your eyes that same day—there was a real immediacy to it. I lived in the darkroom. I'd spend all night there. You'd go in and you'd never want to go out." Leibovitz took night courses in photography in addition to her day classes in painting, and at age twenty she made her first photo sale to *Rolling Stone*.

A picture of counterculture poet Allen Ginsberg at a peace rally with a marijuana cigarette got Leibovitz started. Urged by a photographer friend to market the photo, she took her portfolio to *Rolling Stone*, which immediately bought the Ginsberg picture. Although she had not yet graduated from the art institute, Leibovitz quickly found a niche on the *Rolling Stone* staff. As she remarked in a 1983 *New York* article: "They really needed someone.... The good photographers in San Francisco were art-oriented and didn't want to do commercial work." If Leibovitz shared those qualms, she overcame them, and in three years she became *Rolling Stone*'s chief photographer.

Her style was journalistic in the beginning. Using black-and-white film, Leibovitz shot straightforward, unposed portraits, often spending large amounts of time living with her subjects to get her pictures. In a 1984 *American Photographer* article by Laurence Shames she explained: "I'd just sit in the corner for three or four days ... and when something happened, I'd shoot it." One of Leibo-

Leibovitz focuses on actress Meryl Streep's versatility and role-playing ability in this 1981 cover.

vitz's longest such outings came in 1975, when the popular British band the Rolling Stones asked her to be their tour photographer. For six months she traveled and lived with the group, documenting their performances and their private lives. She even snapped a color close-up of lead singer Mick Jagger's sutured wrist after he put his hand through a plate glass window. The tour took a heavy personal toll, however. Immersed in the fast-living, drug-taking rock culture, Leibovitz started using cocaine and spent the next several years battling the drug.

After *Rolling Stone* adopted color covers early in the 1970s, Leibovitz traded in her black-and-white journalistic approach for the brilliant colors and intense lighting that became hallmarks of her work. She had to learn new skills and approaches to make the most of the new medium. As she explained in *ARTnews:* "When I was in school, I wasn't taught anything about lighting, and I was only taught black-and-white. So I had to learn color myself.... I soon realized that I couldn't shoot subtle tones. I had to do something that would survive [*Rolling Stone's*] printing process."

Revealing Poses

As Leibovitz's photography career progressed, she also learned to pose her subjects instead of simply taking whatever shots presented themselves. Sitters with only a few hours to spare began asking what she wanted them to do. "I was a very reluctant director at first because I was quite happy just photographing things as they were," Leibovitz remarked in *Esquire*. But in the late 1970s and early 1980s, she admitted, "I started thinking conceptually ... and I would try to outdo myself with each cover."

Leibovitz started posing her subjects in ways that brought out hidden aspects of their personalities or captured their public images. The Blues Brothers appear in blue face paint, Bette Midler's success with the song "The Rose" resonates through a shot of her lying amidst dozens of roses, and versatile actress Meryl Streep, in mask-like face makeup, pulls at the edges of her face as if to remove her mask. Some of Leibovitz's subjects went topless or totally undressed. Although her goal was often simply to reveal hidden aspects of her sitters' characters, Leibovitz became known for her ability to get sitters to disrobe.

During her thirteen years with *Rolling Stone,* Leibovitz had a powerful impact on the magazine's image. Editor Jann Wenner acknowledged her contributions to his publication in Shames's *American Photographer* story: "Annie's covers did a great deal to define what we wanted *Rolling Stone* to be.... Very witty, very intimate, very bold." Fronted with Leibovitz photographs, the magazine became so highly regarded in the rock culture that "there was even a song about a rock group's passionate yearning to see itself thereon portrayed," Shames noted. "The *Rolling Stone* cover was *it,* and Annie Leibovitz *was* the *Rolling Stone* cover."

Reviewers expressed various opinions on what made Leibovitz's photographs stand out. In Hagen's *ARTnews* article, critic Andy Grundberg asserted that Leibovitz "exaggerates the distinctive characteristics of [her subjects'] public images in a way that's funny and deflating." Hagen was impressed by how "physical" her portraits are: "Leibovitz gets her sitters to use their whole bodies." In a similar vein, several writers traced Leibovitz's success to her skill at getting her subjects actively involved in their photo sessions. As Shames put it, "What sets Leibovitz apart ... has almost nothing to do with her handling of the camera, and almost everything to do with her handling of the subject." Leibovitz herself stated in a *New York* article by Vicki Goldberg: "I don't even think I was a very good photographer to begin with. I could just get people to do these things."

Two qualities that have helped Leibovitz "get people to do things" are persistence and what Shames called "a *kamikaze* intimacy that virtually no one can resist." She has been known to prolong a photo session for hours to get through a wary subject's guard. Once, with actor William Hurt, Leibovitz worked continuously from midafternoon to early the next morning. Observed George Lange in a 1984 *American Photographer* article, "She often told people that she was trying to photograph them as they really were, minus the attitudes and *personae* that celebrities usually adopt in formal portrait sessions." Leibovitz herself has proved free enough of pretense to jump into a swimming pool fully clothed, lie down on a wet beach, stand in a cold rain, and spend hours in desert heat to get the pictures she wants. Commenting on her rigorous photo sessions in *American Photographer,* Shames wrote, "There may be easier ways to do the job, but getting a picture the easy way seems to fill Leibovitz with guilt, self-doubt, and depression."

Rolling away from Stone

Leibovitz's drive to create expressive portraits eventually led to her 1983 break with *Rolling Stone.* According to editor Wenner, quoted by Shames in *American Photographer,* "Annie got a little too far out on a limb.... And I sawed the limb off." Shames reported that "her own vision was taking her farther into a sort of expressionism," while Wenner was leaning more toward straight-forward "head-shots." Other commentators blamed personality conflicts. In a 1988 *New York* article, Leibovitz offered this comment on herself: "I've resisted working with someone who tells me what to do.... Basically, I've always just listened to myself. I consider myself difficult to work with—a temperamental artist." Whatever the reason for the split, by the time Leibovitz left she had become "as famous as many of her subjects," as Maddy Miller wrote in *People.*

The year Leibovitz left *Rolling Stone* was also marked by the publication of her book *Photographs,* the first major collection of her portraits. Containing approximately seventy images, the volume drew a range of critical responses. Characterizing Leibovitz's approach in general as "witty, humane, affectionately mocking," a *New York Times Book Review* writer described some of the pictures as "poignant" but criticized a few as "pointless sleaze." The critic ultimately praised the book as "arresting proof" of how she "has revitalized the portrait to illuminate the less obvious sides of people we had just started to grow bored with." Writing in *Washington Post Book World,* Tighe commented that "celebrity in the razzle-dazzle sense is the *raison d'etre* of Leibovitz's pictures" and that her subjects' fame was what made most of the photos memorable. Certain exceptional images, such as that of singer-songwriter John Lennon, curled nude around his fully clothed, impassive wife, Yoko Ono, earned her approval for transcending mere glitz and suggesting "that Leibovitz can answer a higher calling than that of the circulation manager."

That controversial photo of John and Yoko, described by Miller in *People* as "probably Leibovitz's most famous," was significant for Leibovitz as well. In *New York,* Kanner observed that it is one of the photographer's "favorite pictures." Said Leibovitz: "It's significant historically—because it was taken hours before Lennon died—and graphically.... It told the story of their relationship, that he was a child to the woman and they were still together." After Lennon was killed outside his

New York apartment building in December 1980, the photo appeared on the cover of a special *Rolling Stone* issue commemorating his life and death—despite the designers' interest in a simple head shot but in accord with Lennon's agreement with Leibovitz. According to a note in that issue, Lennon himself had said of the pose, "You've captured our relationship exactly."

After Leibovitz left *Rolling Stone,* she joined *Vanity Fair* to be what Shames called the magazine's "Major Photographic Artist"—at least in theory. Promised the creative freedom to shoot whatever she liked, she nevertheless soon found illustrative covers giving way once again to portraits—snapped by another prominent photographer, Irving Penn. Leibovitz found herself "underutilized," Kanner reported. She began to consider a change in direction, a change of image. For one thing, she told Shames, "I've got to shake this reputation as the girl who gets people to undress. Besides," she added, "I've been realizing lately that the real intimacy is in the eyes. The real challenge is to get the shirt-off feeling but with the shirt *on.*" Leibovitz also thought of returning to black-and-white photography and straight journalistic work. "Anything to move beyond this narrow little category of what people insist on calling the celebrity portrait," she said.

Within a year of changing jobs Leibovitz also expressed second thoughts about her usual hectic work life. In a 1984 interview with *Harper's Bazaar,* she noted that she "used to do nothing but work," but that now she was beginning to date. Still driven by a competitive streak—"I can't stand it when I see a better picture. I really go crazy," she told *Harper's*—she nonetheless had begun to entertain thoughts of changing her priorities. "I find that having been a photographer for so many years makes me better at it," she observed, "and more relaxed about it. For the first time in my life, I can conceive of putting my work to one side, getting it into perspective and getting on with my life."

Shots That Sell

The lull was temporary. When a colleague suggested Leibovitz try spending some of her time on advertising work, she was "floored" at first, Kanner quoted. "I never figured I should be doing that." But Leibovitz took the advice. A stint with the American Express credit card company proved particularly suited to her talents. The company did not require their product to appear in her photographs, and they gave her a great deal of latitude in posing her sitters. Leibovitz depicted Christian pop singer Amy Grant walking on water, Speaker of the House Tip O'Neill lounging in a beach chair with a cigar stubbed out in the sand, and jazz singer Ella Fitzgerald in a leopard-skin coat with her 1959 Mercedes convertible, among others.

For Leibovitz, advertising was both familiar territory and a startling new world. In Kanner's *New York* article, the photographer observed a similarity between advertising and her previous work, as distinguished from journalism: "Journalism is creeping in on events happening in front of you over which you have no control. I've moved into the terrain of making pictures, composing, theater. I don't see much difference between this and my editorial work." But she found another aspect of advertising strange and somewhat daunting: "Before American Express, I truly didn't know what advertising was. But then I saw my pictures on the back cover here, on the inside cover there, and ... I felt a little panic. I didn't know it would be this big. Suddenly, I worried that the work wasn't good enough." Hundreds of cardholders requesting reprints of her ads proved that worry unfounded, however, and another client reported an eight percent increase in sales after her ad ran. Leibovitz received several awards for her American Express work, making the "Portraits" advertising campaign one of the most acclaimed ever.

In 1990 Leibovitz got her wish to return to black-and-white photography, at least for a while, with the bonus of indulging her long-standing interest in dance. Asked to document the White Oak Dance Project in Florida, she did posed and casual pictures of the choreographers and the dancers, including the internationally renowned dancer Mikhail Baryshnikov. The experience, which spanned three weeks, inspired her to continue to "explore the possibilities of blending her posed work and her more casual imagery," Hagen reported.

By 1991 Leibovitz had attained such stature that the International Center for Photography and the National Portrait Gallery in Washington, D.C., mounted a retrospective of her twenty-year career—only the second time such an exhibition was held for a living photographer. Record crowds turned out for the show. The total attendance for its five-week run at the Portrait Gallery equalled a year's normal attendance at the gallery, or around three hundred thousand. Leibovitz's career was also celebrated in an accompanying book of more than two hundred pages titled *Photographs—Annie*

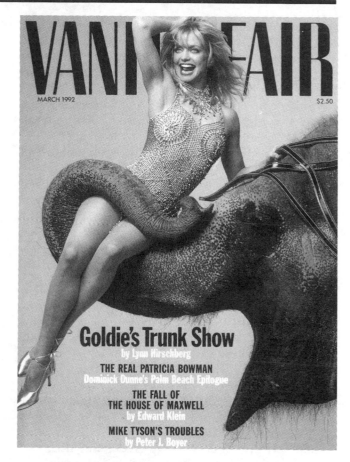

After her 1983 break with *Rolling Stone*, Leibovitz moved on to the slick world of *Vanity Fair*, where she has photographed such stars as Goldie Hawn.

Leibovitz, 1970-1990. Reviewing the book for the *New York Times Book Review*, Christine Schwartz dubbed Leibovitz "the modern equivalent of a court painter." Echoing Tighe's opinion that her work's significance hinges on the public's love of celebrities, she nevertheless commended Leibovitz's ability to "achieve the combination of glamour, intimacy and wit we demand of celebrity pictures." To Schwartz, the collection confirms Leibovitz as "our day's most gifted photographer of the stars." Richard Lacayo, writing in *Time*, assessed her portraits with reservations, finding them somewhat paradoxical. Asserted Lacayo, "Leibovitz's best-known work ... tries to twit propriety in the slickest possible style." In a more favorable appraisal, Maddy Miller of *People*, noting that Leibovitz is "still making waves," suggested that "this extraordinary 20-year retrospective may quickly be eclipsed by the photographer's continuing triumphs."

Judging from her 1992 comments to Hagen in *ARTnews*, Leibovitz is unlikely to rest on her laurels. She regards her work as art that continues to develop. "I don't think, How is the work going to look in history," she remarked. "But I've always been interested in how the pictures will look as a body of work, over my lifetime. My interest has always been in how the work changes and grows." Reflecting on her beginnings and her career, she noted how her direction has shifted. "I've realized in the last year that I can't go back to being a street photographer.... The early work was about not altering what you see, and the later work is about being involved, wanting to arrange things. But more important than whether it's altered or not is whether it's really what I want to do. I think I'm starting to finally do work for myself that I don't expect to see published—which is a whole new idea for me."

Regardless of what the future may hold for her, Leibovitz has secured her place in American popular culture. According to Lacayo, "She brought a pagan abandon to the authorized depiction of celebrities, a bit of primeval fire for the image machine." Even more, Shames reported, she became "the most resourceful and influential portraitist of her generation." In comments quoted in *Esquire*, Leibovitz described her career in more modest terms: "In the early days at *Rolling Stone*, I remember thinking that I was documenting our times. And if I photograph Soledad prison or [actress] Jodie Foster, I'm still photographing my time." Her career has remained a crucial part of her life. "I work most of the time," she observed in *ARTnews*. "I've learned to live inside the work. It's what I like to do most, and the things I do outside of it usually feed back into it." As a result of her years of working, Leibovitz has won a prominence that makes her take her work seriously. As she told Hagen, "I'm in the luxurious position to act on how I think. And I really believe it would be a major mistake not to take advantage of that."

■ Works Cited

"Celebrities in Composed Disarray," *New York Times Book Review*, October 23, 1983, p. 31.

Goldberg, Vicki, "Annie Leibovitz: A Close-up of the Rock-'n'-Roll Photographer's Greatest Hits," *New York*, September 19, 1983, pp. 88-89.

Hagen, Charles, "Annie Leibovitz Reveals Herself," *ARTnews*, March, 1992, pp. 90-95.

Kanner, Bernice, "Annie in Adland: Photo Opportunities," *New York*, March 14, 1988, pp. 24, 26, 28.

Lacayo, Richard, "Shadows and Eye Candy," *Time*, September 30, 1991, pp. 72-74.

Lange, George, "Riding Shotgun with Annie," *American Photographer*, January, 1984, pp. 56-59.

Leibovitz, Annie, "Behind the Photographs," *Esquire*, December, 1991, pp. 124-33.

Miller, Maddy, "Pages: *Photographs Annie Leibovitz 1970-1990*," *People*, November 18, 1991, p. 31.

Rolling Stone, January 22, 1981, p. 5.

Schwartz, Christine, "Shooting Stars," *New York Times Book Review*, January 26, 1992, p. 20.

Shames, Laurence, "On the Road with Annie Leibovitz," *American Photographer*, January, 1984, pp. 38-39, 44-55.

Tighe, Mary Ann, "Portraits of Grandeur and Decadence," *Washington Post Book World*, November 27, 1983, pp. 5, 9, 11.

"Your 30s: The More Decade," *Harper's Bazaar*, June, 1984, pp. 146-47, 180.

■ For More Information See

BOOKS

Leibovitz, Annie, *Photographs*, Pantheon, 1983.

Leibovitz, Annie, *Photographs—Annie Leibovitz, 1970-1990*, HarperCollins, 1991.

Marcus, Adrianne, *The Photojournalist, Mary Ellen Mark and Annie Leibovitz*, Crowell, 1974.

Newsmakers 88, Cumulation, Gale, 1988, pp. 248-49.

PERIODICALS

Adweek, February 1, 1988.

American Photographer, February, 1988.

Art in America, April, 1984.

Arts, February, 1984.

Chicago Tribune, December 23, 1983; May 5, 1991, p. 1.

Christian Science Monitor, November 17, 1983.

Los Angeles Times, November 9, 1983.

Newsday, December 4, 1983.

New York Daily News, November 30, 1986, p. 3.

New York Times, October 9, 1983.

New York Woman, September, 1988, p. 100.

Publishers Weekly, November 16, 1990, pp. 34-35.

Vanity Fair, September, 1991.

Wall Street Journal, September 10, 1987.

Washington Post, December 4, 1984, p. 1; April 19, 1991, p. 1.

—Sketch by Polly A. Vedder

N. Scott Momaday

■ Personal

Full name is Navarre Scott Momaday; surname is pronounced "*ma*-ma-day"; born February 27, 1934, in Lawton, OK; son of Alfred Morris (a painter and art teacher) and Mayme Natachee (a teacher and writer; maiden name, Scott) Momaday; married Dorothy Gaye Mangold, September 5, 1959 (divorced, 1973); married Regina Heitzer, July 21, 1978; children: (first marriage) Cael, Jill, Brit (all daughters); (second marriage) Lore (daughter). *Education:* University of New Mexico, A.B., 1958; Stanford University, M.A., 1960, Ph.D., 1963.

■ Addresses

Home—1041 West Roller Coaster Rd., Tucson, AZ 85704. *Office*—Department of English, University of Arizona, Tucson, AZ 85721. *Agent*—IMG-Julian Bach Literary Agency, 22 East 71st St., New York, NY 10021.

■ Career

University of California, Santa Barbara, assistant professor, 1963-67, associate professor of English,

1967-69; University of California, Berkeley, professor of English and comparative literature, 1969-72; New Mexico State University, visiting distinguished professor of the humanities, 1972-73; Stanford University, Stanford, CA, professor of English and comparative literature, 1973-80; University of Arizona, Tucson, professor of English, 1980—, Regents Professor of English, 1988—. Moscow State University, visiting professor of American literature, 1974; visiting professor at Columbia University, 1979, Princeton University, 1979, and University of Regensburg, Germany, 1985 and 1987; School of American Research, resident scholar, 1989-90; fellow of the Gihon Foundation Council on Ideas, 1992, and American Academy of Arts and Sciences, 1992—.

Artist; has exhibited paintings and drawings in galleries in Arizona, North Dakota, Texas, Oklahoma, New Mexico, and Germany; exhibitions include "N. Scott Momaday: The Man Made of Words and Images," Wheelwright Museum, Santa Fe, 1992-93. Consultant to the National Endowment for the Humanities and the National Endowment for the Arts; trustee of the Museum of the American Indian, Heye Foundation, 1978-83, the National Museum of the American Indian, Smithsonian Institution, 1984—, and the Grand Canyon Trust, 1991—. Pulitzer Prize Jury in Fiction, member, 1981 and 1990, chair, 1986. *Member:* Modern Language Association of America, American Studies Association, Gourd Dance Society of the Kiowa Tribe.

■ Awards, Honors

Academy of American Poets Prize, 1962, for the poem "The Bear"; Guggenheim fellowship, 1966-67; Pulitzer Prize for fiction, 1969, for *House Made of Dawn;* National Institute of Arts and Letters grant, 1970; received honorary degrees from Central Michigan University, 1970, Lawrence University, 1971, University of Massachusetts, 1975, University of Wisconsin, 1976, College of Ganado, 1979, Yale University, 1980, Hobart and William Smith Colleges, 1980, Morningside College, 1980, College of Santa Fe, 1982, University of Vermont, 1991, Ohio University, 1992, and Wheelock College, 1993.

Geographic Society of Chicago Publications Award, 1973; shared Western Heritage "Wrangler" Award with David Muench, 1974, for *Colorado, Summer/Fall/Winter/Spring;* University of New Mexico Alumni Association Zimmerman Award, 1975; Premio Letterario Internazionale Mondello (Italy), 1979; Author of the Year Award, California Association of Teachers of English, 1980; Western Literature Association Award, 1983; New Mexico Endowment of the Humanities Service Award, 1987; inducted into the Oklahoma Hall of Fame, 1987; Jay Silverheels Achievement Award, National Center for American Indian Enterprise Development, 1990; Wallace Stegner Award, Center of the American West, 1991; special commendation, Harvard Foundation of Harvard University, 1992; UCSD Medal, University of California, San Diego, 1993.

■ Writings

(Editor) *The Complete Poems of Frederick Goddard Tuckerman,* Oxford University Press, 1965.

The Journey of Tai-me (Kiowa Indian folktales), limited edition, etchings by Bruce S. McCurdy, University of California, Santa Barbara, 1967, enlarged edition published as *The Way to Rainy Mountain,* illustrated by father, Alfred Momaday, University of New Mexico Press, 1969.

House Made of Dawn (novel), Harper, 1968.

Colorado, Summer/Fall/Winter/Spring (nonfiction), photographs by David Muench, Rand McNally, 1973.

Angle of Geese and Other Poems (includes "Simile," "Four Notions of Love and Marriage," "The Delight Song of Tsoai-talee," and "The Horse That Died of Shame"), David Godine, 1974.

(And illustrator) *The Gourd Dancer* (poems), Harper, 1976.

(And illustrator) *The Names* (memoir), Harper, 1976.

(Editor and author of foreword) An Painter, *A Coyote in the Garden,* Confluence, 1988.

(And illustrator) *The Ancient Child* (novel), Doubleday, 1989.

(And illustrator) *In the Presence of the Sun: A Gathering of Shields,* limited edition, Rydal, 1991.

(And illustrator) *In the Presence of the Sun: Stories and Poems, 1961-1991* (includes "The Bear" and "The Wound"), St. Martin's, 1992.

Also author of film script of Frank Water's novel, *The Man Who Killed the Deer.* Illustrator of *Flight of the Seventh Moon,* by Lynn Andrews, Harper, 1983; and *Ancestral Voice: Conversations with N. Scott Momaday,* by Charles L. Woodard, University of Nebraska Press, 1989. Author of introductions to books, including *Keepers of the Earth: Native American Stories and Environmental Activities for Children,* by Michael J. Caduto, Fulcrum Publishing, 1988; and *Turtle Island Alphabet: A Lexicon of Native American Symbols and Culture,* St. Martin's, 1992. Contributor of articles and poems to periodicals, including *Paris Review;* a frequent reviewer on Native American subjects for the *New York Times Book Review.* Excerpts from Momaday's work read by the author on the audiocassette *N. Scott Momaday: Storyteller,* Lotus Press, 1990.

■ Work in Progress

The Storyteller and His Art, a study of story and storytelling centered upon Native American oral tradition, for Oxford University Press; *A Dark, Indifferent Rage,* a novel, for Doubleday; *The Circle of Wonder,* a children's Christmas book, for Clear Light Publishers; and *The Indolent Boys,* a play commissioned by the Yale School of Drama.

■ Sidelights

Dubbed "the man made of words," N. Scott Momaday is a Native American poet, novelist, storyteller, and artist. "It is an identity that pleases me," the author wrote in the preface to *In the Presence of the Sun: Stories and Poems, 1961-1991.* "In a sense, a real sense, my life has been composed of words. Reading and writing, talking, telling stories, listening, remembering, and thinking (someone has said that thinking is talking to oneself) have been the cornerstones of my existence. Words inform the element in which I live my daily life."

Considered one of the foremost writers of Native American literature, Momaday won a Pulitzer Prize in 1969 for his first novel, *House Made of Dawn*. His work is heavily influenced by the legends, oral tradition, and spirituality of his Kiowa Indian background. "I would say that much of my writing has been concerned with the question of man's relationship to the earth," the author told Joseph Bruchac in *American Poetry Review*. "Another theme that has interested me is man's relationship to himself, to his past, his heritage. When I was growing up on the reservations of the Southwest, I saw people who were deeply involved in their traditional life, in the memories of their blood. They had, as far as I could see, a certain strength and beauty that I find missing in the modern world at large. I like to celebrate that involvement in my writing."

Momaday's father, acclaimed painter Alfred Morris Momaday, is a Kiowa Indian and his mother, writer Mayme Natachee Scott, is of English, French, and Cherokee descent. Despite their white blood, both the author and his mother identify more readily with their Indian heritage. "I know about that part of me which is descended from a Cherokee great-great-grandmother, and about my ancestors who were European—English and French," Momaday told Charles L. Woodard in *Ancestral Voice: Conversations with N. Scott Momaday*. "In [my memoir] *The Names*, I pay some attention to that side of the family. But I'm not moved as much to understand that as I am to understand my Kiowa heritage. I think that's because my Kiowa heritage is quite exotic, and it represents to me a greater challenge in certain respects."

Born in Oklahoma in 1934, the author spent his childhood living on Navajo reservations in New Mexico and Arizona and at Jemez Pueblo, which is also in New Mexico. To Momaday, "'home' was particularly the Navajo country, Dine bikeyah," the author related in *The Names*. "My earliest playmates and schoolmates were Navajo children and the children of Indian Service employees. Just at the time I was learning to talk, I heard the Navajo language spoken all around me. And just as I was coming alive to the wide world, the vast and beautiful landscape of Dine bikeyah *was* my world, all of it I could perceive."

Living among various Indian tribes as well as whites made Momaday comfortable in both worlds. "From early childhood," surmised Woodard, "it was apparent to him that his parents valued education, and the development of bicultural skills, and very physical and emotional understandings of cultural and spiritual origins." Though his parents were both teachers, Momaday remarked in *The Names* that he "was not much interested in the process of learning at school. I can only barely remember the sort of work that was put to us; it was a thing that was not congenial to my mind. The evil of recitation was real; I hated to be called upon. And even worse was the anticipation of it. I knew of no relief equal to that of the bell." The author continued, noting that he did enjoy it when "my mother read to me, or she told me stories in which I had the leading part. And my father told me the old Kiowa tales. These were many times more exciting than anything I found at school; they, more than the grammars and arithmetics, nourished the life of my mind."

Momaday Discovers Bear Power

One Kiowa tale that particularly inspired Momaday was the story of Devils Tower, a volcanic rock formation known to the Kiowas as the sacred Rock Tree. Before he was a year old, Momaday was named for the Rock Tree; his Kiowa name is Tsoai-talee, which means "Rock Tree Boy." According to Kiowa legend, a boy and his seven sisters were playing at the spot when suddenly the boy turned into a bear. He then chased his sisters, who ran, terrified, until they came to a tree stump. The stump spoke to the sisters, telling them to climb upon it. When they did, the tree began to grow, lifting the sisters into the sky where they became the stars of the Big Dipper constellation.

Of the boy who turned into a bear, Momaday told Woodard, "I identify with that boy. I have for many years. And I have struggled with my bear power through those years. . . . My notion is that the boy and the bear are divisible. That after the end of the story, the bear remains and the boy remains and they come together now and then. The boy becomes a boy again and becomes a bear again, and this goes on and has gone on through the centuries, and probably in every generation there is a reincarnation of the bear—the boy bear. And I feel that I am such a reincarnation, and I am very curious about it. The way I deal with it, finally, is to write about it—to imagine it and to write a story about it. All things can be accepted, if not understood, if you put them into a story."

Bears have indeed surfaced in several works by Momaday, including poems, stories, a novel, and paintings. Momaday's 1988 graphite and wash "Self Portrait with Leaves," for instance, is a depiction of a bear. "I'm never more alive than when I'm really in touch with my bear power," the author told Woodard. "It is difficult to describe.... There is an energy, an agitation, an anger, perhaps. A power that rises up in you and becomes dominant. The feeling is unmistakable. And you deal with it in various ways. You become very spiritual. You feel a greater kinship with the animal world and the wilderness. You feel strong when you're most in touch with this bear. You become very intense in your work. And in your life. You accelerate your activity—writing, painting, whatever. You tend to be reckless, careless, self-destructive. You drink too much. You drive too fast. You pick on guys bigger than you are.... You become a magnificent lover, storyteller—it's just a great burst of vitality."

Though storytelling was an important part of his childhood, Momaday did not begin writing seriously until he was in college. He spent his last year of high school at the Augusta Military Academy in

THE WAY TO RAINY MOUNTAIN

N. SCOTT MOMADAY

Illustrated by
AL MOMADAY

Each chapter in this 1969 book is broken down into three sections containing a Kiowa tale, a historical anecdote, and Momaday's autobiographical musings.

Fort Defiance, Virginia, in order to obtain a college-preparatory education that was unavailable in the remote areas where he lived. Momaday then enrolled at the University of New Mexico at Albuquerque, where he earned a degree in political science and won prizes for public speaking and creative writing. "I think I had wanted to be a writer, as so many young people do, but I didn't know what that meant until I was an undergraduate," the author explained in an interview with Jean W. Ross in *Contemporary Authors*. "Then I started writing poems and kept up the writing of poetry pretty much through graduate school. Then I turned to prose."

After earning his bachelor's degree in 1958, Momaday taught school for a year on the Jicarilla Apache reservation in Dulce, New Mexico. The author fondly recalled the experience to Woodard, who asked how Momaday's life might be different had he settled there. Momaday replied, "I can't imagine staying there a possibility.... I did love the time I spent there. But if I were still there, I'd be principal at the school, maybe, and I'd be married to a Jicarilla Apache girl and we'd have thirteen children. Maybe I would be a writer and maybe not.... That was a very interesting time in my life.... I was becoming an adult when I went to Dulce. It was a wonderful environment.... Well away from distraction and temptation. Lots of time in which to write, and I used it well. I think back upon that as a very happy and productive time in my life."

The Way to Rainy Mountain

Following his stay in Dulce, Momaday attended Stanford University as a graduate student in literature, earning his master's degree in 1960 and his doctorate in 1963. The author's doctoral dissertation, a compilation of the work of New England poet Frederick Goddard Tuckerman, became his first published book in 1965. And though Momaday's own first literary efforts were poems, he turned to a different genre with his second book, a collection of Kiowa folktales titled *The Journey of Tai-me*. These legends became the basis for *The Way to Rainy Mountain*, an experimental work that tells the story of the Kiowa people through myth, objective observation, and the author's personal impressions.

The Way to Rainy Mountain, which was published in 1969, consists of twenty-four numbered chapters. Each chapter is divided into three passages, with the first passage of each chapter being a

Kiowa tale, the second containing a historical anecdote, and the third consisting of Momaday's autobiographical observations. Near the end of *The Way to Rainy Mountain*, Momaday has "transformed his threefold division into mythic, historic, and autobiographical journeys into a single, all encompassing but nonetheless personal one," according to Charles A. Nicholas in the *South Dakota Review*.

In *The Way to Rainy Mountain* Momaday details the migration of the Kiowas from the mountains of the northwestern United States to the southern Great Plains. The tribe acquired horses along the way to Rainy Mountain, which is in Oklahoma, and became "a lordly society of sun priests, fighters, hunters, and thieves, maintaining this position for 100 years, to the mid-nineteenth century," wrote *Saturday Review* contributor John R. Milton. In the late nineteenth century, the Kiowas were almost annihilated by the U.S. Calvary, and the sacred buffalo herds that sustained them were being destroyed as well. To the Kiowa, the buffalo were earthly representations of their sun god. "Momaday's own grandmother," reported Kenneth Fields in the *Southern Review*, "who had actually been present at the last and abortive Kiowa Sun Dance in 1887, is for him the last of the Kiowas." The reviewer continued, noting that "the real subject of [Momaday's] book is the recognition of what it means to feel himself a Kiowa in the modern American culture that displaced his ancestors."

Referring to *The Way to Rainy Mountain*, Roger Dickinson-Brown wrote in the *Southern Review* that "the story is simple, and dignified, and rich in coherent detail." The book was praised enthusiastically by other critics, some of whom pointed out its unusual form and sometimes elegiac tone. "When I say that I know of no book like *Rainy Mountain* the reader may react with understandable skepticism," Fields commented. "But it must be seen to be believed. . . . As Momaday alternates his voices we watch his cultural past, endlessly fascinating and forever irrecoverable, taking its life in his mind." According to Milton, "Momaday stresses three things in particular throughout the book. . .: a time that is gone forever, a landscape that is incomparable, and a human spirit that endures."

"After I wrote *The Way to Rainy Mountain*, a number of people came up to me and said, 'Oh, this is wonderful, that you are able to look back into your ancestry to this degree. We wish we could do that.' It hadn't occurred to me that most people can't do that," Momaday remarked to

"Superb." —NEW YORK TIMES

HOUSE MADE OF DAWN

N. SCOTT MOMADAY

WINNER OF THE PULITZER PRIZE

A Native American man is caught between the world of his Indian ancestors and white society in this 1968 Pulitzer Prize-winning novel.

Woodard. "But just about that time, there was a growing interest in that sort of thing. I think it is still there, and may be still growing. We have such things as roots, after all, and there seems to be a great hunger to discover and understand those roots, those origins, in many people these days."

House Made of Dawn Wins Pulitzer

The search for a cultural identity is a major theme in Momaday's most famous work, the Pulitzer Prize-winning novel *House Made of Dawn*. Published in 1968, the book "presents the heartbreaking effort of [Momaday's] hero to live in two worlds," wrote Marshall Sprague in the *New York Times Book Review*. The protagonist, Abel, is a young Native American who returns from serving in World War II to live on an Indian reservation in the desert Southwest. There he becomes involved in a brief romantic affair with a white California woman before killing a contemptible albino. Abel serves a prison sentence for his crime and is then paroled to a Los Angeles relocation center. Though he attempts to adapt to the white world and his new factory job, Abel drinks in his spare time and eventually returns to the reservation. There he carries on the tradition of his dying grandfather by participating in an ancient ritual, the dawn footrace against evil and death.

In *House Made of Dawn* Momaday employs an episodic narrative that led Dickinson-Brown to describe the book as "a batch of often dazzling fragments" rather than a novel. "The result," Dickinson-Brown added, "is a successful depiction but not an understanding of what is depicted." Writing in *Southwest Review*, Baine Kerr called the first part of *House Made of Dawn* "a staggeringly difficult interrupted narrative," but conceded, "the fact is that it works." Commenting in the same vein, Sprague noted that "there is plenty of haze in the telling of this tale—but that is one reason why it rings so true. The mysteries of cultures different from our own cannot be explained in a short novel, even by an artist as talented as Mr. Momaday."

Though some reviewers were not completely satisfied with *House Made of Dawn*, others responded enthusiastically to the novel, which *Best Sellers* contributor Charles Dollen judged to be "as exquisite as its title suggests" and Sprague found to be "as subtly wrought as a piece of Navajo silverware." Kerr described *House Made of Dawn* as "a creation myth—rife with fabulous imagery, ending with Abel's rebirth in the old [Indian] ways at [his grandfather's] death—but an ironic one, suffused with violence and telling a story of culture loss." The reviewer continued, "Momaday is a preserver of holiness in *House Made of Dawn*. He has transported his heritage across the border; in a narrative and style true to their own laws, he has mythified Indian consciousness into a modern novel." In the *Village Voice*, Ann Gottlieb remarked that "Momaday blends the ancient Indian belief in the literal creative power of the Word with a poet's mastery of the resources of English. Here, if anywhere, we may see how English might be tuned to communicate the essence of Indian experience."

Momaday's success with *House Made of Dawn* and his winning of the Pulitzer Prize came as a surprise to the author. "It's probably not the best thing for a man in his thirties to win a major prize like that," he commented to Woodard. "It was all on the basis of that one book, and when I did win the prize, it placed pressure on me. I thought, What do I do now? I don't know to what extent it was a deterrent

to subsequent writing, but I'm sure it was a deterrent. Especially in the first two or three years."

House Made of Dawn's success also gave Momaday the opportunity to become a spokesman for Native Americans, a role that the author rejects. "I had the good sense from the very beginning not to take on the responsibility of speaking for the Indian," he explained to Woodard. "I think that was an expectation on the part of many people. . . . When I was asked if I was speaking for the American Indian . . . I was quick to say, 'No, I'm not. What I'm doing is mine. It's my voice and my ideas, and I don't want to be that, and I don't think I'm entitled to be that. I can write about the Indian world with authority because I grew up in it. I know a lot about it, but I would be the last person to say that my opinions are anybody else's—Indian or not.'"

After *House Made of Dawn*, Momaday published two volumes of poetry, *Angle of Geese and Other Poems* and *The Gourd Dancer*. Momaday's poems are known for their rich imagery; in "The

Momaday exercised his artistic abilities by illustrating his poetry collection *The Gourd Dancer*, a large portion of which he wrote while serving as a visiting professor in Moscow.

Wound," which was reprinted in *In the Presence of the Sun: Stories and Poems, 1961-1991*, he writes: "The wound gaped open; / it was remarkably like the wedge of an orange / when it is split, spurting." Much of Momaday's poetry is inspired by nature, especially the landscape of the Southwest, which "few people have described . . . with such love and precision," commented Bruchac. Along with his native landscape, Momaday expresses his Indian heritage in poems such as "The Gourd Dancer," "Carriers of the Dream Wheel," and "Sun Dance Shield." The award-winning "The Bear" and "Angle of Geese" are considered by critics to be among Momaday's best works, and Dickinson-Brown judged the poems in *Angle of Geese* to be "astonishing in their depth and range." In the interview with Bruchac, the poet read "The Bear" and remarked that he considered it one of his "first really successful poems." In his verse, Momaday describes the bear as "more scarred than others / these years since the trap maimed him, / pain slants his withers, / drawing up the crooked limb. / Then he is gone, whole, / without urgency, from sight, / as buzzards control, / imperceptibly, their flight."

"Man Made of Words" Paints

Momaday wrote much of *The Gourd Dancer*, which he also illustrated, while serving as a visiting professor at Moscow State University in 1974. "Something about that time and place made for a surge in me, a kind of creative explosion," the author explained in his preface to *In the Presence of the Sun: Stories and Poems, 1961-1991*. "I wrote numerous poems, some on the landscapes of my native Southwest, urged, I believe, by an acute homesickness. And I began to sketch. Drawing became suddenly very important to me, and I haunted museums and galleries and looked into as many Russian sketchbooks as I could find. When I came out of the Soviet Union I brought with me a new way of seeing and a commitment to record it."

The desert Southwest that Momaday renders in his paintings and poems is "a much more spiritual landscape than any other I know personally," the author told Bruchac. "And it is beautiful, simply in physical terms. The colors in that landscape are very vivid, as you know, and I've always been greatly moved by the quality of light upon the colored landscape of New Mexico and Arizona. . . . And I think of it as being inhabited by a people who are truly involved in it. The Indians of the Southwest, and the Pueblo people, for example, and the Navajos with whom I grew up, they don't live on the land; they live *in* it, in a real sense. And

that is very important to me, and I like to evoke as best I can that sense of belonging to the earth." In his poem "The Delight Song of Tsoai-talee" in *Angle of Geese*, Momaday writes: "You see, I am alive, I am alive / I stand in good relation to the earth / I stand in good relation to the gods / I stand in good relation to all that is beautiful."

Momaday followed *Angle of Geese* and *The Gourd Dancer* with the publication of *The Names* in 1976. As with *The Way to Rainy Mountain*, the author experiments with form in this memoir; he traces his lineage and tells the story of his childhood using stream-of-consciousness passages, recreated conversations, and occasional poems and Indian tales in addition to straightforward narrative. *The Names* "is an Indian book, but not a book about wrongs done to Indians. It is a search and a celebration, a book of identities and sources," remarked Wallace Stegner in the *New York Times Book Review*. The critic continued, "Momaday has not invented himself, as many Americans have tried to do. He has let the blood speak, looked for tracks, listened and remembered." *The Names*, according to Stegner, is a "mystical, provocative book." In *American Indian Quarterly* Jack W. Marken noted that "the book is closely related to all other major works by Momaday. In all of them he transmutes memories into art." *The Names*, wrote Mick McAllister in *Southern Review*, "offers a sharp and moving portrait of what it was—and is—to grow up Indian in America."

When asked by Woodard why he titled his memoir *The Names*, Momaday replied: "I meant to indicate how important names are to me. Because it's an autobiographical narrative, the great principle of selection in the book is the principle of naming. I wanted to tie all kinds of varied experiences together, and the common denominators of those experiences were the names of people who were important to me, growing up. And the names of places. . . . Naming is very complicated, and a sacred business. . . . If there is one unimaginable tragedy, it is to be without a name, because then your existence is entirely suspect. You may not exist at all without a name. . . . So an awful lot is involved in this business of names, and I meant to indicate that in the title of the book. I don't see how you could find a more intrinsically powerful title than *The Names*."

The Ancient Child

After *The Names*, Momaday concentrated on writing poetry and nonfiction pieces and did not

THE ANCIENT CHILD

A NOVEL

N. SCOTT MOMADAY
PULITZER PRIZE-WINNING AUTHOR OF HOUSE MADE OF DAWN

A middle-aged Kiowa man is put in touch with his Native American heritage through his relationship with a young medicine woman in this 1989 novel.

publish another major work until his novel *The Ancient Child* appeared in 1989. "I don't often think of myself as a novelist," Momaday commented to Woodard. "I started out writing poetry, and I identified with poetry and the poet when I was earning my wings, and I still think of myself as a poet. I haven't had, until [*The Ancient Child*], a strong desire to write a novel."

The Ancient Child is the story of Locke "Set" Setman, a successful middle-aged Kiowa artist residing in San Francisco, and Grey, a young Kiowa and Navajo medicine woman who often fantasizes about the infamous outlaw Billy the Kid. The protagonists meet in Oklahoma after the funeral of Grey's great-grandmother, a wise medicine woman. Grey gives Set a medicine bundle that belonged to his father, who was killed when Set was a child. Because Set's mother died in childbirth, the death of his father left Set an orphan and he was raised by a white couple in California. Though Set is initially

out of touch with his Kiowa background, Grey and the medicine bundle cause Set to look inward and eventually identify with his Indian heritage.

During Set's time with Grey, he searches "for his fierce, bearlike Kiowa self," wrote Ed Marston in the *New York Times Book Review*. "Man into bear—that is Set's transformation at its basic level," *Tribune Books* contributor Charles R. Larson explained, "aided by Grey's loving tutelage and her own renewal with the Navajo world. In the process of describing this symbolic metamorphosis, Momaday's writing soars to heights of poetic beauty." Though praise for *The Ancient Child* was not as enthusiastic as for *House Made of Dawn*, Marston called the book a "mythic and romantic novel." According to Howard Meredith in *World Literature Today*, in *The Ancient Child* Momaday "provides a living sense of the framework of myth that remains important to Native American existence."

Several aspects of *The Ancient Child* are derived from Momaday's own experience and interests. The novel "is about the boy who turns into a bear, and in a sense I am writing about myself," he told Woodard. "I'm not writing an autobiography, but I am imagining a story that proceeds out of my own experience of the bear power. It is full of magic." Grey's mystical visions of Billy the Kid in *The Ancient Child* originated in Momaday's own fascination with the nineteenth-century outlaw. When Woodard asked the author about his interest in Billy the Kid, he replied: "I think it might be because I grew up in New Mexico and heard about Billy the Kid from the time I was very young.... I'm now probably one of the authorities on Billy the Kid. I've thought so much about him.... Billy the Kid is opposed to one part of my experience—to the Indian side of me. He's diametrically opposed to that, but at the same time he's very much a reflection of the world I love. The Wild West."

Billy the Kid, the landscape of the Southwest, and Momaday's Indian heritage all figure prominently in his 1992 collection *In the Presence of the Sun: Stories and Poems, 1961-1991*. The book is also illustrated with Momaday's paintings, with subjects ranging from Native American shields to bears and buffalo. *In the Presence of the Sun* is divided into sections: "Selected Poems," "New Poems," "The Strange and True Story of My Life with Billy the Kid," which contains poems and stories about the outlaw, and "In the Presence of the Sun: A Gathering of Shields," a previously published grouping that includes illustrated vignettes such as "Walking Bear's Shield" and "The Shield That

This 1992 collection features a sampling of Momaday's paintings and focuses on the American Southwest, Billy the Kid, and the author's own Indian background.

Was Touched by Pretty Mouth.'' Momaday finds shields fascinating. ''They're like coats of arms, but they're more personal,'' he explained to Woodard. ''They're individual and they're magic.... It's a wonderful symbolic representation of the ideal of the self.'' Much as if he had created a shield, Momaday reveals his personality in *In the Presence of the Sun*. In the preface to the volume Momaday writes, ''The poems and stories, the drawings here, express my spirit fairly, I believe. If you look closely into these pages, it is possible to catch a glimpse of me in my original being.''

Acknowledging the similarities of theme and subject matter in his writings, Momaday told Bruchac, ''I think that my work proceeds from the American Indian oral tradition, and I think it sustains that tradition and carries it along. And vice versa.... I've written several books, but to me they are all parts of the same story. And I like to repeat myself,

if you will, from book to book, in the way that [American writer William] Faulkner did—in an even more obvious way, perhaps. My purpose is to carry on what was begun a long time ago.... In a sense I'm not concerned to change my subject from book to book. Rather, I'm concerned to keep the story going. I mean to keep the same subject, to carry it further with each telling.''

Through the years Momaday has become more interested in telling his story with both words and illustrations. His drawings and paintings have been exhibited in various galleries, including the University of North Dakota Art Galleries and a retrospective show at the Wheelwright Museum in Santa Fe, New Mexico. As he explained to Woodard, Momaday sees a relationship between writing and visual art. Drawings and paintings, the author noted, ''can be very powerful and can draw upon some sort of universal power in the way that language does.'' Momaday continued, ''I think that I need to paint. I certainly need to write, and painting seems to come from the same impulse.... If I didn't write, I would cease to be.... Painting, now that I have discovered it, is becoming a necessary activity for me—a necessary expression of my spirit.''

Momaday commented further to Woodard that he is slowly becoming as well known for his art as he is for his writings, a phenomenon he considers ''progress.'' The author continued, ''I think that my talents are becoming steadily more nearly equal. I have a long way to go, and I get some resistance. There are people who don't want to believe that I can paint, because they have already accepted me as a writer, and there is in human nature, I think, a tendency to resist new definitions.'' Momaday went on to tell about a German friend who attended an exhibition of his artwork in Heidelberg. As Momaday related to Woodard, his friend remarked: ''Scott, I like your paintings. They're very nice. But you are a great writer and you're wasting your time.''

Whether as a poet, novelist, or painter, Momaday has infused his work with myth, spirituality, and a reverence for nature. His writings, which draw on the Native American oral tradition in both form and subject matter, have inspired a number of Native American authors. In the years since *House Made of Dawn* was published, Momaday has retained his position as an influential literary figure, though it's a designation that the author rarely thinks about. ''I'm afraid that if I started thinking of myself as the dean of American Indian writers I might not work so well,'' Momaday told Bruchac. ''I might be tempted to slow down and accept the deanship when I really want to be out there among the subordinates doing my thing.'' And ''doing his thing,'' whether writing or painting, brings ''the man made of words'' much enjoyment. The author expressed to Woodard that ''it is exciting to be Scott Momaday, alive at this time and presented with stimuli all around me. In fact, it is wonderful.''

■ Works Cited

Bruchac, Joseph, interview with N. Scott Momaday in *American Poetry Review*, July/August, 1984, pp. 13-18.

Dickinson-Brown, Roger, *Southern Review*, winter, 1978, pp. 30-45.

Dollen, Charles, review of *House Made of Dawn*, *Best Sellers*, June 15, 1968, p. 131.

Fields, Kenneth, ''More Than Language Means,'' *Southern Review*, winter, 1970, pp. 196-204.

Gottlieb, Ann, ''A Sense of the Land,'' *Village Voice*, January 29, 1970, p. 8.

Kerr, Baine, ''The Novel as Sacred Text: N. Scott Momaday's Myth-Making Ethic,'' *Southwest Review*, spring, 1978, pp. 172-79.

Larson, Charles R., ''Tribal Roots: Exploring the Fate of an American Indian Artist,'' *Tribune Books* (Chicago), October 1, 1989, p. 3.

Marken, Jack W., ''Book Reviews: 'The Names: A Memoir,''' *American Indian Quarterly*, May, 1978, pp. 178-80.

Marston, Ed, ''Splendor in the Grasslands,'' *New York Times Book Review*, December 31, 1989, p. 14.

McAllister, Mick, review of *The Names*, *Southern Review*, spring, 1978, pp. 387-89.

Meredith, Howard, review of *The Ancient Child*, *World Literature Today*, summer, 1990, pp. 510-11.

Milton, John R., review of *The Way to Rainy Mountain*, *Saturday Review*, June 21, 1969, pp. 51-52.

Momaday, N. Scott, ''The Delight Song of Tsoai-talee,'' *Angle of Geese and Other Poems*, David Godine, 1974.

Momaday, N. Scott, interview with Jean W. Ross in *Contemporary Authors New Revisions Series*, Volume 14, Gale, 1985, pp. 335-40.

Momaday, N. Scott, ''The Bear'' and ''The Wound,'' *In the Presence of the Sun: Stories and Poems, 1961-1991*, St. Martin's, 1992.

Momaday, N. Scott, *The Names*, Harper, 1976.

Nicholas, Charles A., ''N. Scott Momaday's Hard Journey Back,'' *South Dakota Review*, winter, 1975-76, pp. 149-58.

Sprague, Marshall, ''Anglos and Indians,'' *New York Times Book Review*, June 9, 1968, p. 5.

Stegner, Wallace, ''The Names,'' *New York Times Book Review*, March 6, 1977, p. 6.

Woodard, Charles L., *Ancestral Voice: Conversations with N. Scott Momaday*, University of Nebraska Press, 1989.

■ For More Information See

BOOKS

Contemporary Literary Criticism, Gale, Volume 2, 1974, pp. 289-90, Volume 19, 1981, pp. 317-21.

PERIODICALS

Library Journal, March 1, 1990, p. 132.

MELUS, winter, 1983, pp. 66-72; spring, 1985, pp. 79-87.

School Library Journal, October, 1976, p. 125.

Times Literary Supplement, May 22, 1969, p. 549.

—Sketch by Michelle M. Motowski

John Neufeld

■ Personal

Full name, John Arthur Neufeld; has also written under pseudonym Joan Lea; born December 14, 1938, in Chicago, IL; son of Leonard Carl (a manufacturer) and Rhoda (Padway) Neufeld. *Education:* Yale University, B.A., 1960.

■ Addresses

Home—1015 North Kings Rd., No. 316, Los Angeles, CA 90069. *Agent*—Arthur Pine, 1780 Broadway, New York, NY 10019.

■ Career

Television scriptwriter and novelist. Has also worked as a publicist, advertising copyeditor, and middle-school teacher.

■ Writings

YOUNG ADULT NOVELS

Edgar Allan, S. G. Philips, 1968.
Lisa, Bright and Dark (also see below), S. G. Philips, 1969.
Touching, S. G. Philips, 1970.

Sleep Two, Three, Four!, Harper, 1971.
For the Wrong Reasons, Norton, 1973.
Freddy's Book, Random House, 1973.
Sunday Father, New American Library, 1975.
Sharelle, New American Library, 1983.

ADULT NOVELS

(Under pseudonym Joan Lea) *Trading Up*, Atheneum, 1975.
The Fun of It, Putnam, 1977.
A Small Civil War, Fawcett/Ballantine, 1982.
Rolling the Stone, New American Library, 1984.
Family Fortunes, Atheneum, 1988.

TELEPLAYS

Lisa, Bright and Dark (*Hallmark Hall of Fame* presentation), National Broadcasting Company, Inc., 1973.
You Lie So Deep, My Love, American Broadcasting Companies, Inc. (ABC-TV), 1975.

Also author of *Death Sentence*, ABC-TV.

■ Adaptations

Edgar Allan, *Freddy's Book*, *For All the Wrong Reasons*, *The Fun of It*, *A Small Civil War*, and *Sharelle* have all been optioned for television.

■ Sidelights

A girl is horribly injured when she walks through a glass door to get her parents' attention. A teen repeatedly tries to lose her virginity—and ends up a young mother in a failing marriage. A boy tries to understand the meaning of a slang term and becomes involved in some very strange discussions about sex.... Topics that encompass a broad range of experience—mental illness, teen sexuality, sex education, interracial adoption, and governmental repression—are all fair game in John Neufeld's books for young adults. In large part, Neufeld makes these themes accessible to his readers by placing well-drawn, often terribly misunderstood, youthful protagonists at the center of the action. In an essay for the *Something about the Author Autobiography Series (SAAS)*, the author explained some of his inspiration: "The things that interest me are ideas and problems that face us all, but which we often first meet when we're young. If by writing how imaginary people meet and overcome certain problems helps real young people when *they* meet the same problems, then I was doing something useful as well as fun."

A Boy and His Books

Neufeld's early interest in books was fostered by his mother, a former English teacher. "During her lifetime, she was a driven reader and for the three of us, Director of Studies," the author remembered in his essay. "I can recall at the age of eleven sitting with her in our library reading *Macbeth* or *The Merchant of Venice* aloud to each other." Neufeld was encouraged to read anything he could get his hands on, from plays by Henrik Ibsen and George Bernard Shaw to children's books like *Ferdinand the Bull*. While still in junior high school, Neufeld began writing stories based on those he'd read in the *Saturday Evening Post*. He noted that "fame and fortune seemed only a matter of putting a blond heroine in the path of a dark stranger. I wrote tens of stories then and bravely, or innocently, sent them off to the magazine. Each was returned, always with an identical note of rejection."

Over time, Neufeld began to write less and less (although he often had ideas for stories "floating" around in his head). It was not until he began college that Neufeld again became seriously interested in literature and writing. He began consuming all types of books, often using reading as an escape from the rigors of college life. The young Neufeld repeatedly used the time he'd set aside for studying to read the longest books he could find in the school library; as a result, he had to pull a lot of "all nighters" to prepare for tests.

Despite his unorthodox study habits, Neufeld managed to graduate. Having no solid career plans, he decided to go on a "Grand Tour" of Europe

This 1968 novel, Neufeld's first, is based on a true incident about a white family who adopts a young black boy.

(ostensibly to get fodder for new stories). Although his original itinerary included countries such as Germany and Spain, Neufeld ended up spending most of his time in England. "There were endless associations to be made from my reading and studying," he reminisced in his essay. "London seemed more like home than any place I'd ever been.... It was a grand and simple time."

Soon after his return from England, Neufeld was drafted into the Army for a six-month tour of duty at Fort Leonard, Missouri. After "learning how to kill people" in basic training, the fledgling author was assigned to a special duty: teaching English to clerk-typist trainees. In spite of the bad food and often dismal conditions, Neufeld enjoyed his Army service, feeling "proud as hell to have weathered basic ... despite crawling under live tracer bullets on a muddy obstacle course in the middle of the night," he noted in his essay.

Upon his release from the service, Neufeld began to think seriously about his future plans. He realized that it was time to get a "real job," but felt that he had no marketable skills. Using his love for books as a guide, Neufeld turned to what seemed like a logical choice: publishing. After looking for positions in New York and Boston, he initially settled in as an advertising copy writer for Harcourt, Brace and World, later moving on to Franklin Watts as a publicist. Despite the demands of his career, Neufeld continued to write on the side—television dramas, one-act plays, short stories, and poetry. "None of this—I repeat, NONE—was any good," he concluded in *SAAS*.

Real Life—Real Inspiration

Neufeld's first novel, *Edgar Allan*, had an interesting beginning. While attending a publishing convention, Neufeld met an editor from a small publishing house named Marjorie Thayer. Thayer had read a newspaper article that she thought would make a perfect book—for the right author. Neufeld remembered in his essay: "She told me the bare bones of a story about a [white] family who had adopted a black child and, because of community pressures and their own fears, gave him up." Neufeld was very interested in the topic, but had some reservations about adapting it into a fictional format. He wanted the story to "be his own," different from that of the original family; with this in mind, he returned to New York without reading any of the newspaper chronicles. Eventually, he produced an often heart-wrenching account of a family torn apart by social forces they feel powerless to control.

Edgar Allan's exploration of racism, intolerance, and community pressure won kudos from many critics. "*Edgar Allan* is a success for many reasons," exclaimed Jean C. Thompson in *School Library Journal*. "Such irony, perhaps, will not touch children at first, but this book about a family on trial is one to save, share, and discuss. Certainly its reflection of reality will be noted and praised by the young people who read it." "It is about parents and children, young people, and older people, about love and failure, loss and discovery, coming to terms with oneself and others," concurred Richard Horchler in the *New York Times Book Review*. "In short, *Edgar Allan* is really a novel, a serious work of art, and therefore about what it means to be human being."

Neufeld's follow-up to *Edgar Allan*, entitled *Lisa, Bright and Dark*, is also based on a true incident. In a conversation with a psychiatrist, the author learned about one of the doctor's new patients. The patient was a young woman in deep emotional trouble whose parents did not understand her need for therapy. The author was touched by the story; on paper, the young girl became Lisa Shilling, a teenager slowly drifting into madness. Lisa's harrowing descent is made all the more terrible by the fact that her parents seem unwilling, or unable, to sense their daughter's plight. In the end, Lisa's only hope for help lies with three close friends—compassionate Betsy, up-tight Mary Nell, and former psychiatric patient Elizabeth. Much of Lisa's tragedy lies in that she *knows* she is going crazy, a fact Sada Fretz of *School Library Journal* found important to the book's structure. "The story does not delve into the gruesome details of

SIGNET●451-W8775●$1.50
"ONE OF THE OUTSTANDING BOOKS OF THE YEAR"
THE NEW YORK TIMES BOOK REVIEW.

lisa, bright and dark
JOHN NEUFELD, AUTHOR OF EDGAR ALLAN
A NOVEL OF A YOUNG GIRL'S JOURNEY TOWARD THE STRANGE, HYPNOTIC WORLD OF MADNESS

THE ACCLAIMED NBC-TV "HALLMARK HALL OF FAME" DRAMA!

An intelligent young girl's descent into madness is related in this 1969 novel.

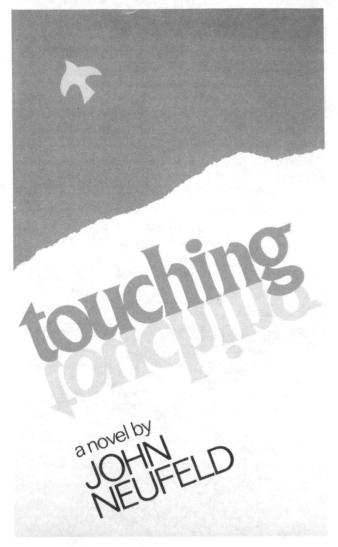

In this 1970 novel, Neufeld examines the relationship between a hip young boy and his stepsister, who has cerebral palsy.

mental illness,'' she wrote, "but it does present a serious subject previously untouched in children's books, and its disintegrating heroine is convincing in her desperation.''

Teen Worlds Falling Apart

Touching also features a teenager dealing with a life-threatening condition. In this case the teen is sixteen-year-old Twink Walsh, whose brave battle with cerebral palsy becomes the focus of her family's world—to the frequent disdain of her very hip, popular stepbrother Harry. Much of the novel addresses Harry's emotional state as he tries to handle the myriad of feelings he has for his embattled sister—disgust, shame, revulsion, and ultimately, love and understanding. Georgess McHargue, writing in the *New York Times Book*

Review, found the book "quite effective," while, in a review of the novel for *School Library Journal*, Thompson asserted that "the story is replete with honesty.''

Social drama is at the center of *Sleep Two, Three, Four!* Set in a totalitarian regime in the year 1983, the novel traces a group of young people as they try to rescue a crippled friend held captive in a "reeducation" facility. Along the way, the small band has a number of adventures, ranging from sleeping in a mystic's cave to hiding from gun-toting government authorities. Writing in *English Journal*, John W. Connor found that the author's "masterful use of simple language ... to build suspense enhances the ending.... John Neufeld will make his readers cherish their ability to question and will make them uneasy about accepting seemingly easy solutions to sociological issues.''

The action of *For All the Wrong Reasons* revolves around sixteen-year-old Tish Davies, who loses both her virginity and childhood at the same time (a problem also facing the fourteen-year-old protagonist of Neufeld's *Sharelle*). When she finds herself pregnant, Tish opts for an abortion; her young lover, however, wants to "be adult" and get married. Tish reluctantly agrees, but the young newlyweds' struggle eventually becomes complicated by sickness, family interference, and the heady day-to-day demands of being young parents. According to the author, it was very important that his heroine's plight be depicted as realistically as possible. Neufeld wrote in *SAAS* that his conditions for writing the book included "that the heroine actually knew how she got pregnant, had had sex more than once and liked it; that she would have the baby—no accidents on horseback or stairways.'' In a review of *For All the Wrong Reasons* for *School Library Journal*, Carol Starr concluded that the subject of teen marriage is "handled better here than in most other novels of the kind.''

Freddy's Book addresses the issue of sexuality from the aspect of education. After young Freddy sees the word "fuck" written on a bathroom wall, he embarks on an often amusing adventure to discover what the word *really* means. From both adults and his peers, Freddy gets interesting—if not always accurate—definitions. While lauding Neufeld's forthright approach to a potentially sensitive issue, Zena Sutherland of the *Bulletin of the Center for Children's Books* found the novel a bit flawed, writing that *Freddy's Book* "isn't quite convincing in constructing a situation in which so many people do a bad job of giving information: that enables the author to make a long story out of Freddy's quest, but the contrivance weakens the story."

Divorce is the backdrop for *Sunday Father*, as fourteen-year-old Tessa O'Connell tries to deal with the inevitable dissolution of her family. As her parents fight over the debris of their marriage, the young teen struggles with her own emotional burdens, including the pressure of conflicting loyalties and a sometimes overwhelming sense of loss. "Neufeld has depicted Tessa's conflict of loyalties and emotions with sensitivity," remarked Michael McCue and Evie Wilson in *Wilson Library Bulletin*. "The interrelationships among characters are well drawn. This contemporary novel should enjoy wide readership among" young adults.

Many of the themes introduced in Neufeld's works for young people—such as new love, loss, and family division—are also present in his adult novels, including *The Fun of It* and *Family Fortunes*. As with Neufeld's young adult works, the key to the success of these stories lies in the author's ability to present realistic characters struggling with honestly-depicted problems. In his *SAAS* entry, Neufeld summed up some of the "rules" that make for a successful writer—no matter what his or her intended audience may be: "Learning to understand the *similarities* between you and other people is desperately important. It's what can pull you down if you let it (it needn't) but also what can make your work ... understandable and likeable.... It's what we all have in common—our humanity, our joys, our disappointments. Being special is wonderful. Being human is more so."

■ Works Cited

Connor, John W., review of *Sleep Two, Three, Four!*, *English Journal*, February, 1972, pp. 305-06.

Fretz, Sada, review of *Lisa, Bright and Dark*, *School Library Journal*, February, 1970, p. 90.

Horchler, Richard, review of *Edgar Allan*, *New York Times Book Review*, November 3, 1968, p. 33.

McCue, Michael, and Evie Wilson, "Elderly Books for Youngerly Readers: *Sunday Father*," *Wilson Library Bulletin*, April, 1977, pp. 674, 687.

McHargue, Georgess, review of *Touching*, *New York Times Book Review*, November 29, 1970, p. 38.

Neufeld, John, essay in *Something about the Author Autobiography Series*, Gale, 1986, pp. 175-87.

Starr, Carol, review of *For All the Wrong Reasons*, *School Library Journal*, September, 1973, p. 98.

Sutherland, Zena, review of *Freddy's Book*, *Bulletin of the Center for Children's Books*, March 7, 1974, p. 116.

Thompson, Jean C., review of *Edgar Allan*, *School Library Journal*, December, 1968, p. 47.

Thompson, J. C., review of *Touching*, *School Library Journal*, November 15, 1979, pp. 121-22.

■ For More Information See

PERIODICALS

Library Journal, October 15, 1973, p. 3022.

New York Times Book Review, November 3, 1968, p., 33; November 11, 1969, p. 60; November 16, 1969, p. 52; February 12, 1972, p. 12.°

Jill Paton Walsh

■ Personal

Full name, Gillian Paton Walsh; born April 29, 1937, in London, England; daughter of John Llewellyn (an engineer) and Patricia (Dubern) Bliss; married Antony Edmund Paton Walsh (a chartered secretary), August 12, 1961; children: Edmund Alexander, Margaret Ann, Helen Clare. *Education:* St. Anne's College, Oxford, Dip. Ed., 1959, M.A. (English; with honours), 1962. *Politics:* None. *Religion:* "Skepticism." *Hobbies and other interests:* Photography, gardening, cooking, reading.

■ Addresses

Home—72 Water Lane, Histon, Cambridge CB4 4LR, England.

■ Career

Enfield Girls Grammar School, Middlesex, England, English teacher, 1959-62; writer, 1962—. Whittall Lecturer, Library of Congress, Washington, DC, 1978. Visiting Faculty Member, Center for the Study of Children's Literature, Simmons College, Boston, 1978-86. Founder, with John Rowe Townsend, of Green Bay Publishers, 1986.

Member: Society of Authors (member of Management Committee), Children's Writers Group, Children's Literature New England (adjunct board member).

■ Awards, Honors

Book World Festival award, 1970, for *Fireweed;* Whitbread Prize (shared with Russell Hoban), 1974, for *The Emperor's Winding Sheet; Boston Globe-Horn Book* Award, 1976, for *Unleaving;* Arts Council Creative Writing Fellowship, 1976-77, and 1977-78; Universe Prize, 1984, for *A Parcel of Patterns;* Smarties Prize Grand Prix, 1984, for *Gaffer Samson's Luck; School Library Journal* Best Book, 1992, for *Grace.*

■ Writings

FICTION FOR YOUNG READERS

Hengest's Tale, illustrated by Janet Margrie, St. Martin's, 1966.
The Dolphin Crossing, St. Martin's, 1967.
Fireweed, Macmillan, 1969.
Goldengrove, Farrar, Straus, 1972.
Toolmaker, illustrated by Jeroo Roy, Heinemann, 1973, Seabury Press, 1974.
The Dawnstone, illustrated by Mary Dinsdale, Hamish Hamilton, 1973.
The Emperor's Winding Sheet, Farrar, Straus, 1974.
The Huffler, Farrar, Straus, 1975, published in England as *The Butty Boy,* illustrated by Juliette Palmer, Macmillan, 1975.
Unleaving, Farrar, Straus, 1976.

Crossing to Salamis (first novel in a trilogy; also see below), illustrated by David Smee, Heinemann, 1977.

The Walls of Athens (second novel in a trilogy; also see below), illustrated by Smee, Heinemann, 1977.

Persian Gold (third novel in a trilogy; also see below), illustrated by Smee, Heinemann, 1978.

Children of the Fox (contains *Crossing to Salamis*, *The Walls of Athens*, and *Persian Gold*), Farrar, Straus, 1978.

A Chance Child, Farrar, Straus, 1978.

The Green Book, illustrated by Joanna Stubbs, Macmillan, 1981, illustrated by Lloyd Bloom, Farrar, Straus, 1982, published as *Shine*, Macdonald, 1988.

Babylon, illustrated by Jenny Northway, Deutsch, 1982.

A Parcel of Patterns, Farrar, Straus, 1983.

Lost and Found, illustrated by Mary Rayner, Deutsch, 1984.

Gaffer Samson's Luck, illustrated by Brock Cole, Farrar, Straus, 1984.

Torch, Viking Kestral, 1987, Farrar, Straus, 1988.

Birdy and the Ghosties, illustrated by Alan Marks, Macdonald, 1989.

Grace, Viking, 1991, Farrar, Straus, 1992.

When Grandma Came (picture book), illustrated by Sophy Williams, Viking, 1992.

Matthew and the Sea-Singer, illustrated by Marks, Simon & Schuster, 1992.

NOVELS FOR ADULTS

Farewell, Great King, Coward McCann, 1972.

Lapsing, Weidenfeld & Nicolson, 1986.

A School for Lovers, Weidenfeld & Nicolson, 1989.

OTHER

(With Kevin Crossley-Holland) *Wordhoard: Anglo-Saxon Stories*, Farrar, Straus, 1969.

The Island Sunrise: Prehistoric Britain, Deutsch, 1975, published as *The Island Sunrise: Prehistoric Culture in the British Isles*, Seabury Press, 1976.

Five Tides (short stories), Green Bay, 1986.

Some of Paton Walsh's manuscripts and papers are housed in the Kerlan Collection, University of Minnesota, Minneapolis.

■ Sidelights

The baby entered the world with some difficulty, wedged into the breech position and wrenched from the womb in such a way that her right arm was permanently damaged. In 1937 doctors be-lieved the arm's resulting limited movement was due to brain damage; they said her parents would have to wait and see how serious her condition, known as Erb's Palsy, would become. Their worry compounded until, at age two-and-a-half, the child began to speak—in full sentences.

The baby grew up to be author Jill Paton Walsh, free of mental deficiency and prevented only from "lifting heavy objects from high shelves, being a bell-ringer, and putting curlers in my own hair," as she wrote in an essay for the *Something about the Author Autobiography Series* (SAAS). "Looking back, I am not surprised that I was chary of talking until I had got the grammar straight in my head, for my entire family made a nonstop game ... of pedantically correcting each others' speech for the most minuscule errors of form or usage," Paton Walsh recalled. Her first words, in response to a neighbor's inquiry as to her daily routine, were, "Normally I play with bricks."

Her parents soon realized that their Jill would possess unimpeded intelligence but continued to limit her physical activities. Her response when told that she would be unable to do a certain thing was to try it, succeed, and infer from the experience that she was much more able-bodied than her family and doctors thought. "This has left me with a lifelong disposition to have a shot at things," Paton Walsh wrote. "Confronted with a difficult task, as constructing a built-in wardrobe, making a ballgown, or writing a publishable book, I am still inclined to tackle it, reflecting that if someone else can do it, I probably can. This is arrogant, of course, but it often proves true.... If I had been contented to do only what the doctors told my parents I would be able to do, I would have led a very narrow life!" Though she was sometimes discouraged from some activities, Paton Walsh's childhood was devoid of any prejudices or special treatment based on her status as a girl. In a family interested in academic accomplishments, the criteria for achievement were the same for Paton Walsh and her sister as for their brothers.

A Child of War

Paton Walsh's childhood was indelibly colored by World War II. "For five crucial years of my childhood—from the year I was three to the year I was eight—the war dominated and shaped everything around me," Paton Walsh wrote. "And then for many years, until well into my teens, postwar hardships remained." Paton Walsh and her family evacuated their home in the London suburb of

North Finchley when it was bombed on a night that her grandmother's new husband was visiting. After three trips to the garden bomb shelter that night, he insisted that everyone return with him to St. Ives in Cornwall. Paton Walsh's father was away, helping the war effort in radar research. After a while her mother returned to London to be closer to him.

The oldest child, Paton Walsh had begun nursery school in St. Ives and was allowed to stay with her grandmother, who insisted that another move would be too traumatic. She enjoyed several years of doting and praise from her grandmother in the tranquil bayside setting but was jolted back to the reality of life in London at age eight when her grandmother died of a heart attack. Paton Walsh recalled a curious conversation that night in which her grandmother misspoke, saying "goodbye" instead of "goodnight." Her step-grandfather's children told Paton Walsh that her grandmother was too ill to see her, but when she crept into her grandmother's room, she found it empty, the bed not slept in the night before. It was her mother, arriving that evening to take her home, who finally told Paton Walsh the truth.

As a child in 1944 London, Paton Walsh's life reflected the ever present danger of bombings. Residents abided by blackout conditions, snuffing all lights at night to prevent detection by German bombers overhead. Yards were scattered with aluminum foil strips to confound enemy radar. Each person wore a numbered disc on his or her wrist for identification purposes in the event of a bombing; the number of residents in the house was chalked on the gatepost. Paton Walsh recalled in *SAAS* that children "think it must have been a time of excitement and danger, whereas it was actually dreadfully boring. There was nothing to do. The cinemas were closed, the swimming pool was closed. . . . Television was closed down, and we were before the age of pop music directed at young people on the radio. There was only reading; and how we read!" New books weren't available, so Paton Walsh worked her way through her grandfather's library of classic literature, not always understanding what she read but staving off boredom nonetheless. Paton Walsh found schoolwork easy, a trait to which she attributed the treatment she received from the nuns who taught her in a small Catholic girls' school. Suspicious and critical of girls who excelled in academics, the nuns were in such an uproar when Paton Walsh was accepted to Oxford University that they not only prayed but offered an entire mass for her soul.

As a student at Oxford, Paton Walsh had the privilege of attending lectures by literary luminaries C. S. Lewis and J. R. R. Tolkien. "The subject of the lectures and tutorials was always literature or philology—we wouldn't have dared ask those great men about their own work!—but the example they set by being both great and serious scholars, and writers of fantasy and books for children was not lost on me," Paton Walsh wrote in *SAAS*. She met her husband while a student there; they married two years after Paton Walsh's graduation. When her first child was born two years later, Paton Walsh left a short-lived teaching position for full-time motherhood, but found the experience stifling. "I was bored frantic," she recalled. "I went nearly crazy, locked up alone with a howling baby all day and all night." Baby Edmund was constantly hungry but unable to stomach the milk he managed to drink. Doctors insisted that breast milk was the only acceptable food for babies; when in desperation Paton Walsh finally rebelled and fed Edmund a preparation of dried milk, he finished it

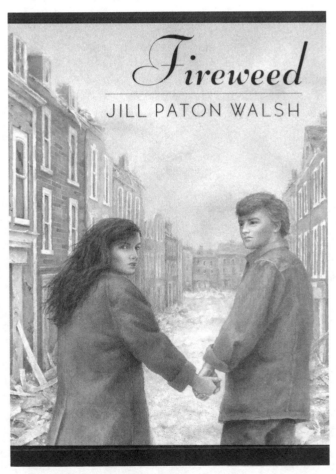

This 1969 novel, a *Book World* Festival award winner, tells the story of friendships between teenagers of differing social classes.

all and slept peacefully. "While he was asleep I *thought*," she wrote. "I thought about my own situation more intently than I ever remember doing, before or since. As plants need water and light, as the baby needed milk, I needed something intellectual, cheap, and quiet. I hauled out of the cupboard an old portable typewriter that my brother had given me, on leaving for America. I began to write a book. It was a children's book. It never occurred to me to write any other kind."

Writing Begins with "Blood, Blades, and Betrayals"

A serendipitous meeting with author Kevin Crossley-Holland, also an Oxford alumnus and then working as a children's book editor at Macmillan Publishing, provided a springboard for Paton Walsh's fledgling career. After reading her first book, Crossley-Holland recommended against having it published but offered her a £ 50 option on a new book. *Hengest's Tale* was the result. "Blood, blades, and betrayals are the hallmarks of this story of Hengest the Jute, invader and settler of fifth century Kent," Arthur T. Leone noted in the *New York Times Book Review*. The story is based on the legend of Hengest and fellow warrior Horsa, who conquered British King Vortigern and settled in Kent. *Horn Book* reviewer Paul Heins described *Hengest's Tale* as "a memorable historical narrative."

Paton Walsh's second child, Margaret, was born while she worked on *Hengest's Tale*. Daughter Helen Clare had arrived by the time she started work on *Fireweed*. Paton Walsh's experiences during World War II prompted her to write *The Dolphin Crossing* and *Fireweed*, her second and third books. Since she was so young when the war began, Paton Walsh set out to research the war, reading everything she could find in newspapers and magazines to supplement her memory. *The Dolphin Crossing* and *Fireweed* "tell of friendships between upper-class and working-class teenagers," Louise L. Sherman observed in *School Library Journal*. The relationships developed in each book are the result of wartime evacuations. Two boys from differing social classes become friends and set sail for Dunkirk in *The Dolphin Crossing*. In *Fireweed*, a boy and girl run away from their evacuation sites to return to London, then band together to survive the blitz. "A haunting, truly impressive novel," Ellen Lewis Buell declared in *Book World*.

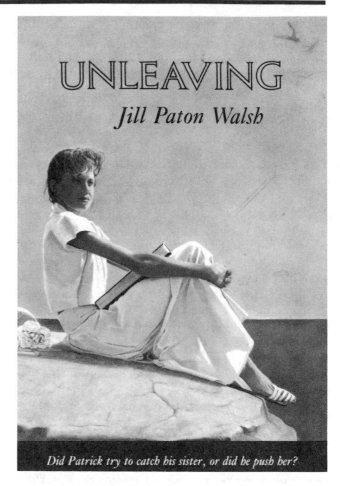

Did Patrick try to catch his sister, or did he push her?

Paton Walsh received the *Boston Globe–Horn Book* Award for this 1976 book about a young woman who inherits her familial home.

A Chance Child and *The Huffler* resulted from a holiday cruise through England's canals. While most of the trip provided views of beautiful countryside, Paton Walsh was struck by the ugliness of the factories and mines in the cities they also passed through. Wondering how the landscape could have become so blighted and abused, Paton Walsh set out to research the Industrial Revolution. As research for *A Chance Child*, Paton Walsh ventured into an operating coal mine. Once again she wore an identifying numbered disc on her wrist. A waif named Creep is the principal character of *A Chance Child*, which focuses on child labor in the mines, mills, and factories of the Victorian era. An abused child himself, Creep runs away from home, climbs aboard a rickety canal boat, and finds himself carried back in time to the nineteenth-century. From accounts of real children Paton Walsh found in old reports, the author recounts the beatings, accidents, and deaths that were a common consequence of nineteenth-century child labor. "Tenderly and carefully, Jill Paton

Walsh adds horror to horror, painting a foul darkness against which the stunted limbs of the children gleam with a lurid pallor," Jane Langton commented in the *New York Times Book Review*. Naomi Lewis, writing in the *Observer*, found *A Chance Child* "an eerie, memorable novel."

Paton Walsh's childhood home in St. Ives provided the setting for *Goldengrove* and *Unleaving*, both about a teenager, Madge, who enters the precipitous stage of adolescence the summer she learns that her cousin Paul, with whom she has spent every vacation at her grandmother's Goldengrove, is actually her brother. In *Unleaving*, Madge, now grown up, inherits Goldengrove and along with it the "reading group" to whom the house has been rented for the summer. Friendship and love develop between Madge and Patrick, the son of one of the professors inhabiting the house. "*Unleaving* loses everything in a synopsis," Elizabeth S. Coolidge wrote in *Washington Post Book World*, "for its significance lies in what the characters think and feel, not in what they do." While death and its effects on each of the characters is the central theme of *Unleaving*, it is "in no way a gloomy book, but one that leaves the reader with a warm and optimistic view of humankind," Coolidge concluded. "[Paton] Walsh doesn't tidy up the blight for which man was born," Alice Bach noted in the *New York Times Book Review*. "She's too wise to attempt answers about growing, living, dying, ethical choices. She exalts the mystery, the unknowing itself."

Settings Fuel Her Imagination

Paton Walsh noted in *SAAS* that most of her stories begin with a place. While some are memories, others result from trips for pleasure or research. Her first adult novel, *Farewell, Great King*, features details of the Greek countryside; the children's stories *The Emperor's Winding Sheet* and *Children of the Fox* also are infused with realistic settings by trips to Greece and Turkey. In *The Emperor's Winding Sheet*, Paton Walsh "brilliantly projects the dying splendor of Constantinople and the agony of its fall," a *Kirkus Reviews* contributor noted. Young Piers Barber ventures from his Bristol home to the far-off land, where he becomes the protector of Emperor Constantine. *Children's Book Review*'s C. S. Hannabuss found that, like *The Dolphin Crossing*, "war is used dramatically; it is a place full of real terrors, and not tied down with wishy-washy abstractions about courage and endurance."

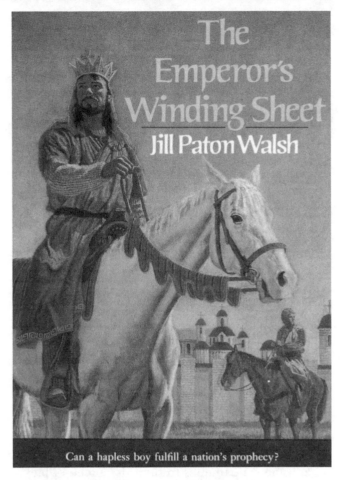

A winner of the 1974 Whitbread Prize, this historical tale tells of the Emperor Constantine and his great city of Constantinople, which later became Istanbul, Turkey.

One story that diverged from Paton Walsh's pattern of writing about places was *A Parcel of Patterns,* inspired by an account of the devastation the Plague brought to the village of Eyam that was told to her by her friend and fellow author, John Rowe Townsend. The story does, however, share another similarity with Paton Walsh's previous works: it features a group of ordinary people behaving courageously in a time of need. When Paton Walsh first heard of the villagers, who banded together to quarantine themselves from other villages in an effort to prevent the disease's spread, she was reminded of the acts of bravery, great and small, that she witnessed in the air raid shelters of her childhood London. Especially prominent is her recollection of the neighborhood milkman who had a knack for calming people and encouraging them to work together during the raids but who became simply Mike the milkman the next morning. She confided that Mike also appears to some degree in the wartime accounts of *Fireweed* and *The Emperor's Winding Sheet.*

The title's "parcel of patterns," a bundle of dressmaking diagrams, is what brings the Plague to Eyam in 1665. When the villagers realize they are infected, they agree to quarantine themselves for the sake of their neighbors. Supplies are delivered to the town boundaries; vinegar-soaked money is left as payment. The story's narrator, Mall, relates the villagers' efforts to prevent others from coming into contact with them, including Thomas, the man she loves. When Thomas refuses to stay away, Mall finds a way to make him believe she has died; Thomas's grief leads him to join the villagers to die as well. "This is a most dreadful, moving story, and it is related ... with a quiet, unerring restraint which will disturb and possess the reader long after the frenzy aroused by a sensational approach would have died away," Neil Philip asserted in the *Times Educational Supplement.*

Paton Walsh's inspiration for *Gaffer Samson's Luck* was once again a place, this time the cottage that she and her husband bought in a desolate area near Cambridge known as the Fens. When young James arrives in his new village, he finds friendship not among the other youths but with an elderly neighbor, Gaffer Samson. When Samson is hospitalized, he sends James to find his "piece of luck," which he buried seventy years earlier in the marshes. James's quest to find the item leads him to a confrontation with the leader of the village gang. In a *School Library Journal* review, Cynthia K. Leibold predicted that "this eloquent story of friendship and responsibility will prove a rewarding adventure for persistent readers."

In the primitive future society depicted in *Torch*, two teens are entrusted with the last Olympic torch and charged with delivering it to the Games. Having no idea what or where the Games are, the pair nevertheless set out to fulfill their obligation. The Games they eventually find, however, are now played for evil purposes, such as selecting slaves and identifying weak children for death. In a *School Library Journal* review, Christine Behrmann found the book "a rewarding challenge to readers who will not emerge with answers but rather an added ability to ask some important questions," while a *Kirkus Reviews* contributor described *Torch* as "a richly textured novel with a strong theme concerning the value to society—in any age—of cooperation and choices freely made."

Paton Walsh employed her research skills again in *Grace*, based on the true story of the 1838 rescue of nine shipwreck victims by Grace Darling and her father, a lighthouse keeper. Having lived peacefully and simply before the rescue, Grace finds unbearable the constant attention she receives after the rescue. Even worse, many of the mainland townspeople accuse Grace of attempting the rescue for monetary gain: rescuers traditionally received a generous reward for their efforts, and Grace had in effect taken money from the lifeboat crew by doing their job. While others recognized Grace's heroism, the uproar was nonetheless too much for her, and she died four years later. "Paton Walsh has brought [Grace] back to life for today's readers in a way that is completely engrossing," Connie C. Rockman declared in *School Library Journal.*

While most of her work has been in the realm of children's fiction, Paton Walsh has also written several adult novels. *Lapsing* presents "an unusual, fastidiously focused tale of a spiritual journey to disillusionment by a bright, deeply committed young Roman Catholic woman," a *Kirkus Reviews* contributor noted. A mutual attraction develops between Tessa and Father Theodore; Tessa marries in an unsuccessful effort to resolve the conflict. *Publishers Weekly* reviewer Diane Roback found *Lapsing* "an arresting novel, nuanced and clever."

The *New York Times Book Review*'s Barbara Wersba admired Paton Walsh's ability to capture the fears and emotions of childhood, something she believes many adults have forgotten. "Jill Paton Walsh, however, has not forgotten—and I am rather in awe of her," Wersba reflected. "She writes as though she were still twelve years old, choking back angry tears." Paton Walsh attributes her affinity for writing children's literature to her own childhood experiences. "The epoch in life in which people first meet a crisis, in which they first begin to define themselves, their own needs, feelings, opinions, is the epoch which they will always feel the most important," she stated in *SAAS*. "The upheavals and changes and conflicts which the war brought to my life mean that for me childhood is the important and interesting stage of life."

■ Works Cited

Bach, Alice, review of *Unleaving, New York Times Book Review*, August 8, 1976, p. 18.

Behrmann, Christine, review of *Torch, School Library Journal*, May, 1988, p. 111.

Buell, Ellen Lewis, review of *Fireweed, Book World*, May 17, 1970, p. 3.

Coolidge, Elizabeth S., "Two Modern English Morality Tales," *Washington Post Book World*, May 2, 1976, p. L13.

Review of *The Emperor's Winding Sheet, Kirkus Reviews*, May 1, 1974, pp. 490-491.

Hannabuss, C. S., review of *The Emperor's Winding Sheet, Children's Book Review*, summer, 1974, p. 71.

Heins, Paul, review of *Hengest's Tale, Horn Book*, August, 1967, p. 478.

Langton, Jane, review of *A Chance Child, New York Times Book Review*, June 17, 1979, pp. 24-25.

Review of *Lapsing, Kirkus Reviews*, October 1, 1987, p. 1419.

Leibold, Cynthia K., review of *Gaffer Samson's Luck, School Library Journal*, February, 1985, p. 80.

Leone, Arthur T., review of *Hengest's Tale, New York Times Book Review*, April 9, 1967, p. 26.

Lewis, Naomi, "Castles Dangerous," *Observer*, December 10, 1978, p. 38.

Paton Walsh, Jill, *Something about the Author Autobiography Series*, Volume 3, Gale, 1987, pp. 189-203.

Philip, Neil, "A Terrible Beauty," *Times Educational Supplement*, January 13, 1984, p. 42.

Roback, Diane, review of *Lapsing, Publishers Weekly*, October 16, 1987, p. 70.

Rockman, Connie C., review of *Grace, School Library Journal*, July, 1992, p. 91.

Sherman, Louise L., "In the Homes of Strangers: The World War II Evacuation of British Children in Children's Literature," *School Library Journal*, April, 1989, p. 42.

Review of *Torch, Kirkus Reviews*, March 1, 1988, p. 371.

Wersba, Barbara, "The Damage Called Growing Up," *New York Times Book Review*, November 5, 1972, p. 6.

■ **For More Information See**

BOOKS

Children's Literature Review, Volume 2, Gale, 1976.

Contemporary Literary Criticism, Volume 35, Gale, 1985.

PERIODICALS

Listener, November 9, 1972, pp. 644-645.

New York Times Book Review, June 16, 1985, p. 30.

Publishers Weekly, December 11, 1978, p. 69.

Punch, December 17, 1969, p. 1016.

School Library Journal, January, 1979, p. 63.

Times Literary Supplement, March 29, 1985, p. 349.

—*Sketch by Deborah A. Stanley*

Kin Platt

■ Personal

Born December 8, 1911, in New York, NY; son of Daniel (a singer) and Etta (Hochberg) Platt; married twice (divorced); children: Christopher. *Hobbies and other interests:* Physical fitness, golf.

■ Addresses

Home—Los Angeles, CA. *Agent*—Marilyn E. Marlow, Curtis Brown Inc., 10 Astor Place, New York, NY 10003.

■ Career

Cartoonist, painter, sculptor, and writer. Worked as political and theatrical caricaturist for New York newspapers, including *Brooklyn Daily Eagle, Sun,* and *World-Telegram,* beginning in 1930; radio scriptwriter for comedy shows such as *Stoopnagle and Bud* and *Jack Benny,* beginning in 1936, and for variety program, *National Biscuit Show;* writer for radio comics, such as Edgar Bergen and George Burns; New York Herald Tribune Syndicate, New York City, cartoonist (writer and illustrator) of comic strip *Mr. and Mrs.,* 1947-63, and *The Duke and the Duchess,* 1950-54; book author, 1961—.

Also worked as caricaturist for *Village Voice* and *Los Angeles Times;* as cartoonist and comic strip creator for advertising agencies; and as sports comic creator for various periodicals. *Military service:* U.S. Army Air Force, Air Transport Command, 1943-46; served in China-Burma-India theater; received Bronze Star, Good Conduct medal, two combat stars, and other decorations. *Member:* Writers Guild of America, Mystery Writers of America, National Cartoonist Society.

■ Awards, Honors

Edgar Award for juvenile mystery, Mystery Writers of America, 1967, for *Sinbad and Me;* Edgar Award runner-up, 1969, for *Mystery of the Witch Who Wouldn't;* award for distinguished fiction, Southern California Council on Literature for Children and Young People, 1974, for *Chloris and the Creeps; Headman* was a 1975 American Library Association notable book; outstanding contribution to children's literature award, Central Missouri State University, 1986.

■ Writings

FOR YOUNG ADULTS

Big Max, Harper, 1965, revised edition illustrated by Robert Lopshire, HarperCollins, 1992.
The Boy Who Could Make Himself Disappear, Chilton, 1969.
Hey, Dummy, Chilton, 1971.
Chloris and the Creeps, Chilton, 1973.
Chloris and the Freaks, Bradbury, 1975.
Headman, Greenwillow, 1975.

Big Max in the Mystery of the Missing Moose, illustrated by Robert Lopshire, Harper, 1975.

The Terrible Love Life of Dudley Cornflower, Bradbury, 1976.

Run for Your Life, photographs by Chuck Freedman, F. Watts, 1977.

Chloris and the Weirdos, Bradbury, 1978.

The Doomsday Gang, Greenwillow, 1978.

Dracula, Go Home, illustrated by Frank Mayo, F. Watts, 1979.

The Ape Inside Me, Lippincott, 1979.

Flames Going Out, Methuen, 1980.

Brogg's Brain, Crowell, 1981.

Frank and Stein and Me, F. Watts, 1982.

Crocker, Lippincott, 1983.

Darwin and the Great Beasts, Greenwillow Books, 1992.

"STEVE FORRESTER" YOUNG ADULT MYSTERIES

The Blue Man, Harper, 1961.

Sinbad and Me, Chilton, 1966.

The Mystery of the Witch Who Wouldn't, Chilton, 1969.

The Ghost of Hellsfire Street, Delacorte, 1980.

FOR ADULTS

Dead as They Come (a Molly Mellinger mystery), Random House, 1972.

A Pride of Women (suspense), Robert Hale, 1974.

Murder in Rosslare, Walker, 1986.

"MAX ROPER" ADULT MYSTERIES

The Pushbutton Butterfly, Random House, 1970.

The Kissing Gourami, Random House, 1970.

The Princess Stakes Murder, Random House, 1973.

The Giant Kill, Random House, 1974.

Match Point for Murder, Random House, 1975.

The Body Beautiful Murder, Random House, 1976.

The Screwball King Murder, Random House, 1978.

EDITOR

Jack London, *The Call of the Wild,* illustrated by Fred Carrillo, Pendulum Press, 1973.

Robert Louis Stevenson, *Dr. Jekyl and Mr. Hyde,* illustrated by Nestor Redondo, Pendulum Press, 1973.

Arthur Conan Doyle, *The Great Adventures of Sherlock Holmes,* Pendulum Press, 1974.

Robert Louis Stevenson, *Kidnapped,* Pendulum Press, 1974.

OTHER

Author of the unpublished musical *Let Freedom Ring* written during World War II.

■ Adaptations

Platt's novel, *The Boy Who Could Make Himself Disappear,* was filmed under the title *Baxter* in 1973. *Big Max* was adapted for audiocassette, Listening Library, 1986.

■ Work in Progress

My Sound Gone, The Baddest Thing, Tending to Witches, and *A Puzzle for Thoreau.*

■ Sidelights

Life as a teenager can be difficult for anyone, whether they are from an affluent city neighborhood, an average-income family in suburbia, or a poor farming community. Peer pressure to experiment with drugs, alcohol, and sex, vices that eagerly await new initiates, is commonplace. But life as a teenager on the streets of a poverty-stricken, aging metropolis can lend new meaning to the word "difficult," as crime, random violence, and death are added to the pressures of adolescence.

Destructive forces like those outlined above marked the life of Owen Kirby, a young white youth who ran afoul of the law after he was attacked in an alleyway by three teenaged gang members because he ventured onto their "turf." After stabbing the others in his defense, Kirby was given a chance to reform, being placed in a progressive work camp in the woods, away from the clutches of city corruption. The facility became a form of sanctuary for the boy, as its counselors listened to his problems and offered alternatives. Yet in the protective atmosphere of the camp, Kirby met and began to admire the leader, the "headman," of a local gang and came to see benefit of membership—safety and power in numbers.

After he was sent home, Kirby tried avoiding trouble, obtaining a job through his parole officer's assistance. But his efforts were short-lived as he again became the victim of gang members. Robbed of his first week's pay, he disregarded the past and continued efforts to reform him, gave in to the pressures antagonizing him, and formed his own crowd. His tortured existence came to a screeching halt as a quicker kid with a corkscrew planted the devise in Kirby's body during a fight. Fatally stabbed, he fell to the floor, conveying his frustration and surprise. His death became another statistic; that of another tormented teen killed in the battle against his environment.

Never fear, the saga of Kirby's tragic demise is only a story in a book, a work simply entitled *Headman*. Yet it is a tale made all the more distressing due to its roots in true-life situations. Its presentation by prolific author and cartoonist Kin Platt caused considerable controversy among librarians, parents, and reviewers upon the book's release in 1975. Its realistic depictions, complete with varying expletives, led some adults to ban their children from reading the volume.

But Platt is no stranger to attempts at censorship of his books. Such portrayals of graphic violence and candid dialogue appear in a number of his works for young adult readers and have earned him the reputation as an author who writes vivid accounts of the harsh realities of adolescence. Many of Platt's characters come from dysfunctional homes, suffer from mental anguish, or are negatively influenced by their desperate lives in blighted urban areas. The concern Platt's books receive from some adults "is based on the not unreasonable assumption that anyone who manages to shock so many adults must be telling it like it is," asserted Joyce Milton in *New York Times Book Review*. The commentator added that the author's frank presentations have worked well for him.

With over thirty years of experience behind him, the outspoken Platt has had frequent problems with publishers, teachers, librarians, and others. In his first book, a 1961 adventure story called *The Blue Man*, the young protagonist, Steve Forrester, attempts to hunt down the blue-bodied alien that he believes killed his uncle. Armed with a rifle, the youth takes the law into his own hands when local police officials ignore his request for help. "They [librarians and critics] objected to the book because the kid was carrying a rifle," Platt told *Authors and Artists for Young Adults* (*AAYA*) in an interview. "I remember Chris, my son, would have to go around to libraries in the Los Angeles area and he'd go to the librarian and say, 'How about taking this book by my pop; it's really a great book.' And so the librarians would read it and would take it, but they were afraid to put it on the shelves. They would hold it under the counter and it would become like a bootleg item. If a kid came in and asked for it, then he would get it. So that's when I first found out the intricacies of the trade."

Platt recalled that he encountered further problems with another adventure tale featuring the Steve Forrester character. Called *The Mystery of the Witch Who Wouldn't*, the work profiled the efforts of two teenagers who try to solve a series of crimes with the help of a local woman, who happens to be a witch. Much of the concern over the book stemmed from Platt's references to the works of English author and black magician Aleister Crowley. "This book was banned and burned in Michigan," Platt explained. "I was accused of witchcraft and in assisting witchcraft. Then I wrote a book called *The Terrible Love Life of Dudley Cornflower* and that was banned because of the language." His books about a brain-damaged child and other troubled teens have also received criticism due to their subject matter, language, or sexual content.

"All of my early books were banned in one way or another because people didn't understand the kind of excitement that I was trying to give readers," Platt recalled for *AAYA*. "I knew what kids wanted to read."

Platt has a history of nonconformity and independent thinking. Born in New York City on December 8, 1911, he began running away from home when he was just seven years old. He eventually hooked up with a rodeo and a circus. During his youth, the would-be author was interested in reading and sports. "In public school I was reading five to seven books a day, so I was always a great reader," Platt told *AAYA*. "As a matter of fact, I was reading [the psychoanalytical theories of Sigmund] Freud and other psychologists by the time I was twelve and thirteen." Recalling that he was especially fascinated with other languages and different types of people, Platt professed that he also enjoyed history, particularly the myths, legends, and peoples of ancient history. American novelist Jack London was one of his favorite authors. Some five decades later, Platt would pursue his interest in London's work by editing the novelist's popular *Call of the Wild* for Pendulum Press.

Like the characters in some of his books, Platt acknowledges that he had a difficult childhood. Commenting on his troubled home life, he asserted, "One of the things that I've tried to do in my children's books is to have kids understand that maybe their lives aren't as bad as some of the characters' lives I was writing about." Although Platt himself was never in a street gang, he had friends who ran with them. "As I recall going through high school, I guess I was probably the only one of my group of friends who didn't go to jail. I wasn't arrested, but I did spend a little time in reform school. I forget what that was about now, but it didn't last too long."

Pursues Career in Art

During his adolescence, Platt knew he wanted to become a cartoonist and an author, although he aspired to write plays, not necessarily children's books. He remembers drawing a lot. "I think the thing that got me out of reform school was that I was drawing all over the walls," Platt revealed to *AAYA.* "One of the facility's directors suggested that drawing might be a way out of my troubles." The young Platt was also interested in sports, as are many of the protagonists in his books. "I've always been a runner. I ran before running became popular," he noted. "Then when everybody started doing it, I thought it couldn't be any good if everybody is doing it, so I stopped for awhile. I really only stopped later on in my seventies when it got kind of silly—you know, when you're not really running anymore, just demonstrating that you can still move."

Still an avid reader at the time of his high school graduation, Platt had no ambitions to attend college. "I was on my own at a very early age; I never thought much of college," Platt said. "I had read more than most college people anyway, and I never could stand being regimented. I think that's why I liked running—because I was on my own." Platt's graduation, however, coincided with the advent of the Great Depression—a time marked with mass unemployment, homelessness, and starvation. "Everybody had trouble finding work," he remembered. "I finally started my professional career as a cartoonist in about 1930. Getting paid in between days of starving, I was doing political and theatrical drawings for the *Brooklyn Daily Eagle.* I was always cartooning. And when I wrote, it wasn't much in a way of anything meaningful. I would start stories and never finish them." Platt also earned money by doing odd jobs in theaters. "I remember hiring myself out and setting up a stand in the lobby. As people came out, I would flash them a drawing of themselves. I worked out of various theaters around the country. It was a way of existing."

As his career was beginning, Platt also prepared short spots for advertising agencies and did some cartooning for the New York *Sun.* "For the *Brooklyn Daily Eagle,* I did one of the first political drawings in this country against Nazi leader Adolf Hitler," Platt told *AAYA.* "By 1936 I was doing radio comedy as a result of having worked in advertising art agencies." Among the radio comedians for which Platt worked were Jack Benny and Stoopnagle and Bud. "I guess my big show was the *National Biscuit Comedy Hour* in 1936, which starred Victor Moore, Helen Broderick, and Mary Martin, who became one of my dear friends."

Moving from New York to Hollywood to be nearer to the new heart of the show-biz empire, Platt quickly became disillusioned with the entertainment world. "I was always very natural and quick at what I did, never having to refer to anything," Platt voiced to *AAYA.* "But the comedy writers in Hollywood worked in cliques and gangs. They all had their card files, and they knew if one joke worked on one show, it would work on another. So here I was trying to put in original humor—which is why I was hired—but when it came down to writing with the writers' groups, I found they were all getting out gags and jokes that everybody laughed at before, and they were trying to revise them, trying to use the tried and true formula. I only lasted three years with that."

In Hollywood he had continued to write for radio comics, most notably for Edgar Bergen. In an autobiographical essay that appeared in *Speaking for Ourselves,* Platt noted that "my flaring temper cost me too many shows and I returned to New York." Elaborating to *AAYA* on his decision to leave, Platt said he now recognizes those years as "a growing period." He added, "I found out that I didn't have much respect for a lot of the comedians and gag writers.... But I was kind of crazy myself. I was so reckless when I was young. I'm completely different from what I used to be."

Platt freely admits that part of his problem in Hollywood can be attributed to his own stubbornness. Noting that he was very proud of his work, he confessed that he was fairly ignorant of how the show biz writing circuit operated. "I wouldn't let anybody change anything that I wrote," Platt related to *AAYA.* "Other people would give up everything to have their idea put in the skit in some form. As a result I bounced around from one comic to another down through the years. I quit a lot of jobs." He later added, "My temper or impatience was always a problem. I never could accommodate phonies or those in authority who were incompetent or regarded their own ideas as unassailable. Too much ego, I suppose, and conflict with editors, too."

On his return to New York, Platt began cartooning again, creating comic books and the animated hero Supermouse. In the early to mid-1940s, Platt took on a new form of employment—service in the U.S. Army Air Force. America was in the heat of World War II, and the former comic writer was drafted,

Part of Platt's "Steve Forrester" series, this 1966 book won the Edgar Award for juvenile mysteries.

classified as an entertainment specialist, and assigned to stints in China, Burma, and India. Part of his duties entailed cartooning for a service newspaper called *Broad Views.* He refers to his work for the publication as "girly cartoons." He also wrote a musical called *Let Freedom Ring* that sparked some controversy as many of his superior officers wanted to become involved in its production. A recipient of a Bronze Star and a Good Conduct Medal for his work, Platt said he also found time to visit other servicemen in the hospital, often drawing their pictures for them.

"I was kind of independent even in the Army, which gave me a lot of trouble because I would write my own papers, which as an enlisted man I wasn't allowed to do," Platt explained to *AAYA.* "I would do caricatures insulting officers and things like that. Officers and I were always fighting."

Upon his release from service in 1946, Platt secured a job with the *New York Herald Tribune.* He had tried to find work with his own comic strip, but was asked to prepare the strip *Mr. and Mrs.* started years earlier by Clare A. Briggs. After Briggs's death in 1930, other cartoonists had continued the work that was syndicated throughout the United States and Europe. "The strip was dying and they wanted to revive it," Platt remarked. "So they asked me to do it. So for a while I would draw it and someone else would write it. But the editor thought I could save the whole strip so they gave me the complete thing to do for Saturdays and Sundays."

Platt illuminated the nature of the comic strip to *AAYA:* "*Mr. and Mrs.* was about what an ordinary man and wife would do in suburban life. He was kind of elderly with a brush mustache. It was a very stupid comedy of, more or less, manners in a man's inability to cope with his wife. The man had a temper much like my own." The strip's characters, the often-feuding Vi and Joe Green, had a very loyal following. Platt said that when he began crafting the cartoon, he tried to readjust the drawing of Mrs. As a result, he received a number of letters from people complaining about the changes made to Vi's hair, her nose, or her chin.

In the 1950s, Platt continued work on *Mr. and Mrs.* and began a strip called *The Duke and the Duchess.* The cartoonist encountered some controversy after he began using the latter strip to comment on political issues of the day. At one point, he attacked Senator Joseph McCarthy, who was attempting to rid the country of alleged Communists through congressional hearings on "un-American" activity. McCarthy was successful in spreading mass paranoia and in getting many people blacklisted from their professions. "I remember getting a letter from the publisher of the *Tribune* that said, 'Mr. Platt, if you were hired for your political opinions you'd be on the political page, not in the entertainment section,'" he divulged. However, Platt worked for the *Tribune* until it folded in 1963. At that point Platt was out of a job.

But the author had already started writing books for young readers: he penned *The Blue Man* in 1961. "I was always so prolific," Platt stated to *AAYA.* "I'd done thousands of animated cartoons, radio scripts, and comic book stories. I had numbers that I can't even tell you about because it would sound preposterous. I told my wife at that time that I was just going to do one thing from then on—just one single thing and it was going to be books. You know, I could actually fill up a room with all the stuff I've done."

Platt did not let the censorship difficulties he encountered with *The Blue Man* impact his decision to write. In 1965 he saw publication of *Big Max*, a detective story with the title character trying to find a missing elephant. Billed as "the world's greatest detective," the protagonist was compared to Arthur Conan Doyle's famous sleuth Sherlock Holmes. A *Horn Book* reviewer called the book "spontaneous fun."

Writes Book for Son

His next book, the second in the Steve Forrester series, was the Edgar Award-winning *Sinbad and Me*. At the core of the adventure tale is the story of

The protagonist of this novel, young Roger Baxter, must deal with his parents' divorce and an abusive mother.

a boy and his bulldog named Sinbad. Inspired by Platt's son Christopher and his pet bulldog Romeo, *Sinbad and Me* is set in Hampton, Long Island, and features a twelve-year-old protagonist with a curiosity and knowledge of old houses and antiques. Steve's interests lead him into an eighteenth-century mystery with twentieth-century complications. As the duo explores an old house, they find passageways, secret codes, and puzzles that point to pirates, sunken treasure, and even murder. Included in the book are actual secret puzzles so the reader can assist in the crime solving.

Sinbad and Me is interspersed with bits of Platt's unique humor. His wit is even evident on the book's dust jacket, which quotes Platt: "'English bulldogs,' he says, 'are supposed to be dumb but they don't write books, proof enough that they are very intelligent.'" Critical response to *Sinbad and Me* was positive, although some reviewers called the story illogical but thoroughly enjoyable. In a commentary for *Young Readers Review*, Phyllis Cohen described the work as "a mystery story with character! It's breezy, funny, brash, clever, and frightening." She added that because of the volume's humor, "this one stands out like a beacon!" Sarah Law Kennerly in a *School Library Journal* review called the book, "outrageously illogical, long and rambling, and refreshingly funny."

In books like *Sinbad and Me*, Platt was trying to inspire children to read. "When I first started out as a writer, I wanted to write books that were so exciting that kids would love to read," he told *AAYA*. "I wanted to be the most exciting writer for kids. I remember when I went up to Harper's and told them about my idea [to inspire children], they said 'Well, Mr. Shakespeare, what would you like to do,' and I promised them a book that was going to be better than Robert Louis Stevenson's *Treasure Island*. They said 'great' and tried not to laugh. On the way home, I remembered how *Treasure Island* was about something like fifteen men on a dead man's chest, with a black spot, caves, pirates, and all that stuff. So I wrote *Sinbad and Me*."

In preparation for the book, Platt made numerous trips to the library to research various concepts contained in the story. He sent his final version to Harper's editors, who cut the tale down about fifty thousand words in Platt's estimation. Not liking his words to be cut or altered, Platt looked for another publisher and was turned down several times before he succeeded. He dedicated the book to the family's bulldog Romeo. "The dog would knock you down just to kiss you, he was just so ferocious," Platt disclosed to *AAYA*. "*Sinbad and Me* was the best thing I ever did for my son because it was very true. They slept in the same bed, often ate off the same plate, things like that. Chris was always having a tough time with me and with his mother, and the dog gave him unremitting, unquestioning love. They had a really wonderful relationship; the dog grew up with him and became a big sturdy rock." He added, "So whenever Chris says I've written a good book, I take that seriously because he's hard to please."

Platt's other major children's books in the 1960s were *The Boy Who Could Make Himself Disappear* and another Steve Forrester adventure, *The Mystery of the Witch Who Wouldn't*. The former title concerned the life of an only child named Roger Baxter. Trapped in a dysfunctional home—his parents have divorced and he is persecuted by his mother—Roger tries to deal with his difficulties, including a speech defect. His problems mount as his mother's abusive nature goes unrecognized by those around him, and he tries to adjust to new surroundings after a move to New York City. The boy finally learns to cope through the help of his friends and therapy.

Critics voiced a mix response to *The Boy Who Could Make Himself Disappear*. Zena Sutherland in a review for *Bulletin of the Center for Children's Books* deemed the work "so moving and so well written," while *School Library Journal*'s John Gillespie called it a story "that will remain with thoughtful young people long after it is read." Platt, however, remembers being stung by other reviewers. He told *AAYA* that he saw some library notices that read, "Don't bother with this. This is not a real Kin Platt book. They expected me to bleed and show my heart for them afterward, and I refused." He also related, "Other reviewers said 'who wants to read about an American bitch mother?'"

Hollywood was interested in *The Boy Who Could Make Himself Disappear*, however, and adapted it into the film *Baxter*. "It was an art film and was

The Boy Who Could Make Himself Disappear was adapted as the 1973 motion picture *Baxter*.

really quite well done. They changed the book around a lot, but what I objected to was the title, *Baxter,*" Platt opined. "That was the only one of my books that was made into a film. I've had other opportunities, but nobody ever wanted to pay enough money or give me a decent contract."

In the 1960s Platt also continued his caricaturing, working for the *Village Voice.* His work in children's literature increased during the 1970s, and he began writing adult mysteries. In all, he saw publication of some twenty of his books during the decade. Among these volumes was the controversial *Hey, Dummy,* the story of a brain-damaged, thirteen-year-old boy named Alan Harper and the twelve-year-old youth Neil Comstock, who gives Alan his nickname "Dummy." Neil is initially cruel to the slow and stumbling Alan, failing to sympathize with or understand the older boy's limitations. But when Alan begins following Neil, the two eventually become friends, much to the chagrin of the Comstock parents. Trying to understand the plight of his new companion, Neil decides to try being Alan for a time. Neil's parents discourage him from seeing Alan, and the retarded youth later runs into trouble when residents falsely accuse him of attacking a neighborhood girl. Neil steps in to help his pal, but the boys are soon caught. During the ordeal Neil further identifies with Alan, and when they are found Neil has begun to use the same simplistic speech pattern as the "Dummy."

After *Hey, Dummy* was published, "critics said it was too depressing," Platt told *AAYA.* "They said, 'who wants to read about brain-damaged children?' So I guess I was always a little ahead of my time." Some commentators were complimentary about the work, however. In the *New York Times Book Review,* Betsy Byars noted that writing a story about a mentally retarded boy was undoubtedly difficult. However, she added, "Platt says more than anybody so far," telling his tale "with gentleness and guts." Zena Sutherland in the *Bulletin of the Center for Children's Books* called Platt's portrayal "a perceptive treatment of a child's sensitivity." She contended that "artistically [the book] suffers somewhat because" the story continually presents adults as angry and unjust.

Anger and resentment were two of the emotions that Platt explored in a series of books that he produced beginning in 1973 with *Chloris and the Creeps.* Delving into the lives of two sisters, the "Chloris" books chart the hostility that the title character feels toward the men in her divorced mother's life. The first installment—told through the narration of the youngest sister, the somewhat well-adjusted Jenny—finds Chloris failing to accept her parents' divorce, her father's subsequent remarriage and suicide, and her mother's attempts to find a new mate. When her mother eventually weds the kind and patient Fidel Mancha, a man of Mexican heritage, Chloris treats her stepfather with contempt and disrespect, idolizing her late father. Poor Jenny is caught in the middle. She likes Fidel, but tries to maintain her loyalty to her sister, while acknowledging Chloris's irrational behavior.

Chloris's mother and stepfather's concern is evident in the following excerpt from the book: "'Why doesn't that one like me?' [asked Fidel.] Mom's tone was bitter. 'She doesn't like me, either. Not since I divorced my husband. But it became worse after he killed himself.' Mr. Mancha was silent for a while. 'Don't worry,' he said at last. 'She will come around. She is too young to keep such a hate bottled up inside her.'. . . Fidel kept on acting as if he didn't know a thing one way or the other. He always treated me with affection, and he didn't change any for Chloris. Whatever he offered me he offered her. She would back off, or pretend she wasn't interested, or that she was too busy, or too tired, or too this or that. Fidel didn't seem to mind. He would nod, his brown eyes soft and understanding. Then he would laugh."

Chloris and the Creeps further delineates Fidel's attempts to win over the eldest child, charting his eventual progress. The "Creeps" of the title—and the subsequent "freaks" and "weirdos"—are Chloris's names for adults, particularly her mother's boyfriends. In the sequel *Chloris and the Freaks,* the angry teenager again displays animosity toward Fidel, hoping and predicting that his marriage to her mother will end in divorce, which it does. Jenny tries to preserve her loyalty to Chloris, and she turns to astrology to escape her woes. The third book in the series, *Chloris and the Weirdos,* continues to describe the youngsters' lives and problems as their mother begins dating anew.

Real-life Experiences Inspire "Chloris" Books

Platt's inspiration for the Chloris books was based on personal experience. He, like Fidel, had remarried, only to find resentment from one of his stepdaughters. "I inherited two daughters that I couldn't handle, so I suppose I made myself into a god-like figure like Fidel," Platt joked. He admitted, however, that parts of the Chloris series are autobiographical, but a lot was invented. "You can't just take things as they are," he said. "You have to improve on life." Platt did use some teenage jargon in his books to lend a more realistic tone. In *Chloris and the Creeps,* for example, little sister Jenny says "gy" a lot, meaning "gosh." Such slang he picked up from one of his stepdaughters.

Platt's personal experience was evident to critics, who noted the realistic portrayal of his characters. "The author writes with incisive candor and clarity, albeit a bitter clarity," asserted Zena Sutherland in the *Bulletin of the Center for Children's Books.* And a *Kirkus Review* commentator surmised that *Chloris and the Freaks* shows "a startlingly truthful portrait of a psychologically mixed up girl." *Booklist*'s Betsy Hearne assessed that Platt displays knowledge of his subject matter, "revealing a flair for funny dialogue in conjunction with serious issues."

Among Platt's other notable works during the 1970s are two novels about gangs, *Headman* and *The Doomsday Gang.* In a synopsis of the former work, *New York Times Book Review* contributor Robert Berkvist called the volume a "taut and very tough novel about growing up dead in the white, black and Chicano ghettos of Los Angeles." *School Library Journal*'s Jack Forman commented on the book's harsh four-letter-word vocabulary, stating that the book's message is that "the only law which is real is the law of the street."

In *The Doomsday Gang,* set in Los Angeles, Platt told the story of a group of teens involved in crime and drug dealing. Outlining the uselessness of gang life, the tale concluded with a neighborhood war erupting between three factions. Death is the result for one gang member, hospitalization for many others. As he did in *Headman,* Platt provides realism by allowing his characters to use the strong language of the street. While many critics complained about the inclusion of vulgar speech, others found it necessary. In a review for *Wilson Library Bulletin,* Patty Campbell compared Platt's use of obscene language in *The Doomsday Gang* to that used by J. D. Salinger in *Catcher in the Rye.* Noting that the frequency of foul language "is numbing and very effectively conveys the flatness and boredom of the limited lives of street kids," Campbell added that Platt's presentation of such language "is completely justified by the subject."

Concerning complaints that some of his books contain too much vulgar language, sex, and violence, Platt told *AAYA:* "Librarians try to protect teachers and they give them this very, very gentle world—a very lovely, sweet world. I know the world's not like that at all and I love to protect

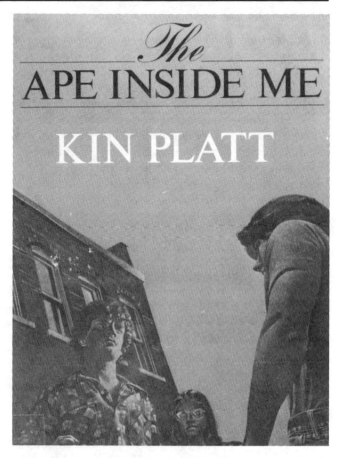

This 1979 novel tells the story of a disturbed boy who manifests his anger in an ape-like alter ego that he calls "Kong."

children too. But I like to get them ready for the world—to acquaint them with what's going to happen with the kind of people and situations they can expect." He added, "And teachers, they try to cut out any essence of truth or what's really going on in the world, putting kids in a cocoon."

In addition to his writings for young readers in the 1970s, Platt debuted a series of adult detective novels, featuring protagonist Max Roper. In titles such as *The Pushbutton Butterfly, The Princess Stakes Murder,* and *The Screwball King Murder,* the private eye combines intelligence and humor to solve cases that baffle police. In the first title, for example, Roper searches for the missing daughter of a millionaire. In *The Screwball King Murder,* the detective solves a series of killings linked to the alleged accidental drowning of a star baseball pitcher. The course of Roper's investigation leads him to an assortment of the player's old girlfriends, each with an axe to grind, and into a dangerous drug ring.

Commenting on the nature of the Roper character, Platt told *AAYA:* "Every mystery writer who presents a bullet-proof character likes to think of the detective as like himself. But that's not true with me." Noting that Roper is "one of the few intelligent detectives able to take care of himself," the author described his creation as "human, bright, funny, and a martial arts expert. He also exhibits good reasoning and wants to expose crime." He added, "Sure Roper is based on aspects of myself, but also on parts I can't possibly be." Platt was approached for the television rights to the first Roper tale, but turned down the offer as he believed the story was worth more money.

As Platt entered the early 1980s, he published two more books featuring troubled teens and several stories for little children. Like his earlier works for young adults, his books *Flames Going Out* and *The Ape Inside Me,* were met with some concern by critics and librarians. In the former title, a disturbed sixteen-year-old girl equates her life with a burning match. She gets professional help via a psychiatrist, but runs into more problems when she becomes involved with her doctor's drug-addicted son. Platt ends the book on a positive note, however, as the teen determines to take charge of her own life.

With *The Ape Inside Me,* Platt unveiled the angst-filled life of scrawny, fifteen-year-old Eddie. The story's title refers to the boy's inner turmoil—an anger that builds so much within him that it becomes difficult to control. Coming from a dysfunctional family, Eddie receives help from other adults in his life, including his employer (he works part time at an auto body shop) and coach. The latter suggests that the boy channel his fury into boxing. As Eddie tries to sort out his life, however, he finds more trouble—this time in the form of love. *The Ape Inside Me* received mixed reviews from critics. Some were adverse to the story's violence, others lauded its believability.

Has Difficulty Finding Publishers

During the mid- to late-1980s, times were tough for Platt as he had problems getting his books printed. "Publishers have been afraid of the kind of books that I've wanted to do, as far as public opinion and sales are concerned. I've tried to write about a kid who's deaf and dumb, and that was considered too depressing," he told *AAYA*. "I've been more or less blocked out because I didn't want to keep doing ordinary books. I always felt that I had to stay ahead of everybody else, in my own mind at least. . . . I don't write to make money; I write because the story has to be told." Despite

his standoff with publishers, Platt managed to debut detective Bill Stanwood in the 1986 adult mystery *Murder in Rosslare.*

Continuing to have problems with publishers even today, Platt acknowledges that his current woes are similar to those he had with comics and writers in Hollywood. "I would never let anybody make corrections unless there was a good reason for it; I never let anybody change me or the book. My problem with publishers was the result of two things—I got angry at my editors and the editors got fed up with me. And there just came a time when I wasn't able to sell anything. I couldn't believe it. After a while you start wondering, 'What the hell am I writing for?' I would write books and the editors would say, 'Well, we like the book but we can't use it right now.'. . . I would have rather heard somebody say, 'I hate your book and we don't want it' than 'I loved your book, but we can't take a chance on it.'"

Platt's comeback as a children's book author came with *Darwin and the Great Beasts* in 1992. "I had to do something that I could control more or less; something that would be safe and educational—something that would sell," Platt confided. "I had

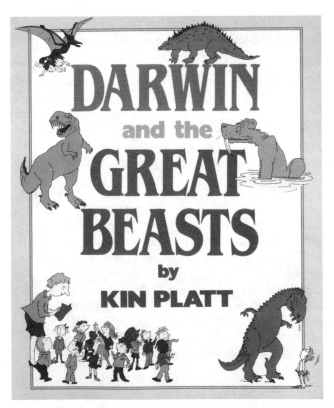

In this 1992 novel for children, Platt combines his writing and cartooning abilities to weave a tale about a young boy named Darwin who travels back in time to the age of dinosaurs.

to create and sell something to stop the bleeding, the rejections." His book was turned down several times before he found a publisher in Greenwillow. While proving that the author was still able to write entertaining stories for young audiences, *Darwin* also served as the first book that Platt self-illustrated. The cartoonist had considered drawing the art for *Big Max* some three decades earlier, but realized that his animated style did not reflect the nature of the book. His technique was ideal for *Darwin*, however, so he created the artwork despite his failing eyesight.

With *Darwin*, Platt tells the story of a boy who goes on a class field trip to California's La Brea Tar Pits. On their tour through the museum, the students learn what life was like during the dinosaur era, viewing skeletal remains of the once-dominant creatures. After Darwin hears how such mammals and reptiles became extinct, he begins envisioning how he would have helped them survive. His ideas are explored in the book as the boy travels back into time. Coupled with the adventure tale is factual information about the creatures he encounters on his journey.

Darwin and the Great Beasts received favorable reviews. A commentator for *Publishers Weekly* noted that "the ingenious juxtaposition of fact and fiction proves enticing." Cathryn A. Camper of *School Library Journal* also commented on Platt's mixing of truth and fantasy. She asserted that such texts "create the kind of comedy that makes children giggle (and adults groan)."

Looking back on his more than sixty-year career, Platt related to *AAYA*: "What I did have from the very beginning was a magical gift for writing. I never realized it until much later on. Things just came automatically. It's only now that I have to really think of stories." When asked what he perceives as his best work, Platt related that he didn't believe his writing was his greatest achievement. "Caricaturing is what I do best," he explained. "I like to think I'm the best caricaturist alive today. It's something that I feel I do better than anyone else." Upon further reflection, Platt said that one of his most important accomplishments concerns the impact that his books have had on various children. Through correspondence he has heard from youngsters who claim that his writings have influenced them or inspired them to read more.

Depicting his humorous side, Platt's advice to aspiring young writers was "find another profession." On a more serious note, he suggested, "Learn to endure." He added, "Everyone has something worthwhile to say, but not everyone is concerned with the truth." He also noted, "Books can't have an effect if no one is willing to publish them. The important thing is to write the book and complete the package."

■ Works Cited

Berkvist, Robert, review of *Headman, New York Times Book Review*, December 14, 1975, p. 8.

Review of *Big Max, Horn Book*, October, 1965, p. 498.

Byars, Betsy, review of *Hey, Dummy, New York Times Book Review*, March 12, 1972, p. 8.

Campbell, Patty, review of *The Doomsday Gang, Wilson Library Bulletin*, December, 1978, pp. 340-41.

Camper, Cathryn A., review of *Darwin and the Great Beasts, School Library Journal*, June, 1992, p. 124.

Review of *Chloris and the Freaks, Kirkus Reviews*, December 15, 1975, pp. 1379-80.

Cohen, Phyllis, review of *Sinbad and Me, Young Readers Review*, October, 1966, pp. 1-2.

Review of *Darwin and the Great Beasts, Publishers Weekly*, June 15, 1992, p. 103.

Forman, Jack, review of *Headman, School Library Journal*, December, 1975, p. 61.

Gillespie, John, review of *The Boy Who Could Make Himself Disappear, School Library Journal*, October, 1968, p. 172.

Hearne, Betsy, review of *Chloris and the Freaks, Booklist*, November 15, 1978, p. 548.

Kennerly, Sarah Law, review of *Sinbad and Me, School Library Journal*, December, 1966, p. 71.

Milton, Joyce, review of *Flames Going Out, New York Times Book Review*, February 1, 1981, p. 28.

Platt, Kin, *Sinbad and Me*, Chilton, 1966.

Platt, Kin, *Chloris and the Creeps*, Chilton, 1973.

Platt, Kin, autobiographical essay in *Speaking for Ourselves: Autobiographical Sketches by Notable Authors of Books for Young Adults*, compiled and edited by Donald R. Gallo, National Council of Teachers of English, 1990, pp. 176-78.

Platt, Kin, interviews with Kathleen J. Edgar for *Authors and Artists for Young Adults*, February 11, 1993, and March 9, 1993.

Sutherland, Zena, review of *The Boy Who Could Make Himself Disappear, Bulletin of the Center for Children's Books*, September, 1968, pp. 14-15.

Sutherland, Zena, review of *Chloris and the Freaks, Bulletin of the Center for Children's Books*, April, 1976, p. 131.

Sutherland, Zena, review of *Hey, Dummy, Bulletin of the Center for Children's Books,* June, 1972, p. 162.

■ For More Information See

BOOKS

Contemporary Literary Criticism, Volume 26, Gale, 1983, pp. 348-56.

PERIODICALS

Best Sellers, February, 1980, p. 410.

Booklist, January 1, 1980, p. 662; April 15, 1992, p. 1529.

Bulletin of the Center for Children's Books, January, 1974, p. 84; January, 1978; December, 1978; March, 1979, p. 124; September, 1979, p. 16; May, 1980, pp. 180-81; November, 1980, p. 62; October, 1981, pp. 35-36; January, 1984.

Interracial Books for Children Bulletin, Volume 10, number 7, 1979, p. 15.

Kirkus Reviews, May 15, 1968, p. 556; November 15, 1971, p. 1213; February 15, 1973, p. 188; July 15, 1975, p. 783; February 1, 1980, p. 136; March 1, 1986, pp. 347-48.

New York Times Book Review, September 24, 1961, p. 40; March 1, 1970, p. 45; November 16, 1975, pp. 50, 52; August 10, 1986, p. 23.

School Library Journal, December, 1969, p. 64; November, 1979, p. 92; December, 1980, pp. 63-64, 74.

Voice of Youth Advocates, December, 1981, p. 34.

Wilson Library Bulletin, February, 1981, pp. 454-44.

—Sketch by Kathleen J. Edgar

Sandra Scoppettone

both for *Trying Hard to Hear You;* California Young Readers Medal (high school), California Reading Association, 1979, for *The Late Great Me;* (as Jack Early) Shamus Award, Private Eye Writers of America, and Edgar Allan Poe Award nomination, Mystery Writers of America, both 1985, both for *A Creative Kind of Killer;* Edgar Allan Poe Award nomination, 1986, for *Playing Murder.*

■ Personal

Also writes under pseudonym Jack Early; born June 1, 1936, in Morristown, NJ; daughter of Casimiro Radames and Helen Katherine (Greis) Scoppettone; partner of Linda Crawford (a writer). *Hobbies and other interests:* Old movies, reading, gambling (in moderation), computers and on-line connections with bulletin boards, tennis.

■ Addresses

Home—131 Prince St., New York, NY 10012. *Agent*—Charlotte Sheedy, Charlotte Sheedy Literary Agency, 611 Broadway, New York, NY 10012.

■ Career

Full-time professional writer.

■ Awards, Honors

Eugene O'Neill Memorial Theatre Award, 1972, for *Stuck;* Ludwig Vogelstein Foundation grant, 1974; American Library Association best young adult book citation, 1975, and New Jersey Institute of Technology New Jersey Authors Award, 1976,

■ Writings

PICTURE BOOKS

Suzuki Beane, illustrated by Louise Fitzhugh, Doubleday, 1961.
Bang Bang You're Dead, illustrated by Fitzhugh, Harper, 1968.

YOUNG ADULT NOVELS

Trying Hard to Hear You, Harper, 1974.
The Late Great Me, Putnam, 1976.
Happy Endings Are All Alike, Harper, 1978.
Long Time between Kisses, Harper, 1982.
Playing Murder, Harper, 1985.

ADULT NOVELS

Some Unknown Person, Putnam, 1977.
Such Nice People, Putnam, 1980.
Innocent Bystanders, New American Library, 1983.
Everything You Have Is Mine ("Lauren Laurano" mystery), Little, Brown, 1991.
I'll Be Leaving You Always ("Lauren Laurano" mystery), Little, Brown, 1993.

NOVELS UNDER PSEUDONYM JACK EARLY

A Creative Kind of Killer, F. Watts, 1984.

Razzamatazz, F. Watts, 1985.
Donato and Daughter, Dutton, 1988.

PLAYS

Home Again, Home Again Jiggity Jig, produced at Cubiculo Theatre, 1969.
Something for Kitty Genovese (one-act), performed by Valerie Bettis Repertory Company, 1971.
Stuck, produced at Eugene O'Neill Memorial Theatre, Waterford, CT, 1972, produced at Open Space Theatre, New York City, 1976.

SCREENPLAYS

Scarecrow in a Garden of Cucumbers, Maron-New Line, 1972.
The Inspector of Stairs, Independent, 1975.

TELEPLAYS

Love of Life, Columbia Broadcasting System, Inc. (CBS-TV), 1972.
A Little Bit Like Murder, American Broadcasting Companies, Inc. (ABC-TV), 1973.

OTHER

Scoppettone's manuscripts are housed in the Kerlan Collection at the University of Minnesota.

■ Work in Progress

A third "Lauren Laurano" mystery; a new mystery under the pseudonym Jack Early.

■ Adaptations

The Late Great Me was adapted into a film directed by Anthony Lover, Daniel Wilson Productions, 1982; *Donato and Daughter* was adapted into a television movie starring Charles Bronson and Dana Delany, CBS-TV, 1993.

■ Sidelights

"One thing I would like to say is that I'm a lesbian," proclaims Sandra Scoppettone in an interview for *Authors and Artists for Young Adults* (*AAYA*). "I mean, that should be clear. I also want to say that I've been with the same person for twenty years—I think it's important for people to know that it can be done." Author of both young adult novels that deal with homosexuality, alcoholism, and murder, and adult novels that depict a hallucinatory seventeen-year-old, a single-parent male detective, and a witty lesbian private investigator, Scoppettone has been accused of writing about such controversial topics merely for the money. "But it isn't true," she asserts in *Speaking*

for Ourselves. "The books I've written have been about important issues in my own life or in the lives of people I've known." Among the personal topics covered in Scoppettone's novels are alcoholism, homosexuality, and incest. "I think my childhood traumas had a lot to do with shaping me as a writer," she explains in her *AAYA* interview. Michael Lassell, writing in the *Advocate* in 1991, invited readers to meet Scoppettone, "comfortably ensconced in the SoHo loft she shares with her lover of [twenty] years, writer Linda Crawford, and two bushy felines named Nick and Nora. The award-winning author of [thirteen] novels—including three mysteries written under the pseudonym Jack Early—is 55 but looks 40. She's short and half Italian, a recovering alcoholic with 18 years sobriety, and an out lesbian since 1954."

Growing up in South Orange, New Jersey, Scoppettone knew as early as the age of five that she wanted to be a writer. And right from the start, her parents encouraged this ambition. "They gave me the feeling that I could do this," recalls Scoppettone in her interview. "They certainly encouraged it and said I could do whatever I wanted and were very supportive the whole time." An only child, Scoppettone remembers being both active and reserved, depending on the situation. "When I was with other kids I certainly was active," she observes. "When I would come in after playing I was all alone. My mother was there, and later my father, but there were no other children for me to play with, so I used my imagination a great deal to make up stuff."

One thing that set Scoppettone apart from other children was the overprotectiveness of her parents, especially that of her father. "I wasn't allowed to do a lot of physical stuff that other kids were allowed to do, like riding bikes or going down our hill all the way on a sled. It was hard, so it made me feel a little different." To compensate for these feelings, Scoppettone would escape into her imagination and write stories when she was alone. One of her favorite activities took place at her grandparent's house when she was about five or six and the only grandchild. "It was a fairly big family, and I would get under the table and listen to everything and spy," relates Scoppettone. "I loved to listen and loved to hear adults tell stories and talk. I made up my own stories a lot. I remember playing with marbles, not playing regular marble games, but making a marble a person, giving them a name and moving them around."

Other aspects of her childhood, including grammar school, were also enjoyable for Scoppettone. When she reached seventh grade, however, her feelings about school suddenly changed. "I seemed to have a personality change," she remarks to *AAYA*. "I was a very good little girl up till then, and then I became sort of a bad little girl." Leaving school early at the end of seventh grade when she was diagnosed as having chorea, a disease that required a great deal of rest, Scoppettone returned the next year with a totally different attitude. "I was no longer quiet, I was no longer a goodie two shoes. I had a complete personality change."

From Picture Books to Young Adult Tragedy

After finishing high school, Scoppettone had no interest in attending college; she wanted to move to New York City and write. Her parents supported her in her endeavors, and she took on various jobs within the city. "I really began to support myself with my writing around the age of thirty," observes Scoppettone. Children's author and illustrator Louise Fitzhugh collaborated with Scoppettone on her first published work—the picture book *Suzuki Beane*. "Louise came over one day with all these little drawings, dumped them all over my bed, and said we should do a book," Scoppettone tells *AAYA*. "When she left I started to lay them out. I remember sitting on my bed and putting them around, and then putting them into notebook form. In some places I wrote under her pictures, others I left blank. She then took it back and we sold it practically overnight."

Scoppettone's next book was another picture book with Fitzhugh. In the meantime, she also wrote for other media, including television, film, and stage. "Writing for television, film, or theater is a cooperative thing, and I don't like it much because you usually don't have the final word like you do with books," Scoppettone points out. And because of the lack of control a writer has in these media, she doesn't plan on writing for them again. "I've had productions and it's very exciting to hear your words on one hand. On the other hand, it's horrifying when you know they've skipped three pages of an act and they don't know it. It's a very out of control situation. Something I like about writing books is that you have control."

It was Scoppettone's ability to handle and control a touchy situation that inspired the subject matter for her first young adult novel. "I was living on the North Fork of Long Island where there was a thing called 'Youth on Stage,'" she remembers. "They needed someone to direct the summer musical and I had directed adult things, so I volunteered. There

THE HAUNTING NOVEL OF AN UNFORGETTABLE SUMMER THAT CHANGED THE LIVES OF THREE LOVING FRIENDS.

TRYING HARD TO HEAR YOU
BY SANDRA SCOPPETTONE

This 1974 novel, which won an American Library Association award, tells the story of three friends whose lives are forever changed during one fateful summer.

were two high school boys who were obviously having an affair, and the kids were being awful to them. I stepped in and didn't let all the awful things that happen in the book happen, but that was the basis for *Trying Hard to Hear You.*"

Published in 1974, *Trying Hard to Hear You* tells a similar tale. Set in the summer of 1973 on the North Fork of Long Island, the story is told by sixteen-year-old Camilla Crawford. A summer production of the musical *Anything Goes* is under way, and Camilla and her group of friends are all participating in one way or another. During the course of rehearsals, Camilla falls for one of the actors, Phil Chrystie. The two go out on a couple of dates, but Camilla is confused when Phil asks more than a few questions about her best friend and next-door neighbor Jeff Grathwohl. Things come to a head when Jeff and Phil are caught kissing during a Fourth of July party. The group then proceeds to ostracize the two boys and violence ensues. Breaking under the pressure, Phil decides to "prove" his sexuality with a girl; the two get drunk and are killed in a car crash. "The confrontation between the gentle sincerity of the lovers and the tittering shock of the 'straights' is . . . the most emotionally genuine and moving thing in the book," maintains Annie Gottlieb in the *New York Times Book Review*. A *Booklist* reviewer asserts that "plot threads are credibly interwoven" and "adult as well as teenage characters are well developed and interrelated" in *Trying Hard to Hear You* to create "a teenage story of unusual depth for mature readers."

Controversial Individuality

Scoppettone's next young adult novel, *The Late Great Me*, also has somewhat personal origins. "*The Late Great Me* deals with alcoholism," she tells *AAYA*. "I had done my research because I'm a recovered alcoholic. When I wrote it I was sober, but I have had years of being an active alcoholic. This was not my story, however—I didn't write about myself. Things such as hangovers and blackouts are the same, but this is not my story. I do think I was a teenage alcoholic, though, in the sense that I think I was an alcoholic the first time I picked up a drink. I didn't get sober until I was in my thirties."

Geri Peters, the young alcoholic in *The Late Great Me*, is able to overcome her drinking problem approximately a year after it starts. Considering herself one of the "freaks" in her high school, Geri is thrilled at the beginning of her junior year when Dave Townsend, a handsome new student, picks her to befriend. Her mother, who constantly relives and talks about her "popular" teenage years, desperately wants Geri to fit in and is ecstatic that her daughter has a new friend. The two start dating, and Dave introduces Geri to drinking the first time they go out. As time goes by, Geri's drinking escalates until she has bottles stashed in her school locker and in her closet at home. Nothing can make Geri realize she has a problem, not even the death of Dave's mother— another alcoholic. It is finally one of her teachers, a member of Alcoholics Anonymous (AA) herself, who spots the signs, and Geri grudgingly accepts her help. Scoppettone "has a swift, engaging style but the story is centered on a problem rather than on empathetic characters," asserts a *Publishers Weekly* contributor. Karen McGinley, however,

concludes in *Best Sellers* that "*The Late Great Me* is a book which will make us all more aware of a problem that is growing around us. It will help us to grow in our own awareness and understanding."

Scoppettone deals with another "controversial" issue in *Happy Endings Are All Alike*, a book which has been banned in several areas. "That's the one that got the least attention when I wrote it, the least reviews, the least anything. It sold the least because it's about girls," relates Scoppettone in her *AAYA* interview. The novel, published in 1978, focuses on the lesbian relationship between two teenage girls in a small American town. Jaret and Peggy are spending a loving summer together when Peggy decides to test her sexual orientation by dating a young man. In the meantime, a jealous youth who has been spying on the two girls

A BANTAM STARFIRE BOOK

THE LATE GREAT ME

THE SHATTERING NOVEL BY
SANDRA SCOPPETTONE

"My name is Geri Peters. I'm your everyday average girl next door; an alcoholic at seventeen."

In this award-winning 1976 book, Scoppettone uses her own experiences to chronicle a teenage girl's bout with alcoholism.

savagely beats and rapes Jaret, threatening to reveal her lesbianism if she tells anyone. With the support of her family, Jaret bravely brings charges against the boy.

Linda R. Silver, writing in *School Library Journal*, finds *Happy Endings Are All Alike* to be full of "dimensionless characters, a formless, melodramatic plot, and dialogue that substitutes repetitive jargon for human speech." Although many critics found the rape scene unnecessarily brutal, Lenore Gordon writes in the *Interracial Books for Children Bulletin* that Scoppettone's "intent is not to shock, but to leave the reader with no illusions about the violence inherent in the act." Geraldine DeLuca, writing in the *Lion and the Unicorn*, sees *Happy Endings Are All Alike* as successfully exposing the prejudice against homosexuals and maintains that "it is a book that challenges many of our conventional assumptions about life, particularly the belief that certain patterns lead to happiness and that they are the same for all of us. And it encourages

Scoppettone examines sexual prejudice in this 1978 novel about a lesbian couple.

the individual to stand for what he or she needs and believes."

Long Time between Kisses, Scoppettone's next young adult novel, also touches on the subject of individuality. Billie James, who resides in a loft in New York City's SoHo district, refers to the people in her life as The Mother, The Father, The Organic Woman, and The Bonus Boy. Her divorced parents lead rather unusual lives: her mother is an artist turned carpenter, and her father, who lives with a younger woman, is a failed musician who spends most of his time doing drugs. During the summer of her sixteenth year, Billie, who thinks she has an unremarkable personality, chops off all her brown hair and dyes her new crewcut bright purple. Dumping her boyfriend, she finds herself falling for twenty-one-year-old Mitch, who has recently discovered he has multiple sclerosis. In the meantime, she and her best friend Elissa start taking care of an old man, Captain Natoli, who's been forgotten by his family and is barely surviving. After realizing that Mitch has left behind his family and fiancee because of his disease, Billie does the right thing and tracks them down. In the end, she discovers that she does have quite a remarkable talent—a tremendous capacity to care for other people.

"*Long Time between Kisses* is a refreshing and well-written novel that explores the discovery and change inherent in adolescence," describes Liz Williams in *Young Adult Cooperative Book Review Group of Massachusetts*. Annie Gottlieb, writing in the *New York Times Book Review*, maintains that the emotional aspect of the book is on target, but also believes that "the moralizing has that whiff of condescension; under the hip surface is a sugar pill." Joseph A. Szuhay, on the other hand, writes in *Best Sellers* that *Long Time between Kisses* "is a serious yet humorous presentation of life not too infrequently faced by our youth." And *Voice of Youth Advocates* contributor Jorja Davis concludes: "Wit and humor, and finely drawn characters . . . work together to flesh out this bittersweet identity crisis and first love."

Donning Cloak and Dagger

Scoppettone's young adult novel *Playing Murder* is similar to many of her adult novels: it concerns a murder and the solving of a crime. Anna Parker has just moved to Blue Haven Island, Maine, with her mother and father, her twin brother Bill, and her younger sister. The move was necessary after Bill was caught stealing money from his football team's

A friendly game turns deadly in Scoppettone's 1985 young adult novel.

uniform fund; his parents want to avoid embarrassment and start a new life. Upon arriving in Maine, the entire Parker family starts to work at the restaurant they've bought. The family that previously owned the establishment includes handsome young Kirk Cunningham and his sister and brother, who all continue to work at the restaurant. Despite the fact that she still has a boyfriend, Tony, in her old hometown, Anna falls for Kirk and begins to see him even though he has a girlfriend himself. The action reaches a turning point one night when the group is playing an after dark game called "Murder," and Kirk, who is playing the "victim," is actually killed. In an attempt to clear her brother, who's been arrested for the crime, Anna learns that Kirk wasn't what he appeared to be and eventually discovers the true murderer.

Finding "several . . . questionable bits in the whodunit," a *Publishers Weekly* reviewer, however, goes on to add that *Playing Murder* "is nevertheless fine escape reading." Susan Levine, writing in

Voice of Youth Advocates, finds Anna's narrative to be a bit repetitive at times, but nonetheless asserts that "the book is interesting" and that "its suspense holds it together well." And a *Bulletin of the Center for Children's Books* contributor points out that "the plotting and the plethora of suspects are somewhat contrived," but concludes that *Playing Murder* "has the sort of danger and suspense that appeal to thriller fans, and it paints a devastating picture of the murder victim."

In addition to her young adult novels, Scoppettone has written several novels for adults, under both her own name and the pseudonym Jack Early. The first, written under her own name, combines fact with fiction in a tale of sex and scandal. *Some Unknown Person* concerns the events leading up to and surrounding the actual death of twenty-five-year-old playgirl Starr Faithfull. A drug addict and alcoholic, Faithfull had been seduced at the age of eleven by her forty-five-year-old uncle—Andrew J. Peters, then Mayor of Boston. The details of their nine-year affair made the Faithfull murder case infamous. The autopsy results pointed to drowning, but Faithfull was a champion swimmer, and the family insisted that she was murdered even after suicide notes were found. The Faithfull case was never actually solved. "Scoppettone has blended fact and fiction in this novel, creating her own conjecture of who the 'Unknown Person' responsible for Starr Faithfull's death might be," notes a *New York Times Book Review* contributor. The book introduces most of the people who were important in Faithfull's life, alternating back and forth in time between 1906 and 1977. *Some Unknown Person*, the reviewer concludes, "is an entertaining [and] interesting idea presented in an interesting way."

Sticking with the subject of murder, Scoppettone published *Such Nice People* in 1980. The Nashes, who on the surface seem to be a normal suburban family, are really plagued by several problems. Cole, the father, is hoping to disappear after the Christmas holiday to start a new life alone. Anne, the mother, is wrapped up in a new affair and plans to divorce Cole after the holidays. Kit, the oldest daughter, is away at college and seeing a therapist to work through the aftermath of several love affairs. Sara, the youngest daughter, is fat and unhappy. Steven, one of the younger sons, constantly smokes pot. And Tom, the oldest of the boys, is delusionary and intent on following the instructions of his imaginary leader SOLA, who has told him to kill all the members of his family except for Kit (she will be the Duchess in the new order).

On the appointed day, Tom follows through with SOLA's orders, killing everyone in his family except for his brother Max, who manages to escape, and Kit, who is late getting home because of a flat tire. Tom himself is then killed by his mother's lover, who senses that something is wrong and rushes over to the house.

Many critics found the violence that fills *Such Nice People* to be sensationalistic and unnecessary. "If this were straightforward reportage, then there might be some reason for all the lurid bloodletting," relates a *Publishers Weekly* contributor, adding that as a novel all it amounts to is "ugly and pointless ... occult fiction at its worst." *Such Nice People* provides "enough family pathology to keep a Psych. 101 class busy all semester—but the clinical potpourri doesn't add up, leaving this an unconvincing and unimaginative sick-a-thon that's ultimately just exploitational and more than a little loathsome," maintains a *Kirkus Reviews* contributor. Michele M. Leber, writing in *Library Journal*, concludes: "Scoppettone's readable enough style and canny handling of adolescent characters are not reasons enough to buy this."

Jack Early Mysteriously Appears

Scoppettone next turned to detective and mystery writing for adults under the pseudonym Jack Early. "One day this voice came to me in first person male, and I thought, 'This is a private eye and his name is Fortune Fanelli,'" she explains in her *AAYA* interview. "He started talking to me. This sounds crazy, but that's what happened. I started writing in that voice and it was a forty-two-year-old man and in first person. I thought it would be very jarring to put a woman's name on the book, so I just picked the name Jack Early. Jack got prizes and all kinds of reviews that Sandra had never gotten, and so I just sort of stuck with the name for a while. It was very nice to be anonymous—people didn't know until the third book who Jack Early was."

Scoppettone's first Jack Early book, *A Creative Kind of Killer,* was published in 1984 to favorable reviews. The book features Fortune Fanelli, an ex-cop and long-divorced single parent whose good investments have enabled him to become a part-time private detective. When the body of teenager Jennifer Baker is found in New York's SoHo district, Fanelli is hired by her uncle to find both Baker's killer and her younger runaway brother. During the investigation Fanelli is threatened, another body is found, and a kiddie porn ring is uncovered. "Early has filled his book with well-drawn characters and believable dialogue," writes a *Library Journal* contributor. And *Washington Post Book World* reviewer Jean M. White concludes that *A Creative Kind of Killer* is "a solid, well-crafted mystery, although not without flaws. But Fortune himself is a refreshingly different narrator-shamus."

Early's next novel, *Razzamatazz,* concerns a homicide in peaceful Seaville, Long Island. The crime is especially painful for Colin Maguire, who works for the *Seaville Gazette.* Just a few years earlier, his wife and children were murdered in their Chicago home while he was out drinking—the crime was never solved. As more corpses begin to appear, Colin and the police chief Waldo Hallock search for leads. In the meantime, the *Gazette*'s competition runs a story which insinuates that Colin killed his family, and he is threatened by an angry mob of citizens who believe him to be the Seaville killer. He and Hallock flee to look for Annie (Colin's new lover), who has been abducted by the killer. "Crisp writing plus abundant surprises and quaint community tidbits from Colin's 'Looking Back' column will keep readers riveted until the last page," observes a *Publishers Weekly* contributor. Newgate Callendar, writing in the *New York Times Book Review,* similarly observes that *Razzamatazz* "is one of those down-to-the-wire stories, very well written, guaranteed to keep you flipping the pages."

Scoppettone's third Early novel was made into a television movie starring Charles Bronson and Dana Delany. *Donato and Daughter* concerns both the alienated members of the Donato family and a psychopath on the loose in New York City who is killing nuns. Lt. Dina Donato is in charge of the detective team, and appoints Sgt. Mike Donato, her father, as her partner, despite the difficulties the two have been having relating to each other since her brother's suicide. "Events move at a breakneck pace," relates a *Publishers Weekly* contributor, adding that the "suspense is unremitting" and that "numerous side plots and intriguing characters enliven" *Donato and Daughter.*

Private Eye Laurano Leaps into Action

"I had three years after I finished *Donato and Daughter* where I couldn't write at all," reveals Scoppettone in her *AAYA* interview. "When I was able to write again it was under my own name and it was *Everything You Have Is Mine.*" The first installment of a three book contract, *Everything*

You Have Is Mine introduces the character Lauren Laurano and is "the first book I've ever written directly about myself," adds Scoppettone. "Meet Lauren Laurano," invites Lassell. "She's short, Italian, and 42 (although she looks younger). She's a witty, articulate feminist, a lesbian chocoholic who gets queasy at the sight of blood. She's a wise-cracking sweetheart of a pistol-packing private eye and the protagonist of one of the summer's hottest novels."

Published in 1991, *Everything You Have Is Mine* details Laurano's attempts to solve a rape case that quickly turns into a murder investigation. Laurano resides in Greenwich Village with her long-time lover Kip, a psychologist who has a large family that is very accepting of the couple's relationship. The young victim, who is date-raped and then murdered a short time later, is called Lake Huron and was born during the 1960s to a very complicated family. To find first the rapist and then the murderer, Laurano must overcome her fear of computers and untangle Huron's family ties from amid lies that have been told over the years. Jean M. White, writing in the *Washington Post Book World*, finds the plot of *Everything You Have Is Mine* to be overcomplicated, but concedes that Scoppettone "is a sharply observant writer and captures the flavor of the Greenwich Village scene with its quirky characters and sassy-smart talk." A *Publishers Weekly* contributor concludes that "a lively pace, convincing characterization, colorful scene setting and sensitive observations about complications among families ordinary and unusual far outweigh the overwrought elements of the plot; readers will want to follow Lauren on her next case."

The next novel featuring Lauren Laurano, *I'll Be Leaving You Always*, has the detective dealing with the death of a close friend and solving the murder at the same time. Scoppettone explains to *AAYA* that she hopes that the books featuring Laurano will help women "feel prouder and have more self-esteem as lesbians. I think it's already happening. *Everything You Have Is Mine* is the first mainstream lesbian private eye book and it took a courageous publisher to print it. I got my first daily *New York Times* review for that book—I don't know if you know what that means. After writing for all these years, to finally be reviewed in the daily *Times* was really exciting. I had gotten other reviews in the Sunday *Times*, but that's not quite as prestigious. It was this book, and it was reviewed very well without making a big number about the lesbianism

either. It is what it is and that's the way the reviewer took it and it was really great."

Although she has written for both young adult and adult audiences, Scoppettone now chooses to write for the older group. "I do prefer writing for adults now only because I feel I've said everything I have to say to young adults," she tells *AAYA*. "However, if something should come to mind that I feel would be best in that form I would do it. I think my young adult books have been fairly successful because I don't write down, I pretty much write the same." The several young adult novels that Scoppettone has written deal with issues not normally presented to teens and have had a greater impact on them because of it. "My young adult books have had a tremendous effect. I've known people who have gotten sober after reading *The Late Great Me*; it

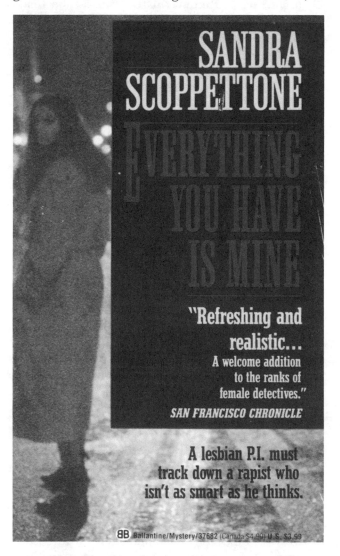

Scoppettone's 1991 adult mystery introduces readers to the character of Lauren Laurano, a witty private eye on the trail of a rapist.

ticked off something in their head. Certainly the gay and lesbian books have affected people's lives. I wish that I'd had such books when I was a kid. What I really hoped was that the books would let them know it was okay. It was amazing, because when I was doing readings for *Everything You Have Is Mine* a number of people came up to me and said, 'I was a fan of yours when I was a little girl and your books changed my life.' It's very thrilling. So I guess I hope these books change people's lives in a positive way."

■ Works Cited

Callendar, Newgate, "Crime," *New York Times Book Review*, October 13, 1985, p. 29.

Review of *A Creative Kind of Killer, Library Journal*, April 1, 1984, p. 736.

Davis, Jorja, review of *Long Time between Kisses, Voice of Youth Advocates*, August, 1982, p. 37.

DeLuca, Geraldine, "Taking True Risks: Controversial Issues in New Young Adult Novels," *Lion and the Unicorn*, winter, 1979-80, pp. 125-48.

Review of *Donato and Daughter, Publishers Weekly*, January 15, 1988, p. 79.

Review of *Everything You Have Is Mine, Publishers Weekly*, February 22, 1991, p. 213.

Gordon, Lenore, review of *Happy Endings Are All Alike, Interracial Books for Children Bulletin*, Volume 10, number 6, 1979, p. 16.

Gottlieb, Annie, review of *Trying Hard to Hear You, New York Times Book Review*, January 12, 1975, p. 8.

Gottlieb, Annie, "Young but Not Innocent," *New York Times Book Review*, April 25, 1982, p. 44.

Lassell, Michael, "Murder, She Writes," *Advocate*, July 2, 1991, p. 93.

Review of *The Late Great Me, Publishers Weekly*, November 10, 1975, p. 47.

Leber, Michele M., review of *Such Nice People, Library Journal*, April 15, 1980, p. 1005.

Levine, Susan, review of *Playing Murder, Voice of Youth Advocates*, June, 1985, p. 135.

McGinley, Karen, review of *The Late Great Me, Best Sellers*, May, 1976, p. 40.

Review of *Playing Murder, Bulletin of the Center for Children's Books*, May, 1985.

Review of *Playing Murder, Publishers Weekly*, August 16, 1985, p. 71.

Review of *Razzamatazz, Publishers Weekly*, March 22, 1985, p. 54.

Scoppettone, Sandra, in an essay for *Speaking for Ourselves*, compiled and edited by Donald R. Gallo, National Council of Teachers of English, 1990, pp. 186-87.

Scoppettone, Sandra, in an interview with Susan M. Reicha for *Authors and Artists for Young Adults*, January 14, 1993.

Silver, Linda R., review of *Happy Endings Are All Alike, School Library Journal*, February, 1979, p. 65.

Review of *Some Unknown Person, New York Times Book Review*, September 25, 1977, p. 22.

Review of *Such Nice People, Kirkus Reviews*, March 1, 1980, p. 319.

Review of *Such Nice People, Publishers Weekly*, February 22, 1980, p. 92.

Szuhay, Joseph A., review of *Long Time between Kisses, Best Sellers*, June, 1982, p. 123.

Review of *Trying Hard to Hear You, Booklist*, November 15, 1974, p. 340.

White, Jean M., review of *A Creative Kind of Killer, Washington Post Book World*, May 20, 1984, pp. 8-9.

White, Jean M., review of *Everything You Have Is Mine, Washington Post Book World*, April 21, 1991, p. 10.

Williams, Liz, review of *Long Time between Kisses, Young Adult Cooperative Book Review Group of Massachusetts*, April, 1982, pp. 57-58.

■ For More Information See

BOOKS

Contemporary Literary Criticism, Volume 26, Gale, 1983.

PERIODICALS

English Journal, September, 1975, pp. 80-83.

Horn Book, August, 1982, pp. 417-18.

Kirkus Reviews, October 15, 1974, p. 1110; November 15, 1975, p. 1304; September 15, 1978, p. 1022.

Library Journal, September 15, 1974, pp. 2297-98; May 1, 1985, p. 81.

New York Times Book Review, February 22, 1976, p. 38; April 14, 1991, p. 25.

Publishers Weekly, November 10, 1975, p. 47; June 20, 1977, p. 66; July 24, 1978, p. 100; December 3, 1982, p. 50; February 17, 1984, p. 73.

School Library Journal, January, 1976, p. 58; May, 1980, p. 92.

Village Voice, December 16, 1974, pp. 51-52.

Wilson Library Bulletin, December, 1978, p. 341.

—*Sketch by Susan M. Reicha*

Jerry Seinfeld

■ Personal

Born April 29, 1954, in Brooklyn, NY; son of Kalman (in business) and Betty Seinfeld. *Education:* Queens College, graduated with degree in communications and theater, 1976. *Hobbies and other interests:* Baseball, sports cars.

■ Addresses

Home—Los Angeles, CA; and New York, NY. *Office*—c/o Lori Jonas, Jonas Public Relations, Inc., 417 South Beverly Dr., Suite 201, Beverly Hills, CA 90212.

■ Career

Stand-up comedian, actor, and screenwriter. Worked variously as a light bulb salesman, a waiter, and a jewelry street vendor. Creator, with Larry David, *Seinfeld*, National Broadcasting Company, Inc. (NBC-TV), 1989; appears as Jerry Seinfeld, and producer, *Seinfeld*, NBC-TV, 1989—. Tours frequently as a stand-up comic. Made regular appearances on *The Tonight Show* and *Late Night with David Letterman.* Appeared briefly as the Governor's joke writer, *Benson,*

American Broadcasting Companies, Inc. (ABC-TV), 1980. Appeared in a number of television specials, including *The Tonight Show Starring Johnny Carson 19th Anniversary Special,* NBC-TV, 1981; *Tonight Show Starring Johnny Carson 24th Anniversary,* NBC-TV, 1986; *Disneyland's Summer Vacation Party,* NBC-TV, 1986; "Rodney Dangerfield—It's Not Easy Bein' Me," *On Location,* HBO, 1986; "Jerry Seinfeld—Stand-Up Confidential," *On Location,* HBO, 1987; *An All-Star Celebration: The '88 Vote,* ABC-TV, 1988; *Late Night with David Letterman Seventh Anniversary Show,* NBC-TV, 1989; "Montreal International Comedy Festival," *HBO Comedy Hour,* HBO, 1989; *Night of 100 Stars III,* NBC-TV, 1990; *Funny Business with Charlie Chase II,* The Nashville Network, 1990; *The 4th Annual American Comedy Awards,* ABC-TV, 1990; *42nd Annual Primetime Emmy Awards Presentation,* Fox, 1990; *Spy Magazine Presents How to Be Famous,* NBC-TV, 1990; *The Second Annual Aspen Comedy Festival,* Showtime, 1990; *The 43rd Annual Primetime Emmy Awards Presentation,* Fox, 1991; and *Today at 40,* NBC-TV, 1992. Also appeared on stage in *Night of 100 Stars III,* Radio City Music Hall, New York City, 1990.

■ Awards, Honors

American Comedy Award, funniest male comedy club stand-up, 1988; Clio Award, best announcer radio commercial, 1988; Emmy Award nomination, outstanding writing in a comedy series, 1991, best actor in a comedy series, 1992, and American Comedy Award, funniest actor in a television series, 1992 and 1993, all for *Seinfeld.*

■ Writings

"Jerry Seinfeld—Stand-Up Confidential," *On Location* (television special), HBO, 1987.
(With others) *Seinfeld* (television series), NBC-TV, 1989—.

Also author of stand-up routines.

■ Adaptations

Seinfeld greeting cards, T-shirts, mugs, buttons, and wall calendars are available.

■ Work in Progress

A book of wit and widsom for Bantam to be published September, 1993.

■ Sidelights

Double parked on the streets of New York, George Costanza, a neurotic, short, balding man, looks on incredulously as his current girlfriend, Allison, screams, "I don't want to live. I don't want to live!" "Because of *me*?," he skeptically asks. "You must be joking. Who wouldn't want to live because of me? I'm nothing." "No, you're something," Allison assures him. "You can do better than me," continues George. "You could throw a dart out the window and hit someone better than me. I'm no good." "You're good. You're good," Allison says passionately. "I'm bad. I'm bad," counters George, shaking his head. "You're killing me!" screams Allison violently.

The scene shifts to the local coffee shop. George is sitting in one of the fake leather booths with Elaine Benes, a sarcastic beauty who's in publishing. Jerry Seinfeld, a stand-up comic whose jeans and white tennis shoes are always immaculately clean, is on the other side of the restaurant talking on the telephone. "So what could I do?," George asks Elaine. "I couldn't go through with it. She threatened to kill herself." "Over *you*?," questions Elaine, desperately trying not to laugh. "Yes. Why? Is that so inconceivable?," asks George indignantly. "Well . . .," laughs Elaine. The camera moves across the room to Jerry, who's talking into the phone. "Yeah, I'm trying to get in touch with Sharon Leonard. She works for the NYU paper. This is Jerry Seinfeld. She was supposed to meet me at a coffee shop to do an interview."

Back at the booth, Elaine glances to see if Jerry is coming back and leans across to George: "What are you going to get Jerry for his birthday?" "I got him a great gift," replies George smugly. "Really,

what?," asks Elaine. "I got two tickets to see *Guys and Dolls*," declares George, smiling happily. "That is a *good* gift. Maybe he'll take me," says Elaine hopefully. "No, I, um, I'm gonna go with him," asserts George a little unsurely. "What did you get?" Jerry starts walking back to the table as Elaine replies, "I got him a two-line phone." Reaching the booth, Jerry throws his arms up in the air and says, "Unbelievable. She's not there." He sits down next to George, who asks, "What paper does she write for?" "She writes for the NYU school newspaper," replies Jerry a little impatiently. "She's a grad student in journalism. Never been to a comedy club. Never even seen me—has no idea who I am." "Never even seen you?," asks Elaine. Jerry shakes his head, taking a drink of his coffee. "Gotta kind of envy that," says Elaine facetiously. "You know," responds Jerry, "you've been developing quite the acid tongue lately." "Really?," asks Elaine happily, a huge grin engulfing her face. "Hey," she continues, "who do you think is the most unattractive world leader?" "Living or all time?," asks Jerry. "All time," says Elaine. "Well, if it's all time, then there's no contest," contends Jerry. "It begins and ends with Brezhnev." Elaine looks up at the ceiling deep in thought, smacks her lips, and retorts, "I don't know. You ever get a good look at de Gaulle?" Unable to keep quiet, George offers his opinion: "Lyndon Johnson was uglier than de Gaulle." Elaine points at George, "I got news for you. Golda Meir could make 'em all run up a tree." "Golda Meir," agrees Jerry, pointing at Elaine. "Good one."

At this point, Elaine realizes that the two young women in the booth behind Jerry and George are eavesdropping, and she decides to give them a show. Speaking in a loud voice, Elaine proceeds to tell George and Jerry that they should really come out of the closet and be open homosexuals. George plays along with the game, but Jerry is disgusted by the whole thing. It is only later that he discovers that Sharon Leonard, the reporter, was one of the young women listening to their conversation. Remembering Jerry and George from the restaurant, Sharon includes a discussion of their "relationship" in her article, which takes on a snowball effect when the Associated Press picks up the story. George and Jerry spend the remainder of the episode trying to make their friends and families believe that they are in fact heterosexual.

The four principal characters of *Seinfeld*—from left to right: Jerry, Julia Louis-Dreyfus as Elaine, Michael Richards as Kramer, and Jason Alexander as George.

Talk, Chatter, and Gab

So goes another episode of *Seinfeld*, the popular NBC sitcom that views the world a little differently than most. The show centers on the days and nights of a stand-up comedian, Jerry Seinfeld, and the things that happen in his everyday life. He then works these events and conversations into his routines, which are shown at the beginning and the end of each episode. Basically, Seinfeld plays himself. "*Seinfeld* defines itself best by what it doesn't do," maintains Richard Panek in *Mirabella*. "The dialogue doesn't follow the typical setup-and-punchline formula of the typical sitcom. The acting doesn't follow the broad-gesture-and-bombast technique of the typical sitcom. And the sensibility doesn't follow any sitcom, period." Chris Smith, writing in *New York*, points out that "the cast of *Seinfeld* is getting the cranky rhythms of New York just right. . . . Most TV shows would try to conjure New York atmosphere by using zany dese-and-dose accents. *Seinfeld*, set in a gray prewar apartment on West 81st Street, has got the *attitude* down: Jerry and his pals obsess comically over the tiny annoyances and dramas of urban life, circa [1993]—stuff like standing in bank lines or hassling with the dry cleaner." Smith also observes that "*Seinfeld* doesn't feel like sitcom television; it feels more like a conversation with your funniest friends."

It is Seinfeld's background as a stand-up comedian, as well as that of the show's co-creator, Larry David, that sets *Seinfeld* apart from other sitcoms, which tend to be more formula driven. Growing up in Massapequa, Long Island, Seinfeld was not the member of the family that earned the most laughs, though—it was his father. "My dad was very funny," recalls Seinfeld in an interview with Mark

Goodman and Lorenzo Benet for *People*. "He turned me on that it's fun to be funny. That's really why I do it." As far as childhoods are concerned, Seinfeld's was a pretty mild one. "His was a Long Island life, a quiet suburban existence with happy parents and happy children," describes Stephen Randall in *Playboy*. "The only unusual aspect of it was the fact that both parents had been raised without parents of their own, which gave them an independence they passed on to their two kids."

This independence was evident in Seinfeld at an early age; he got things the way he wanted them, or he wouldn't take them at all. "As family lore has it," relates Jerry Lazar in *Us*, "on Seinfeld's third birthday, he wanted not just a slice of birthday cake but the whole thing. When he was refused, he opted to eat no cake at all rather than back down on his demand." Seinfeld's older sister, Carolyn Liebling, similarly observes in a *GQ* interview with Alan Richman: "He had a very ordinary childhood, but he was very driven. If he wanted a toy, he'd sit at the table crying or arguing or carrying on. He'd obsess about things like that." Seinfeld's main obsession as a child, however, was television. "Jerry was *chained* to the television," complains his mother, Betty, in her interview with Randall. "At one point, I had to get rid of it. I couldn't stand it." This didn't solve the addiction, though. Seinfeld "simply went next door to the neighbors' to get his fix," explains Randall. "Looking back, one realizes that it wasn't wasted time. He talks in TV metaphors, makes jokes about both old and new TV shows and commercials and still harbors a desire to grow up to be Bud on *Flipper*." Seinfeld tells Randall: "I swear to God, I've learned most of what I know about life from TV."

Around the age of thirteen or fourteen, Seinfeld started taping interviews that he conducted with his pet parakeet. This experience, along with watching comedians on television, prompted Seinfeld to choose his career aspiration at an early age. As a teenager, though, he was not very sociable or overly popular. "When you retreat from contact with other kids, your only playground left is your own mind," Seinfeld explains in his interview with Richman. "You start exploring your own ability to entertain yourself." So Seinfeld became the type of kid who fell somewhere between obnoxious and funny. He wouldn't hang out and smoke with the other guys in school, but he would pass notes in class just to get a laugh.

The cast of *Seinfeld* on the diner set, one of the central settings for the show.

Minimal Beginnings

Graduating from Queens College in 1976 with a double major in theater and communication arts, Seinfeld immediately began his quest for a career as a stand-up comedian; his first night out was not very promising, however. "July 1976. Jerry Seinfeld takes the stage at Catch A Rising Star, the storied New York comedy club," describes Steven Rea in *Entertainment Weekly*. "He clears his throat, mumbles hello, and launches into a carefully honed 15-minute act. The launch is aborted. He freezes." Recalling his first performance, Seinfeld tells Rea, "I was only able to remember the subjects I wanted to talk about. So I stood up there and went, 'The beach ... Driving ... Your Parents. ...' I did that for about a minute and a half and then just left." The performance went over better than expected. "They thought that was what I meant to do," adds Seinfeld.

This rocky beginning didn't discourage Seinfeld. In fact, he reveals in his interview with Barbara Walters for *The Barbara Walters Special* that the anxiety and uncertainty of stand-up fascinate him. "I'm really attracted to tension, you know. Maybe that's one of the reasons I became a stand-up comedian. When you walk on that stage there is a palpable tension, and if you can diffuse it that's a wonderful release." Seinfeld soon learned to do just that through tireless hard work, and eventually became a regular at Catch A Rising Star, the Improv, and the Comic Strip. "There was no work anywhere else," remarks Seinfeld in an interview with Glenn Collins for the *New York Times*. "So we saw everyone, every night. We did a lot of hanging out—from, say, 9 to 1 or 2 A.M. at the clubs, and then in the coffee shop till 3 or 4.... I took no more than a day off. Four years of pretty much working for free, picking up $30 and $50 dollar gigs to support yourself. I think it takes five years just to learn how to express yourself, to know what to say."

In order to support himself while he was learning and perfecting the craft of stand-up, Seinfeld worked at a variety of part-time jobs. He sold light bulbs over the telephone, recounting in his interview with Richman that it was a "tough job. There's not many people sitting home in the dark going, 'I can't hold out much longer.'" Seinfeld also worked the streets, selling costume jewelry in front of Bloomingdales—his cart even had wheels for quick escapes from the police. "Running from the police on the streets of Manhattan—this is a parents' dream come true," he assures Richman. After putting in four years on the New York circuit, Seinfeld had twenty-five minutes of solid material and decided to make the big move to Los Angeles.

Although he moved to Los Angeles to make a name for himself as a stand-up comedian, Seinfeld's career took a brief detour into the world of television sitcoms shortly after his arrival. Cast as the governor's joke writer on the ABC comedy *Benson* in 1980, his part ended up lasting for only a few episodes. "The day the show was supposed to start shooting again after the break, I flew in from New York and showed up at the studio," explains Seinfeld in an interview with Stewart Weiner for *TV Guide*. "I sat down at the table to read the script, but there was no script and no chair for me. Then the assistant director called me aside to tell me that they forgot to tell me I wasn't on the show anymore." The whole experience left Seinfeld feeling annoyed, mostly because he'd wasted his time on television shows when he should have stuck to his stand-up work. "Honing his mind with new comic routines and his body with yoga, he set out to become the consummate comic," relates Richman. "I wanted to wind up like George Burns, but with a little more spinal flexibility," explains Seinfeld to Richman.

Seinfeld's big break as a stand-up comedian came about a year after his *Benson* experience—he appeared on *The Tonight Show*. "I remember the date, May 7, 1981," recalls Seinfeld in his *New York Times* interview. "Every comedian knows that date—their own, I mean. So, here I had five years of going out every night and developing my act, and I was going to take all the chips I'd developed and put them into the center of the table on one five-minute bit." His act was a success: "Suddenly I was lifted from the pack, in L.A." Since then, Seinfeld has appeared on the show over twenty times, as well as being a regular on *Late Night with David Letterman*. Throughout the early 1980s, stand-up was all Seinfeld did—he was interested in neither television nor movies. "He traveled across America with his yellow legal pad and his No. 2

pencils, always writing, picking up nothing in the way of residuals except jet lag," relates Richman. "He believed that he was suffering for his craft, until one day in the late Eighties, in Boston's Logan Airport, when he had what might be called a financial epiphany." Seinfeld recounts the revelation: "I had this job in Boston at a college. I landed, they didn't pick me up, and I'm waiting at the airport, like, three hours. I'm really getting pissed off, and I'm thinking, The hell with it, I'm getting on a plane, going back to New York, screw them, I'm not doing the show. What do they expect me to do, get a rental car, pay for it? Then I looked in my book and I realized I was making, like, $17,000 for this. I had gone from a $1,500 comic to a $15,000 comic without noticing. I go, Wait a minute. I can afford a rental car."

A Show about Nothing

By the time 1989 rolled around, Seinfeld was up to over three hundred appearances a year; television seemed like the last thing he would do, so he did it. NBC and Castle Rock Entertainment approached him about doing a special, and Seinfeld went to his friend and fellow stand-up comedian Larry David for help. The two spent an evening at the Westway

Elaine helps an insecure George cheat on a test in another humorous, though characteristically pointless, episode from *Seinfeld*.

Diner on Ninth Avenue coming up with and discussing ideas. Seinfeld recollects the conversation in his interview with Smith. "The No. 1 question when you're a stand up comedian, is where do you get your material." David replied with: "That's what the show should be. How comedians come up with their material." Seinfeld's answer: "They do this. They hang around with their friends." NBC liked the idea so much that they wanted *Seinfeld* as a series.

"Seinfeld and David structured the show to take advantage of Seinfeld's talent for conversational humor—and not stretch his meager abilities as an actor," asserts Smith. "Seinfeld would play himself, a 37-year-old stand-up comic whose emotional age is holding steady at 25, endearingly immature yet smart. You know the type: the kind of guy who pulls his turtleneck up over his nose, turns around, and says slyly, 'Bazooka Joe.'... Most of the time, TV Jerry would hang out in a Greek coffee shop or in his living room yapping with his buddies." Jerry's main buddy would be George, played by Jason Alexander. Modeled after Larry David, George would be a balding, brooding, neurotic nerd who couldn't keep a girlfriend or a job. "My relationship with George is the glue of the show," points out Seinfeld in his *New York* interview. "Our conversation is basically the conversation between me and Larry. Two idiots trying to figure out the world."

Two more characters were added to round out the main cast of *Seinfeld.* Michael Richards, a comedian with Eraserhead-type hair who slides in and out of rooms as if he's on skates, plays Jerry's goofball neighbor Kramer. And finally, former *Saturday Night Live* player Julia Louis-Dreyfus was cast as Elaine, Jerry's hip ex-girlfriend. "We needed some estrogen," Seinfeld explains in his *New York* interview. "It was getting to be too much of a guy show." During *Seinfeld*'s initial run, NBC moved the show around frequently, yet it was still able to build up somewhat of a "cult" audience. And since 1990 this audience has grown considerably, consisting of the advertising world's most coveted group—eighteen to thirty-four-year-olds.

Seinfeld is "micro-concept TV," observes Seinfeld in his interview with Weiner, who adds: "It's long bank lines, subway muggings, missing rent-a-car reservations, rude waiters. Sneezing is good. No cute kids, no morals tacked onto the end." The most important aspect of *Seinfeld* is the conversation: "It was conceived as a show about conversation," points out Seinfeld in his interview with Rea. "The stories are incidental to us. We're more interested in the interplay of the dialogue." Consequently, many *Seinfeld* episodes appear to have no plot. One show has Jerry, George, Elaine, and Kramer looking for their car in a shopping mall parking garage. Another begins with the first three waiting for a table in a Chinese restaurant and ends with them still waiting. More recent episodes incorporate elements of satire. In an hour-long show, Jerry meets New York Met player Keith Hernandez, who subsequently starts dating Elaine. Kramer, and his pal Newman, hold a grudge against Hernandez because they think he spit at them after one of the baseball games they attended. In a classic scene, Jerry reenacts the spitting incident, mirroring a sequence in the popular movie *JFK*.

Will the Real Seinfeld Please Stand Up?

A series of episodes run during the 1992-93 season continue along the same vein, blurring the line between reality and fiction even further. Jerry is approached after one of his stand-up performances by a couple of NBC executives, who ask him if he's interested in doing a show for them. He and George then come up with the idea for the show—it will be about "nothing," with characters modeled after Jerry, George, Elaine, and Kramer. The executives don't go for the idea, though, and the show ends up being about a guy sentenced to be a butler because he was in a car accident and had no insurance—typical sitcom fare, and everything that *Seinfeld* is not.

"*Seinfeld* episodes are loosely structured, with the anecdotal, stream-of-consciousness style of monologue material," describes Richard Zoglin in *Time*, adding: "Seinfeld seems totally at ease as a sitcom leading man, all gawky insouciance and whiny sarcasm." Mike Duffy, writing in the *Detroit Free Press*, has only praise for the show: "Taking ordinary, everyday situations and embarrassing moments of modern life, *Seinfeld* routinely turns them inside out—and then transforms them into sublimely inventive, nontraditional TV comedy." And John J. O'Connor asserts in the *New York Times* that *Seinfeld* is "a brilliant riff on contemporary anxieties and foibles of the unmistakably urban persuasion. Nothing never had it so good."

One of the main things that sets *Seinfeld* apart from other sitcoms is that its star is not really acting—that's the "real" Seinfeld up there. "That's me up there every week," reveals Seinfeld in his *New York* interview. "I just do what I'd do in real life." Many of the conversations on the show are actual conversations between Seinfeld and David, and everything that happens to the "real" Seinfeld, such as getting a television series at NBC, also happens to the "TV" Seinfeld. "I'm the guy. I am the guy," he asserts when Walters asks him the differences between himself and the character he "plays" on television. "First of all, I would say we look a lot alike.... It's a strange thing to be that public, I mean, people really know me now. I can't act. That's it, you know."

Seinfeld never expected the show to be as successful as it is. "We figured we'd do six shows and that would be it," he relates in his interview with Smith. "We wanted to be a legend, the show they *should* have left on. People would say, 'Boy, did you guys get screwed.'" Despite his television achievements, however, Seinfeld will always consider himself a stand-up comedian. Back in 1990, before he achieved "star" status, Seinfeld revealed his thoughts on this subject in his interview with Randall: "I really feel the key to having a successful career in comedy is never taking the bait of stardom per se. If you think you're a star, you're not a comedian anymore, because a comedian is one of us. Anyway, being a stand-up is a grimy gig. A big star—well, short of an Eddie Murphy—you get up there and the audience will give you a free ride for five, maybe ten minutes. That's it. If you're not funny that night, I don't care how famous you are. It doesn't matter. As long as I'm doing my stand-up, the audience will keep me in my place. It keeps me from being a show-business asshole. Stardom can exist on its own, but laughs do not."

Still holding true to this belief, Seinfeld seeks out comedy venues to try out his new ideas for the show or for a routine. "Two or three times a week I'll go around to a local club and I'll just go on stage and work on some things," he explains to Walters. "I'm having an affair with these people and it's very intimate, and it's not like anything else. They tell me things about myself, [like] if I'm getting a little too big a head. If I'm too confident the audience picks it up and I can feel it in the laughs." Seinfeld goes on to reveal in his *TV Guide* interview that "being on TV is not my first love. I'm a stand-up comedian, first and foremost. I'm obsessed with the mechanism of comedy; it's unconquerable, dark, and mystical. A sitcom could never give me that."

What *Seinfeld* has given its star is fame, and with the fame comes a loss of privacy. Stories of Seinfeld's neatness and need for control and perfection run rampant. He owns over twenty pairs of Nike Air sneakers, giving them away to charity as soon as they get a smudge on them. If someone moves something in his apartment or his house and puts it back exactly where it was, he can still tell it's been moved. And as soon as he finishes eating something, he flosses. "Seinfeld's spotless Porsche Carrera 4 is a four-wheel-drive vehicle capable of doing 150 mph on wet pavement in a city where it never rains," describes Richman. "His spotless Manhattan apartment, which he likens to Superman's Arctic lair, is gray and chrome, filled with highly polished German and Italian fixtures, the latest in post-Axis decor. The kitchen cabinets seem constructed of titanium. The minute he walks in, having been away for a few months, he adjusts the clock. This is only a sampling. He insists that everything in his life be spotless, including himself."

Seinfeld views his sudden and overwhelming fame as being really "out of hand. People are interested in me now way beyond what's appropriate," he contends on *The Barbara Walters Special*. "It's very odd, very curious to me, very interesting. And I can feel it, boy. It's like being on a ferris wheel and this is the top of the wheel. I am right now at the top of the ferris wheel, and I know what's coming." When the show's popularity does finally abate, and Seinfeld finds himself at the "bottom" of the ferris wheel, he'll continue to do what he's always done—travel the world as a stand-up comic. "When men are growing up, reading about Batman, Spiderman, Superman, these aren't fantasies,

On the set of Jerry's humble yet immaculate apartment, Elaine, George, and Jerry await the thunderous laughter from the studio audience.

these are career options," maintains Seinfeld in his *New York* interview. "Superman is my role model. I have this very romantic image of the stand-up comic, the solitary challenge of being out there on your own, using whatever you have on you. Every man thinks of himself as a low-level superhero. And it came true for me. I got to do what I wanted to do in life. To me, that's being Superman."

■ Works Cited

Charles, Larry, *Seinfeld,* NBC-TV, February 11, 1993.

Collins, Glenn, "How Does Seinfeld Define Comedy? Reluctantly," *New York Times,* September 29, 1991, Section H, pp. 33-34.

Duffy, Mike, "Tonight's 'Seinfeld' Gives Guy Pals a Lot to Get Straight," *Detroit Free Press,* February 11, 1993, Section D, p. 6.

Goodman, Mark, and Lorenzo Benet, "Comedy Abounds," *People,* December 2, 1991, pp. 87-88.

Lazar, Jerry, "Mr. Clean," *Us,* April 4, 1991, pp. 16-19.

O'Connor, John J., "Seinfeld's Quirky Road to Reality," *New York Times,* September 16, 1992, Section C, p. 20.

Panek, Richard, "Jerry Seinfeld," *Mirabella,* October, 1991, pp. 48, 50.

Randall, Stephen, "Jerry Seinfeld's Bland Ambition," *Playboy,* August, 1990, pp. 104-06, 132, 142-43.

Rea, Steven, "Very Jerry," *Entertainment Weekly,* March 1, 1991, pp. 29-30.

Richman, Alan, "You're a Comic. Make Me Laugh!," *GQ,* May, 1992, pp. 136-41, 202, 204-05.

Seinfeld, Jerry, in an interview with Barbara Walters, *The Barbara Walters Special,* ABC-TV, November 24, 1992.

Smith, Chris, "City Slicker," *New York,* February 3, 1992, pp. 32-37.

Weiner, Stewart, "Stand-Up Seinfeld Settles Down for a Stay," *TV Guide,* May 23, 1992, pp. 11-15.

Zoglin, Richard, "Comedian on the Make," *Time,* August 24, 1992, p. 63.

■ For More Information See

PERIODICALS

Detroit Free Press, November 20, 1992, Section F, p. 4; December 22, 1992, Section B, p. 6.

Entertainment Weekly, September 11, 1992, p. 35; April 9, 1993, pp. 14-21.

People, June 4, 1990, p. 14.

USA Today, October 2, 1991, Section D, p. 1.

—*Sketch by Susan M. Reicha*

Stephen Sondheim

"Broadway Sings: The Music of Jule Styne," PBS, 1987, and "Bernstein at 70," PBS, 1989. *Member:* American Academy and Institute of Arts and Letters, American Society of Composers, Authors, and Publishers, Authors League of America, Writers Guild of America, Dramatists Guild (president, 1973-81).

■ Personal

Full name, Stephen Joshua Sondheim; born March 22, 1930, in New York, NY; son of Herbert (a dress manufacturer) and Janet (a fashion designer and interior decorator; maiden name, Fox; present surname, Leshin) Sondheim. *Education:* Williams College, B.A. (magna cum laude), 1950. Informal apprentice to Oscar Hammerstein II, mid-1940s; studied composition with Milton Babbitt, early 1950s. *Hobbies and other interests:* Mathematics, crossword puzzles.

■ Addresses

c/o Flora Roberts, 157 West 57th St., New York, NY 10019.

■ Career

Composer and lyricist. Visiting professor of drama and musical theater and fellow at St Catherine's College, Oxford, 1990. Appeared in television specials, including *June Moon,* PBS, 1974, and *Putting It Together—The Making of the Broadway Album,* HBO, 1986. Appeared in episodes of the television series *Great Performances,* including

■ Awards, Honors

Antoinette Perry ("Tony") Award nominations, League of American Theatres and Producers, 1958 (with composer Leonard Bernstein), for *West Side Story,* 1960 (with composer Jule Styne), for *Gypsy,* 1965 (with composer Richard Rodgers), for *Do I Hear a Waltz?,* 1976, for best score in *Pacific Overtures,* 1982, for best score in *Merrily We Roll Along,* and 1984, for best score in *Sunday in the Park with George;* Antoinette Perry Awards, 1963, for *A Funny Thing Happened on the Way to the Forum,* 1971, two awards for best music and best lyrics in *Company,* 1972, for best score in *Follies,* 1979, for best score in *A Little Night Music,* 1979, for *Sweeney Todd,* and 1988, for best score in *Into the Woods;* New York Drama Critics' polls conducted by *Variety,* 1969-70, named best composer for *Company,* and 1970-71, named best composer and lyricist for *Follies;* Drama Desk Awards, 1969-70, for music and lyrics in *Company,* 1970-71, for music and lyrics in *Follies,* 1972-73, for music and lyrics in *A Little Night Music,* 1978-79, for music and lyrics in *Sweeney Todd,* 1981-82, for lyrics in *Merrily We Roll Along,* 1983-84, for lyrics in *Sunday in the Park with George,* and 1987-88, for lyrics and outstanding musical *Into the Woods;*

New York Drama Critics' Circle Awards for best new musical, 1970, for *Company*, 1971, for *Follies*, 1973, for *A Little Night Music*, 1976, for *Pacific Overtures*, 1979, for *Sweeney Todd*, 1984, for *Sunday in the Park with George*, and 1988, for *Into the Woods*; Los Angeles Drama Critics' Circle Awards, 1974-75, for music and lyrics in *A Little Night Music*, and 1989, for original musical score in *Into the Woods*; Pulitzer Prize for drama, Columbia University Graduate School of Journalism, 1985, for *Sunday in the Park with George*; *Evening Standard* Drama Awards for best musical, 1987, for *Follies*, and 1989, for *Into the Woods*; Laurence Olivier Award for musical of the year, Society of West End Theatre (England), 1988, for *Follies*, and 1991, for *Sunday in the Park with George*.

Grammy Awards, National Academy of Recording Arts and Sciences, 1970, for best musical cast album *Company*, 1973, for musical cast album *A Little Night Music*, 1975, for song of the year "Send in the Clowns" from the musical *A Little Night Music*, 1979, for best musical cast album *Sweeney Todd*, 1984, for best musical cast album *Sunday in the Park with George*, 1986, for best musical cast album *Follies in Concert*, and 1988, for best musical cast album *Into the Woods*; Edgar Allan Poe Award (with Anthony Perkins), Mystery Writers of America, 1973, for best motion picture screenplay *The Last of Sheila*; Academy Award, Academy of Motion Picture Arts and Sciences, 1990, for best original song "Sooner or Later (I Always Get My Man)" from the film *Dick Tracy*; Golden Globe Award nominations, Hollywood Foreign Press Association, 1990, for original songs "Sooner or Later (I Always Get My Man)" and "What Can You Lose?" from the film *Dick Tracy*.

Hutchinson Prize, Williams College, 1950; honorary doctorate, Williams College, 1971; musical salute given by the American Musical and Dramatic Academy and the National Hemophilia Foundation at Shubert Theatre, 1973; Elizabeth Hull-Kate Warriner Award, Dramatists Guild, 1979, for *Sweeney Todd*; Brandeis University Creative Arts Award in theatre arts, 1982; Unique Contribution Award, Drama League of New York, 1983, "for initiating an American Young Playwrights Festival"; Common Wealth Award of Distinguished Service in dramatic arts, Bank of Delaware, 1984; named Lion of the Performing Arts, New York Public Library, 1989; National Medal of Arts Award, National Endowment for the Arts, 1992 (declined).

■ Writings

STAGE PRODUCTIONS

(Composer of incidental music) *The Girls of Summer*, produced at Longacre Theatre, New York City, 1956.

(Lyricist) *West Side Story* (also see below; first produced at Winter Garden Theatre, New York City, September 26, 1957, revived at New York State Theatre, New York City, June 24, 1968, revived at Minskoff Theatre, February 14, 1980), music by Leonard Bernstein, Random House, 1958, published in *Romeo and Juliet and West Side Story*, Dell, 1965.

(Lyricist) *Gypsy* (also see below; first produced at Broadway Theatre, New York City, May 21, 1959, revived at Winter Garden Theatre, September 23, 1974, revived at St. James Theatre, New York City, November 16, 1989), music by Jule Styne, Random House, 1960.

(Composer of incidental music) *Invitation to a March*, produced at Music Box Theatre, New York City, 1960.

(Composer and lyricist) *A Funny Thing Happened on the Way to the Forum* (also see below; first produced at Alvin Theatre, New York City, May 8, 1962, revived at Lunt-Fontanne Theatre, New York City, April 4, 1972), Dodd, 1963.

(Composer and lyricist) *Anyone Can Whistle* (also see below; first produced at Majestic Theatre, New York City, April 4, 1964), Dodd, 1965.

(Lyricist) *Do I Hear a Waltz?* (also see below; first produced at 46th Street Theatre, New York City, March 18, 1965), music by Richard Rodgers, Random House, 1966.

(Lyricist with others) *Leonard Bernstein's Theatre Songs*, produced at Theatre De Lys, New York City, 1965.

(Composer and lyricist) *Company* (also see below; first produced at Alvin Theatre, April 26, 1970), Random House, 1970.

(Composer and lyricist) *Follies* (also see below; first produced at Winter Garden Theatre, April 4, 1971), Random House, 1971.

(Composer) *The Enclave*, produced at Theatre Four, New York City, 1973.

(Composer and lyricist) *A Little Night Music* (also see below; first produced at Shubert Theatre, New York City, February 25, 1973, produced at Majestic Theatre, 1973-74), Dodd, 1974.

(Coauthor of additional lyrics with John LaTouche) *Candide* (revival; also see below), original lyrics by Richard Wilbur, music by Leonard Bernstein, produced at Chelsea Theatre Center of Brooklyn, Brooklyn, NY, 1973-74, produced at Broadway Theatre, March 10, 1974, revived at New York State Theatre, October 13, 1982.

(Composer and lyricist) *The Frogs*, produced at Yale Repertory Theatre, New Haven, CT, May 20, 1974, produced at Odyssey Theatre, Los Angeles, 1983.

(Composer with John Kander and Giuseppe Verdi) *Once in a Lifetime*, produced by Public Players Inc., Central Arts Theatre, 1975.

(Lyricist with others) *By Bernstein*, produced at Chelsea Theatre Center Westside, New York City, 1975.

(Composer and lyricist) *Pacific Overtures* (also see below; first produced at Winter Garden Theatre, January 11, 1976, revived at Promenade Theatre, New York City, October 25, 1984), Dodd, 1977.

(Composer and lyricist) *Sweeney Todd: The Demon Barber of Fleet Street* (also see below; first produced at Uris Theatre [now Gershwin Theatre], New York City, March 1, 1979, revived as an opera at New York State Theatre, October 11, 1984), Dodd, 1979.

(Composer and lyricist with others) *The Madwoman of Central Park West*, produced at 22 Steps Theatre, 1979.

(Composer and lyricist) *Merrily We Roll Along* (also see below), first produced at Alvin Theatre, November 16, 1981, revived at La Jolla Playhouse, La Jolla, CA, June 16, 1985.

(Composer and lyricist) *Sunday in the Park with George* (also see below; workshop produced at Playwrights Horizons, New York City, July 6, 1983, produced at Booth Theatre, New York City, 1984-85), Dodd, 1986.

(Composer and lyricist) *Into the Woods* (also see below; produced at Old Globe Theatre, San Diego, CA, c. 1986, produced at Martin Beck Theatre, New York City, 1987-89), Theatre Communications Group, 1989.

(Composer and lyricist with others) *Jerome Robbins' Broadway*, produced at Imperial Theatre, New York City, 1989-90.

(Composer and lyricist) *Assassins* (first produced at Playwrights Horizons, 1991), Theatre Communications Group, 1991.

Also provided music for *Twigs*, first produced at Fisher Theatre, Detroit, MI, c. 1972. Composer with Mary Rodgers of song "The Boy from . . ." for *The Mad Show*, produced at New Theatre, New York City, 1966.

STAGE MUSICAL ANTHOLOGIES

Sondheim: A Musical Tribute (benefit production), produced at Shubert Theatre, March 11, 1973.

Side by Side by Sondheim (also see below), includes music by Leonard Bernstein, Mary Rodgers, Richard Rodgers, and Jule Styne, produced in London, 1976, produced at Music Box Theatre, April 18, 1977, revised version first performed as *A Stephen Sondheim Evening*, produced at Sotheby's, New York, March 3, 1983.

Marry Me a Little (also see below), first produced in October, 1980, produced at Actor's Playhouse, New York City, 1981.

Follies in Concert with New York Philharmonic, first produced at Lincoln Center, New York City, September 6, 1985.

Julie Wilson: From Weill to Sondheim—A Concert (one act devoted to Sondheim's work), produced at Kaufman Theatre, 1987.

You're Gonna Love Tomorrow: A Stephen Sondheim Evening, produced at New Playwrights' Theatre, Washington, DC, c. 1987.

Sondheim: A Celebration at Carnegie Hall, produced in New York City, 1992.

Putting It Together, produced by Manhattan Theatre Club, City Center Theatre, New York City, 1993.

FILM COMPOSITIONS

(Lyricist) *West Side Story* (also see below), United Artists (UA), 1961.

(Lyricist) *Gypsy* (also see below), Warner Bros., 1962.

(Composer and lyricist) *A Funny Thing Happened on the Way to the Forum* (also see below), UA, 1966.

(Composer of the score) *Stavisky* (also see below), Cinemation, 1974.

(Composer and lyricist) *A Little Night Music* (also see below), New World, 1977.

(Composer of score with Dave Grusin) *Reds*, Paramount, 1981.

(Composer and lyricist with others) *Dick Tracy*, Touchstone-Buena Vista, 1990.

Also author of music and lyrics for "The Madam's Song," in *The Seven-Per-Cent Solution*, Universal, 1977.

SCREENPLAYS

(With Anthony Perkins) *The Last of Sheila*, Warner Bros., 1973.

TELEVISION PRODUCTIONS

(Composer and lyricist with Burt Shevelove) *The Fabulous 50s* (special), Columbia Broadcasting System (CBS-TV), 1960.

(Composer and lyricist) *Evening Primrose* (special), American Broadcasting Cos. (ABC-TV), 1966.

(Composer and lyricist) *Annie, the Woman in the Life of a Man* (special), CBS-TV, 1970.

(Composer and lyricist) *Sweeney Todd, The Demon Barber of Fleet Street* (special; also see below), Entertainment Channel, 1982.

(Lyricist) "Candide," *Great Performances*, Public Broadcasting Service (PBS-TV), 1986.

(Composer and lyricist) "Follies in Concert," *Great Performances*, PBS-TV, 1986.

(Composer and lyricist) "Sunday in the Park with George" (also see below), *Broadway on Showtime*, Showtime, 1986, broadcast on *American Playhouse*, PBS-TV, 1986.

(Composer and lyricist) "A Little Night Music" (also see below), *Live from Lincoln Center* (broadcast from New York State Theatre), PBS-TV, 1990.

(Composer) *Time Warner Presents the Earth Day Special*, ABC-TV, 1990.

(Composer and lyricist) "Into the Woods" (also see below), *Great Performances*, PBS-TV, 1991.

Also author of song "The Saga of Lenny," included in "Bernstein at 70," *Great Performances*, PBS-TV, 1989, and of lyrics to "Somewhere," included in *Putting It Together—The Making of the Broadway Album* (special), HBO, 1986.

TELEPLAYS

(With others) *Topper* (series), National Broadcasting Co. (NBC-TV), 1953.

The Last Word (series), CBS-TV, 1957-59.

RECORDINGS

West Side Story, Columbia, 1957, released as film soundtrack, 1961.

Gypsy, Columbia, 1959.

A Funny Thing Happened on the Way to the Forum, Capitol, 1962.

Anyone Can Whistle, Columbia, 1964.

Do I Hear a Waltz?, Columbia, 1965.

Company, Columbia, 1970.

Follies, Capitol, 1971, released as *Follies in Concert*, RCA, 1985.

A Little Night Music, Columbia, 1973.

Stavisky, Polydor, 1973.

Sondheim: A Musical Tribute (anthology), Warner Bros., 1973, released as *Sondheim Evening: A Musical Tribute* (includes Sondheim singing "Anyone Can Whistle"), RCA, 1990.

Pacific Overtures, RCA, 1976.

Side by Side by Sondheim, RCA, 1977.

Sweeney Todd, The Demon Barber of Fleet Street, RCA, 1979.

Marry Me a Little, RCA, 1981.

Merrily We Roll Along, RCA, 1981.

Sunday in the Park with George, RCA, 1984.

Music of Stephen Sondheim, Book of the Month Records, 1985.

Into the Woods, RCA, 1988.

I'm Breathless (Music from and Inspired by the Film "Dick Tracy") (contains "Sooner or Later (I Always Get My Man)" and "What Can You Lose?"), Sire, 1990.

Sondheim songs are also featured in Barbra Streisand's *Broadway Album*, 1985, and *Stephen Sondheim: A Collector's Sondheim* (compilation of original cast recordings), RCA.

OTHER

(Author of introduction) Richard Lewin and Alfred Simon, *Songs of the American Theatre*, Dodd, 1973.

(Contributor) Otis L. Guernsey, Jr., editor, *Playwrights, Lyricists, Composers on Theatre*, Dodd, 1974.

(Author of introduction) Hugh Fordin, *Getting to Know Him* (biography of Oscar Hammerstein), Random House, 1977.

Stephen Sondheim's Crossword Puzzles, Harper, 1980.

(Editor) *Lyrics by Oscar Hammerstein II*, revised edition, Hal Leonard Publishing, 1985.

Also author of *The Hansen Treasury of Stephen Sondheim Songs*, 1977, *The Stephen Sondheim Songbook*, 1979, and *All Sondheim*, 1980. Contributor of crossword puzzles to *New York* magazine, 1968-69.

■ Adaptations

Into the Woods has been adapted into a juvenile book by Hudson Talbott, published by Crown, 1988.

■ Sidelights

"My experience with Sondheim musicals—and I expect that of most Sondheim enthusiasts—has inevitably been the same," *New York Times* theater critic Frank Rich once remarked. "One sits in a theater where people are cheering or sneering; the pitch and conflict of battle drift into intermission, where heated arguments ensue. At the packed closing performance of *Follies* at the Winter Garden in 1972, people threw flowers at the stage in the same theater where, only a week or so earlier, audiences had greeted the same production with indifference and coughing. At an early preview of *Sweeney Todd* (1979), dozens of unprepared theatergoers ran for the exits once it became apparent that cannibalism was on the evening's menu. At a final-week performance of the short-lived *Merrily We Roll Along* (1982), scattered clumps of theatergoers rose to give every song an ovation while the majority of the house looked on in perplexed, dumbfounded silence. I never saw a performance of *Sunday in the Park With George* (1984) at which some members of the audience didn't walk out early—often not even waiting until intermission to do so—while others, sobbing in their seats, refused to budge until well after the house lights were up."

Widely recognized as the most prominent composer on Broadway today, Stephen Sondheim is also renowned for consistently arousing heated critical and popular debate. A large number of theater reviewers love him for his ingenuity and inventiveness—he has garnered a record seven New York Drama Critics' Circle Awards for best new musical, as well as an Oscar, a handful of Grammys, and a Pulitzer. He can boast, moreover, of being the only composer to be honored with Tonys three years in a row. Critics celebrate the sharp wit and sophistication of his lyrics and credit him with redefining the American theater because of his high intellectual ambitions. He is acclaimed for tackling hefty, innovative subjects that range from revenge and injustice in *Sweeney Todd* to aestheticism and creativity in *Sunday in the Park with George* to Western imperialization in *Pacific Overtures,* and his productions are among the most highly anticipated on Broadway.

His appeal among general audiences, however, has been limited. Though many of his shows have enjoyed lengthy runs, the majority of them have lost money, like his Pulitzer Prize-winning *Sunday in the Park with George,* as well as *Sweeney Todd* and *Follies,* which lost all $800,000 of its investment. To theatergoers anticipating blithe, escapist fare reminiscent of the "traditional" American musical, his productions are perceived as disturbing and called inaccessible, cold, and calculated. He has been labelled "all mind, no heart," as he writes in *Sunday in the Park,* and many conservative theatergoers charge him with, as Herbert

Kretzmer reported in a London *Times* piece, "bring[ing] the U.S. musical to its present moribund state by draining it of the warmth, humanity and vulgar excitements that once constituted the life blood of Broadway." Kretzmer added: "Sondheim is not a people's man."

Sondheim himself is perhaps one of his own worst critics. Religious about not bowing to public taste, he constructs songs that are integral to the musical's story line and that enhance and develop its characters—no matter what the current pop music fad. Many critics point out that his songs are dramatic vignettes in and of themselves and become self-contained playlets when performed outside the context of the drama. Intricate rhymes and tricky wordplay infuse his works, and he carefully pieces together words and melodies much like he would approach the solving of one of the crossword puzzles he enjoys so much. Lyric writing is "an elegant form of puzzle," he was quoted as saying in a *Los Angeles Times* article by Barbara Isenberg. As thorough as he is about composing, he admits he still experiences self-doubt when his songs are performed. "When I first hear a song sung," he said in a *New York Times* article by Samuel G. Freedman, "I'm worried that I'm going to be embarrassed by what I wrote. . . . Out there in front of other people with performers, it's got to carry its own weight and I'm worried it won't. I'm less nervous than I used to be. The agony is at a lower level. But it's not entirely free from nerves, from apprehension."

"I write generally experimental, unexpected work," Sondheim continued. "My kind of work is caviar to the general. It's not that it's too good for people, it's just that it's too unexpected to sustain itself very firmly in the commercial theater." Hardly afraid of failure, he has candidly admitted that as long as he has attempted something enterprising and inventive, he will not be mortified if the work flops. As he acknowledges in his song 'Live, Laugh, Love' from *Follies:* "Success is swell / And success is sweet / But every height has a drop. / The less achievement / The less defeat."

In spite of a rocky childhood, Sondheim realized a love for music and the theater from an early age. He was born in 1930 New York to moderately wealthy parents, who divorced when Sondheim was ten and were often too busy with professional pursuits to spend time with him. His father he remembers as a dress manufacturer, whose constant worrying endowed Sondheim with a tendency toward cynicism. His mother he recalls as a dress designer who, following the venomous divorce,

In the climactic scene from the 1961 film version of *West Side Story*, starring Natalie Wood and Richard Beymer, Maria runs to Tony after a fatal fight.

vented her hostility toward her former husband on her son. "From her I get my tendency to hysteria," Sondheim later admitted to William A. Henry III and Elizabeth L. Bland in *Time*. Lyrics from at least one Sondheim song, "The Little Things You Do Together" from *Company*, his 1970 musical about marriage, hint at the trauma the songwriter experienced over the divorce: "The concerts you enjoy together, / the neighbors you annoy together, / the children you destroy together."

Sondheim Meets Hammerstein

Fortunately for Sondheim, in the summer of 1942 he became friends with neighbor Jamie Hammerstein, the young son of celebrated Broadway lyricist Oscar Hammerstein. Sondheim developed an affinity for the family so quickly that "by Christmas," Jamie quipped in Henry and Bland's *Time* article, "Stephen was more a Hammerstein than a Sondheim." The most pivotal relationship developed between Sondheim and Oscar Hammer-

stein, who at the time was working on the Broadway musical *Oklahoma!* "Oscar was everything to me," Sondheim recalled to Charles Michener in *Newsweek*. "He was a surrogate father and I wanted to be exactly like him." Hammerstein encouraged the youngster's burgeoning enthusiasm for the theater and music (Sondheim had taken piano lessons sporadically from the time he was seven), and the teenager responded by collaborating with a few other schoolmates on *By George*, a musical for their school in Pennsylvania. "I really thought it was terrific," Sondheim told Craig Zadan in *Sondheim and Co.* "And when I finished it, I not only wanted Oscar to see it but I wanted him to be the first to read it, because I just knew he and [collaborator Richard] Rodgers would want to produce it immediately and I'd be the first fifteen-year-old ever to have a musical done on Broadway." Hammerstein didn't agree. "'It's the worst thing I've ever read.' And he probably saw that my lower lip began to tremble," Sondheim continued, "and he said, 'Now, I didn't say that it was untalented, I said it was terrible. And if you want to know *why* it's terrible I'll tell you.'" Hammerstein went on to explain to the youngster such artistic techniques as how to compose songs within the framework of the story, how to write lyrics that encompass one-act dramas, and how to build character. Hammerstein also illuminated the relationship between words and music as well as the significance of content. "At the risk of hyperbole," Sondheim later recalled, "I'd say that in that afternoon I learned more about songwriting and the musical theater than most people learn in a lifetime. I was getting the distillation of thirty years of experience."

Hammerstein mapped out an informal apprenticeship for the young composer, which involved the writing of four musicals over a span of six years, and allowed Sondheim the opportunity to observe while he and Rodgers collaborated on what would ultimately become the classic musicals *The King and I* and *South Pacific*. While Sondheim was an eager pupil, he had no intention of continuing his study of music in college, preferring instead to enter Massachusetts's Williams College in 1946 to pursue his love of mathematics. Then a freshman music course changed his mind. "The professor, Robert Barrow, was cold and dogmatic," Sondheim remembered for Henry and Bland. "I thought he was the best thing I had ever encountered, because he took all the romance away from art. Instead of the muse coming at midnight and humming *Some Enchanted Evening* into your ear, music was *constructed*. It wasn't what other people wanted to hear, but it turned me into a music major." Following his graduation in 1950 with honors in composition and music theory, Sondheim won the Hutchinson Prize, a two-year fellowship that allowed him to study both structure and theory with avant-garde American composer Milton Babbitt. Five years later, after gaining some professional experience writing for the short-lived television series *Topper* and composing music for a production that was shelved when its producer died, Sondheim got his break in the mid-1950s. Playwright Arthur Laurents, familiar with Sondheim's apprentice musicals and in need of a lyricist for an upcoming project, hooked Sondheim up with Leonard Bernstein, the project's composer. The meeting was concise: Sondheim played; Bernstein "freaked out," as he admitted in *Broadway Song and Story*; and the youngster was hired.

"I Like to Be in America"—On Broadway, That Is

Unaware that Laurent's project—*West Side Story*—would launch his career, Sondheim at first hesitated to accept the position, hoping instead to break into Broadway as both a composer *and* lyricist. Prodded by Hammerstein, though, he took the job—a decision that ultimately made him, at the tender age of twenty-seven, lyricist for what has become a classic of American musical theater. *West Side Story*, a modernized version of William Shakespeare's tragedy *Romeo and Juliet*, opened in September of 1957 and quickly gained recognition for its innovative subject matter. The production, which ran for 732 performances, greeted theatergoers accustomed to traditionally optimistic American musicals with examinations of violence, hatred, delinquency, prejudice, passion, and death. Audiences and critics were impressed by the bold musical that blended song, choreography, music, and book for the first time into an integrated whole. Much of *West Side Story*'s critical accolades were reserved for the collaborative efforts of its creators: Laurents, Bernstein, Sondheim, and Jerome Robbins, a gathering of talent "which should remain for many seasons as the most fortunate union in the history of money," decided John McClain in *Journal American*. Sondheim's lyrics garnered some attention as well, though: His words are "biting and tender," judged Robert Coleman in the *Daily Mirror*, while John Chapman of the New York *Daily News* asserted they possess "simple grace."

Sondheim himself did not view his work as kindly. Even though such pieces as "Gee, Officer Krupke," "America," "Maria," "I Feel Pretty," "Somewhere," "Tonight," and "Cool" became audience favorites after the release of the film version in 1961, Sondheim never felt completely satisfied with many of them and even admitted they embarrassed him. "I changed the lyric of 'I Feel Pretty' after seeing the run-through in New York because I was ashamed of it," he disclosed in *Broadway Song and Story*. "Later the others said they liked it better the way it was before, so I went home. I'm not fond of a lot of the *West Side Story* lyrics. To me, they seem very 'written.' I like 'Something's Coming' and 'Jet Song' because they have a kind of energy to them. The more contemplative lyrics I find very self-conscious and a mite pretentious every now and then. I hear a writer at work instead of a character."

On the heels of *West Side Story*'s stage success, Sondheim was offered the chance to write for another Laurent show—a prime opportunity, but a job Sondheim was not completely convinced he wanted. "I really didn't want to wait another couple of years to write a score myself," Sondheim remembered in *Broadway Song and Story*. "But I went to Oscar [Hammerstein], and he persuaded me to do *Gypsy*. He said that the chance to work with these people and particularly to write a show for a star (which I had never done before) was invaluable.... Because I liked the piece enough and because I knew and liked [composer Jule Styne]'s stuff a lot, I said O.K.... I haven't regretted it for one second. Not only do I love the score, I love the show."

An enormous theatrical triumph upon its May, 1959, Broadway opening, *Gypsy* starred Rosalind Russell and Jack Klugman and ran for more than seven hundred performances. A re-creation of the old vaudeville and burlesque shows, the musical revolves around Rose, the domineering and some-times brutal mother of Gypsy Rose Lee, the real-life American striptease queen of the mid-1900s. In *Gypsy*, the coldly ambitious Rose epitomizes the quintessential stage mother who is willing to sacrifice virtually anything to make her daughter a star. "The first half of [*Gypsy*] brings together in effortless coalition all the arts of the American musical stage at their highest point of development," decided Kenneth Tynan in *Curtains*. "So smooth is the blending of skills, so precise the interlocking of song, speech, and dance, that the sheer contemplation of technique becomes a thrilling emotional experience." Sondheim's work garnered particular acclaim: William K. Zinsser of *Horizon* stressed that "if [Sondheim] were merely a brilliant technician, [*West Side Story* and *Gypsy*] would not have made such an impact. It is because his lyrics so surely fit not only the moment but the total mood and character of the story that *West Side Story* and *Gypsy* have an extra unity, maturity, and dramatic strength."

Stars Karl Malden, Rosalind Russell, and Natalie Wood belt out a tune from the 1959 production of *Gypsy*.

Zero Mostel stars in this 1966 film adaptation of Sondheim's Tony Award-winning musical *A Funny Thing Happened on the Way to the Forum.*

The Music Finally Comes

Even with two Broadway successes to his name, Sondheim still had not accomplished what he really wanted to do—compose. Then he got his wish. Teaming up with playwrights Burt Shevelove and Larry Gelbart, he found in the comedies of classical Roman playwright Titus Maccius Plautus the inspiration for what would become his debut work as both composer and lyricist. The result was a smash hit. Running for almost a thousand performances, *A Funny Thing Happened on the Way to the Forum* premiered on Broadway in 1962 and a year later snatched the Tony Award for best new musical. One of the most conventional of Sondheim's works, the outrageous, farcical work blends vaudeville bits, sight gags, and spoofs, and is considered the composer's most purely comedic production. *Forum* is "about the funniest musical comedy ever written," lauded *New York Times* theater critic Frank Rich. Unfortunately, the wave of accolades was short-lived. Throughout the remainder of the

decade, Sondheim never came close to realizing the enormous success of *Forum*. The next two projects he wrote for—*Anyone Can Whistle*, an ephemeral 1964 show about insanity in a corrupt town, and *Do I Hear a Waltz?* (with music by Richard Rodgers), a 1965 musical detailing an American tourist's search for love abroad—flopped.

Five years later Sondheim turned himself around by joining forces with noted director and producer Harold Prince. Together the two would create seven musicals over the span of a decade and forge a reputation for experimental, conceptual works that most often find their inspiration in such cheerless and atypical Broadway themes as desolation, disillusionment, and despair. *Company*, their first collaboration, was a landmark hit that offers an unsentimental and pessimistic look at marriage and the loneliness of a citified life filled with answering machines, beepers, and intercoms. The production is structured as a series of vignettes and focuses on

Robert, a thirty-five-year-old New York bachelor who, though intensely afraid of commitment, realizes he must make some human connection. His surprise birthday party given by his married friends opens *Company*, while flashbacks reveal his prior troublesome, and generally disheartening, encounters with his wedded friends. Ultimately he moves from protesting against "Someone you have to let in, / Someone whose feelings you spare," to a dire plea that "Somebody crowd me with love, / Somebody force me to care."

Sondheim's score and lyrics were among the most applauded elements of *Company*. Many critics found his jeering, brittle words an exact match for the empty, vacuous lives of the matrons who spend days "Keeping house but clutching a copy of *Life* / Just to keep in touch," as proclaimed in "Ladies Who Lunch." John Lahr in *Harper's* called the particular piece "a superb song . . . [in which] Sondheim lets mockery have a field day. With her checklist of the various bourgeois pastimes, the sozzled singer uses anger to stir things up and create the illusion of movement in a stalled life." His music was lauded as clever, sophisticated, and eclectic, prompting one critic, Martin Gottfried in *Women's Wear Daily*, to assert that Sondheim "is the most exciting, stimulating, theatre-minded composer at work today. His freedom from standard forms, his meters, harmonies, modulations, long-lined constructions . . ., dissonances and plain music are so superior to what we hear in the theatre that comparisons are absurd." "Sondheim and Prince," *Newsweek*'s Michener ventured, "[have] given the Broadway musical comedy a new lease on life."

The triumph of the Sondheim-Prince musical continued a year later with *Follies*, a musical throwback to the 1920s and 1930s that examines the progression of time as well as the disintegration of optimism. In *Follies*, a troupe of retired showgirls reunite in a crumbling vaudeville theater three decades after the close of the fictional Weismann Follies. Throughout the show, ghosts of the past continually "bump" into the characters of the present, as each individual's former and current self is portrayed by two different actors. "It is this idea," assessed Gottfried in *Women's Wear Daily*, "and the awesomeness of its execution that give the show its monumental feeling—a breath away from the living." Four partygoers are spotlighted in particular in the production: Phyllis, who married the prosperous and charming Ben, and her best friend Sally, who wed the unfaithful Buddy and still longs for Ben, her old flame. The folly of

Actors Len Cariou and Elizabeth Taylor in a scene from *A Little Night Music*.

trying to recapture what the characters remember as the youthful innocence of their past is played out when old rivalries and relationships are revived. "Middle-aged compromise intervenes," described Irving Wardle in the London *Times*, "and the party breaks up in disenchantment and a return to the old domestic treadmill."

Despite its reputation as a significant musical work and the handful of Tonys it won, *Follies* failed to recoup its investment and incited widely contradictory criticism. Sondheim's score, which many critics described as a salute to his Broadway predecessors, generated both wide acclaim as well as halfhearted recognition. *Follies* "is an incredible display of musical virtuosity," declared T. E. Kalem in *Time*. "It is a one-man course in the theatrical modes of the '20s, '30s, and '40s musicals, done not as a parody or mimicry, but as a passionately informed tribute." Arlene Croce was less enthusiastic about the composer's effort, arguing in *Stereo Review* that "to his credit, Sondheim seems to have offered his pastiches in a genial spirit, like a host showing us his collection of old movies; but to some critics this is enough to make him the king of a new genre." Criticism of *Follies'* emotional content sparked debate as well: on one hand reviewers complained that the work was bleak, and that a more compelling and engaging story was needed. On the other hand, many lauded the intense feelings expressed in Sondheim's lyrics. Fury surfaces, they pointed out, in "Could I live through the pain / On a terrace in Spain? / Would it pass? / It would pass. / Could I bury my rage / With a boy half your age / In the grass? / Bet your ass"; while ambivalence emerges through "God why don't you love me / Oh you do, I'll see you later / Blues."

Love, Politics, and Gore

Turning from the acerbic wit of *Follies* and *Company,* Sondheim and Prince achieved a rare commercial success with 1973's *A Little Night Music,* a bittersweet love story set in turn-of-the-century Sweden. Based on the Ingmar Bergman film *Smiles of a Summer Night,* the work turns on the foolishness of love among members of a debauched Swedish elite and is one of the few Sondheim musicals that ends optimistically. *Night Music* follows such individuals as Frederick Egerman, a middle-aged attorney whose marriage to a giddy eighteen-year-old has never been consummated despite his pleas; his gloomy, seminarian-pupil son, who craves his stepmother; and Frederick's mistress, who is coupled with a dragoon who considers his beautiful wife "irrelevant." As Sondheim writes, all involved are arrested in a state of "perpetual anticipation . . . Playing a role / Aching to start / Keeping control / While falling apart."

In critiques of *Night Music,* theater reviewers especially pointed out Sondheim's innovative approach to the production's score. Imposing a stylistic constraint on the music, he composed each piece in a variant of 3/4 time, creating a lilting, waltz-like backdrop for the romantic encounters on stage. "The warm, beating heart of this tender, witty musical for lovers and other grownups is Steve Sondheim's music and words," conjectured Michener in *Newsweek.* "His music fits *Night Music* as perfectly as the lace-over-chiffon bodices and long skirts fit its leading ladies. In keeping with an age of grand, stylized gestures, his score is something of a tour de force." *A Little Night Music* also marked the first time a Sondheim song broke outside the Broadway theater circuit to become a pop hit. "Send in the Clowns" was subsequently recorded by Frank Sinatra, as well as Barbra Streisand, and captured a Grammy for best song of the year. Later Bernstein wrote in *Sondheim and Co.* that the work "really breaks your heart . . . that's a real piece of poetry both musically and verbally."

Sondheim and Prince aspired to a new artistic form three years later with *Pacific Overtures,* a musical that examines the metamorphosis of an entire culture. Called "bold," "audacious," and "ambitious," the critically successful production turns on the westernization of Japan, which began in the mid-nineteenth century when American Commodore Matthew Perry arrived in the Orient on an expedition. Relations opened between the two nations, and Japan—which had been isolated from the world for 250 years—was thrust into the modern age. Tackling a political issue for the first time, the collaborators question in *Pacific Overtures* the "triumph" of Western civilization and suggest at the close of the work that the conquest (or exploitation) of Japanese culture has come full circle: the "students" have become the "teachers."

Though disregarded for the most part by theatre audiences, *Pacific Overtures* met with an enthusiastic reception among many reviewers, who especially found Sondheim's score impressive and evocative of traditional Japanese music. "Sondheim didn't pretend to write Oriental music, but instead grasped its texture," determined Gottfried in the *New York Post.* "Sondheim's feeling for the weight and wit of measured language allows him to deftly absorb Japanese poetic forms such as haiku into his lyrics," asserted Jack Kroll in *Newsweek.* "His parallel gift for the histrionic shapes and gestures of music lets him slip with sneaky grace between Western and Eastern modes." "Sondheim is the most remarkable man in the Broadway musical today," judged Clive Barnes in *New York Times* piece. "Here he shows it victoriously."

Sondheim and Prince swapped politics for injustice, cannibalism, and Hitchcockian gore with 1979's *Sweeney Todd, The Demon Barber of Fleet.* Considered a major contribution to the American theater, the grim, gruesome musical is based on one of the most popular plays in British theater history, which was originally penned by nineteenth-century playwright George Dibdin Pitt. *Sweeney Todd* revolves around the title character, a barber who is wrongfully exiled to Australia by an unscrupulous judge and then returns to London to exact his revenge. Obsessed with vengeance, Sweeney Todd slits the throats of unsuspecting patrons, then donates the bodies to his industrious landlady Mrs. Lovett, who blends the carcasses into her acclaimed meat-pies.

A moderate success with more than five hundred performances on Broadway, *Sweeney Todd* roused considerable critical debate. Some theater reviewers faulted Sondheim for his macabre choice of subjects: "This 'musical thriller' about a homicidal barber, a tonsorial Jack the Ripper in Dickensian London, slashes at the jugular instead of touching the heart," observed Kroll in *Newsweek*. Other critics, such as *High Fidelity*'s Alan Rich, considered the production a "musical masterpiece," emphasizing in particular the range, depth, and innovation of Sondheim's music. "Sondheim has composed an endlessly inventive, highly expressive score that works indivisibly from his brilliant and abrasive lyrics," declared Richard Eder in the *New York Times*. "In some ways it is [Sondheim's] most melodic, richest work," appraised Howard Kissel in *Women's Wear Daily*, "yet, even at its lushest moments, the context never lets the music seem merely 'beautiful.' The tenderest moment, musically, for example, is a love song the vengeful barber sings to his razor." Broadway composer Jule Styne, commenting in a 1985 interview excerpted in *Sondheim and Co.*, insisted that "the most unbelievable job of music writing . . . and I say this with deep reverence and envy, the most brilliant job of music writing ever in my life, is *Sweeney Todd*." With *Sweeney Todd*, opined Lahr in *Harper's*, "Sondheim has become the American musical: a king on a field of corpses."

The Sondheim-Prince Regime Ends

Sondheim's reign as king did not last long. In late 1981 Prince and Sondheim's next musical, *Merrily We Roll Along*, opened, then just as quickly closed after only sixteen performances. Considered a critical flop, the work follows in reverse chronological order the lives of a trio of Broadway writers, whose success at the outset of the production is offset by the realization at the close that their lives are empty and loveless. "Sondheim has given this evening a half-dozen songs that are crushing and beautiful—that soar and linger and hurt," conceded Rich in the *New York Times*. "But the show that contains them is a shambles." Decrying a weak, awkward book, Walter Kerr of the *New York Times* advised Sondheim and Prince to "take fresh stock of their imaginative energies. They are much too innovative to allow themselves to become so predictable."

After *Merrily*'s bitter failure, Kretzmer reported in the London *Times* that "Sondheim became severely depressed and announced that he would renounce the theatre. 'I felt the hatred on Broadway that was directed at Hal [Prince] and me,'" Sondheim was quoted as saying. "'I really don't like that whole aspect of show business and I wish it would go away.'" Sondheim subsequently severed his partnership with Prince, marking the first time in his career he was without a veteran collaborator. Some critics have speculated that this separation finally gave Sondheim the opportunity to create a project entirely his own. They also asserted that after a career spent collaborating with such innovators as Rodgers, Michael Bennett, and Robbins, Sondheim was finally free to explore an issue he has felt passionate about throughout his career—the dramatic creation of art.

Enlisting the talents of James Lapine, a commercially unseasoned playwright and director, Sondheim embarked on the project, which ultimately became the 1985 Pulitzer Prize-winning *Sunday in the Park with George*. A novel work inspired by the landmark nineteenth-century painting "A Sunday Afternoon on the Island of La Grande Jatte," the musical revolves around the painting's creator, French artist Georges Seurat, a pointillist who fashioned the work using multitudinous dots of paint. In two acts, *Sunday in the Park* turns on a

Mandy Patinkin and Bernadette Peters star in the Pulitzer Prize-winning *Sunday in the Park with George*, Sondheim's lament for the growing commercialization of the art world.

single idea—how an innovative, principled artist works. The musical opens in Paris, where Seurat set his painting, and follows the creation of the piece from sketch to final canvas. The second act jumps more than one hundred years to 1984 and Seurat's fictional great-grandson, an avant-garde laser artist who aspires to reach the artistic heights his great-grandfather did. In the twentieth century, however, art is no longer a valued commodity; the art world has become flashy, high-tech, commercial, and empty, much like the musical theater Sondheim was facing, many critics suggested. Commentators also pointed out that parallels exist between Seurat himself and Sondheim, both of whose works have been labelled inventive, yet emotionally cold. As Rich wrote in the *New York Times*: "*Sunday* allows Sondheim at last to channel his own passion into a musical that is not about marriage, class inequities or other things he doesn't seem sincerely to care about, but is instead about what does matter to him—art itself, and his own predicament as a driven artist whose austere vision, like Seurat's, is often incorrectly judged as heartless."

Sondheim opted to stage *Sunday in the Park* at Playwrights Horizons, a nonprofit, Off-Broadway theater known for presenting innovative works. Following the production's successful 1983 run, Sondheim moved the musical to Broadway's Booth Theatre, where it remained for another five hundred performances. The critical reception, characteristically enough, was decidedly mixed. Although most reviewers acknowledged the fresh concept of the work, many complained of flat dialogue and static, underdeveloped characters that generated no empathy among theatergoers. "The sad fact," concluded Kissel in *Women's Wear Daily*, "is that despite [Sondheim's] obvious intention to treat the subject in a mode as experimental as it deserves,... *Sunday* is a thin and lifeless evening." "I found *Sunday in the Park with George* ... empty and pretentious," held Victoria Radlin in *New Statesman*. Conversely, many other reviewers commended Sondheim and Lapine for their ambitious vision of struggling artists and judged *Sunday in the Park* a major contribution to the American theater. "To say that this show breaks new ground is not enough," emphasized Kroll in *Newsweek*, "it also breaks new sky, new water, new flesh and new spirit."

Frolics with Fairy Tales

Invigorated by his recent collaboration with Lapine, Sondheim teamed with the librettist a second time to produce 1986's *Into the Woods*. A somewhat philosophical examination of what happens after the "happily ever after" in children's stories, the two-act intertwines two Jacob and Wilhelm Grimm fables, one traditional yarn, and one original tale. As the musical opens, a humble, childless couple is doggedly combing the woods in search of four objects that when delivered to an evil witch will restore their fertility. On their quest they cross paths with well-known fairy tale characters like Little Red Ridinghood, Cinderella, and Jack, who are traipsing merrily through the forest seeking to fulfill their own adventures—which more often than not involve the loss of innocence. After Jack climbs the beanstalk and slays the giant, for example, he sings about his brief encounter with Mrs. Giant: "She holds you to her giant breast ... You know things you never knew before." Little Red Ridinghood, too, emerges from her confrontation with the lecherous wolf crooning, "He showed me things ... many beautiful things ... He got me excited and scared." By the close of the first act, all appears to be well: Jack has slaughtered the giant, Cinderella has found her prince, Little Red Ridinghood has been rescued from the wolf, and the baker has secured all of his goods. The contentment, however, is short-lived. "Ever-after lasts until the second act," explained Gerald Weales in *Commonweal*, "when the characters find that they have left fairy-tale land for Sondheim country, where they find betrayal, infidelity, boredom, recrimination, the taste of ashes in the mouth of realized desire. And pain. And death."

With advance sales reaching $3.7 million, *Into the Woods* opened on Broadway in November of 1987 to widely disparate reactions that ranged from awful to superb. Many critics complained that with *Into the Woods* Sondheim finally caved in to public demands and created a show that ultimately sacrificed innovation for light, frothy fare. As Ray Conlogue explained in the Toronto *Globe and Mail*: "There is a kind of desperation about this show, a desperation to be clever and witty, to please, to be original and yet loved by everybody." "Sondheim's songs are largely unmemorable, uninteresting, and bereft of sophistication," declared John Podhoretz in the *American Spectator*. "Apparently, in his quest to save the musical, he has decided to jettison his greatest strength as a lyricist in order to appeal to the greatest number." Other reviewers raved about the production. "*Into the Woods* is the best show yet from the most creative mind in the musical theater today," asserted William A. Henry, III, and Elizabeth L. Bland in *Time*. "It is also that

"Ever After"

Rapunzel in her tower

In the woods

Sondheim's successful *Into the Woods* speculates about what might have happened after the "happily ever after" endings in various fairy tales.

joyous rarity, a work of sophisticated artistic ambition and deep political purpose that affords nonstop pleasure."

Sondheim's compositions from *Into the Woods* provoked just as wide a variety of reactions. Among the most critically discussed was the production's final song, "No One Is Alone." The lyrics, sung by Cinderella to Little Red Ridinghood in the wake of the musical's final disaster, read: "Mother cannot guide you / Now you're on your own ... Only me beside you / Still, you're not alone. / No one is alone, truly. / No one is alone." *Los Angeles Times* critic Dan Sullivan observed that "this false-positive solution seems unworthy of a show that elsewhere won't settle for formula. It would be more honest at this point in the story to have a song where the characters admit that everybody is alone—which is why it's necessary for them to band together. The woods are a place for tough thinking, not platitudes." At the other end of the spectrum was Rich of the *New York Times*, who declared that "To hear 'No One Is Alone,' the cathartic and beautiful final song of *Into the Woods*, is to be overwhelmed once more by the continuity of one of the American theater's most extraordinary songwriting careers. The lyric's terrifying opening admonition—'Mother cannot guide you'—sends one reeling back three decades to the volcanic finale of *Gypsy*, in which the mother ... at last casts her children into the woods

of adulthood with the angry outburst, 'Mama's got to let go!'"

Shoots to Kill

Serving up conventional fare was hardly a critical reaction to Sondheim's 1991 *Assassins*, a musical many reviewers judged his most daring to date. Called alternately "disturbing," "audacious," "intellectually ambitious," and "grotesque," *Assassins* offers a dark look at the men and women who throughout history have attempted to kill United States presidents. Among the assassins featured are John Wilkes Booth, the actor who murdered Abraham Lincoln and who reappears throughout the production prodding others to kill; John Hinckley, the Jodie Foster-obsessed criminal who clipped President Ronald Reagan in 1981; Samuel Byck, the lunatic who in 1974 hijacked a commercial jetliner in the hope that it would crash into Richard Nixon's White House; and Lynette "Squeaky" Fromme, the woman obsessed with serial killer Charles Manson who in the mid-1970s attempted to kill Gerald Ford. Sketches, songs, and monologues pepper the ninety minute revue-type production, which opens at a fairgrounds shooting gallery game that boasts: "Hit the Prez and Win a Prize." The work climaxes as the assassins gather at the Texas School Book Depository and goad Lee Harvey Oswald—who is contemplating suicide—to "join the family" by slaying President John F. Kennedy.

Although many theatergoers expressed dismay at Sondheim's choice of subjects—objecting to what they considered to be a glorification of assassins—the production sold out before its limited run at Playwrights Horizons and ticket cancellations were snatched up by eager customers. Theater critics, however, were a bit less enthusiastic. For example, *New York*'s John Simon found the closing scene with Oswald "preposterous and tasteless" and felt the musical never should have reached the stage while the United States was engaged in the Persian Gulf War. "When the terrible events in the gulf began, Sondheim & Co.—all affluent folks in no great need of turning a buck—could have done the gallant thing and shut down, or shot down, their not very viable brainchild." Those critics who applauded the effort pointed to the production's emphasis on America as the land of opportunity, explaining that many of the assassins, frustrated by their failed attempts at realizing the American dream, became crazed destroyers intent on killing the chief executive and perhaps ensuring their own renown. "This songwriter gives genuine, not mocking, voice to the hopes, fears and rages of two centuries' worth of American losers, misfits, nuts, zombies and freaks," asserted Rich in the *New York Times*. "These are the lost and underprivileged souls who, having been denied every American's dream of growing up to be President, try to achieve a warped, nightmarish inversion of that dream instead." Rich added: "Sondheim has real guts. He isn't ashamed to identify with his assassins to the extreme point where he will wave a gun in a crowded theater, artistically speaking, if that's what is needed to hit the target of American complacency." Other admirers commended Sondheim's work for its originality. "No musical in the last decade has ever dared this much," judged David Richards in the *New York Times*. "It turns the musical's traditional values inside out and delivers a rebuke to [famed American playwright, producer, and actor] George M. Cohan on his very own turf." The entire range of reactions, however, were summed up by Kroll in his *Newsweek* assessment of the piece: *Assassins* is "a show that will disturb many, enrage some and even move others."

Throughout his entire career Sondheim has routinely disturbed, enraged, and moved audiences, prompting many critics to highlight his repeated ventures into the unexpected when reviewing his work. "The biggest challenge for me is the opportunity to constantly try new things," Sondheim commented in *Sondheim and Co*. "I believe it's the writer's job to educate the audience ... to bring them things they would never have expected to see. It's not easy, but writing never has been." He added: "I learned a long time ago to write what I care about and what I want to see, so of course there's always the danger that not everyone is going to agree with our shows or even like them." He has defied tradition by selecting unusual, and sometimes bizarre, subjects, and has stretched the traditional boundaries of the American musical by tackling such ambitious issues as artistry, vengeance, imperialization, loneliness, obsession, and disillusionment. Sondheim "has steadily pushed toward—or beyond—the limits of what the score, the narrative, the very premise of a musical can be," exclaimed William A. Henry, III, in *Time*. "More than anyone else writing today, perhaps more than anyone who came before, he emerges a consummate master of what musicals have been with a vision of what they should become."

Sondheim's vision throughout the years has been complimented by an enormous musical talent that his contemporaries have readily recognized. "It was self-evident that Steve Sondheim was incredi-

bly gifted before any of his work was seen by anybody but some friends around a piano," recalled Prince in *Broadway Song and Story*, who first met the composer in the late 1940s. "I wish more people could write with his sophistication and elegance of lyrics and music and present such challenging material," *Sweeney Todd* actor George Hearn told Sheryl Flatow in *Opera News*. Lyricist Alan Jay Lerner joked in the London *Times* that "it's a federal offence ... to criticize Steve Sondheim in any way." Sondheim's "music sings to me, and I respond to it," emphasized *Sunday in the Park* star Mandy Patinkin in *Opera News*, "It takes me away, and God knows that's all I want in life." And Herbert Kretzmer, himself winner of a Tony Award for his lyrics for *Les Miserables*, proclaimed in the London *Times* that "Sondheim is simply the best songwriter alive, inspiring an immeasurable awe."

Sondheim experienced a surge of popularity in the late 1980s and early 1990s, when anxious Londoners swarmed to the British revival of *A Little Night Music*; excitement grew over his yet-to-be produced *Assassins*; copies of Streisand's *Broadway Album*, which features Sondheim songs, were selling in the millions; and "Sooner or Later (I Always Get My Man)," his nightclub-type song composed for 1990's *Dick Tracy*, earned him his first Academy Award. But applause or no applause, Sondheim has been steadily plugging away at composing and writing for more than three and a half decades—a length of time he prefers not being reminded of. "I'm really 22 years old," he laughingly confessed to the *New York Times*'s Mervyn Rothstein. "Don't you know I'm just very precocious?"

■ Works Cited

Barnes, Clive, "Theater: *Pacific Overtures*, Musical about Japan," *New York Times*, January 12, 1976, p. 39.

Chapman, John, "*West Side Story*: A Splendid and Super-Modern Musical Drama," *Daily News*, September 27, 1957.

Coleman, Robert, "*West Side Story* a Sensational Hit!," *Daily Mirror*, September 27, 1957.

Conlogue, Ray, "Sondheim Musical Loses Itself in the Woods," *Globe and Mail* (Toronto), November 7, 1987.

Croce, Arlene, "Stephen Sondheim's *Follies*: A Pretty Girl Is Like a Malady, Etc.," *Stereo Review*, July, 1971, pp. 110-11.

Eder, Richard, "Stage: Introducing *Sweeney Todd*," *New York Times*, March 2, 1979, p. C3.

Flatow, Sheryl, "Making Connections," *Opera News*, November, 1985, pp. 18, 20, 22.

Freedman, Samuel G., "The Creative Mind: The Words and Music of Stephen Sondheim," *New York Times*, April 1, 1984.

Furth, George, *Company*, music and lyrics by Stephen Sondheim, Random House, 1970.

Goldman, James, *Follies*, music and lyrics by Sondheim, Random House, 1971.

Gottfried, Martin, review of *Company*, *Women's Wear Daily*, April 27, 1970.

Gottfried, Martin, "*Follies*: '. . . Monumental,'" *Women's Wear Daily*, April 5, 1971.

Gottfried, Martin, "*Overtures*—A Remarkable Work of Theater Art," *New York Post*, January 12, 1976.

Guernsey, Otis L., Jr., editor, *Broadway Song & Story: Playwrights, Lyricists, Composers Discuss Their Hits*, introduction by Terrence McNally, Dodd, 1985.

Henry, William A. III, and Elizabeth L. Bland, "Master of the Musical," *Time*, December 7, 1987, pp. 80-82.

Henry, William A. III, and Elizabeth L. Bland, "Some Enchanted Evening," *Time*, November 16, 1987, pp. 96-97.

Henry, William A. III, and John Edward Gallagher, "More Than Song and Dance," *Time*, June 16, 1986, p. 90.

Isenberg, Barbara, "Sondheim Isn't Quite Out of the 'Woods,'" *Los Angeles Times*, January 8, 1989, pp. 4-5, 75.

Kalem, T. E., "Seascape with Frieze of Girls," *Time*, April 12, 1971, p. 78.

Kerr, Walter, "A Libretto Has to Face the Music," *New York Times*, December 13, 1981, pp. D3, D6.

Kissel, Howard, review of *Sunday in the Park with George*, *Women's Wear Daily*, May 3, 1984.

Kissel, Howard, review of *Sweeney Todd*, *Women's Wear Daily*, March 2, 1979.

Kretzmer, Herbert, "Hullabaloo of Broadway," *Times* (London), July 11, 1987.

Kroll, Jack, "The Blood Runs Cold," *Newsweek*, March 12, 1979, pp. 101, 103.

Kroll, Jack, "The Killing of Presidents: Sondheim's New Musical Probes America's Dark Side," *Newsweek*, February 4, 1991, p. 72.

Kroll, Jack, "Sondheim Paints a Picture," *Newsweek*, May 14, 1984, pp. 83-84.

Kroll, Jack, "Zen and Zap," *Newsweek*, January 26, 1976, p. 59.

Lahr, John, "Sondheim's Little Deaths," *Harper's*, April, 1979, pp. 71-4, 76, 78.

Lapine, James, *Into the Woods*, music and lyrics by Sondheim, Theatre Communications Group, 1989.

Lapine, James, *Sunday in the Park with George*, music and lyrics by Sondheim, Dodd, 1986.

McClain, John, "Music Magnificent in Overwhelming Hit," *Journal American*, September 27, 1957.

Michener, Charles, "Words and Music—by Sondheim," *Newsweek*, April 23, 1973, pp. 54-56, 61, 64.

Podhoretz, John, "The American Musical's Last Hope," *American Spectator*, March, 1988, pp. 28-29.

Radlin, Victoria, review of *Follies*, *New Statesman*, August 7, 1987, pp. 23-24.

Rich, Alan, "Sweeney Todd Triumphs on Disc," *High Fidelity*, August, 1979, pp. 80-81.

Rich, Frank, review of *Merrily We Roll Along*, *New York Times*, November 17, 1981.

Rich, Frank, "Sondheim and Those Who Would Kill," *New York Times*, January 28, 1991, pp. C19-20.

Rich, Frank, "Sondheim's Winding Paths," *New York Times*, November 29, 1987.

Rich, Frank, "Stage: *Into the Woods*, From Sondheim," *New York Times*, November 6, 1987.

Rich, Frank, review of *Sunday in the Park with George*, *New York Times*, October 21, 1984.

Richards, David, "They Shoot Presidents, Don't They?," *New York Times*, February 3, 1991, Section 2, pp. 1, 28.

Rothstein, Mervyn, "With Three Hits Running on Broadway, Sondheim Keeps Writing," *New York Times*, November 27, 1989, pp. C13, C15.

Simon, John, "Dumb, Dumb Bullets," *New York*, February 4, 1991, p. 38.

Sullivan, Dan, "*Into the Woods* Finds Its Way on Broadway," *Los Angeles Times*, November 6, 1987.

Tynan, Kenneth, *Curtains: Selections from the Drama Criticism and Related Writings*, Atheneum, 1961, pp. 319-22.

Wardle, Irving, "Songs without an End," *Times* (London), July 23, 1987.

Weales, Gerald, "Tales and Dragons: *Into the Woods* and *Nixon in China*," *Commonweal*, January 15, 1988.

Weidman, John, *Assassins*, music and lyrics by Sondheim, Theatre Communications Group, 1991.

Wheeler, Hugh, *A Little Night Music*, music and lyrics by Sondheim, Dodd, 1974.

Zadan, Craig, *Sondheim & Co.*, 2nd edition, Harper & Row, 1986.

Zinsser, William K., "On Stage: Stephen Sondheim," *Horizon*, July, 1961, pp. 98-99.

■ For More Information See

BOOKS

Contemporary Literary Criticism, Gale, Volume 30, 1984, pp. 375-403, Volume 39, 1986, pp. 172-75.

Gordon, Joanne, *Art Isn't Easy*, Southern Illinois University Press, 1990.

Rockwell, John, *All American Music: Composition in the Late Twentieth Century*, Knopf, 1983, pp. 209-20.

PERIODICALS

America, December 12, 1987, p. 458.

Atlantic Monthly, December, 1984, p. 121.

Chicago Tribune, October 14, 1983; May 3, 1984; April 29, 1985; December 7, 1986; December 14, 1986; November 6, 1987; June 12, 1988.

Chicago Tribune Book World, April 15, 1984.

Daily News, April 6, 1964; April 27, 1970; February 26, 1973; May 3, 1984.

Insight, August 28, 1989, p. 59.

Journal of Popular Culture, winter, 1978, pp. 513-25.

Los Angeles Times, March 18, 1983; May 20, 1984, p. 3; November 26, 1984, pp. 1, 5.

Maclean's, December 24, 1984, p. 41.

Musical Quarterly, April, 1980, pp. 309-14.

Nation, December 12, 1987, pp. 725-27.

New Leader, December 28, 1987, pp. 18-19.

New Republic, June 18, 1984, pp. 25-26; December 21, 1987, pp. 28-30; April 3, 1989, pp. 28-29; January 1, 1990, pp. 27-28.

Newsweek, November 16, 1987, pp. 106-07; June 22, 1992, p. 52.

New York, November 16, 1987, p. 109; October 2, 1989, p. 82; August 20, 1990, pp. 120, 124.

New Yorker, August 11, 1975, pp. 74-76; November 16, 1987, pp. 147-48; February 11, 1991, pp. 68-69.

New York Post, March 19, 1965; April 19, 1977; May 3, 1984.

New York Times, March 6, 1983; July 24, 1983; April 4, 1984; May 3, 1984, p. C21; May 13, 1984, pp. 7, 31; October 13, 1984; October 26, 1984; May 24, 1985; September 9, 1985; July 23, 1987; October 9, 1987; November 1, 1987; May 10, 1988; January 22, 1990; September 30, 1990; November 7, 1990.

People, September 23, 1985, p. 78.

Saturday Review, May 1, 1971, pp. 16, 65.

Stereo Review, July, 1973, pp. 94-95.

Sunday Times (London), May 3, 1970.

Time, September 25, 1989, p. 76; February 4, 1991, p. 62.

Times (London), May 5, 1984; August 2, 1989; January 28, 1991, p. 16.

U.S. News and World Report, February 1, 1988, pp. 52-54.

Variety, April 8, 1964, p. 80; November 19, 1975, pp. 64-65; November 22, 1989; February 4, 1991, p. 95.

Vogue, April, 1984, p. 85.

Washington Post, November 18, 1981; November 6, 1987.

Women's Wear Daily, February 26, 1973.

—Sketch by Denise Kasinec

Jerry Spinelli

Personal

Born February 1, 1941, in Norristown, PA; son of Louis A. (a printer) and Lorna Mae (Bigler) Spinelli; married Eileen Mesi (a writer), May 21, 1977; children: Kevin, Barbara, Jeffrey, Molly, Sean, Ben. *Education:* Gettysburg College, A.B., 1963; Johns Hopkins University, M.A., 1964; attended Temple University, 1964. *Hobbies and other interests:* Tennis, country music, travel, pet rats.

Addresses

Home—331 Melvin Rd. Phoenixville, PA 19460. *Agent*—Ms. Ray Lincoln, Ray Lincoln Literary Agency, 7900 Old York Rd., 107-B, Elkins Park, PA 19117.

Career

Chilton Company (magazine publishers), Radnor, PA, editor, 1966-89; writer. *Military service:* U.S. Naval Reserve, 1966-72. *Member:* Philadelphia Writers Organization.

Awards, Honors

Boston Globe/Horn Book Award, 1990, Newbery Medal, American Library Association, 1991, and D. C. Fisher Award, 1992, all for *Maniac Magee;* Carolyn Field Award, 1991.

Writings

YOUNG ADULT NOVELS

Space Station Seventh Grade, Little, Brown, 1982.
Who Put That Hair in My Toothbrush?, Little, Brown, 1984.
Night of the Whale, Little, Brown, 1985.
Jason and Marceline, Little, Brown, 1986.
Dump Days, Little, Brown, 1988.
Maniac Magee, Little, Brown, 1990.
The Bathwater Gang, illustrated by Meredith Johnson, Little, Brown, 1990.
There's a Girl in My Hammerlock, Simon & Schuster, 1991.
Fourth Grade Rats, illustrated by Paul Casale, Scholastic, 1991.
The Bathwater Gang Gets Down to Business, illustrated by Johnson, Little, Brown, 1992.

"SCHOOL DAZE" SERIES

School Daze: Report to the Principal's Office, Scholastic, 1991, published as *Report to the Principal's Office!,* 1991.
Who Ran My Underwear Up the Flagpole?, Scholastic, 1992.
Do the Funky Pickle, Scholastic, 1992.

OTHER

Contributor to books, including *Our Roots Grow Deeper Than We Know: Pennsylvania Writers— Pennsylvania Life,* edited by Lee Gutkind, University of Pittsburgh Press, 1985; and *Noble Pursuits,* edited by Virginia A. Arnold and Carl B. Smith, Macmillan, 1988. Work also represented in anthologies, including *Best Sports Stories of 1982,* Dutton; and *Connections* (short stories), Dell.

■ Sidelights

Jerry Spinelli is "a master of those embarrassing, gloppy, painful and suddenly wonderful things that happen on the razor's edge between childhood and full-fledged adolescence," according to Deborah Churchman in the *Washington Post Book World.* Perhaps best known for his Newbery award-winning book, *Maniac Magee,* Spinelli is a noted teller of adolescent tales, recreating the teenage years with accuracy and humor. Popular with his young adult audience, Spinelli covers such controversial topics as racism and sex, writing in a youth-oriented style that sometimes brings him into conflict with parents who feel he is perhaps too realistic in his stories. Many critics, however, have noted that Spinelli presents adolescents as they are, acne, pubescent curiosity, and all. "He neither judges nor berates but shakes everyone up in his own bag of tricks and watches to see what will spill out," commented Ethel R. Twichell in the *Horn Book.* John Keller, also writing in the *Horn Book,* remarked: "Jerry has listened and observed, and, in language that is never self-consciously literary, he illuminates that rough magic children carry around with them."

Spinelli was born and raised in Norristown, Pennsylvania, and like many boys dreamed of becoming a major league baseball player when he grew up. But at sixteen his thoughts turned to professional writing when he wrote a poem commemorating the victory of his high school football team in a big game. The poem was published in the local newspaper and suddenly writing seemed as fascinating as baseball had once been. As an adult, Spinelli tried his hand at writing what he once called in *Contemporary Authors* "grown-up novels about important stuff," but they remained unpublished.

It wasn't until Spinelli married another writer, and became an instant father to her five children, that his career as a writer took a new direction. The children became the inspiration for much of his writing—the sibling rivalry, fighting, and general mayhem, combined with his own childhood memo-

ries. In his Newbery Medal acceptance speech published in *Horn Book,* Spinelli claimed, "For my first two books, I didn't even have to look outside my own house." And he once told *Contemporary Authors:* "One night one of our angels snuck into the refrigerator and swiped the fried chicken that I was saving for lunch the next day. When I discovered the chicken was gone, I did what I had done after the big football victory: I wrote about it. I didn't know it at the time, but I had begun to write my first published novel, *Space Station Seventh Grade.*" In his Newbery acceptance speech, Spinelli also described speaking before a group of children, answering the question of where he "got all that stuff" he wrote about. "I pointed to them. . . . 'You're the funny ones. You're the fascinating ones. You're the elusive and inspiring and promising and heroic and maddening ones.'" Instead of writing the "important stuff" about adults, Spinelli found his inspiration and his audience in young adults.

Of Girls and Space Stations

Spinelli began his writing career with the novel *Space Station Seventh Grade.* Jason Herkimer, the protagonist, is a thirteen-year-old boy, curious about his maturing pubescent body, interested in girls, and building a model space station in his spare time. He's also trying to survive his first year in junior high school. "Spinelli has written a marvelous, often hilarious, expose of Jason during his seventh-grade year," declared Virginia Marr in the *School Library Journal.* Falling in love with a cheerleader is only one of Jason's learning experiences, as he struggles through pimples, coping with the death of a friend's brother, and trying to get along with his parents and stepfather. James J. McPeak called *Space Station Seventh Grade* a "first-rate story of that age when boys are neither fish nor fowl, but simply fun."

Space Station Seventh Grade "is not . . . as frivolous as it seems at first; but it is consistently zippy and bright—and all the better for not waving its colors prematurely," stated a reviewer in *Kirkus Reviews.* The issue of racism enters the story subtly, through Jason's friend, Peter Kim, a Korean-American, and through an episode in a black neighborhood. Spinelli also touches on the role of women in today's society through Jason's relationship with Marceline McAllister, a classmate and fellow track team member. At first, Jason insults Marceline with one of his famous moose calls, for which he is suspended. But when she eventually beats him up his macho attitude diminishes drastically. Told in a

Is junior high the beginning of the end?

Space **S**tation **S**eventh **G**rade

Jerry Spinelli

CAN $3.95

In this 1982 novel, young Jason must contend with his maturing adolescent body and the trials of surviving junior high.

series of short, episodic chapters, the story is narrated by Jason and reads as if an adolescent had written it, complete with swearing, slang, and complaints about parents. "Jason is often racist, sexist, crude in his speech and gross in his habits. He is also sometimes sensitive and always uproariously funny," commented Marilyn H. Karrenbrock in the *ALAN Review*.

Some critics, however, found *Space Station Seventh Grade* "humorous, episodic, but weakly constructed," as noted by a reviewer for the *Bulletin of the Center for Children's Books*. Other critics found the language "crude" and Jason's behavior sometimes inappropriate, as when he and his friend Richie carry groceries for an elderly woman. Thinking that she is rich, the boys hope to be rewarded financially, but all they are offered is a glass of ice

water. "They behave outrageously" in response to this offering, commented Barbara A. Bannon in *Publishers Weekly*, wandering around the woman's house and looking in closets and rooms as the woman falls asleep. Twichell concluded: "For those who view adolescence from a comfortable distance, the author has produced a truly funny book; those presently at the precarious stage may find Jason's hilarious adventures all too painfully recognizable."

The adventures continue in *Jason and Marceline*, the sequel to *Space Station Seventh Grade*. Ninth-grader Jason has a crush on the individualistic Marceline, but she rejects him because of his macho attitude towards women. It is only after saving a choking seventh grader, and returning the boy's grateful, terrified hug, that Jason is reconciled with Marceline. "Spinelli's teenagers are fresh and funny, sometimes crude, sometimes poignant, and always very real," noted Diane Roback in *Publishers Weekly*.

As in *Space Station Seventh Grade*, Jason is the narrator of *Jason and Marceline*, and the reader watches events unfold through his eyes, from his first kiss with Marceline to drinking beer with his male friends. "Jason . . . truly sounds like a teenager," wrote Twichell, calling *Jason and Marceline* an "equally funny and often earthy sequel to *Space Station Seventh Grade*." Denise M. Wilms, writing in the *Booklist*, contended that "the crudeness here grates but is true to life, and the message is worthwhile." And *School Library Journal* contributor Robert Unsworth concluded: "It's a quick, witty read, and even the print is big."

The Best Laid Plans

"He calls her Megamouth. She calls him El Grosso," begins Karen Jameyson's *Horn Book* review of *Who Put That Hair in My Toothbrush?*, Spinelli's second published book. The story of twelve-year-old Megin Tofer and her older brother, fifteen-year-old Greg, *Who Put That Hair in My Toothbrush?* explores family relationships, especially sibling rivalry. In just one of many arguments, fights, and stunts, Greg is the one who puts "that hair" on his sister's toothbrush, much to her disgust. Subplots enliven the tale, as Greg falls in love with a dream girl and eventually realizes that what he really wants is the girl who is pursuing *him*. Megin is a tomboy, and ice hockey is her passion. She makes friends with another tomboy during the course of the story—Emilie Bain, a resident of the local nursing home whom Megin adopts as her grandmother.

In alternating chapters of *Who Put That Hair in My Toothbrush?*, Megin and Greg narrate their story as they fight each other, struggle with their parents and with their own emotions and problems, and relate the details of their individual lives. "The humor of the writing" alleviates the sometimes repetitive dialogue as Megin and Greg express their animosity, commented a reviewer in the *Bulletin of the Center for Children's Books.* By the end of the book, Greg and Megin realize the strength of family bonds, with Greg offering support to Megin when Emilie dies. "Spinelli keeps things very light most of the way through, shading into more serious feelings—with considerable finesse—only at the end," judged a critic in *Kirkus Reviews.* Jameyson concluded: "With a sure ear for adolescent dialogue—especially for that of boys—the author has again succeeded in creating a lively, absorbing novel."

In *Dump Days,* Spinelli writes for a slightly younger audience, telling of two sixth grade friends, J. D. and Duke, who spend part of their summer trying to make money so that they can afford to have the "Perfect Day." Through various schemes and plans, the boys try to improve their finances. Unfortunately, they never seem to prosper from their efforts. They forget to charge for their goods and services on one occasion, and on another they lose the money in a flood. The local dump provides a place to hang out, plot the Perfect Day, see rats, and find hidden treasures that they can sell. "Spinelli spins a story . . . of a friendship based on trust, humor, compassion and imagination," declared a reviewer in *Publishers Weekly.* Roger Sutton, writing in the *Bulletin of the Center for Children's Books,* also noted the "solid friendship" between the boys.

Finally, J. D. and Duke raise money at a block party, but only enough to replace their Vietnamese friend's violin that gets destroyed during the gathering. At story's end, they may not be the richer for all their efforts, but the boys are happier in the knowledge that they have helped a friend, and that there is always the next summer to try again for the Perfect Day. Sutton noted the "nostalgic glow" present in the novel, especially in the boy's "squeaky clean, overdone, and dated" slang, as in their expression, "krymineez." Twichell's review was more favorable, noting that "J. D. and Duke are as lighthearted a pair of adolescents to have ever slapped a high five" with "their entertaining and usually disastrous adventures."

For the Modern Age

"A blending of tall tale and actuality" is how Spinelli described his novel, *Maniac Magee,* to *Authors and Artists for Young Adults.* Fiction and reality merge "to the point where it makes no difference which is which," but his lesson against racism comes clearly across. This award-winning novel features Jeffrey Lionel Magee, an orphan who earns the name "Maniac" through his extraordinary running speed, abrupt appearances, and talent for hitting baseballs. The idea for Maniac grew out of Spinelli's and his friends' experiences and brushes with prejudice as youths. In his Newbery Medal acceptance speech, Spinelli recalled a black friend who had been raised in an orphanage. One summer he tried to get into a public pool with a group of other orphanage kids and was refused admittance. "He does not know if the running began that day. He recalls only that he ran everywhere he went. . . . That was the first patch in the quiltwork that became *Maniac Magee.*"

Among the numerous honors bestowed upon this 1990 book were the Newbery Medal and the *Boston Globe-Horn Book* Award.

"Spinelli, in his best book to date, creates a provocative slice of life," proclaimed Deborah Abbott in *Booklist*. When Maniac Magee loses his parents at an early age, he is sent to live with his unloving aunt and uncle. At age eleven he decides to leave and ends up in the segregated town of Two Mills. The East End of town is the black neighborhood, the West End is where the white families live. Maniac is the white boy who runs everywhere, lives with both white and black families, and is homeless in between. Amanda Beale and her loving family take Maniac in initially, but because he is white and they are black, he is forced to leave for their sakes after societal pressure becomes too much. He then lives with an older man, Earl Grayson, through fall and early winter in a basement, but unfortunately Grayson dies and Maniac is alone again. In the white West End, a family of beer drinking racists finally take Maniac in. There is a "feel-good ending," according to *School Library Journal* contributor Joel Shoemaker, in which tensions start to be resolved and Maniac finds a true home. "Spinelli writes humorously and bravely about a touchy subject," concluded Cathryn A. Camper in the *Five Owls*.

While racism may be the central concern in *Maniac Magee*, other issues surface, including homelessness and illiteracy. In between families, Maniac lives on the streets as a homeless child. And while he may not go to school, he reads everything he possibly can, even teaching others to read. He also teaches blacks and whites about one another, trying to lessen the tension between residents of Two Mills. His experiences as a white child who eventually lives on both sides of town give him the aura of a legend as a contemporary folk hero. *New York Times Book Review* contributor Alison Teal noted that "Spinelli grapples here with a racial tension rarely addressed in fiction for children in the middle grades." Presenting his tale in a manner that his readers will enjoy, Spinelli "brightens the story with exaggeration, humor, and melodrama," described Twichell.

In *There's a Girl in My Hammerlock*, Spinelli takes on another social issue, that of gender bias. Eighth-grader Maisie Potter, one of the school's best athletes, has a crush on Eric Delong. Told in a first-person narrative style, "Maisie's is an original and vibrant adolescent voice—curious, confident, and very alive," judged Susan Knorr in the *School Library Journal*. When her try-out for the cheerleading squad fails, Maisie joins the wrestling team, all in an effort to get closer to sports-minded Eric. Once on the team, she faces opposition from teammates, friends, and just about everyone else. Luckily, she has a supportive family to help her through and encourage her when she needs it. She also has a stubborn streak and the toughness to complete the season, especially after her one date with Eric doesn't turn out as she had expected. "A rattling good sports story that is clever, witty and tightly written," proclaimed a reviewer in *Publishers Weekly*. A reviewer in *Horn Book* commented that "the action zips along . . . with plenty of lively, believable dialogue," noting that *There's a Girl in My Hammerlock* is "likely to spark some serious thinking about gender stereotypes."

While Maisie is able to overcome the peer pressure surrounding her, fourth-grader Suds Morton, the narrator of *Fourth Grade Rats*, isn't nearly that tough. When Suds's best friend, Joey Peterson, decides to live up to the rhyme—"Third grade angels! Fourth grade rats!"—he drags Suds into the mischief, doing such awful, rat-like things as pulling first-graders off their swings. Joey's mother finally puts a stop to the antics, and Suds is

This 1992 book is the second of Spinelli's more recent "School Daze" series.

relieved. He's more interested in Judy Billings than rebellion, although he tries to fit in with his peers. "Unfortunately this story never feels authentic, and Joey and Suds's predicament and its resolution are pat and contrived," judged Claudia Logan, writing in the *Washington Post Book World*. Other critics were more positive, with a reviewer in *Publishers Weekly* writing that "rapid-fire dialogue and a hilarious string of episodes . . . unfold a story with a valuable message." Spinelli makes a statement about the hazards of peer pressure with his tale, and a reviewer in *Horn Book* noted: "The message is clear, but presented in a low-key and unobtrusive way that does not detract one whit from the fast-paced yarn."

Spinelli is a writer whose style and content have drawn a loyal following of readers—young adults facing social, moral, and personal problems and full of questions, just like his characters. A family man who draws on real-life events to both teach and entertain, Spinelli, as Keller wrote, "is a man who shines forth with the desire to be a writer, a man whose great drive is to share his vision of the world with his readers. As he creates the honest and accurate worlds reflected in so many of the passages of his novels, he is also a man whose enthusiasm for what he does is infectious."

■ Works Cited

Abbott, Deborah, review of *Maniac Magee*, *Booklist*, June 1, 1990, p. 1902.

Bannon, Barbara A., review of *Space Station Seventh Grade*, *Publishers Weekly*, December 24, 1982, p. 65.

Camper, Cathryn A., review of *Maniac Magee*, *Five Owls*, July/August, 1990, p. 108.

Churchman, Deborah, "Tales of the Awkward Age," *Washington Post Book World*, January 13, 1985, p. 8.

Contemporary Authors New Revision Series, Volume 30, Gale, 1990.

Review of *Dump Days, Publishers Weekly*, April 29, 1988, p. 77.

Review of *Fourth Grade Rats*, *Horn Book*, September, 1991, p. 594.

Review of *Fourth Grade Rats*, *Publishers Weekly*, September 27, 1991, p. 58.

Jameyson, Karen, review of *Who Put That Hair in My Toothbrush?*, *Horn Book*, June, 1984, pp. 343-44.

Karrenbrock, Marilyn H., review of *Space Station Seventh Grade*, *ALAN Review*, winter, 1985, p. 35.

Keller, John, "Jerry Spinelli," *Horn Book*, July/August, 1991, pp. 433-36.

Knorr, Susan, review of *There's a Girl in My Hammerlock*, *School Library Journal*, September, 1991, p. 260.

Logan, Claudia, review of *Fourth Grade Rats*, *Washington Post Book World*, August 11, 1991, p. 11.

Marr, Virginia, review of *Space Station Seventh Grade*, *School Library Journal*, October, 1982, p. 156.

McPeak, James J., review of *Space Station Seventh Grade*, *Voice of Youth Advocates*, April, 1983, p. 42.

Roback, Diane, review of *Jason and Marceline*, *Publishers Weekly*, November 28, 1986, p. 78.

Shoemaker, Joel, review of *Maniac Magee*, *School Library Journal*, June, 1990, p. 138.

Review of *Space Station Seventh Grade*, *Bulletin of the Center for Children's Books*, November, 1982, p. 56.

Review of *Space Station Seventh Grade*, *Kirkus Reviews*, November 1, 1982, pp. 1196-97.

Spinelli, Jerry, "Newbery Medal Acceptance," *Horn Book*, July/August, 1991, pp. 426-32.

Sutton, Roger, review of *Dump Days*, *Bulletin of the Center for Children's Books*, September, 1988, p. 21.

Teal, Alison, review of *Maniac Magee*, *New York Times Book Review*, April 21, 1991, p. 33.

Review of *There's a Girl in My Hammerlock*, *Horn Book*, September/October, 1991, p. 599.

Review of *There's a Girl in My Hammerlock*, *Publishers Weekly*, July 25, 1991, p. 54.

Twichell, Ethel R., review of *Dump Days*, *Horn Book*, May, 1988, p. 355.

Twichell, Ethel R., review of *Jason and Marceline*, *Horn Book*, March, 1987, p. 217.

Twichell, Ethel R., review of *Maniac Magee*, *Horn Book*, May, 1990, p. 340.

Twichell, Ethel R., review of *Space Station Seventh Grade*, *Horn Book*, February, 1983, p. 54.

Unsworth, Robert, review of *Jason and Marceline*, *School Library Journal*, February, 1987, p. 95.

Review of *Who Put That Hair in My Toothbrush?*, *Bulletin of the Center for Children's Books*, July, 1984, p. 213.

Review of *Who Put That Hair in My Toothbrush?*, *Kirkus Reviews*, May 1, 1984, pp. 51-2.

Wilms, Denise M., review of *Jason and Marceline*, *Booklist*, January 1, 1987, p. 712.

■ For More Information See

PERIODICALS

Best Sellers, February, 1983, p. 448.
Horn Book, January/February, 1991, pp. 40-41; July/August 1991, pp. 433-436.
Kirkus Reviews, May 1, 1990, p. 655.
Los Angeles Times, May 9, 1987.

School Library Journal, September, 1984, p. 134; June, 1990, p. 138; February, 1991, pp. 12-13; August, 1991, p. 169.
Voice of Youth Advocates, December, 1990, p. 290.
Washington Post Book World, January 13, 1985, p. 8.

—*Sketch by Terrie M. Rooney*

John Rowe Townsend

■ Personal

Born May 10, 1922, in Leeds, England; son of George Edmund Rowe (a clerk) and Gladys (a secretary; maiden name, Page) Townsend; married Vera Lancaster, July 3, 1948 (died May 9, 1973); children: Alethea Mary, Nicholas John, Penelope Anne. *Education:* Emmanuel College, Cambridge, B.A., 1949, M.A., 1954.

■ Addresses

Home—72 Water Ln., Histon, Cambridge CB4 4LR, England.

■ Career

Journalist for the *Yorkshire Post,* 1946, and *Evening Standard,* 1949; *Manchester Guardian,* Manchester, England, sub-editor, 1949-54, art editor, 1954-55, editor of *Manchester Guardian Weekly,* 1955-69, part-time children's books editor, 1968-79, columnist, 1968-81; writer and lecturer, 1969—. Simmons College Center for the Study of Children's Literature, adjunct professor, 1978-86; Children's Literature New England, faculty member, 1987—, board member, 1990—. Member of

Harvard International Seminar, 1956. Visiting lecturer, University of Pennsylvania, 1965, and University of Washington, 1969 and 1971; May Hill Arbuthnot Honor Lecturer, Atlanta, GA, 1971; Anne Carroll Moore Lecturer, New York Public Library, 1971; Whittall Lecturer, Library of Congress, 1976. Founder, with Jill Paton Walsh, of Green Bay Publishers, 1986. *Military service:* Royal Air Force, 1942-46; became flight sergeant. *Member:* Society of Authors (chairman of children's writers and illustrators group, 1977-78 and 1990-91; member of management committee, 1982-85).

■ Awards, Honors

Carnegie Medal honors citation, 1963, for *Hell's Edge;* Carnegie Medal honors citation, 1969, Silver Pen award, English Centre of International PEN, and *Boston Globe-Horn Book* Award for excellence in text, both 1970, and Edgar Allan Poe Award, Mystery Writers of America, 1971, all for *The Intruder;* Christopher Award, 1982, for *The Islanders; Trouble in the Jungle, Good-bye to the Jungle, Pirate's Island, The Intruder, The Summer People, Noah's Castle,* and *Good-night, Prof, Dear* appeared on the American Library Association notable books list; *Trouble in the Jungle, The Intruder, The Islanders,* and *A Sense of Story* appeared on the *Horn Book* Honor List.

■ Writings

"JUNGLE" SERIES; FOR CHILDREN

Gumble's Yard, illustrated by Dick Hart, Hutchinson, 1961, published as *Trouble in the Jungle*, illustrated by W. T. Mars, Lippincott, 1969.

Widdershins Crescent, Hutchinson, 1965, published as *Good-bye to the Jungle*, Lippincott, 1967, revised edition published as *Good-bye to Gumble's Yard*, Penguin, 1981.

Pirate's Island, illustrated by Douglas Hall, Lippincott, 1968.

FOR CHILDREN

A Wish for Wings, illustrated by Philip Gough, Heinemann, 1972.

Top of the World, illustrated by Nikki Jones, Oxford University Press, 1976, illustrated by John Wallner, Lippincott, 1977.

Clever Dick, Oxford University Press, 1982.

Dan Alone, Lippincott, 1983.

Gone to the Dogs, Oxford University Press, 1984.

Tom Tiddler's Ground, illustrated by Mark Peppe, Kestrel, 1985, Lippincott, 1986, published as *The Hidden Treasure*, Scholastic, Inc., 1988.

The Persuading Stick (novel), Lothrop, 1986.

Rob's Place (novel), Viking Kestrel, 1987, Lothrop, 1988.

FOR YOUNG ADULTS

Hell's Edge, Hutchinson, 1963, Lothrop, 1969.

The Hallersage Sound, Hutchinson, 1966.

The Intruder (novel), illustrated by Graham Humphreys, Oxford University Press, 1969, illustrated by Joseph A. Phelan, Lippincott, 1970.

Good-night, Prof, Love, illustrated by Peter Farmer, Oxford University Press, 1970, published as *Good-night, Prof, Dear*, Lippincott, 1971, published as *The Runaways*, edited by David Fickling, Oxford University Press, 1979.

(Compiler) *Modern Poetry: A Selection*, reproductions chosen by Doreen Roberts, Oxford University Press, 1971, photographs by Barbara Pfeffer, Lippincott, 1974.

The Summer People, illustrated by Robert Micklewright, Lippincott, 1972.

Forest of the Night, illustrated by Farmer, Oxford University Press, 1974, illustrated by Beverly Brodsky McDermott, Lippincott, 1975.

Noah's Castle, Lippincott, 1975.

The Xanadu Manuscript, illustrated by Paul Ritchie, Oxford University Press, 1977, published as *The Visitors*, Lippincott, 1977.

King Creature, Come, Oxford University Press, 1980, published as *The Creatures*, Lippincott, 1980.

The Islanders, Lippincott, 1981.

A Foreign Affair, Kestrel, 1982, published as *Kate and the Revolution*, Lippincott, 1982.

Cloudy-bright (novel), Lippincott, 1984.

Downstream (novel), Lippincott, 1987.

Cranford Revisited, Green Bay Publications, 1989.

The Golden Journey (novel), Viking Kestrel, 1989, published as *The Fortunate Isles*, Lippincott, 1989.

The Invaders, Oxford University Press, 1992.

Contributor to *The Friday Miracle and Other Stories*, edited by Kaye Webb, Puffin, 1969; and *Hundreds and Hundreds*, edited by Peter Dickinson, 1984.

OTHER

Written for Children: An Outline of English-language Children's Literature, J. Garnet Miller, 1965, Lothrop, 1967, 5th edition, Bodley Head, 1990.

A Sense of Story: Essays on Contemporary Writers for Children, Lippincott, 1971, revised edition published as *A Sounding of Storytellers: New and Revised Essays on Contemporary Writers for Children*, Lippincott, 1979.

(Selector) *Twenty-five Years of British Children's Books*, National Book League, 1977.

Contributor to books, including *Only Connect*, edited by Sheila Egoff, G. T. Stubbs, and L. F. Ashley, Oxford University Press, 1969; *Cross-currents of Criticism*, edited by Paul Heins, Horn Book, 1977; and *The Openhearted Audience: Ten Authors Talk about Writing for Children*, edited by Virginia Haviland, Library of Congress, 1980. Contributor of articles and reviews to periodicals, including *Manchester Guardian*, *Times Literary Supplement*, and *Horn Book*.

Townsend's works have been translated into over a dozen languages.

■ Adaptations

ITV television series were produced for *The Intruder*, 1972, and *Noah's Castle*, 1980; *Gumble's Yard* was adapted for television.

■ Sidelights

In some of the books John Rowe Townsend read as a child, "wicked children—that is, children who did almost any of the things that children would the Number One Field Intelligence Unit, Townsend followed the British troops into the territory they captured and reported on the goods their enemy had left behind as they had retreated. When the troops themselves did not move forward, however, neither did Townsend's outfit, and he soon found himself detained in Florence, a historic city celebrated for its works of art. Of the city, Townsend wrote: "There my education began.... I suddenly found myself aware of art and architecture, and, arising rapidly out of this awareness, literature." The atmosphere of Florence inspired Townsend; he began to read poetry, study paintings, and wonder how other people had interpreted or reacted to the art he had seen. He finally realized that he wanted to return to school so he could learn more.

It Looked Like a College

Back in England in 1946, Townsend did not follow the normal procedures someone hoping to be

Published in 1969, this novel tells the story of children left alone to survive by their own wits.

admitted to a university would have. He took a train and then a bus from Leeds to the University of Cambridge, walked into a building that he thought must be a college, and found his way to a Senior Tutor. A three-hour conversation convinced the Tutor to offer Townsend admission. This was an unheard of manner of getting into Cambridge, a highly respected institution constantly beset by a considerable number of qualified applicants. But the following year, Townsend became a student and, not long after that, a husband. In 1948, he married Vera Lancaster, whom he had met early in the war while he worked in the civil service.

Townsend decided that he would major in English. He and Vera lived happily and simply on a grant. The university was full of veterans and their wives, and Cambridge "was an idyll," Townsend wrote in *SAAS*. Aside from his studies, Townsend became interested in journalism and joined the student newspaper. He quickly rose to chief editor, and though the time needed for his spot on the paper took away from the time he could dedicate to his studies, Townsend never looked back. In the manner of many collegiate newspaper staffs, Townsend and his colleagues wrote articles criticizing the university's administration as well as penning the necessary columns and editorials. In *SAAS*, Townsend admitted, "I never enjoyed journalism so much again."

Though Townsend still considered writing books his main ambition, when he graduated from Cambridge he was heavily involved with his journalistic pursuits and thought he should try for a position on a major paper. Ideally, he wanted to work for the *Manchester Guardian*, so he wrote the editor a letter. When he received no reply, he wrote again. He still didn't get an answer. Then, after writing the chairman of the Gas Board a stinging letter in response to a billing error, Townsend wrote a third time to the editor of the *Guardian*, A. P. Wadsworth, criticizing him for not responding to his business correspondence. Much as Townsend had innocently walked into Cambridge and had been offered admission in a singular way, this final, untraditional letter opened the door for him: Wadsworth replied to Townsend's heated letter, requested an interview, and finally gave Townsend a position on the staff.

Aside from the editor's interest in outspoken, uninhibited candidates, Townsend believes that Wadsworth was attracted to his application because of his interest in newspaper design at a time when few others were. Townsend's first three years at the *Guardian* were spent as a sub-editor, normally want to do—were duly punished and warned where their sins would ultimately lead them," he wrote in an autobiographical essay for the *Something about the Author Autobiography Series (SAAS)*. "Goody-goodies were praised and rewarded. It was all rather alarming." When Townsend was eight, he decided to write his own book, one more to his liking. *The Crew's Boat*, which covered the pages of five notebooks, was written in pencil and illustrated with crayon. It told the story of a family whose twelve children decide to build a boat by hollowing out a tree trunk. Then they set sail around the world, from ocean to ocean, conquering the primitive tribes they find on distant islands and teaching them civilized ways. After completing this debut, Townsend didn't write another book for thirty years. The next book, more realistic than the first, began his career as an author of children's books. Now Townsend is the author of an extensive list of respected titles, which include both young adult novels and volumes of criticism on children's literature.

When Townsend was born in 1922, his hometown, Leeds, England, was crowded with industries and shops. The particular district in which the Townsends lived always seemed tilted: it was built on a hillside that the streetcar would crawl up on its way to the suburbs and then, once it had reached the top of the hill, scream back down. "It was a small, urban world—a maze of narrow streets and alleyways, a world of little cramped dwellings and corner shops," Townsend wrote in *SAAS*. Mr. Townsend's clerking job made his family somewhat prosperous until he developed Parkinson's disease when Townsend was still a boy. Eventually, Mr. Townsend was unable to work, and the small pension that the family had to depend on for daily needs made circumstances difficult. Townsend's youth was shadowed by his father's affliction.

A strong student in elementary school, Townsend received a scholarship to attend Leeds Grammar School. Though the scholarship paid for books and tuition, the other obligatory expenses (uniforms, field trips) proved to be a heavy burden for the already financially despondent family. Though Townsend remained a top student at Leeds, he considered school just a duty he owed his parents out of respect and thought of education itself merely as a means to acquire the diplomas necessary for adult life. The literature he studied interested him only as the material that would later show up on exams, not as an art form, though he did think throughout school that he would be a writer someday.

Artist Francoise Taylor's depiction of Townsend i office when he worked for the *Manchester Guard*

Because they would not have been able to aff send Townsend to college even if he had another scholarship, the Townsends took the out of school when he was seventeen and him in a job at the Inland Revenue (incom department of the civil service. There, Tow became interested in the lives that were hir in the department's files. "Contrary to what be supposed," he noted in his *SAAS* essay, "v the Revenue gave one remarkable insight people's histories, ways of life and private s as well as their finances. I used to read th with eager interest while eating my lun sandwiches. [The files] were an education ways of the world."

Another education would come when, with War II being waged, Townsend joined the Air Force at the age of twenty. He kn eyesight would prohibit him from beco pilot but hoped to land a position as a navigator. He failed the vision test for that however, and was given a job encoding After being stationed in Egypt and Pa Townsend landed in Italy in 1944. As a me normally want to do—were duly punished and warned where their sins would ultimately lead them," he wrote in an autobiographical essay for the *Something about the Author Autobiography Series (SAAS)*. "Goody-goodies were praised and rewarded. It was all rather alarming." When Townsend was eight, he decided to write his own book, one more to his liking. *The Crew's Boat*, which covered the pages of five notebooks, was written in pencil and illustrated with crayon. It told the story of a family whose twelve children decide to build a boat by hollowing out a tree trunk. Then they set sail around the world, from ocean to ocean, conquering the primitive tribes they find on distant islands and teaching them civilized ways. After completing this debut, Townsend didn't write another book for thirty years. The next book, more realistic than the first, began his career as an author of children's books. Now Townsend is the author of an extensive list of respected titles, which include both young adult novels and volumes of criticism on children's literature.

When Townsend was born in 1922, his hometown, Leeds, England, was crowded with industries and shops. The particular district in which the Townsends lived always seemed tilted: it was built on a hillside that the streetcar would crawl up on its way to the suburbs and then, once it had reached the top of the hill, scream back down. "It was a small, urban world—a maze of narrow streets and alleyways, a world of little cramped dwellings and corner shops," Townsend wrote in *SAAS*. Mr. Townsend's clerking job made his family somewhat prosperous until he developed Parkinson's disease when Townsend was still a boy. Eventually, Mr. Townsend was unable to work, and the small pension that the family had to depend on for daily needs made circumstances difficult. Townsend's youth was shadowed by his father's affliction.

A strong student in elementary school, Townsend received a scholarship to attend Leeds Grammar School. Though the scholarship paid for books and tuition, the other obligatory expenses (uniforms, field trips) proved to be a heavy burden for the already financially despondent family. Though Townsend remained a top student at Leeds, he considered school just a duty he owed his parents out of respect and thought of education itself merely as a means to acquire the diplomas necessary for adult life. The literature he studied interested him only as the material that would later show up on exams, not as an art form, though he did think throughout school that he would be a writer someday.

Artist Francoise Taylor's depiction of Townsend in his office when he worked for the *Manchester Guardian*.

Because they would not have been able to afford to send Townsend to college even if he had won another scholarship, the Townsends took their son out of school when he was seventeen and placed him in a job at the Inland Revenue (income tax) department of the civil service. There, Townsend became interested in the lives that were hinted at in the department's files. "Contrary to what might be supposed," he noted in his *SAAS* essay, "work in the Revenue gave one remarkable insights into people's histories, ways of life and private secrets, as well as their finances. I used to read the files with eager interest while eating my lunchtime sandwiches. [The files] were an education in the ways of the world."

Another education would come when, with World War II being waged, Townsend joined the Royal Air Force at the age of twenty. He knew his eyesight would prohibit him from becoming a pilot but hoped to land a position as a radio-navigator. He failed the vision test for that as well, however, and was given a job encoding reports. After being stationed in Egypt and Palestine, Townsend landed in Italy in 1944. As a member of the Number One Field Intelligence Unit, Townsend followed the British troops into the territory they captured and reported on the goods their enemy had left behind as they had retreated. When the troops themselves did not move forward, however, neither did Townsend's outfit, and he soon found himself detained in Florence, a historic city celebrated for its works of art. Of the city, Townsend wrote: "There my education began. . . . I suddenly found myself aware of art and architecture, and, arising rapidly out of this awareness, literature." The atmosphere of Florence inspired Townsend; he began to read poetry, study paintings, and wonder how other people had interpreted or reacted to the art he had seen. He finally realized that he wanted to return to school so he could learn more.

It Looked Like a College

Back in England in 1946, Townsend did not follow the normal procedures someone hoping to be

Published in 1969, this novel tells the story of children left alone to survive by their own wits.

admitted to a university would have. He took a train and then a bus from Leeds to the University of Cambridge, walked into a building that he thought must be a college, and found his way to a Senior Tutor. A three-hour conversation convinced the Tutor to offer Townsend admission. This was an unheard of manner of getting into Cambridge, a highly respected institution constantly beset by a considerable number of qualified applicants. But the following year, Townsend became a student and, not long after that, a husband. In 1948, he married Vera Lancaster, whom he had met early in the war while he worked in the civil service.

Townsend decided that he would major in English. He and Vera lived happily and simply on a grant. The university was full of veterans and their wives, and Cambridge "was an idyll," Townsend wrote in *SAAS*. Aside from his studies, Townsend became interested in journalism and joined the student newspaper. He quickly rose to chief editor, and though the time needed for his spot on the paper took away from the time he could dedicate to his studies, Townsend never looked back. In the manner of many collegiate newspaper staffs, Townsend and his colleagues wrote articles criticizing the university's administration as well as penning the necessary columns and editorials. In *SAAS*, Townsend admitted, "I never enjoyed journalism so much again."

Though Townsend still considered writing books his main ambition, when he graduated from Cambridge he was heavily involved with his journalistic pursuits and thought he should try for a position on a major paper. Ideally, he wanted to work for the *Manchester Guardian,* so he wrote the editor a letter. When he received no reply, he wrote again. He still didn't get an answer. Then, after writing the chairman of the Gas Board a stinging letter in response to a billing error, Townsend wrote a third time to the editor of the *Guardian,* A. P. Wadsworth, criticizing him for not responding to his business correspondence. Much as Townsend had innocently walked into Cambridge and had been offered admission in a singular way, this final, untraditional letter opened the door for him: Wadsworth replied to Townsend's heated letter, requested an interview, and finally gave Townsend a position on the staff.

Aside from the editor's interest in outspoken, uninhibited candidates, Townsend believes that Wadsworth was attracted to his application because of his interest in newspaper design at a time when few others were. Townsend's first three years at the *Guardian* were spent as a sub-editor, self, and he sets out to try to determine who he could be if this mysterious stranger's claim is correct. As Arnold looks for clues to the real truth of his past, Sonny turns murderous, and chases Arnold across the sands on the night of a tempest. Sonny dies in the ensuing storm, and Arnold's guilt at having caused another's death overcomes him. Finally, however, he accepts that his identity is determined not by what his name happens to be or who his father is, but instead by who he makes himself to be through his actions. "Over the whole novel," Barnes wrote, "there hangs a sense of the transience of mortal things in comparison with the permanence of the natural world." Neil Millar described *The Intruder* in the *Christian Science Monitor* as "unsentimental, unsweetened, [and] uncompromisingly honest." In *The Nesbit Tradition: The Children's Novel in England, 1945-1970*, Marcus Crouch called the novel "one of the outstanding books of its decade."

Fantasies Real and Imagined

For his 1982 book *A Foreign Affair* (published in the United States as *Kate and the Revolution*), Townsend built on a game he and his friends had played while at Leeds Grammar School. Though his years at the school were not marked with intellectual vigor, Townsend did secretly create with his friends a complex game in which each of the players was the ruler of a Ruritanian state. They conducted the affairs of state with notes passed between them when the teacher was distracted. The game, Townsend wrote in *SAAS*, was "an escape from what I saw as the necessary drudgery of schoolwork and from the hard times that afflicted my home." Later, the game also gave Townsend the idea for a book, and *A Foreign Affair* was the result. Written to provide fun and enjoyment, the book pairs Kate, a sixteen-year-old Londoner, with Rudi, a prince from a tiny kingdom in the middle of Europe, Essenheim. Kate is suspicious of Rudi's advances at a party, his handsomeness making her skeptical that he could be genuinely attracted to a plain girl like herself. Her suspicions are well-founded: Rudi uses Kate, the type of women respected and found desirable in Essenheim, to get his great uncle, the Prince Laureate, to make him his successor. The ensuing escapades are filled with comedy and satire. A *Growing Point* contributor praised "the sheer professional technique which lies behind the smooth, rapid, easy narrative style," and maintained: "The sentence rhythms and syntax suit perfectly an adventure story illuminated with verbal wit and a most disarming sense of the ridiculous. Indeed, this is a book to enjoy." In the *Times Literary Supplement*, Alan Brownjohn wrote that *A Foreign Affair* "is salted with more than a little wry intelligence and nicely-placed wisdom."

In *The Persuading Stick*, Townsend again moved to new ground, this time touching on the realm of magic. Sarah Casson, routinely overlooked by both her family members and schoolmates, finds a stick beside the canal. Suddenly, she realizes that the stick allows her to make people do the things she wishes them to. At first, those actions are minor and innocent: her family spends more time together and gives her more attention, her teacher dismisses the class early, and her mother makes her special dishes. Sarah soon worries that she shouldn't be using this newfound power, however, because it doesn't seem right to manipulate people. But when Sarah's distressed older brother threatens to kill himself, she manages to change his mind without the benefit of the stick, leaving it up to the reader to decide whether the stick is truly magical or if Sarah herself has been doing the persuading. A *Kirkus Reviews* contributor called *The Persuading Stick* "a thoughtful exploration of the discovery of constructive assertiveness by a naturally nondominant child," and Gerald Mangan identified the novel in the *Times Literary Supplement* as "a very absorbing little parable."

Rob's Place, which was published in 1987, also deals with the plight of a troubled child. After eleven-year-old Rob's parents divorce, his best friend moves away, leaving him to deal with the new home situation alone. Then his mother and new stepfather have a baby, and the child's crying keeps all of them up during the night. To escape the situation, Rob turns to fantasy: he envisions an island that he peoples with characters he has read about in books. He daydreams of the island when his environment is to much for him to handle, but the innocent psychological game becomes more serious as he becomes more depressed and the island begins to invade both his waking and sleeping hours. Eventually, Rob does manage to get help from a new friend. A *School Library Journal* contributor praised the scenes that take place on the island for being "especially vivid," and a *Publishers Weekly* reviewer called *Rob's Place* "an imaginative and thought-provoking depiction of a boy's struggle to adjust."

Further stepping away from the social realism which marked his early novels, Townsend writes of a purely fantastical setting in 1989's *The Golden Journey* (published in the United States as *The*

Fortunate Isles). On a group of islands inspired by the Greek philosopher Plato's descriptions of the legendary city Atlantis, Townsend creates a nation of people consisting of two classes: nobles, who are identified by their blond hair and blue eyes, and plebeians, who all have black hair and dark eyes. Against this backdrop, the poor Eleni stands out: her unique combination of dark hair and blue eyes assigns her the prophesied role of Messenger, to whom legend has given the duty to travel to the Holy Mountain and see the Living God in order to free her people from their unjust king. Though Eleni herself doesn't uphold these religious beliefs, she sets out on a challenging, peril-filled journey with two companions. The setting of *The Golden Journey* was called "believable" by a *Kirkus Reviews* contributor, and a *Horn Book* reviewer praised Townsend's ability to build "some of the scenes into an extravaganza constructed of myth, legend, and fantasy."

About Writing and Writers

Outside of the fictional works Townsend has written, he is also the author of critical literature on children's books. *Written for Children: An Outline of English-language Children's Literature*, which Townsend composed at the suggestion of his editor, examines the evolution of children's books from the fifteenth century to the present. Some of the subjects the book focuses on are illustrations, poetry, and picture books found in England, the United States, Canada, and Australia. In his *SAAS* essay, Townsend described his own approach to evaluating literature: "My personal leaning is toward appreciative criticism. I try to approach every new book in a spirit of hope and excitement, though not without discrimination. One thing I believe most passionately is that a good book for young people must be a good book, period." Townsend also wrote the study *A Sense of Story: Essays on Contemporary Writers for Children*, which overviews the work of nineteen children's books authors—including Madeleine L'Engle, Andre Norton, and Rosemary Sutcliff—in separate chapters, each of which is followed by a short essay by the author and a bibliography of his or her works. These books of criticism helped establish Townsend not only as a children's book author, but also as an author of books about children's books.

Townsend's fiction has touched on many themes, but he specifically noted two in *SAAS*: "One is a theme that a great many writers for children and young people have explored in different ways—the theme of youngsters taking on responsibility for their own and other lives when the adults cannot or will not do so. Other themes are more individual to myself. I am endlessly fascinated by human relationships which have to grow and flower in a brief period of time." As well as allowing the author to explore these themes, Townsend's books have brought him happiness. "Professionally, I'm one of the world's lucky ones," he wrote. "I am what I always wanted to be, a writer." But even a fortunate writer with a long career behind him has a childhood identity, and Townsend acknowledges in his essay that it, too, forms a part of him: "I recognize now that at the deepest roots I am, and shall be until I die, a child from Leeds."

■ Works Cited

Barnes, Ron, "John Rowe Townsend's Novels of Adolescence," *Children's Literature in Education*, winter, 1975, pp. 178-190.

Brownjohn, Alan, review of *A Foreign Affair*, *Times Literary Supplement*, September 17, 1982, p. 1001.

Crouch, Marcus, *The Nesbit Tradition: The Children's Novel in England, 1945-1970*, Ernest Benn, 1972, p. 208.

Review of *A Foreign Affair*, *Growing Point*, September, 1982, p. 3942.

Review of *The Fortunate Isles*, *Horn Book*, March/April, 1990, pp. 211-212.

Review of *The Fortunate Isles*, *Kirkus Reviews*, September 15, 1989, p. 1410.

Review of *Gumble's Yard*, *Times Literary Supplement*, December 1, 1961, p. xx.

Mangan, Gerald, review of *The Persuading Stick*, *Times Literary Supplement*, November 28, 1986, p. 1344.

Manthorne, Jane, review of *Hell's Edge*, *New York Times Book Review*, August 31, 1969, p. 16.

Millar, Neil, review of *The Intruder*, *Christian Science Monitor*, May 7, 1970, p. B6.

Review of *The Persuading Stick*, *Kirkus Reviews*, September 15, 1987, p. 1398.

Review of *Rob's Place*, *Publishers Weekly*, April 29, 1988, p. 78.

Review of *Rob's Place*, *School Library Journal*, March, 1988, p. 201.

Townsend, John Rowe, autobiographical essay in *Something about the Author Autobiography Series*, Volume 2, Gale, 1986, pp. 271-286.

Review of *Widdershins Crescent*, *Times Literary Supplement*, December 9, 1965, p. 1142.

■ For More Information See

BOOKS

Blishen, Edward, editor, *The Thorny Paradise*, Kestrel, 1975, pp. 146-156.

Children's Literature Review, Volume 2, Gale, 1976, pp. 169-175.

PERIODICALS

Best Sellers, May 1, 1967; June 1, 1969.

Books and Bookmen, July, 1968.

Book World, December 3, 1967; May 5, 1968; May 17, 1970; May 9, 1971.

Canadian Children's Literature, Volume 48, 1987, pp. 29-41.

Christian Science Monitor, May 4, 1967.

Cricket, September, 1983.

Horn Book, April, 1967; June, 1967; August, 1968; August, 1970; June, 1971; August, 1971; October, 1971; April, 1973; June, 1973, pp. 241-247; April, 1975; October, 1975; August, 1977; December, 1977; October, 1982; January, 1985; January, 1987; July, 1987; March, 1988; March, 1990.

New Society (London), December 7, 1967.

New Yorker, December 16, 1967; December 14, 1968.

New York Times Book Review, May 7, 1967; November 5, 1967; May 26, 1968; April 26, 1970; May 2, 1971; November 5, 1972; November 19, 1972; December 29, 1974; April 11, 1976; April 3, 1977; November 6, 1977; February 19, 1984.

Times Literary Supplement, November 24, 1966; May 25, 1967; March 14, 1968; October 16, 1969; October 30, 1970; October 22, 1971; December 3, 1971; November 3, 1972; December 6, 1974; April 4, 1975; December 5, 1975; December 10, 1976; July 15, 1977; July 18, 1980; September 18, 1981; September 17, 1982; July 27, 1984; October 11, 1985; November 28, 1986.

Washington Post Book World, May 2, 1976.

Young Reader's Review, May, 1967; April, 1968.

—Sketch by Roger M. Valade III

Keenan Ivory Wayans

■ Personal

Born c. 1958, in New York, NY; son of Howell (in sales) and Elvira (a homemaker) Wayans. *Education:* Attended Tuskegee Institute.

■ Addresses

Home—Los Angeles, CA. *Office*—Ivory Way Productions, 5746 Sunset Blvd., Hollywood, CA 90028.

■ Career

Comedian, actor, director, producer, and screenwriter. Began career as a stand-up comedian at various comedy clubs in New York City and Los Angeles, CA. Television work includes: actor in *Irene* (pilot), 1981, and *For Love and Honor* (series), 1983-84; coproducer and cowriter of *Robert Townsend and His Partners in Crime* (comedy special), 1987; executive producer and writer of *Hammer, Slammer, and Slade* (comedy pilot), 1990; creator, executive producer, actor, and head writer, *In Living Color* (series), 1990-92; guest on specials, including *Motown Thirty: What's Goin' On!*, 1990, *MTV's 1990 Video Music Awards*, 1990,

Comic Relief V, 1991, *The Fifth Annual American Comedy Awards*, 1991, and *The American Music Awards*, 1991; guest on series *A Different World*, *Benson*, and *Cheers*. Film work includes: actor, *Star 80*, 1983; actor and cowriter, *Hollywood Shuffle*, 1987; actor, coproducer, and cowriter, *Eddie Murphy Raw*, 1987; director, actor, and writer, *I'm Gonna Git You Sucka*, 1988; cowriter, *The Five Heartbeats*, 1991. *Member:* Screen Actors Guild, Directors Guild of America, Screen Writers Guild.

■ Awards, Honors

Emmy Award for outstanding variety, music, or comedy program, American Academy of Television Arts and Sciences, 1990, for *In Living Color;* Emmy Award nominations for outstanding writing in a variety or music program, 1990 and 1991, and outstanding individual performance in a variety or music program, 1991, all for *In Living Color*.

■ Writings

SCRIPTS FOR TELEVISION

(With Robert Townsend) *Robert Townsend and His Partners in Crime* (special), HBO, 1987.
Hammer, Slammer, and Slade (pilot), ABC, 1990.
In Living Color (series), Fox, 1990-92.

SCREENPLAYS

(With Townsend) *Hollywood Shuffle*, Samuel Goldwyn, 1987.
(With Eddie Murphy and Townsend) *Eddie Murphy Raw* (sketch portions), Paramount, 1987.

(And director) *I'm Gonna Git You Sucka,* Metro-Goldwyn-Mayer/United Artists, 1988.

(With Townsend) *The Five Heartbeats,* Twentieth Century-Fox, 1991.

■ Work in Progress

Writing comedy film with brother.

■ Sidelights

The second oldest of ten children, Keenen Ivory Wayans grew up in a household where suppertime was filled with humor and laughter. His ready-made audience afforded him the opportunity to develop his unique brand of comedy and to practice for a career in the entertainment business. After his beginnings as a stand-up comedian, Wayans successfully ventured into acting, directing, and writing for film and television. His work, which often pokes fun at the stereotyping of blacks and their culture, has earned him a devoted public following. From his involvement in films like *Hollywood Shuffle* and *I'm Gonna Git You Sucka* to his creation of the prime-time television comedy series *In Living Color,* Wayans has presented controversial, cutting-edge humor that often catches viewers off guard and finds a mixed critical reception. "I want to be an entity," Wayans told *New York*'s Dinitia Smith, adding "a source of product, people."

Wayans was born and raised in New York City. Early in his life he experienced racism firsthand. For example, on occasion one local white police officer would prompt Wayans and his brother to race each other and then trip them. Even though Wayans and his family were victims of prejudice at times, he told *People* contributors Charles E. Cohen and Vicki Sheff that his mother and father "always built up our self-esteem." Wayans's father had a career in sales, and his mother was a homemaker. The family lived in a tenement in Harlem until Wayans was six years old and then moved into a predominantly white housing project where Wayans was frequently harassed by white teenagers. The children shared three rooms, and for privacy Wayans would retreat into a bedroom closet and dream about his future as an entertainer.

The same year they moved, Wayans realized he wanted to become a comedian after he saw actor and comic Richard Pryor delivering a stand-up performance on television. "He was doing routines about being poor, about looking for money, about being beaten up by the school bully. It was all happening to me at the time," explained Wayans to Smith. His penchant for humor was also fueled by his family, who would practice making each other laugh at dinnertime. Wayans recalled for Smith, "All of us sitting around the table, the food would just fly out of our mouths! We'd love it when someone would get mad. That's where we get the edge to our comedy."

Because of his flare for comedy, Wayans stood out in a crowd at his high school. "I was a tall, gangly, Afro-wearing teen-ager who figured his best shot at attracting girls was by making them laugh," he confessed to *Hollywood Reporter* writer Christopher Vaughn. Wayans and his younger brother Damon were inseparable, rattling off jokes as a team; they would make up characters and act them out for their friends and family. (Some of these characters later appeared on Wayans's show *In Living Color,* which also starred Damon.) Wayans told Smith that he stayed away from drugs and alcohol in high school, and he worked long hours as a McDonald's manager to help support his family.

After graduation, Wayans attended Alabama's Tuskegee Institute under a scholarship to study engineering. "I had such culture shock down there.... [Y]ou'd get downtown and it wasn't nothing but a pharmacy and a Goodwill store," recalled Wayans to *Interview* contributor Kevin Sessums. Wayans continued to liberate his comedy in college, and before his senior year began he decided to quit school and follow his dream of becoming a comedian. He began his career in New York City's prominent comedy club, The Improv, where he met then sixteen-year-old actor and comedian Eddie Murphy. Wayans told Smith that he remembers the young Murphy stating, "'I thought I was the only funny black guy in New York. Now I see there are two.'" Later Wayans would help write Murphy's concert film, *Eddie Murphy Raw,* which became the most lucrative concert film made to that date. Wayans also met Robert Townsend, another aspiring young black entertainer, at the Improv. In 1980 Wayans moved to Los Angeles where he continued his stand-up comedy and tried out for parts in motion pictures and television.

Poking Fun at Hollywood's Stereotypes

Landing only an occasional television role in Los Angeles, Wayans decided to venture into filmmaking, which he believed was also more conducive to his outlandish form of comedy. He told Vaughn that the scarcity of quality acting roles for African Americans in the early 1980s also motivated him to

Wayans impressed critics and moviegoers alike with this 1988 film, which marked his directorial debut.

make and act in his own films. Wayans rectified this inequity with Townsend, who had also moved to Los Angeles from New York, in their collaborative 1987 motion picture *Hollywood Shuffle*. Townsend explained the objective for *Hollywood Shuffle* to *Ebony* reporter Marilyn Marshall: "The majority of jobs [acting roles for African Americans] are bogus, [focusing on] stereotypes. Yet people fight for them, and in *Hollywood Shuffle,* I spoke up and said, 'That's not right.' And I tried to do it in a funny way."

A satire, *Hollywood Shuffle* revolves around struggling actor Bobby Taylor, played by Townsend, who must work at a hot dog stand to make enough money to support himself. Taylor perceives that because he is an African American his chances of finding a respectable part in a film are practically nonexistent. Therefore, he auditions and receives the lead role as a pimp in a blaxploitation film—a genre capitalizing on the portrayal of dubious black stereotypes, including pimps, drug dealers, murderers, and thieves. The movie, *Jivetime Jimmy's Revenge,* is being written, produced, and directed by white people. The black actors are trained and coached by whites to act more "black." Disheartened by his role, Taylor imagines himself in satirical situations. For example, he envisions an acting school where black people are taught "black" characteristics by white people; becomes Superman; defeats a bully named Jerry Curl (played by Wayans) by confiscating his curl activator; reviews blaxploitation films in a spin-off of Gene Siskel and Roger Ebert's movie review television show, *At the Movies;* stars in a blaxploitation film called *Rambro: First Youngblood;* and becomes a victim of ridicule by the National Association for the Advancement of Colored People (NAACP) for acting in blaxploitation films. Following his dream sequences, Taylor realizes he has doubts about his involvement in *Jivetime Jimmy's Revenge* and quits. He also pleas for the other minority cast members to leave the production. Later he auditions for a more tolerable acting role as a mailman in a commercial.

Although *Hollywood Shuffle* was written by both Townsend and Wayans, the latter received meager recognition from the critics for his contributions. Wayans told Smith, however, that he felt Townsend deserved the greater publicity. Critics were generally positive about the production. In *New Republic* Stanley Kauffmann called *Hollywood Shuffle* a "lively, knowledgeable film." Armond White, a *Film Comment* contributor, found that the movie "offers a shrewd look at Hollywood's be-

nighted attitudes and nonthinking." "*Hollywood Shuffle* is an exhilarating blast of anger and disgust. Much of it is wildly funny," wrote David Denby in his review for *New York*. And a *Motion Picture Guide* writer found Townsend and Wayans's film to be "downright hilarious."

Following his success with *Hollywood Shuffle,* Wayans began work on a parody of his own. A satire of blaxploitation films, the movie was released as *I'm Gonna Git You Sucka.* Wayans, who wrote, directed, and acted in the film, also cast two family members, Damon and Kim. Like the earlier movie, Wayans's solo comedy pokes fun at Hollywood stereotyping. He admits to receiving inspiration from the 1980 slapstick film *Airplane!* when creating *I'm Gonna Git You Sucka.* Wayans told Sessums that the movie is not intended to "satiriz[e] black people but bad moviemaking." In the film, Jack Slade, played by Wayans, takes leave from the U.S. Army to return to his hometown of "Any Ghetto, U.S.A." He wants to investigate his brother Junebug's death, which was caused by wearing too many gold chains. When Slade learns of a gold-chain pusher named Mr. Big, he vows to attack the malefactor's operations to avenge his brother's death. He solicits help from former stars of 1970s blaxploitation films, including *Slaughter*'s Jim Brown and *Truck Turner*'s Isaac Hayes. However, the heroes have lost their abilities to battle the bad guys, creating havoc as they trip and set off a number of loaded guns and detonate dynamite before breaking through the window of Mr. Big's offices. Eventually Slade finds himself fighting alone, but with help from his mother his mission succeeds.

In *People* Wayans expounded on his aspirations for his film: "I wanted to do something that was true to its ethnicity but not restricted to it. That's important to me as a black filmmaker because I feel that our society is painted to be more racist than it is." In the eyes of some white critics, his film was regarded as being degrading to blacks. "There is no racial issue," responded Wayans to Vaughn. "*Sucka* is a parody of a genre film." He concluded, "these are white guys trying to tell me, a black man, what is funny to black audiences." When asked by *Rolling Stone* contributor Jill Feldman if his movie was just another blaxploitation film, Wayans reflected: "There's really no such thing as blacksploitation. Blacksploitation is just an action-adventure movie with black men in the lead." Other critics gave *I'm Gonna Git You Sucka* rave reviews. A reviewer for *The Motion Picture Guide* stated that "Wayans keeps the jokes coming fast and thick, never giving the audience time to stop laughing.'' The critic concluded, *''I'm Gonna Git You Sucka* is on target often enough to make Wayans a talent worth watching.'' And Stuart Klawans stated in his article for *Nation,* ''No joke is too dumb, no pose too embarrassing, in this amiably slapdash and utterly engaging story.''

Wayans's film received a favorable reception despite some marketing problems. He told *American Film* contributor Betsy Sharkey that United Artists (UA) ''never got beyond the fact that [the movie] was black.'' Sharkey confirmed Hollywood's bias toward black films through a studio marketing executive who told her: ''Historically, there is a belief that black films don't do as well'' as white films. She also quoted producer Dale Pollock as saying, ''Black films do have an extra burden. They have to be better.'' Wayans believes such negative attitudes prevailed at UA when it was time to market *I'm Gonna Git You Sucka.* Forecasting that the film would not do well in white areas, UA only promoted the film in predominantly black neighborhoods. Wayans was upset over the UA decision, thinking that the movie should be advertised to white audiences as well. Wayans told Sharkey, ''I could have set myself on fire, and it wouldn't have changed their minds.'' Yet Wayans's film proved successful, grossing nearly seven times its production costs. In Sharkey's article Wayans also commented on how he deals with negative reactions from the film industry. ''There are times when you ask yourself, 'What does a black man have to do?' '' he related. ''But you have to channel those feelings into something productive. Bitterness will kill you.'' In 1990 when Wayans talked to Cohen and Sheff, he maintained that ''this town still has not embraced the black creator.''

Outrageous Television

After attending a screening for *I'm Gonna Git You Sucka,* Fox television network executives enticed Wayans to produce a television program telling him he could have creative reign over the series. Taking the offer, in 1990 Wayans developed a skit format program titled *In Living Color* that has been compared to veteran sketch show *Saturday Night Live.* The show consists of bawdy comedy skits parodying television shows and commercials, motion pictures, black stereotypes and culture, and celebrities, especially prominent black figures. It also features dancing by a group called The Fly Girls and performances by guest musicians. Wayans explained to Smith that *''In Living Color* shows people different sides of black life and black

culture. It's important that I do it honestly. I don't just show the black bourgeoisie or professionals—or criminals. I try to show every side of black life.'' The cast mainly consists of black actors. Four of Wayans's nine siblings have appeared on the show—Damon, Kim, and Marlon acted, and Shawn, who was at first the D.J. for The Fly Girls, became a member of the acting team in 1991. Kim Wayans told Cohen and Sheff, ''We're a very tight family, almost like the Osmonds''—a family of popular entertainers who had a variety show in the 1970s. According to Cohen and Sheff, ''critics tripped over their adjectives with praise'' for Wayans's show.

In Living Color's writers, who come from a variety of racial backgrounds, work long hours coming up with ribald comedy for the show. Smith observed, ''During production, the writers live in an enclosed world of alternating weariness and mania, with long sessions spent trying to see who can be funnier, dirtier, and sillier.'' Some of the results of the writing include caricaturing famous people, such as actress and talk-show host Oprah Winfrey, fighter Mike Tyson, and the Reverend Jesse Jackson. Some segments, like the sarcastic ''Homey the Clown,'' are presented on a regular basis. In another comedy scene, Damon Wayans makes inappropriate uses of language when playing a prisoner who has educated himself. And the cast depicts a day in the life of a family whose members all have buttocks for foreheads in the comedy skit ''The Buttmans.'' Fox executive Harris Katleman

The original cast of *In Living Color.*

Snackin' Shack.

Tag Team Televangelists.

Anton the Homeless Man.

Men on Film.

A Talk Show Hostess.

A Lawyer's TV Ad.

The Hedleys.

New Faces of '90.

The Fly Girls.

A sampling of popular sketches from Wayans' Emmy Award-winning television show, *In Living Color.*

talked about the show's cutting-edge nature to Andrew Feinberg of *TV Guide*. "Two years ago, no one would have aired *In Living Color*," Katleman opined. "It's too different, too ethnic, and brings up too many issues that standards and practices [censors have] never had to deal with before." "There's nothing subtle about the humor. It's extremely visceral, in-your-face stuff," said *In Living Color* writer John Bowman in Jeffrey Ressner's feature for *Rolling Stone*. Ressner himself concluded his article assessing that "*In Living Color* is about raunch and being raunchy."

While *In Living Color* has received generally favorable reviews, it has been criticized by some viewers for emphasizing stereotypes. One of the skits that received such concern is "The Homeboy

Shopping Network." This sketch, which plays on the stereotype that blacks are hoods, features two young black men who sell stolen goods on a home shopping program. Another skit, "The Equity Express Card: Helping the Right Sort of People," presents a wealthy black man having problems using a credit card. Also, certain skits have proved unsettling to some feminists, including sketches wielding jokes about women's breasts, shaving, and tampon use. In particular, one segment featured a woman's talk show ending with women clawing at each other. Members of the gay community have also voiced complaints, citing the characterizations in the "Men on Film" skit, in which two gay black men review movies. In one episode of "Men on

Film'' the characters stated (as quoted in Smith's article):

"Blaine: 'Eddie Murphy was back in *Another 48 HRS.*'

"Antoine: 'This movie just got off on the wrong track.... I'd like to see more about them old sweaty mens all together in them tiny little cells with no one to turn to but each others.'

"Blaine: 'Ooh, drop the soap!'

"Antoine: 'Finally, we have *Die Harder*. What a way to go! Ninety minutes with Mr. Bruce Willis.'

"Blaine: 'Oooh yes, don't tempt my tummy with the taste of nuts and honey....'"

Some viewers feel that these depictions are supplying a dubious representation of gay people to the public. Wayans responded to the reproaching comments in Harry F. Waters and Lynda Wright's *Newsweek* article: "If the show picked on only one group, I could understand people being uptight. But we get *everybody*."

In light of *In Living Color*'s controversial nature, Fox network censors actively oversee the writing. Tamara Rawitt, the show's former producer, told Smith: "Usually they jump in the car and come right over during taping." The censors' response to the "Men on Film" dialogue cited earlier was to cut the line "Ooh, drop the soap!" In another instance Wayans shot two versions of a sketch, one

racier than the other. The sketch in question was a parody on 2 Live Crew singer Luther Campbell, whose album was banned in several states for being overly sexual. Wayans had hoped the more suggestive version would be chosen, but was disappointed. Wayans did admit to Ressner, however, that he does have certain standards for his comedy. He said that the show would never feature sketches on Nazi skinheads, the Ku Klux Klan, crack cocaine, or AIDS.

Despite these criticisms from viewers and censors, *In Living Color* has been described as a "groundbreaking comedy show" by *Entertainment Weekly* contributors Alan Carter and Juliann Garey. Smith called it "a surprise hit" and also emphasized that the program frequently ranked as one of the top-twenty shows in the Nielsen ratings. Ressner lauded *In Living Color* as being "TV's hottest new comedy show."

After almost three years of producing *In Living Color*, Wayans and Fox officials became entangled in a dispute over the rerun syndication of the show. The program's copyright was scheduled to revert to Wayans during 1993, but in December 1992, Fox declared that they would air the reruns first. Given no time to challenge Fox before they announced their plans, Wayans ultimately decided to leave *In Living Color*. "It was absolutely the most difficult thing I've ever had to do," said Wayans to Carter and Garey. "But I had to. I

Wayans appears onstage at the close of an episode of *In Living Color*.

couldn't condone what they did, and how they did it. No one wanted me to leave, but I couldn't continue in good conscience. I couldn't give them a show that was a certain quality and not have them return that quality." Because of Fox's decision, the other Wayans cast members wanted to leave. Having no obligations to the show, Damon and Marlon left immediately, but Kim and Shawn were required by contract to stay. After departing from *In Living Color*, Wayans revealed he would try to create another comedy show on a different network.

During his career, Wayans has made waves in Hollywood, helping to bring African Americans to the forefront of the entertainment industry. He has not been alone in his efforts, however. Other prominent black males are also working to increase African American participation in quality productions. They include Townsend, Murphy, actor and talk-show host Arsenio Hall, and actor and film-maker Spike Lee. Calling themselves the "black pack," these five entertainers are best friends and provide support to each other in business. Yet each has made his own name in Hollywood. "I've had to be my own big brother in this business," Wayans related to Cohen and Sheff. "I never talk to people about things. I work them out for myself."

■ Works Cited

Carter, Alan, and Juliann Garey, "Wayans's World: Is He Demon Keenan or Deposed King of 'Color'?," *Entertainment Weekly*, January 15, 1993, pp. 6-7.

Cohen, Charles E., and Vicki Sheff, "Bridging the Gap between Black and White, Keenen Ivory Wayans Scores a Raucous Hit with Fox's *In Living Color*," *People*, June 11, 1990, pp. 75-76.

Denby, David, "The Visible Man," *New York*, April 6, 1987, pp. 90-91.

Feinberg, Andrew, review of *In Living Color*, *TV Guide*, June 2, 1990.

Feldman, Jill, "Keenen Wayans's Sucker Punch," *Rolling Stone*, November 3, 1988.

Review of *Hollywood Shuffle*, *The Motion Picture Guide: 1988 Annual*, Cinebooks, 1988, pp. 119-120.

Review of *I'm Gonna Git You Sucka*, *People*, December 12, 1988, p. 185.

Review of *I'm Gonna Git You Sucka*, *The Motion Picture Guide: 1989 Annual*, Cinebooks, 1989, p. 84.

Kauffmann, Stanley, "Stanley Kauffmann on Films: Comedy, Sharp and Otherwise," *New Republic*, May 4, 1987, pp. 26-27.

Klawans, Stuart, review of *I'm Gonna Git You Sucka*, *Nation*, February 13, 1989.

Marshall, Marilyn, "Robert Townsend: Hollywood 'Shuffling' to the Top," *Ebony*, July, 1987, pp. 54, 56, 58.

Ressner, Jeffrey, "Off-Color TV," *Rolling Stone*, April 23, 1992.

Sessums, Kevin, "The Black-Pack Attack," *Interview*, December, 1988, p. 56.

Sharkey, Betsy, "Knocking on Hollywood's Door: Black Filmmakers Like Spike Lee Struggle to See and Be Seen," *American Film*, July/August, 1989, pp. 22-27, 53-54.

Smith, Dinitia, "Color Them Funny: Keenen Ivory Wayans and TV's New Black Comedy Hit," *New York*, October 8, 1990, pp. 29-35.

Vaughn, Christopher, "Filmmakers in Focus," *Hollywood Reporter*, January 25, 1989, p. 13.

Waters, Harry F., and Lynda Wright, "Saturday Night Breakthrough: A New Show Tests Limits," *Newsweek*, May 21, 1990.

White, Armond, "Woody Allen and Robert Townsend.... Class Clowns," *Film Comment*, March/April, 1987, pp. 11-14.

■ For More Information See

BOOKS

Newsmakers 91, Cumulation, Gale, 1991, pp. 455-457.

PERIODICALS

Los Angeles Times, April 15, 1990.
Time, April 27, 1987, p. 79.°

—*Sketch by Jane M. Kelly*

Acknowledgments

Acknowledgments

Grateful acknowledgment is made to the following publishers,
authors, and artists for their kind permission to reproduce copyrighted material.

JUDIE ANGELL. Cover of *Nice Girl from Good Home,* by Fran Arrick. Copyright © 1984 by Bradbury Press. Reprinted by permission of Bradbury Press, an affiliate of Macmillan, Inc./ Cover of *In Summertime It's Tuffy,* by Judie Angell Gaberman. Copyright © 1977 by Judie Angell Gaberman. Reprinted by permission of Dell Books, a division of Bantam Doubleday Dell Publishing Group, Inc./ Jacket of *Secret Selves,* by Judie Angell. Copyright © 1979 by Judie Angell Gaberman. Jacket illustration by George Thompson. Reprinted by permission of Bradbury Press, an affiliate of Macmillan, Inc./ Cover of *Tunnel Vision,* by Fran Arrick. Copyright © 1980 by Fran Arrick. Reprinted by permission of Dell Books, a division of Bantam Doubleday Dell Publishing Group, Inc./ Photograph courtesy of Judie Angell. °ca

PIERS ANTHONY. Cover of *A Spell for Chameleon,* by Piers Anthony. Ballantine Books, 1977. Copyright © 1977 by Piers Anthony. Cover art by Michael Whelan. Reprinted by permission of Ballantine Books, a division of Random House, Inc./ Cover of *Var the Stick,* by Piers Anthony. Bantam Books, 1973. Copyright © 1973 by Piers Anthony. Reprinted by permission of Bantam Books, a division of Bantam Doubleday Dell Publishing Group, Inc./ Cover of *On a Pale Horse,* by Piers Anthony. Copyright © 1983 by Piers Anthony Jacob. Cover art by Michael Whelan. Reprinted by permission of Ballantine Books, a division of Random House, Inc./ Illustration from *Piers Anthony's Visual Guide to Xanth,* by Piers Anthony. Avon Books, 1989. Copyright © 1989 by Bill Fawcett & Associates, Inc. Illustrations by Todd Cameron Hamilton and James Clouse. Reprinted by permission of Avon Books, New York./ Cover of *Firefly,* by Piers Anthony. Avon Books, 1992. Copyright © 1990, 1992 by Piers Anthony Jacob. Reprinted by Avon Books, New York./ Cover of *Chthon,* by Piers Anthony. Berkley Medallion, 1975. Copyright © 1967 by Piers A. D. Jacob. Cover illustration by John Jude Palencar. Reprinted by permission of The Berkley Publishing Group.

STEVEN BOCHCO. Movie stills from *L.A. Law* and *Hill Street Blues,* courtesy of NBC-TV./ Movie still from *Silent Running,* courtesy of Universal Pictures./ Movie stills from *Columbo, Hooperman,* and *Doogie Howser, M.D.,* courtesy of ABC-TV./ Photograph A/P Wide World Photos.

EDGAR RICE BURROUGHS. Illustration from *Michael Whelan's Works of Wonder,* by Michael Whelan. Copyright © 1985 by Michael Whelan. Reprinted by permission of Ballantine Books, a division of Random House, Inc./ Cover of *Tarzan and the Lost Empire,* by Edgar Rice Burroughs. Cover art and title page illustration by Frank Frazetta. Reprinted by permission of The Berkley Publishing Group./ Cover of *John Carter of Mars,* by Edgar Rice Burroughs. Copyright © 1964 by Edgar Rice Burroughs, Inc. Cover art by Gino D'Achille. Reprinted by permission of Ballantine Books, a division of Random House, Inc./ Illustration from *The Pulps: Fifty Years of American Pop Culture,* compiled and edited by Tony Goodstone. Chelsea House, 1976. Copyright © 1970 by Tony Goodstone. Reprinted by permission of TSR, Inc./ Cover of *Pellucidar,* by Edgar Rice Burroughs. Cover art and title page illustration by Roy Krenkel, Jr. Reprinted by permission of The Berkley Publishing Group./ Movie still from *Tarzan, the Ape Man,* courtesy of MGM/UA Entertainment Co.

ORSON SCOTT CARD. Cover of *Red Prophet,* by Orson Scott Card. Copyright © 1988 by Orson Scott Card. Reprinted by permission of Tom Doherty Associates./ Cover of *Ender's Game,* by Orson Scott Card. Copyright © 1977, 1985 by Orson Scott Card. Reprinted by Permission of Tom Doherty Associates./ Cover of *Speaker for the Dead,* by Orson Scott Card. Copyright © 1986 by Orson Scott Card. Cover art by John Harris. Reprinted by permission of Tom Doherty Associates./ Cover of *The Memory of Earth,* by Orson Scott Card. Copyright © 1992 by Orson Scott Card. Cover art by Keith Parkinson. Reprinted by permission of Tom Doherty Associates./ Cover of *Seventh Son,* by Orson Scott Card. Copyright © 1987 by Orson Scott Card. Reprinted by permission of Tom Doherty Associates./ Photograph by Jay Kay Klein.

PAUL FLEISCHMAN. Illustration from *The Birthday Tree,* by Paul Fleischman. Harper & Row, 1979. Illustrations by Marcia Sewall. Reprinted by permission of HarperCollins Publishers Inc./ Illustration from *Graven Images,* by Paul Fleischman. Text copyright © 1982 by Paul Fleischman. Illustrations copyright © 1982 by Andrew Glass. Reprinted by permission of HarperCollins Publishers Inc./ Cover of *Joyful Noise: Poems for Two Voices,* by Paul Fleischman. Text copyright © 1988 by Paul Fleischman. Illustrations copyright © 1988 by Eric Beddows. Reprinted by permission of HarperCollins Publishers Inc./ Cover of *The Half-a-Moon Inn,* by Paul Fleischman. Text copyright © 1980 by Paul Fleischman. Cover art copyright © 1991 by Neil Waldman. Cover copyright © 1991 by HarperCollins Publishers. Reprinted by permission of HarperCollins Publishers Inc./ Cover of *Graven Images,* by Paul Fleischman. Text copyright © 1982 by Paul Fleischman. Reprinted by permission of HarperCollins Publishers Inc./ Photograph by Marilyn Sanders.

Raymond. Reprinted by permission of HarperCollins Publishers Inc./ Movie still from *Baxter*, National General Pictures./ Photograph by Jerry Eisenberg.

SANDRA SCOPPETTONE. Jacket of *Playing Murder: A Novel*, by Sandra Scoppettone. Copyright © 1985 by Sandra Scoppettone. Jacket art copyright © 1985 by Ellen Thompson. Jacket copyright © 1985 by Harper & Row, Publishers, Inc. Reprinted by permission of HarperCollins Publishers Inc./ Cover of *Trying Hard to Hear You*, by Sandra Scoppettone. Bantam Books, 1976. Copyright © 1974 by Sandra Scoppettone. Reprinted by permission of Bantam Books, a division of Bantam Doubleday Dell Publishing Group, Inc./ Cover of *The Late Great Me*, by Sandra Scoppettone. Bantam Books, 1977. Copyright © 1976 by Sandra Scoppettone. Reprinted by permission of Bantam Books, a division of Bantam Doubleday Dell Publishing Group, Inc./ Cover of *Happy Endings Are All Alike*, by Sandra Scoppettone. Copyright © 1991 by Catherine Hopkins. Reprinted by permission of Alyson Publications, Inc./ Cover of *Everything You Have Is Mine*, by Sandra Scoppettone. Ballantine Books, 1992. Copyright © 1991 by Sandra Scoppettone. Reprinted by permission of Ballantine Books, a division of Random House, Inc./ Photograph by Linda Crawford.

JERRY SEINFELD. Photograph of Seinfeld with co-stars by Gino Mifsud./ Movie still from episode #04-0307 of *Seinfeld*, photograph by Barry Slobin, courtesy of Castle Rock Entertainment./ Movie stills from *Seinfeld*; NBC-TV./ Photograph courtesy of Jonas Public Relations, Inc.

STEPHEN SONDHEIM. Scenes from *Into the Woods* and *Sunday in the Park with George* © 1990 by Martha Swope./ Scene from *A Little Night Music*; Viacom Pictures./ Scene from *Something Funny Happened on the Way to the Forum*, copyright © 1982 by United Artists Corporation./ Photograph by Michael Le Poer Trench.

JERRY SPINELLI. Jacket of *Maniac Magee*, by Jerry Spinelli. Jacket photograph by Carol Palmer. Reprinted by permission of Little, Brown and Company./ Cover of *Space Station Seventh Grade*, by Jerry Spinelli. Copyright © 1982 by Jerry Spinelli. Reprinted by permission of Dell Books, a division of Bantam Doubleday Dell Publishing Group, Inc./ Cover of *Who Ran My Underwear up the Flagpole?*, by Jerry Spinelli. Copyright © 1992 by Jerry Spinelli. Reprinted by permission of Scholastic, Inc./ Photograph by M. Elaine Adams.

JOHN ROWE TOWNSEND. Illustration from *Trouble in the Jungle*, by John Rowe Townsend. Text copyright © 1961 by John Rowe Townsend. Illustrations copyright © 1969 by J. B. Lippincott Company. Reprinted by permission of HarperCollins Publishers Inc./ Cover of *Trouble in the Jungle*, by John Rowe Townsend. Text copyright © 1961 by John Rowe Townsend. Reprinted by permission of HarperCollins Publishers Inc./ Cover of *The Intruder*, by John Rowe Townsend. Oxford University Press, 1970. Copyright © 1969 by John Rowe Townsend. Cover design by Graham Humphreys. Reprinted by permission of Oxford University Press./ Drawing of Townsend by Francoise Taylor./ Photograph by Jill Paton Walsh.

KEENAN IVORY WAYANS. Advertisement for *I'm Gonna Git You Sucka*; MGM/UA Home Video./ Wayans with his hands raised to his face; photograph by E. J. Camp/. Copyright © by Fox Broadcasting Company./ *In Living Color* cast on stage; photograph by Jon Delano./ "In Living Color" cast portrait; photograph by E.J. Camp/ © Fox Broadcasting Company./ Scene from *Snackin' Shack*; photograph by Jon Delano./ "The Fly Girls"; photograph by Darius Anthony./ Scenes from "Tag Team Televangelists," "Anton the Homeless Man," "Men on Film," "A Talk Show Hostess," "A Lawyer's TV Ad," "The Hedleys," and "New Faces of '90"; photographs by Joseph Viles.

Cumulative Index

Author/Artist Index

The following index gives the number of the volume
in which an author/artist's biographical sketch appears.